MORGAN GRENFELL

1838–1988

Statue of George Peabody, situated in front of the Royal Exchange, London
(By courtesy of Morgan Grenfell Group)

MORGAN GRENFELL

1838–1988

The Biography of a Merchant Bank

KATHLEEN BURK

OXFORD UNIVERSITY PRESS

1989

Oxford University Press, Walton Street, Oxford OX2 6DP
Oxford New York Toronto
Delhi Bombay Calcutta Madras Karachi
Petaling Jaya Singapore Hong Kong Tokyo
Nairobi Dar es Salaam Cape Town
Melbourne Auckland
and associated companies in
Berlin Ibadan

Oxford is a trade mark of Oxford University Press

Published in the United States
by Oxford University Press, New York

British Library Cataloguing in Publication Data
Burk, Kathleen
Morgan Grenfell 1838–1988: the biography of a
merchant bank.
1. (City) London. Merchant banks. (Firm) Morgan
Grenfell, history
332.66'09421'2
ISBN 0-19-828306-7

Library of Congress Cataloging in Publication Data
Burk, Kathleen.
Morgan Grenfell 1838–1988: the biography of a merchant bank/
Kathleen Burk.
p.   cm.
Includes bibliographical references.
1. Morgan Grenfell & Co.—History. 2. Merchant banks—Great
Britain—History. I. Title.
HG2998.M67B87   1989   89-16276
332.6'6'094212—dc20   CIP
ISBN 0-19-828306-7

Typeset by The Alden Press, London
Printed and bound in
Great Britain by Biddles Ltd,
Guildford and King's Lynn

Preface and Acknowledgements

THE relationship between an institution and its historian is sometimes fraught, especially when the institution is a bank. The history of such attempts to write history is littered with examples of access denied and information withheld, of manuscripts censored and even suppressed. Certainly, when Morgan Grenfell first approached me about writing their history, recent examples of the above were known to me, and encouraged doubts about the desirability of my writing a book over which I might not exercise complete control. Morgans reassured me; and they kept their word. I have seen everything I wished to see, including restricted papers; the subjects I have written about were of my own choosing; and the only excision I have made in the book as it stands was one possibly actionable sentence. The period since 1981 is of a different order. Even for this period I have seen all the documents I asked to see, and members of the Group talked frankly to me about the events of the decade. But writing a chapter of the same type as the first eight in the end proved impossible: there was the undeniable problem of customer confidentiality, and perspectives on the events of the period—including my own—frequently changed. In the end we all agreed that, for now, a brief Epilogue is best.

This book was researched and written to a very tight deadline, and this would have been impossible to meet without the full co-operation of a large number of people, both within and without Morgans. First came the research: and here I am very much indebted to Moira McGuinness and her colleague Marilyn Cranny, who helped me to locate files long dead and buried, and who always remained cheerful, even when my requirements interfered with their current work. Outside of Morgans, I must pay special tribute to Dr John Orbell of Barings, a model bank archivist: while properly concerned about the papers of his own organization, he nevertheless went out of his way to help, both in locating Barings files which might aid my research, and in a careful reading of several chapters of the book. Likewise I must thank Henry Gillett and his colleagues at the Bank of England, who helped to decipher cryptic references to people long departed, and Edwin Green of the Midland Bank archives, whose knowledge of his bank's history helped illuminate my own work. Finally, I must underline my obligation to Judy Slinn, my research assistant, whose labour in gutting dozens of old and frequently filthy ledgers provided the financial backbone of the book.

After the research came the writing, and I would like to acknowledge the efforts of all those who read the manuscript, whether the whole or in part. A full list appears below, but here I must single out four, all of whom read the entire manuscript and took the time to write extensive comments, which were always thoughtful and frequently acute: Mike Hildesley, Sir John Sparrow, Peter Surridge, and Jeremy Wormell. But suggestions from virtually all of the following readers were incorporated in the book: John Baylis, David Bendall, C. B. B. Beauman, Robert Binyon, Sir George Blunden, E. A. Bradman, M. Bullock, Sir Peter Carey, Professor Vincent Carosso, Lord Catto, J. E. H. Collins, John Craven, Dr Stefanie Diaper, David Douglas-Home, John Forsyth, Henry Gillett, Desmond Harney, John Izard, George Law, P. J. McAfee, Janet McCurrie, Sir John Mallabar, Lord O'Brien, Dr John Orbell, Bryan Pennington, Professor Leslie Pressnell, Charles Rawlinson, Christopher Reeves, Anthony Richmond-Watson, Judy Slinn, John Smith, David Suratgar, Richard Webb, Donald Wells, Christopher Whittington, and Philip Ziegler. Successive suggestions, however, required the typing of successive drafts, and here I must thank Ainslee Rutledge, who is fast, accurate, cheerful, and catches inconsistencies in the text. Janet McCurrie, Sue Howson and Chris Beauman helped read the proofs, and Chris also helped see the book through the press, as well as providing invaluable guidance in the final stage of writing. I must also thank Howard Trust for help at a timely moment.

But there are two people of whom it might literally be said that without their help, there would have been no book. Firstly, I must thank Desmond Harney who, on behalf of the bank, commissioned the history. At all stages of the work he has supported, aided, and facilitated, ensuring that my relationship with Morgans was generally most agreeable. Secondly, I want to thank a close friend, Janet Haylett. My acceptance of the commission virtually coincided with the birth of my daughter, and Janet, helped by another neighbour, Liz Nightingale, took on much of the responsibility of caring for her. Only those who are attempting to combine career and family responsibilities will fully understand just what that meant to me, and it is to her that this book is dedicated.

For access to manuscript collections and permission to quote from them I am grateful to the Controller of Her Majesty's Stationary Office for material in the Public Record Office; the Trustees of the British Library and of the Bodleian Library; the House of Lords Record Office; the Guildhall Library; the Bank of England; Baring Brothers & Co.; the Midland Bank Ltd.; the British Steel Corporation Record Centre,

Irthlingborough; Nuffield College, Oxford; and Mr Christopher Reeves and Mrs Fortune Stanley, for papers in their possession. In the United States I am indebted to the National Archives; the Library of Congress; the New York Historical Society; the Essex Institute, Peabody, Mass.; the Harvard Business School, Boston; Amherst College, Mass.; the University of Virginia, Charlottesville, Va.; and Yale University, New Haven, Conn.

Full responsibility for all matters of fact and interpretation remains mine alone.

K.B.

April 1989

Contents

List of Plates

Introduction

THE combination of money, power, and secrecy produces an undeniable allure, and merchant banks have frequently been viewed through an atmosphere of romance denied to their more mundane joint-stock cousins. The furthering of empire, the financing of wars, the developing of once-primitive countries, the advising of swashbuckling industrial tycoons—these are all activities which lend themselves to the Romance of Business genre of writing from which merchant banks and bankers have unduly benefited or suffered. It is probable that the House of Rothschild has attracted the bulk of this attention, which has produced a whole clutch of family sagas, but the House of Morgan, although younger, is not far behind. In the latter case, however, the spotlight has focused to an overwhelming extent on one man, J. Pierpont Morgan, by common consent a titan. But concentration on Pierpont Morgan has meant concentration on the American House of Morgan, and the result until very recently has been almost total ignorance about the connected banks in Philadelphia, Paris, and London. This is particularly ironic in view of the fact that until the 1880s the London bank was the dominant partner; thereafter, until London and New York were forced to separate in the 1930s, the London bank recognized New York as dominant, but the relationship amongst the partners was that of equals.

Morgan Grenfell traditionally date their origins from the day in August 1838 when George Peabody, an American in London, bought a supply of quill pens and ledgers and opened a counting-house. In 1854 George Peabody & Co. took another American, J. S. Morgan, as partner; the bank became J. S. Morgan & Co. in 1864, by which time, having made their reputation as a dealer in American issues and various commodities, they were the leading American house in London. J. S. Morgan's son, J. Pierpont Morgan, returned to New York and eventually established the bank which bears his name. He remained senior partner in the London bank until 1909, when J. S. Morgan & Co. was reconstituted as Morgan Grenfell & Co., and the New York bank, rather than Pierpont Morgan and his son J. P. Morgan, Jr., was a partner taking one-half of the profits. The resident senior partner was the Englishman E. C. Grenfell, who had become a partner in 1904. Grenfell and J. P. Morgan, Jr., known as Jack, were very close friends—Jack was an Anglophile and divided his time equally between the US and Britain —and during the First World War and the 1920s relations, both business and personal, between the London and New York banks and bankers were particularly close. But a change in American banking law in 1933 forced the American partners to withdraw from the London bank, and Morgan Grenfell became a limited liability company, with the New York house retaining a one-third shareholding. The final break came in 1981, when Morgan Guaranty Trust Company of New York sold this shareholding to a group of British institutions: the London and New York banks were by now competitors in a number of areas, and it no longer made sense for the one to hold a substantial shareholding in the other.

It is clear, then, that a predominant theme of the book must be the Anglo-American relationship, not only between the two banks but also between the two financial centres, and indeed, in certain periods, between the two countries. Related to this is a second theme, the international activities of Morgan Grenfell. J. S. Morgan & Co. leapt to prominence as a result of their taking on the issue of a French war loan just before France's capitulation in the Franco-Prussian war of 1870–1. Morgans were behind the first issuing of a British war loan in the United States (during the Boer War in 1900), and in the decade before the First World War were unwillingly involved in China. During the First World War the British government rapidly grew dependent on North America for supplies, and increasingly for the dollars to pay for them: from January 1915 to August 1917 the purchase orders and the loans and exchange transactions necessary to pay for them were channeled through Morgan Grenfell to J. P. Morgan & Co., the British government's purchasing and financial agent in the US. During the 1920s the House of Morgan helped several European countries to return to the gold standard; Morgans were in general the leading bank involved in the 'bankers' diplomacy' of the period, concentrating on the problem of reparations and on the reconstruction of Europe, and Morgan Grenfell led or co-led on the associated issues of loans in London. Morgans extended credits to the British government in 1925 to facilitate Britain's return to gold and in 1931 to aid in the (ultimately futile) attempt to keep her there. After the Second World War Morgan Grenfell began developing business interests overseas, an effort redoubled in the 1970s, as a result of which the bank became a leader in export and project finance.

A third theme is Morgan Grenfell's activities in the corporate finance field. The First World War destroyed much of their international business, and they were one of the first merchant banks to turn determinedly to the issuing of domestic, industrial, and commercial securities.

This lead was lost in the middle years, but during the 1970s continuous effort was put into building up the corporate finance capabilities of the bank, with the result that by the mid-1980s it was acknowledged one of the best, if not the best, in the City.

For a good part of its history, Morgan Grenfell owed its leading position partly to its relationship with J. P. Morgan & Co. The London bank's position relative to that of the New York bank shadowed that of the City of London to Wall Street. In 1838 George Peabody & Co. began developing into one of the earliest 'merchant banks' as such at a period when London was the centre of the international capital market. By the later nineteenth century J. S. Morgan & Co. was the predominant bank in the Morgan group, because it was the original bank and housed the senior partner and because it was situated in London, which contained the expertise, at least where international transactions were concerned. But the balance slowly but ineluctably tipped the other way, both for the House of Morgan and for London and New York City, because New York increasingly had the money. Even so, as late as the mid-1920s J. P. Morgan, Jr. could still write that American investors preferred joint London/New York issues because the approval of the City was reassuring to them—it gave an issue an imprimatur of quality. More than once, Morgan Grenfell negotiated a New York loan over the cables from London on behalf of a client who wanted to borrow in New York but preferred to negotiate in London. Morgan Grenfell benefited too because J. P. Morgan & Co. naturally insisted that, in their joint loans, Morgan Grenfell should have the leading place on the British side. But much of this began to end with the separation of the banks forced by the US Banking Act of 1933. It is possible that the forced withdrawal of the American partners helped contribute to Morgan Grenfell's subsequent hibernation, although few banks did well during the years of depression and war which followed. It is therefore fitting that it was Lord Harcourt, great-grandson of the American J. S. Morgan, who brought in the new men in the late 1960s and early 1970s who helped to awaken Morgan Grenfell and set it once again on its way to resurgence and growth.

CHAPTER ONE

GEORGE PEABODY & CO.
1838–1864

The Birth of the Bank

A MEDIEVAL church building could be said to have a history, not a date, and it is necessary to take the same attitude towards the origins of the firm which eventually became Morgan Grenfell. The firm of George Peabody & Co., the first incarnation of today's bank, emerged rather than was founded, with Peabody himself acting as a merchant banker for some years before he founded a merchant bank. This development was analogous to the whole field of merchant banking, which emerged from general merchanting and evolved into the financial establishments of today. In other words, the date 1838, traditionally seen as the founding date of Morgan Grenfell, must be seen as convenient rather than strictly accurate: George Peabody & Co. itself was founded only in 1851. Yet by the date of Peabody's retirement in 1864, it was the most important American merchant bank in London. The fact that Peabody was, and remained, an American was of crucial importance to the orientation of the firm, and in fact, the United States remained its primary focus for almost a hundred years.

Peabody's Early Business Career

George Peabody was born in 1795 in South Danvers, Massachusetts, which was subsequently renamed Peabody in his honour. The Peabody name was (and is) an honoured one in New England history, but George came from one of the poorer branches of the Peabody family, whose common ancestor had emigrated from Hertfordshire, England, in 1635. George's father was a casual leather-worker and owner of a small farm, as well as the father of eight children. At the age of eleven George started work in a country general store, and it was from the owner of this store that he learnt to keep accounts in a clear handwriting and to organize and discipline his daily activities. Over the following years he changed occupations several times, during one period riding on horseback through Virginia hawking goods.[1]

During the War of 1812 with Great Britain, Peabody met the merchant Elisha Riggs, who traded in a number of commodities, including wheat, whiskey, and hams (and naval stores during the war). In 1814 the two of them went into partnership, and the following year the firm established its headquarters in Baltimore, trading as Riggs, Peabody and Company, and specializing in dry goods imported from Britain. This was the turning-point in Peabody's business career: his face was now turned towards Britain, and in 1827 he made his first business trip there. In 1829 Elisha Riggs retired, and the firm was reconstructed as Peabody, Riggs & Co., with Elisha Riggs's nephew Samuel becoming the junior partner. Each partner contributed $25,000 in capital: Peabody as the senior was to undertake the purchasing in Europe and Riggs as the junior was to concentrate on selling the goods in the US. It should be noted that the partnership agreement left Peabody free to trade on his own account while restricting Riggs to the business of the firm.[2]

In the years 1829–37 Peabody made four further trips to Britain. Clearly he found the experiences more than pleasant, for in 1838 he was to take up residence there. These were prosperous years for both Peabody and the firm: in 1815 Peabody had had very little capital, while by 1837 he had over $300,000, or £65,000.[3] The basic strength of Peabody, Riggs & Co. and of Peabody himself meant that both were to come through the panic of 1837 with enhanced reputations.

The panic of 1837 had roots in both the US and Britain, although only the American situation could be termed a panic. By late 1835 and particularly 1836 prosperity began giving way first to uncertainty and then to growing difficulties, culminating in a crisis in 1837. In the US the problems stemmed from speculative expansion both in land and in transport, fuelled by easy credit, and compounded by political rows between the Whigs and the Democrats over the role of the Bank of the United States.[4] In Britain, the Bank of England experienced an increased outflow of gold, with reserves dropping from £7.4 milllion at the end of the second quarter to £4.3 million at the end of the fourth quarter of 1836.[5] There had been over-expansion in domestic banking in Britain as well as in the US, and by late 1836 and early 1837 there were failures of banks in Ireland and in Manchester (the so-called Northern and Central Bank of England).[6] The 25% fall in cotton prices in the British market between February and March 1837 made things worse for houses involved in American trade. By July and August the Bank of England was forced to announce a high Bank Rate of 5% (the rate at which they would discount bills, at face value minus 5%) and made it clear that they would handle no more cotton acceptances (bills which had been 'accepted' or guaranteed by a bank). The Bank's growing reluctance to rediscount American cotton acceptances—that is, to agree to pay over cash for them to the banks and hold them to maturity, when they would supposedly be repaid—had already doomed the three main American firms in England most deeply involved in the American trade (Wiggins & Co., Wilkes & Co., and Wilson & Co.). The Bank's refusal to rediscount meant that the firms' funds were consequently locked up in uncollectable debts, and on 2 June 1837 all three shut their doors. Their failure destroyed the market for cotton acceptances, and American banks on the east coast, who had masses of them in their vaults as security for loans made for speculative purposes, in turn called in their loans from their correspondent banks in the West. But western banks were in an even worse state, having issued great quantities of paper money and extended credits far above legal limits. Many western banks therefore failed, bringing down with them their clients in the West as well as many eastern banks.

The Bank of England's worries about American credits extended far beyond cotton bills: because of the increasing financial and commercial difficulties in the US the Bank became more and more worried about the amount being borrowed in Britain on American bills (that is, with the bills being used as security). In August 1836, in fact, the Bank refused to discount bills being drawn on houses active in American trading, and this meant that merchants involved in the American trade had great trouble getting credit and keeping sufficiently liquid. In theory this should have hit Peabody, Riggs & Co. very hard indeed, but in fact their financing continued to be carried out successfully. This was because Peabody had begun already to batten down the hatches. Early in 1836, in response to the warning signs he could see for himself as well as the warnings of friends, Peabody had returned to the US and begun curtailing operations. He concentrated on collecting debts owed to the firm and in remitting the funds to England: both of these operations would soon become difficult for other firms, as their customers became unable to pay their bills and as the US exchange rate weakened. At the same time, Peabody ceased operations on his own account and reserved all of his private means and credit for the use of the firm. By the spring of 1837 Peabody was instructing his partner Riggs to realize their assets even if little profit was forthcoming, and Peabody himself made sales at a loss in order to get rid of stock and to get cash. As far as he was concerned, the priority was the state of their credit and reputation: as long as the firm met all of their obligations promptly and at any price they could live and fight another day; if they lost their reputation the firm would never be an important one.[7] By September 1837 Peabody could write to Riggs that 'With respect to the standing of our house . . . I believe we are almost the *only* American importers of European goods that have met every engagement on both sides of the Atlantic with punctuality.'[8]

The reputations of Peabody and of his company were also enhanced by the fact that he had helped others who were caught out by the crisis. Altruism was a necessary but not sufficient reason. He helped W. & J. Brown & Co. of Liverpool (the future Brown, Shipley & Co.), for instance, primarily because they were the major source of his credits in England and he held drafts on them for £18,000; he would have found it difficult to make good such a sum if they had failed. He spent a good deal of time and effort putting together a guarantee for them, and he himself subscribed £5,000 of the sum of £400,000 required by the Bank of England for its help. In addition he also helped several friends who found themselves in financial difficulties.[9]

Peabody was therefore in a good position, with regard both to his financial strength and to his reputation, to put into effect various changes in the firm which he and Riggs had agreed upon during his last sojourn in the States.[10] Basically, they wanted to expand the firm's business while at the same time cutting down expenses, and Peabody decided that the answer was to take a counting-house in London. Firstly, he would himself be able to purchase goods in that market without the need to pay commissions to other firms. Secondly, by means of the counting-house, he could conveniently accept occasional bills drawn on himself, which would help to cut down on the expense of heavy banking commissions; by doing so he would also increase his credit facilities. But thirdly, he would need some trustworthy person to replace him in the North: someone would be needed to keep a close watch on things in Lancashire and Yorkshire during the purchasing season, while Peabody did the same in London as well as taking care of the firm's financial activities. To this end Peabody, Riggs & Co. made two of the employees junior partners. By 1840, then, Peabody, Riggs & Co. consisted of the two senior partners, Peabody (the prior, as the more senior of the two was then called) and Riggs, two junior partners, H. T. Jenkins and A. W. Peabody (the latter a cousin of Peabody's), each of whom received a sixteenth share in the firm (without any contribution to capital), and a bookkeeper and a salesman, each of whom received a twenty-fourth share of the profits if the amount exceeded their salaries.[11]

From Merchant to Merchant Banker

Peabody's move to London was crucial for the future Morgan Grenfell. Now that Jenkins was available to purchase goods in the North and to make annual visits to the US (A. W. Peabody, after a year's experience in Britain, had returned to the US to concentrate on selling), Peabody could afford to spend most of his time in London and concentrate on the financial side of the business. He clearly found this ultimately more interesting and probably more profitable than basic merchanting work: since 1836, after all, his activities on his own account, rather than that of the firm, had been primarily financial rather than trading in dry goods. In August 1838, then, he moved into a 'commodious counting house' with mahogany furnishing at 31 Moorgate,[12] supplying it with a cash box for 10s. 6d. (52½ p), two gross of steel pens at 5s. (25 p) a gross, and a quire of foolscap paper at 1s. (5 p).[13]

It should not be thought, however, that Peabody travelled a singular path as, over the years, he gradually changed from being primarily a merchant to acting primarily as a merchant banker: in fact, most of the leading merchant banks grew up in precisely the same manner. That is, they moved from merchanting to banking when they had built up a sufficient reputation for soundness and reliability—and wealth—which warranted their colleagues' trust. They gradually concentrated on banking because the profits were higher and the risks were lower (at least in commercial credits).[14]

The fact that Peabody, Riggs & Co. had emerged from the 1837 crisis in such relatively good shape seems to have encouraged the partners to implement ambitious plans for expansion. From 1838 they increased their imports of dry goods from Britain, and they also undertook new functions both in terms of widening the range of imports they handled and in venturing into new sources of supply; for example, they turned more of their attention to Russian goods. In addition, they began handling consignments for others, especially of wheat. Yet, the upward trend was of short duration, and the firm found itself dangerously over-extended when another slump hit in 1839.

During the period 1837–9, renewed confidence in American bills—as long as they were not cotton acceptances—meant that British lending to Americans had continued. As two historians note, 'the British shouldered the heavy load of dead canals, railroads, state bonds and mortgages on deflated land'.[15] The British, it must be assumed, were enticed by the high yields and dependent on possibly self-interested publicity for their knowledge of the strength of the various railway and state bonds. By 1839, however, incredulity began to set in, and with Belgian and French banking collapses in 1838, the European liquidations were added to the American difficulties to ensure that the ensuing panic was international in scope. Work stopped on railways and canals, people were thrown out of work, banks closed their doors, and depression settled over the western part of the US. In 1839, $200 million of American securities were owned in England, and by 1841, when the Bank of the United States failed, $120 million of these were in danger of suspension. Banks south of New York suspended payments for the third time since 1837, and the next year Illinois, Indiana, Louisiana, Michigan, Alabama, Maryland, Mississippi, Florida, and Pennsylvania either defaulted on the interest due on their state bonds or repudiated them altogether. This, of course, made the sale of American securities in Britain almost impossible. The British lobbied to have the Federal government assume the obligations of the defaulting states, and when this proved impossible the reaction was ferocious. Sydney Smith, editor of the *Edinburgh Review*, wrote that he never met a citizen of Pennsylvania (one of the defaulting states) at a London dinner

without feeling a disposition to seize and divide him—to allot his beaver to one sufferer and his coat to another—to appropriate his pocket handkerchief to the orphan, and to comfort the widow with his silver watch, Broadway rings, and the London Guide which he always carried in his pockets. How such a man can set himself down at an English table without feeling that he owes two or three pounds to every man in the company, I am at a loss to conceive. He has no more right to eat with honest men than a leper has to eat with clean.[16]

Even the Federal government, when attempting to issue a loan in Europe in 1842, was essentially thrown out of bankers' offices:

'You may tell your government,' said the Paris Rothschild to Duff Green, the American agent, 'that you have seen the man who is at the head of the finances of Europe, and that he has told you that they cannot borrow a dollar, not a dollar.'[17]

George Peabody suffered personally from this reaction. In spite of his high standing—he was referred to by the London *Times* as 'an American gentleman of the most unblemished character'—he was refused admission to the Reform Club because he was a citizen of a nation that did not pay its debts.[18]

Peabody, Riggs and Co. suffered from both the trading slump and the slump in American securities. Their customers found it difficult to pay for the goods imported from Europe. Peabody, Riggs & Co. found it expensive to pay their suppliers because the exchange rate was against the dollar. Because of this, American stocks, especially stock of the Bank of the United States, had been sent to England for Peabody to sell, rather than cash their dollar remittances. Therefore, when the bottom dropped out of the market for American railway and state bonds and Bank of United States paper, Peabody experienced great difficulty, eventually settling for substantial losses. (His problems were increased because he had himself bought stocks with borrowed money, something he swore never to do again.) The firm, however, pulled through, and by late 1842 or 1843 was reasonably secure again.

But George Peabody himself had had enough of the dry goods business, where profits were low and, with the continuing development of American producers, unlikely to increase in the near future. The crisis of 1839, followed by the depression of 1841, had wiped out some of the firm's assets and reduced its profits, and Peabody decided that he wanted to dissolve the partnership. He had been considering such a move since 1839; but when the partnership agreement expired in 1841 he had renewed it rather than see the firm become second in trade, as he put it. However, he withdrew most of his capital from the firm beyond the $50,000 (just under £11,000) stipulated by the 1841 partnership agreement, preferring to use it for his own dealing in securities. In 1843, when the upturn came, Peabody withdrew the rest of his capital from Peabody, Riggs & Co. Nevertheless, the firm continued to use his name: he received an annual fee of $3,000 for executing the firm's financial business, and the firm itself was helped by the Peabody name. By 1845, however, he decided to sever himself completely from the dry goods business, and the firm was closed.[19]

Peabody later said that one reason for closing the firm was that it had not been as efficient as formerly, writing to a friend that 'old houses, after a series of years of success, get indolent and do not make great exertions to obtain business . . .'.[20] Another reason was presumably his disenchantment with the dry goods business itself; after all, he certainly continued his merchanting activities, notably in the China trade and later on with iron rails for the US. But perhaps a more important reason was his enjoyment of trading in securities and financial business in general.

During the period 1837–45, in fact, Peabody had been gradually turning himself more and more into what would later be termed a merchant banker. (In the nineteenth century the term 'merchant banker', rather than just 'merchant', was considered rather *déclassé*.)[21] Any functional definition of the term would have to include a reference to dealing in acceptances, and from the evidence it is clear that Peabody was doing so within four months of establishing himself at 31 Moorgate in August 1838.[22] For himself he was a heavy buyer and seller of American securities: trading in these stocks and bonds was, by 1843, essentially his full-time occupation. But beyond his own and Peabody, Riggs & Co.'s financial activities, Peabody became more and more involved in carrying out financial commissions for others. It is true that these transactions were on a relatively small scale, being carried out primarily for friends. He preferred not to make cash advances during the slump; rather, he performed money services. If funds were made available to him, he would issue a letter of credit; he negotiated bills of exchange for others, since he was active in dealing with foreign exchange for Peabody, Riggs & Co. as well as for himself; he disbursed funds. However, what he did do on some scale for others (as well as for himself) was to execute stock transactions.[23]

Although Peabody appeared to be acting entirely on his own, during the period between 1844 and 1847 he was in fact involved in a secret partnership with a New York firm, Wetmore & Cryder. Because a merchant banker was heavily involved in international trade, almost by definition he needed an 'agency' at the other end in order to originate and carry out transactions: once he had decided to set up on his own, this became an urgent requirement for Peabody. This secret partnership was concluded in 1843 when John Cryder, one of the New York partners, visited England. Peabody was ecstatic, since his new partners were men of wealth and position.

How might the two ends work together? Take the example of an English exporter and an American importer. The American importer would have arranged to import certain goods at a given cost from the British exporter. He would go to Wetmore & Cryder and ask them to arrange a credit for him, which they would agree to do if they were satisfied with his financial standing. The British exporter, once the goods had been put on board ship, would take the bill of lading to Peabody and 'draw' a bill of exchange—essentially an IOU—on Peabody, who would 'accept' it, i.e. guarantee payment at a specified future date. The date, characteristically, might be three months in the future, allowing time for the goods to be shipped. The exporter could then 'discount' the bill at a discount house; that is, he would receive in cash the face value of the bill, minus a discount equal to the short-term interest rate. Peabody would then send the bill of lading to Wetmore & Cryder, who would release the documents to the importer when he gave them the dollar funds necessary to cover the bill accepted by Peabody. Wetmore & Cryder would then send a bill of exchange as remittance to Peabody who would pay the acceptance when it was presented at maturity. Peabody and Wetmore & Cryder would both have received a certain percentage commission on the value of the bill.[24]

This procedure allowed exporters to receive cash promptly for their goods, rather than having to wait for payment until the goods had been sold and the cash remitted. It was an arrangement whereby an importer could borrow money in the exporter's country to pay the producer for the goods: the two firms acted as the intermediaries, arranging for funds and transmitting them as necessary. They also needed each other to pronounce on the credit-worthiness of possible customers: would they and could they pay their bills? If they could not, whoever had accepted the bill was liable for the repayment.

Peabody also set about rearranging his business and his premises to accommodate increased business. He moved from Moorgate to 6 Warnford Court, Throgmorton Street. He engaged a 'first rate Book Keeper', C. C. Gooch, whom he paid £150 a year and who later became his partner; he also employed two other clerks, each of whom received £120 a year. (All of these salaries were very good for this period.) Peabody also opened an account with the Bank of England: this would save on the transfer of funds from other English cities, and he would enjoy certain discount privileges. He was now ready for business.

The aim of the three partners was to start out cautiously and to build up gradually a sound agency and commission business. This was an absolute necessity: young and unproven houses in England had to exercise caution in what bills they accepted, because the refusal of the chief discount houses to rediscount them could destroy their credit. Such a reaction by the discount houses would have prevented Peabody from carrying on the partnership with Wetmore & Cryder, since his chief task as a London partner was the handling of commercial bills of exchange sent to him by his New York partners. The fact that this was the main business between the two probably provides the reason for the partnership's remaining secret: if partners drew bills of exchange on each other this was a matter for criticism. If the partnership remained secret, the business world would only assume that it was a correspondent drawing on a separate house. To this end the partners wrote all letters to each other themselves: even Peabody's confidential clerk, Gooch, remained in ignorance.[25]

Yet the partnership did not prosper as Peabody had hoped. The acceptance business did not grow very much, partly, Peabody felt, because his partners were too cautious, whilst business transacted on a small percentage basis requires large volume to be profitable. Peabody felt he was much more energetic and certainly more daring; as he wrote to Cryder on 3 February 1847, 'with every disposition to be prudent, when I see a great opening for a successful operation, I must embark on it even should I remotely hazard the loss of a few thousands.'[26] Of course, acceptances were not the whole or even the greater part of his business: during the first two years of the partnership Peabody's most profitable operations were in buying and selling American securities, and, as he wrote to his partners, it took up almost all of his 'time by day and thought by night'.[27]

Peabody was still a merchant as well as a merchant banker, and, in addition to his stockjobbing and financial transactions, he participated in, for example, the China trade, both on his own account and as a commission merchant, where he dealt in tea, silk, and 'drugs', presumably opium. But the trade in Chinese goods was uncertain: in 1846 the tea market was depressed, with buyers holding off while waiting to see if the British government would reduce the duty on tea, and in 1847 the silk market was in difficulties. Peabody became disillusioned with dealing in Chinese goods, and when money became tight in 1847 he withdrew from the trade.

Peabody was also involved in sending Indian corn to Ireland. He had been involved in the grain trade in a small way for some time, and when August 1846 brought news of the failure of the Irish potato crop, he began to look at the trade seriously; by October he had made his first profit of $1,200 on 6,000 barrels of flour. This was followed by other small profits, and the partners were soon large operators in the trade, in particular in Indian corn. However, they did not make profits commensurate with the scale of their operations, because promising early returns were followed by substantial losses.[28]

In short, the partnership was only a moderate financial success and it was not renewed in 1847. (For the period 1844–6, the profits of the New York house were just over $96,000, while those of the London house were just under £23,000, about $106,000.)[29] Temporary financial disappointment might have been borne, but Peabody clearly did not think that substantial profits were very likely. Wetmore was one of the ten wealthiest men in New York, but he had a young and demanding wife and was often away from business. Cryder had had to deal with Wetmore's China business and was overburdened, and for whatever reason he had not been very active in building up a general business; he expressed himself as unwilling to drum up 'two penny' business and consignments.[30] Further, the partnership restricted Peabody's securities trading; although the partnership agreement allowed him to utilize up to £25,000 for trading in stocks (and he had on occasion gone beyond), nevertheless Cryder felt very nervous about Peabody's activities. Peabody in short thought his partners were timid and lacking in initiative, and although the two firms remained friends and continued to influence business towards each other, Peabody nevertheless was disillusioned about partnerships, maintaining in 1849 that he would never have another partner. But the partnership had benefited Peabody in certain ways: he had been associated with wealthy and successful businessmen, and he was richer in 1848 than in 1844 and better known.[31]

Peabody on His Own

For the next few years, then, Peabody worked on his own, aided only by his clerk, Gooch, and the assistant clerks. Although he continued to engage in banking business, the bulk of his time for the remainder of the 1840s was spent on transactions in American stocks, for which he seems to have been the major London specialist dealer.[32] He bought and sold securities in the London market, and when prices were higher in the US he shipped them across the Atlantic and sold them there. He took parts of new issues in the US and sold them in Europe, usually on joint account with firms such as Baring Brothers, then the most important English house in American finance.

It was some time before he ventured to lead in issuing American securities in Britain. After the repudiations by the states, American securities were seen as risky, and Peabody spent no little energy in trying to restore confidence in them. He had, in fact, great faith in their ultimate value, so he was prepared to buy at low prices with the confidence that he would eventually reap a profit. Peabody himself attributed his success in American securities to a further factor besides his faith and his detailed knowledge of American conditions. Because there was no regular market for American securities in England, Peabody, as a large and constant buyer, reaped many advantages. He made his office a centre of transactions, and he developed the reputation of being willing to buy or sell any

American securities; as he wrote to Wetmore & Cryder on 3 January 1845, '*Generally* the offers are first made to me and I sometimes buy or sell rather than lose the reputation I have of being ready to do either.'[33] In short, Peabody was, in modern parlance, a 'market-maker', whose willingness to buy and sell, even when conditions were volatile, provided the investor with liquidity. One result of market-making, of course, was and is that investors will show the man in that position the business first, because they know he will always make a price, which has a clear business advantage.[34] Brokers also came to Peabody because he was willing to pay the full brokerage commission, unlike others who tried to save on their commissions.[35]

Even when American securities were not very popular, Peabody made a good business: he turned over his capital often, sometimes at a very small profit, and with his knowledge he had few loss-making transactions (he estimated that between 1842 and 1845 he had bought and sold over $6 million worth of American securities 'with scarcely a transaction which had been attended by loss'). The possibilities after 1848, then, when the whole market for American securities had altered, were exploited to the full.

The market had altered partly because of American actions and partly because of events on the European continent. Firstly, several states resumed interest payments on their bonds and this encouraged the feeling that others might do so and that in general, American state bonds were a more reasonable risk. Secondly, the threatened American war with Mexico seemed to have been called off (although it was only postponed). Thirdly, renewed attention was paid in Britain to the basic strengths of the US, such as its population and natural resources, its growing manufacturing base, and its developing infrastructure. The fact that Federal securities were selling at a premium in the US encouraged confidence. Finally, later in 1848 gold was discovered in California. In Continental Europe itself the spate of revolutions in 1848 caused 'nervous money' to buy American bonds.[36]

Peabody worked to take advantage of the easier climate for American securities. His most important move was to work closely with Baring Brothers. In July 1848 they agreed to 'act in perfect unison in making sales',[37] and in general they worked together to raise prices. Peabody did not like working with the London Rothschilds (N. M. Rothschild & Sons), for example, because they tended to undercut the market; Barings agreed with his view of such matters, and when in 1848 the Rothschilds' underselling of some bonds threatened their success, Peabody and Barings together bought $106,000 worth of the bonds from them and removed them from the market. Their price then rose and sales increased.[38]

But Peabody did not restrict his activities to Britain itself, and he worked to build up a market on the Continent, in particular in Germany. Not only did money frightened by revolution flow into American bonds, but they were bought especially by German emigrants to the States: bearer bonds were easily transferable and preferable to carrying cash on the long voyage. His main trading, then, was in American state and railroad securities, which he sold in Britain and on the Continent, although he also traded in Mexican and Peruvian bonds. Nevertheless, the combination of his knowledge and faith in American securities, and the fact that he had the luck to be able to buy at a low price and sell in a rising market, meant that by the late 1840s he had became a wealthy man. Beyond that, he had prestige and useful business connections, both in the US and in Britain, for example with Barings. It was time, as his friends repeatedly told him, to turn his attention to building up an outstanding American house in London. While trading in securities his general banking business had continued to grow, and in 1849 he decided to give more time to the project.[39]

There was in the late 1840s no important American-run house in London, and had been none since the collapse of the three American trading houses in the panic of 1837. Peabody had the capital and connections, and he also had the ambition to build a house which would be the centre, not only of the American trade, but for Americans in that trade. As usual, his luck was with him, and conditions were favourable for expansion, being a period of commercial optimism and of low interest rates. What he needed were new correspondents, that is, firms with whom he could maintain close connections, in the US; new types of business; and, importantly, new partners with whom to share the work. Over the subsequent five years he fulfilled all three requirements.

A prime requirement for a large merchant bank was a strong agency in New York. He continued to shun partnerships, but he developed a 'very intimate association' with Duncan, Sherman & Co., a new house whose partners were wealthy men with wide experience. He had other important correspondents in New Orleans, San Francisco, and Boston. Their importance was paramount, as David Landes has written:

These correspondents, usually bankers in their own right but sometimes heads of firms that the first banker had a silent interest in or simple subordinates in charge of agencies, were the critical pivots of international exchange business. For one thing, they were indispensable as financial collaborators, remitting payments, receiving drafts and collecting debts, drawing letters of credit, and so on. But equally important, they were in effect the eyes and ears of their distant associate, an intelligence corps whose strategic situation in customer territory enabled the foreign banker to work smoothly and safely with business-men he had never seen.[40]

Peabody and the agencies in the US split the charges, but Peabody insisted on changing the risk involved in acceptance credits. Ordinarily the risk would have been taken jointly, but Peabody insisted that the American agencies guarantee the credits, so that failure to pay would fall entirely on the American agency. Protests were made, but Peabody insisted, writing to Duncan, Sherman & Co. on 12 March 1852, for example, that 'If there is any risk, credits ought not to be given and if there is none you get better paid than we do.'[41] He was apparently afraid that the American houses would grant too extensive credits and he thought that if they had to guarantee the accounts they would be more careful to whom they extended their—and Peabody's—credit.[42]

Peabody had never forsworn dealing in goods as well as in financial services, but had merely decided that dry goods did not provide profit commensurate with the work. As noted before, he dealt in American wheat and in the China trade, but in 1849 he began to deal directly in the exporting of iron rails to the States. He had already granted large credits to rail exporters, but Peabody wished to have a share in the profits, and not just collect financing commissions. Through his various correspondents in the US and agents of the railroad companies who were visiting England, Peabody took an active part in shipping rails. Sometimes he bought cheaply from the iron master and sold more dearly; sometimes he arranged purchases on a commission basis; some-times he merely extended credit. A New York house, Chouteau, Merle and Sanford (later P. Chouteau, Sanford & Co.), sent an agent to London to make arrangements for the banking end of its own transac-tions, and this agent concluded an agreement with Peabody in April 1851. The New York house looked after the American side of the transactions, its members travelling throughout the US looking for orders and studying conditions, and many of the sales were made there; the New York house also attended to collections, remittances, and the sale of railroad bonds in the US. Peabody's part was to buy rails, to attend to their shipment, and to carry on the banking business in England. The latter included giving to iron manufacturers the facility to draw upon him, arranging insurance, and generally looking after the joint interests. If an American railroad agent went to Britain to buy rails, Peabody competed with other merchant bankers to secure the contract. But he soon found the mercantile aspects—the technical business and the travelling—onerous and tedious, and by July 1851 he had secured C. M. Lampson to carry out the work.

By 1852 American railroads were booming: the American government was aiding the railroads with land grants, and various state and local governments helped with issues of bonds. This was very useful, both to the railroads and to George Peabody. Those firms which manufactured rails were in a depressed state and agreed to take railroad bonds in payment for the rails, thus facilitating the financing of the railroads. Someone had to market the securities, and Peabody, among others, dealt in the issues of American railroads. Altogether, Peabody's involvement in railroad financing and exporting of rails was very lucrative and would continue to be so for a good many years.[43]

Because of his growing success, Peabody had for some time felt the need to take a partner. He had, it is true, declared in 1849 that he would never have a partner again, but by 1851 he was working ten hours a day and had not been absent from the office on two consecutive business days for twelve years. He was nearly fifty-seven, and his correspondents in the US were somewhat alarmed at the fact that it was essentially a one-man business: if anything happened to Peabody there would be no continuity. Finding a partner, however, was no easy task: his was an American house and he wanted it to continue to be so in all ways, and therefore he required an American of standing and business talent.[44] He had not found one by 1849, when he had given up the idea of adding an important partner immediately and settled for making G. C. Gooch, his confidential clerk since 1843, a salaried partner at £500 a year.

In 1851, however, Peabody took a further step in regularizing matters: on 22 December a circular announced the formation of George Peabody & Co. The interests of the firm were to include 'American and other Stocks, Foreign Exchange, Banking and Credits, the execution of Railroad Orders, purchase and sale of Produce and general Mercantile Transactions'.[45] Peabody was to provide £250,000 capital at 5% interest; the profits were to be divided at the rate of 92% for Peabody and 8% for Gooch, who continued as a partner. Peabody was to continue to be free to deal on his own account, and with minor exceptions these profits were to go entirely to him.[46] It is this organization which can be said to constitute the institutional beginning of Morgan Grenfell; it was not, however, until 1854 that a Morgan became part of the firm.

The Peabody–Morgan Partnership

Although Junius Spencer Morgan, like George Peabody, came from an old New England family—the Morgan ancestor had arrived in New England from Bristol less than a year after the Peabody ancestor—in most other respects their two backgrounds were very different. While Peabody had come from a poor family and had had only a minimal formal education, Morgan's father was, by the time Junius Morgan was a young man, a prosperous hotelier, businessman, and farmer, one of the founders of the Aetna Insurance Company. Junius was born in 1813, educated at private schools, and apprenticed to Alfred Welles of Boston, a merchant and banker, where he learnt the practical details of running a business. After five years as a clerk with Welles, Junius was briefly his partner, and subsequently the partner in Morris Ketchum's private bank on Wall Street in New York City. In January 1836 Morgan left Wall Street to return to his home town of Hartford, Connecticut, to become a partner in the wholesale dry goods house of Howe Mather & Co.[47]

As the most junior partner, he supervised the clerks and dealt with the firm's correspondence. But his most time-consuming task was to travel on the firm's behalf, paying and collecting bills, buying cotton and wool, and supervising and recruiting the firm's agents and correspondents. Most of his time was spent in New England and New York, but on occasion, as during the panic of 1837, he travelled doggedly through the South trying to collect the firm's bills.

Upon the death of his father in 1847, Junius Morgan, at the age of thirty-four, came into a sizeable fortune. His own record as an established merchant joined with his inherited estate to make him a member of New England's commercial élite. ('The Merchants', wrote a contemporary observer, 'are the prominent class; the most respectable, the most powerful.')[48] His connections, his proven abilities, and his increased capital opened up greater opportunities: in February 1850 he became a senior partner in the firm, now called Mather Morgan & Company, and in May 1850 he left on his first business trip to Europe. His intention was to meet some of London's leading merchant bankers and transatlantic traders and to learn what opportunities there were for his own firm to move into that business.[49] He was clearly looking for larger opportunities than were available in Hartford.

He made his first move shortly thereafter, arranging in the autumn of 1850 to go into business in Boston with James M. Beebe, 'the young and outstandingly successful founder and owner of the city's (perhaps the country's) largest wholesale dry goods and importing house',[50] James M. Beebe & Co. The firm had sales of some $2 million in 1849 and a staff of thirty; the growing volume of imports and the possibilities for expansion made it advisable to add to the firm's capital. Morgan brought some capital and he brought experience, connections, and a high reputation as well. On 1 January 1851 the new firm of J. M. Beebe, Morgan and Co. was announced.[51] It was a successful partnership: by the time Morgan visited London again in 1853, the firm had boosted its annual gross sales to some $7 million, triple what they had been when Morgan joined the firm.[52]

But this visit to London ensured that the Beebe partnership would be of short duration, for one of the people Morgan called on in London was Peabody, who had granted a credit to J. M. Beebe, Morgan & Co. They first met at Peabody's counting-house at 6 Warnford Court on about 15 May 1853. Peabody, now fifty-eight, had been suffering from gout and rheumatism as well as intestinal complaints, and had been away from his business for four months; worse, reports of his illness had appeared in the New York newspapers and disturbed his primary agent, Duncan, Sherman & Co., who hardly wanted thousands of dollars of their business tied up with a firm consisting of a sick man and a junior partner. Friends of Peabody's had been urging him for years to take in another partner, and, of course, he had himself been looking for one. Morgan would prove to be just the man he required.[53]

Peabody invited Morgan and his wife to attend a large dinner, for 150 English and American guests, which he was giving on 18 May at the Star and Garter Hotel in Richmond in honour of Joseph Reed Ingersoll, the new American Minister in London. Peabody was particularly pleased by Morgan's ability to mix well with many kinds of people, an attribute on which he placed very high value. Shortly thereafter, Peabody had a long talk with Morgan and discussed with him a possible partnership. Morgan was interested and promised to think seriously about the proposal, and after his return to the US the two exchanged letters regularly.[54] In November 1853 Peabody initiated serious negotiations, and early in February 1854 Morgan returned to London; he examined the firm's accounts and satisfied himself with the way Peabody and the firm conducted business, and after further discussions the two agreed that he should become a partner.[55]

Congratulations poured in from American clients and associates of Peabody, as well as from British clients; one Englishman wrote to Morgan that as Peabody was 'fast approaching the usual allotment of life, we naturally look to you as the future representative of American credit in this country'.[56] But even more valuable as evidence of Morgan's abilities and of what he and Peabody in tandem were expected to accomplish are letters from Samuel Ward, the American agent of Barings, who wrote to Barings on 11 April 1854 that 'Mr Morgan is highly thought of here as a man of talent, energy & labor. If Mr Peabody was safe before, he will be much safer now with Mr Morgan at his side.' By 27 October he was writing that Morgan had 'a hold on this side which will make the competition more formidable than before'.[57]

Morgan was joining the premier American house in London, although it was not yet the premier house in the American trade: this was a position more likely to be contested between Baring Brothers & Co. and Brown, Shipley & Co., the English branch of Alexander Brown & Sons. But Peabody, and doubtless Morgan, had aspirations, and meanwhile the new arrangements seemed well on track to ensure, as Peabody once wrote, 'that my house will be purely American, that its continuance for many years will not depend on my life, and that my American friends will feel that, in every respect, the house is worthy of their entire confidence'. His offices were arranged in an American manner, with current American newspapers laid out on the table: they were intended to be, as he once remarked, 'a center for his American friends visiting England'.[58] Apparently he entertained every American who arrived at his office with a letter of credit, introducing him around London and perhaps providing a box at the opera, with a corsage for his wife. In July 1855 he remarked that he had entertained eighty Americans for dinner and thirty-five at the opera within a week.[59]

He also went in for rather more lavish celebrations, and in the 1850s he became known for sumptuous Anglo-American dinners in honour of American diplomats and other notables. It was during the Crystal Palace Exhibition in 1851, when the US had several exhibits for which Peabody had advanced funds, that he gave the first of a regular series of dinners to celebrate the Fourth of July: the Duke of Wellington was the guest of honour, and where the Duke led, others followed.[60] Public relations is clearly not a modern concept.

But Peabody could attract this sort of attendance at his dinners not merely because of his jovial personality: what was more important was the standing of his house. Between 1 August 1848 and 30 September 1854 Peabody, and George Peabody & Co., had made £311,546, and by December 1851 Peabody himself was worth £1.2 million. When the articles of partnership were drawn up for Peabody and Morgan, they stipulated that Peabody was to provide £400,000 of the firm's capital of £450,000; Morgan was to provide £40,000, and Gooch £10,000. This was not contemptible for what had been virtually a one-man show, and now, with a young and vigorous partner, considerable gains could be expected. The partnership was to run for ten years, and after paying 5% annual interest on the partners' capital balances, the profits and losses were to be divided as follows: Peabody 65%, Morgan 28%, and Gooch 7%. In addition, Morgan was to receive an entertainment allowance of £2,500 a year, to be devoted to entertaining the firm's clients and contacts; both men agreed on the importance of informal discussions in congenial surroundings to lubricate business dealings.[61]

Morgan started work in a crowded office, but that was soon to change: in November 1854 the firm moved to its new counting-house at 22 Old Broad Street, and he settled down to learn the business. Between 1854 and 1858 most of Peabody & Co.'s business, measured in terms of volume and profits, stemmed from its commercial credit operations. Peabody, as he told Morgan, had organized his house to take advantage of an expanding international economy (he dealt in China and India as well as in the US), and the signs, although now mixed, were on the whole still encouraging. It was worrying that Britain was caught up in the Crimean War, which involved as well Russia, France, and Turkey, all areas of business for the City of London; furthermore, in the US there were growing North–South problems which would lead, within a few years, to the Civil War, as well as more mundane problems of corruption in American railroads. But still, the outlook was generally positive, and the firm looked to increasing business, particularly in the US.[62]

Peabody's commercial credit operations had begun to grow dramatically from around 1850, when he made a grand tour of the US eastern port cities, lining up agency agreements with almost every respectable house which would sign on.[63] He arranged with the various American correspondents (especially Duncan, Sherman & Co. of New York, to whom he allowed 'almost unlimited' credit, and Blake, Ward & Co. of Boston, who had a running bank credit with Peabody of £250,000)[64] that they could issue credits, which they would guarantee, and he would honour them in London. What this agreement did was to leave the management of credit operations largely in the hands of his American correspondents, and they were thus at liberty to alter the terms to make them competitive; all he did, as noted above, was to accept and pay the bills of exchange which customers of his authorized correspondents presented to him in London. Thus he had a total lack of control over his chain of representatives. This was soon to lead to serious trouble for the firm.[65]

Meanwhile, apparently at the suggestion of Morgan, Peabody & Co. began to engage in a very un-English activity: they began soliciting accounts through agents in American and continental ports at $\frac{1}{2}$% commission, which was lower than that normally charged. Barings, whose business was affected, felt that this was very wrong for two reasons: 'it was dishonourable to apply to the correspondent' of a competitor for his business and 'doubly wrong' to offer to work at a reduced commission. Further, Peabody agents emphasized that the two leading partners were American citizens and that arrangements could be made which would eliminate the need for the customer to buy bills for remittance to London. Barings, although the firm most hit by this procedure, merely shared a belief common in the City that this approach was not what was expected of the highest firms.[66] But what Peabody & Co. were doing was quite acceptable in the US: this was not to be the last time that the difference in American and British business practices would be noticeable, and City reaction to American Morgan practices would in the future—and particularly at the turn of the century—rebound to the harm of the firm. The outcome of this push for business would in fact nearly be disastrous: George Peabody & Co. came very close to being a casualty in the panic of 1857.

This particular commercial crisis has been called the first world-wide crisis in history: it broke out first in the US, spread to Britain and Europe, and was then felt in South Africa, Australia, and the Far East. In 1856 between a quarter and a fifth of all British exports went to the US; it has been estimated that British investors held £80 million worth of American stocks and bonds; and there were many substantial lines of credit for American firms in England; therefore, bad news from the US was very bad news indeed for the British financial sector.[67] The origins of the crisis in the US lay in over-expansion and speculation in railroad construction and western lands, a fall in European demand for American wheat, and higher interest rates in England that cut capital exports to the US and lured capital from New York to London.[68] Money therefore became dangerously scarce in the US, business slumped, and many firms found it difficult to collect outstanding debts. Country bankers, particularly in the South and West, withdrew their deposits from New York banks to pay for moving produce from the interior to the Atlantic coast, and New York banks were forced to reduce their loans, with the result that the value of railroad securities fell sharply. Four gold ships from

California were late in arriving, and one, carrying £1,600,000 worth of gold, actually sank. As a result, New York banks found it more and more difficult to pay out depositors' funds. The banks tried to force creditors to repay loans, but they were often in grave difficulties themselves. Finally, on 25 September the Bank of Pennsylvania failed. Within four days other banks in the state had closed, and suspension soon became general; in October alone 1,415 banks stopped and business came to a standstill along the eastern and south eastern seaboards.[69]

The panic soon spread to England, with Liverpool taking the first shock on 27 October when the Liverpool Borough Bank failed. During the rest of October and into November conditions worsened, and then on 11 November the City of Glasgow Bank temporarily suspended payments. Shortly thereafter discounts almost entirely ceased in London except at the Bank of England, and by the 12th the situation for the great bill-brokers was desperate.[70] And then, on 17 November 1857, George Peabody & Co. was forced to ask the Bank of England for help.[71]

How had the firm got into such trouble? The main problem was that all of their American correspondents were suffering from the contraction, and in some cases, such as that of Lawrence, Stone & Co., had failed, owing Peabody & Co. considerable sums (in Lawrence, Stone & Co.'s case, £34,000). Some of those who were still in business, such as Duncan, Sherman & Co., had repudiated their guarantees and were unable to remit payments to Peabody (it was estimated that they alone owed Peabody & Co. as much as £500,000).[72] Peabody at the time was liable for £2,300,000 worth of bills, of which £150,000 were due to Barings, who were urgently pressing for repayment. Peabody needed to protect his reputation and to do that he had to pay out on bills when they matured. But money was also flowing out because English investors were selling their American securities and many did so through Peabody & Co. So he had to protect his own credit and that of his correspondents, such as Duncan, Sherman & Co. The partners came to the conclusion that they had no option but to apply to the Bank of England for a loan of £800,000.[73]

There is no evidence that Peabody and Morgan were particularly apprehensive as to whether the Bank would lend such a sum: after all, they were a large, well-managed firm whose difficulties were not obviously of their own making; furthermore, as noted above, Peabody had in the previous panic in 1837 assisted the Bank in its attempts to aid the Liverpool firm of W. & J. Brown & Co. Indeed, there is no evidence in the Bank's files that there was any moral or financial objection to helping

Peabody & Co., but there was a legal one. By law the Bank was not allowed to make an advance if it could only be secured with foreign issues, and, of course, nearly all of Peabody & Co.'s securities were those of American Federal and state governments and American railroads; the Bank would agree to accept these American securities as collateral for the loan only if the loan was guaranteed by residents in England. Peabody agreed to find the guarantors, and by 20 November the Bank agreed to assist Peabody.[74]

It is notable that during the week when negotiations between Peabody & Co. and the Bank were taking place, commercial rivals tried to take advantage of the firm's weakness to force them out of business. The story goes that a confidential proposal was relayed to Junius Morgan that 'certain individuals' would guarantee a loan to Peabody on the condition that the firm would cease business by the end of 1858. When Morgan told Peabody, 'he was in a rage like a wounded lion, and told Mr Morgan to reply that *he dared them to cause his failure*'.[75]

Far from crashing during the panic, Peabody & Co. appear to have survived with their credit intact. Indeed, the fact that the Bank of England had felt it necessary to come to the firm's aid was taken in the US as evidence of the firm's strength and importance; the *New York Herald* wrote on 3 December 1857 that the loan 'speaks volumes for the character of the house'. J. P. Morgan (known as Pierpont), Junius's son, wrote from New York City to his father that the news of the loan had 'tended to strengthen rather than weaken the character & credit of the house—that the Bk of England should step forward at such a time is considered by everyone as a most convincing proof of the solidity of the house & that nothing but the defalcation of all correspondents upon this side could have brought about the necessity for the aid, so handsomely offered'.[76]

This, of course, was all very reassuring, as was the fact that in the end the partners had to utilize only £300,000 worth of the loan, and were able to divide £50,000 in profit amongst themselves at the end of the year.[77] Furthermore, the firm was able to repay the Bank of England in full by the end of March 1858.[78] But the partners would have been foolish if they had not looked closely at the business and at their procedures to see if lessons could be learnt. They agreed that they had been over-zealous in soliciting clients. However, the firm was not yet of the status—as was Barings, for example—where clients always came to them. The partners realized that they would have to seek clients, but they also agreed that they would not accept too large a volume of bills from any one house;

and certainly, the volume of bills they accepted from, for example, Duncan, Sherman & Co. over the subsequent years was at most only half of what it had been before. They also agreed that they would have to exercise much more control over their agents and correspondents, both in terms of the amounts of credit advanced and in terms of the credit worthiness of the firms to whom they lent their name.[79]

But the favourable outcome of the crisis was also the signal for a change in the leadership of the firm. George Peabody was now sixty-three, tired, and ill. He had many things he wanted to accomplish before he died, and he seems to have felt that time was beginning to run out. He was to remain as the firm's senior partner, but from the spring of 1858 Junius Morgan was the effective head. Peabody returned to the firm for some months in the autumn and winter, but this was his last extended period in the offices, and in February 1859 he gave Morgan full control of the business.[80]

Peabody was a bachelor, with no direct heirs, and he was preoccupied with the dispersal of his fortune; the main reason he wished to retire from active business was to devote his time to philanthropy. Strictly speaking, it is not entirely true to say that he had no possible direct heirs, but he had no acknowledged ones. Peabody had, in fact, a mistress in Brighton, who had borne him a daughter. He was very generous to his mistress during his lifetime—he would regularly withdraw some of his own personal securities in the office, sometimes as much as £2,000 at a time, to be realized and sent to her—and so he left her nothing in his will. The firm continued to help the family. Peabody's daughter married, but her husband, 'who was not a very satisfactory person', lost all of her dowry. As late as the early twentieth century, one of her sons wrote to the firm asking whether he 'could secure a certain amount of help, owing to his connection with Mr Peabody'. One of the office staff, who had known Peabody, was sent to see him, and when the man returned, he reported that 'He is a very impressive young man, he is studying to be a Parliamentary barrister, and his brother is studying to be something in a university, whether in Cambridge or Oxford, I do not know, and both of them have the old man's nose to a dot'. J. Pierpont Morgan, J. S. Morgan's son, gave them some help, and in due course 'the barrister ... reached a very good position at the Parliamentary Bar and the other had become a professor of geology in one of the universities'.[81]

The firm, in fact, did for Peabody's grandsons what Peabody himself spent the last years of his life doing on a very large scale. He wanted to leave London some token of his affection for the city. He thought first

of an elaborate system of drinking fountains; then he considered helping
Lord Shaftesbury's Ragged Schools for the children of the very poor. In
the end, Shaftesbury convinced Peabody that it was more important to
provide better housing conditions for the working classes: in March 1859
Peabody decided that his gift to London would be a number of model
dwellings. The American Civil War began before the gift could be
organized, and it was not until 26 March 1862 that the Peabody Donation
Fund was announced. His donation was to be £150,000 (later increased
to £500,000), which was to be used to build houses to be inhabited by
poor Londoners who had good moral characters and who were good
members of society. (By 1882 the Fund owned 3,500 dwellings and
housed more than 14,600 people, while by 1939 there were more than
8,000 dwellings. During the Second World War thirty blocks of apart-
ments and fourteen cottages were destroyed, but in 1951 a thirteen-storey
block of Peabody flats was erected in Roscoe Street, Finsbury, and in 1962
the Queen Mother unveiled a plaque to Peabody at another new Peabody
Estate in Blackfriars.)[82] As a result of this gift, Peabody in July 1862 was
made a Freeman of the City of London, the first American to receive
the honour. A more enduring monument is the statue of Peabody on
Threadneedle Street near the Royal Exchange: the funds were raised by
popular subscription, and it was unveiled on 23 July 1869.[83]

During the last years of the Peabody–Morgan partnership the major
part of the firm's business was, as before, with the US. The firm
continued to finance a wide variety of commodities, with the most
important continuing to be railroad iron. From January 1859 until
December 1871 the firm had an arrangement with C. M. Lampson & Co.
whereby Lampson & Co. assumed all of the non-financial responsibilities
of the business while Peabody & Co. provided the required credits and
banking services. Profit and loss were divided equally; in addition to the
sums taken out each year, the two firms divided $650,000 in railroad
securities between them in 1871.

The division of duties was significant, and it exemplified a general
trend for Peabody & Co. Banking, rather than dealing in goods, was the
business Peabody and Morgan had decided to emphasize at the outset of
the partnership, and in the years after 1857 their railroad financings in
particular grew significantly. However, until their involvement with the
reorganization of the Ohio & Mississippi Railroad, beginning in 1857, the
firm had not involved itself with the policies or decision-making of
the various railroads whose securities it marketed. But the difficulties
involved with this carrier, the focus of their first major financial

sponsorship of a railroad property, seemed to strengthen a growing conviction on the part of Morgan and Peabody of the need for more effective supervision of the firms whose bonds they sold: after all, their own reputation, as well as money, was at stake.[84] Junius's son Pierpont would spend a substantial portion of his working life acting on this belief.

The partners also tried their hand occasionally at acting as entrepreneurial promoters of enterprise which, while financially risky, could very well be profitable as well as generally beneficial. A good example was their support of Cyrus Field in his attempts to lay a transatlantic telegraph cable. From 1856 until the years beyond the ending of George Peabody & Co. the firm, and the partners individually, supported the enterprise through good times—August 1858, when Queen Victoria wired a message to President Buchanan—and bad—October 1858, when the cable broke. They apparently never lost confidence in the ultimate success of the project, and certainly their reward came in the long term. Their earnings from fees and commissions were slight, but they gained added prestige and recognition through being closely associated with a widely heralded international enterprise; furthermore, over the subsequent eighty years Peabody & Co. and its successor houses in the US and Europe were 'to be intimately associated with most of the communications industry's major financings'.[85]

The American Civil War from 1861 to 1865 disrupted established patterns of trade between Britain and the US, although trade did not cease entirely. Those firms engaged in financing the export of cotton from the South to Britain of course suffered, since the Union (Northern) Navy blockaded Southern ports from April 1861. Peabody & Co., as did other banking firms, found that some of their clients with interests in the South had difficulties remitting funds to cover their debts. But during the war the partners tried to minimize the danger to themselves by extending credits only to known clients and insisting that all advances be covered, either with a trust receipt, the equivalent of a mortgage on the financed merchandise, or with easily saleable first-class securities. Over the course of the war, they earned steady if not spectacular profits on commercial credits (see Appendix I).[86]

On the other hand, the firm's dealings in securities were considerably less profitable. New railroad loans disappeared almost entirely during the war years, and therefore almost all of the firm's dealings were in US government bonds. Unfortunately, demand for such bonds had almost evaporated in Britain as well as in Europe. Not only that, but current holders got rid of most of their American securities. Junius Morgan himself was pretty uninterested in Federal bonds until September 1862, when the victory of the Union Army at Antietam began the turn of the tide against the South. Thereafter Morgan began to trade heavily in Federal issues, but he did most of his buying and selling through his son's firm in New York, J. Pierpont Morgan & Co. In all, the firm's turnover in these issues between April 1862 and November 1866, when it was most active in US long-term bonds, totalled some £299,200. Their net earnings on their Civil War bonds accounts (including interest) amounted to about £16,600.[87]

During these years Morgan began actively to develop the firm's business in European issues, an aspect of the firm's work he considered too long neglected. This was slightly unfair, since Peabody and Gooch had made previous attempts to develop business in Germany, but certainly the fact that the firm's major area of operations was engulfed in civil war encouraged a wider outlook. Furthermore, this was a period of rapid industrial expansion in Europe, and the combination of these two factors helped to convince Morgan of the need to expand the firm's operations in the international securities markets. The immediate results of this decision were not encouraging, since the net earnings in the 1860s were rather low, but it was a pointer for the future (see Appendix I).[88]

In October 1864 the ten-year partnership agreement was due to expire: what was to happen to the firm? J. S. Morgan certainly wanted things to go on as they were: after all, the firm had Peabody's name, a well-known and respected one, and Peabody capital, but he had untrammelled control. The partnership had been a profitable one for all concerned: after setting aside about £241,000 in the firm's 'suspense' account, to cover bad and doubtful debts, the partners had, over the ten-year period, divided a total of £444,468 amongst the three of them (Appendix I). Accordingly, in August 1864 Morgan wrote to Peabody, then staying in the Scottish Highlands, urging him to continue the partnership for some months beyond October: his concern was that many securities held by the firm would have to be sold when the partnership came to an end, and their precipitate sale would result in losses. But Peabody refused: he was nearly seventy, and with the uncertainty of life, a month for Morgan would appear as a year for him; and before he died he wished to arrange his 'wordly affairs' and devote himself to his philanthropies, of which the Peabody Donation Fund was merely a part (Peabody's fortune amounted to something over $10 million).[89] Morgan of course had to accept this. He also had to accept the fact that Peabody refused to allow the firm to remain George Peabody & Co.: he did not wish to have his name used in business affairs over which he had no control. Therefore, on 30 September 1864 George Peabody & Co. ceased to exist, and on 1 October J. S. Morgan & Co. was born.[90]

The career of George Peabody is an exemplification of much which the nineteenth century found admirable. If not precisely a barefoot boy from South Danvers, he certainly began his working life honest but poor. He always worked hard—there are hints all through his career of long hours and endless days without a break—and he did not spurn 'two penny' business, as certain of his colleagues did. He was always willing to take a risk, but by and large they were well-judged risks: it is notable, for example, that for years he refused to issue American securities on his own in London, preferring to work with a larger and better-established firm such as Barings; only in 1853 did he float an issue of railroad bonds on the London market, those of the Ohio & Mississippi Railroad Co., without a co-manager. (He was very successful in disposing of the issue.)[91] Another element in his success was his knack of making useful friends, who tended to include wealthy and influential businessmen. His personal traits encouraged trust: he was personally austere while publicly generous. He ended his life wealthy and respected.

He died on 4 November 1869, and both his native and his adopted countries paid him public honour. His funeral was held in Westminster Abbey, after which his body was carried by special train to Portsmouth. Queen Victoria and W. E. Gladstone, the Prime Minister, had jointly requested the Royal Navy to provide HMS *Monarch*, the Navy's newest ironclad, to take Peabody's body back home, and the *Monarch*, on the orders of President Grant, was escorted by the USS *Plymouth*. The American authorities received the body at Portland, Maine, and there were elaborate services both there and in Peabody (his old home town of South Danvers, renamed in 1868), before he was finally laid to rest near Salem, Massachusetts.[92]

He left behind him in London a firm which he had built from nothing to become the major American house in London. He also left behind him a partner who intended to make the firm more than that: Morgan was determined that J. S. Morgan & Co. would become a major international house, not just an American one. He had already begun dealings in Europe, and would soon reorganize his son's New York firm to provide a strong Anglo-American axis: when his chance came for a daring coup in 1870, which would catapult the bank into the first rank, he was ready.

CHAPTER TWO

J. S. MORGAN & CO.
1864–1910

Per Ardua ad Astra

THE City of London in the second half of the nineteenth century teemed with men aspiring to great fortunes. Bankers, merchants, brokers, and jobbers—the latter two categories sometimes united in the same person—bill-brokers, promoters, those knowledgeable about home and those more interested in abroad, those who were honest and those who were more economical with that commodity, all met in the Square Mile to listen and learn and transact business. At the summit were the private bankers, commercial and merchant, whose watchword was integrity and whose liability was unlimited. But private commercial banks were gradually to disappear, sucked up from the 1890s on into the maelstrom of an amalgamation movement, which by the First World War left the landscape levelled and the great joint-stock banks in command of the field. J. S. Morgan & Co., of course, belonged to a different category of private banker, the merchant banker—or just merchant, as most continued to style themselves until after the First World War. For this group, the period 1864–1910 was one of growth and development, at least for those who salted their ambition with caution.

J. S. Morgan wanted his firm to become, and to be acknowledged as having become, a merchant bank of the first rank. The theme of this chapter is the drive to accomplish this, and it might be said in summary that by 1910 J. S. Morgan & Co. were counted among the first rank, but were not always acknowledged as equals by, for example, Barings and Rothschilds.

As David Landes has noted, membership of the international community of top merchant banks was a way of life as much as a way of business.[1] In their private lives as in their public, such bankers traditionally lived prudently and modestly. The cut of the suit should be sober and made of good quality cloth: flashy clothing was the mark of the speculator. The family home should be solid and spacious, but not too ostentatious: the latter might signify that the partner was spending money on good living which it would be better to put back into the business. Even the working quarters were serviceable rather than luxurious: the great banking palaces of today would have been considered the mark of the *arriviste*. The Morgans, father, son, and grandson, believed strongly in the ethos and way of living of the Victorian private banker. They all lived comfortable lives but they scorned the vulgarly lavish living of men who strove to be public. As late as the turn of the century the offices of J. S. Morgan & Co. exemplified this approach. One writer recalled that, when in London before the First World War,

I found, to my immense surprise, world-famous banking houses tucked away in little courts and alleys. . . . To discover that the office of J. S. Morgan & Company, the great international bankers, was housed in an old-fashioned building, somewhat like a private residence of the American 'brownstone' type, where one was ushered into a front parlor when calling on business, was a real experience . . .[2]

The Morgans themselves within such offices refused to retreat behind great doors: the same writer noted that in New York, ' J. P. Morgan often sat in his shirt sleeves in an open office, where he could keep tabs on all his employees from head clerk to office boy.'[3] Certainly in 1916 the London partners and the staff worked in full view of each other.[4]

Prudence, then, was the external hallmark, that and integrity, because above all it was a calling which was of necessity based upon trust. Merchant banking, after all, dealt primarily in the bill of exchange, which has been defined as the 'acknowledgement of a debt and a promise to pay at some future time in another place and another currency'.[5] Because they frequently never saw the enterprise for which they guaranteed funds, bankers had to depend upon their judgement of people, both those who wished to borrow, and those on whose assessments they often depended as to the credit-worthiness of a potential borrower. To them, the highest praise of a man was that his character was sound: no matter how promising the enterprise seemed, a first-class banker would not lend to anyone he did not trust. 'That subdued méfiance that is the hallmark of the experienced banker'[6] had always to be to the fore.

Yet prudence was not enough for those who were still aspiring to first-class status. The 'slow but steady multiplication of minimal unit gains'[7] would do for those who had no ambition or who already had a position to lose; for others—such as Peabody and J. S. Morgan—an element of daring was required. To a certain extent this had to be part of the make-up of any merchant banker, since of all financial professions it was one of those most open to risk. This daring might take the form of breaking ranks with other bankers by engaging in price competition or by going after clients belonging to other banks: both of these activities were very much frowned upon by reputable and established City bankers, and both had been engaged in by George Peabody & Co. in the years between 1854 and the panic of 1857. But the partners learnt their lesson from that near-disaster, and thereafter behaved as they ought; and in fact, 'George Peabody . . . is an excellent example of professional assimilation. The gradual abandonment by Peabody of the incautious practices of his merchant days and his adoption of more prudent procedures, which he could enforce all the better for his earlier experience',[8] can clearly be seen.

J. S. Morgan, forty-one in 1854, brought energy and a new element of daring to the firm: the ability to judge coolly that an opportunity which his elders and betters thought entirely too risky was in fact safe enough to venture. His courage in ignoring the threats of Otto von Bismarck, Chancellor first of Prussia and then of the German Empire, and agreeing to issue the loan of the soon-to-be-defeated French government was crucial to the consolidation of the firm's position in the ranks of those who were part of the central international group of bankers: those who issued government bonds. The issuing of commercial credits may have been the core business of merchant banking and J. S. Morgan & Co.'s 'bread and butter', but the prestige and the highest rewards accrued to those upon whom governments depended. The French loan of 1870 would greatly enhance the firm's reputation. But it would do more than that: it would bring the firm a substantial addition to its capital.

Developing American Business

In 1864, however, the newly named firm of J. S. Morgan & Co. was still quite clearly of the second rank. It was admittedly the most important American house in London, and one of the most important (along with Barings, Rothschilds, and Brown, Shipley) in the American trade, but its interests were concentrated primarily in the one geographical area, and were not international in the same manner as those of Barings and Rothschilds. The capital of the firm is estimated to have been between £300,000 and £350,000 in 1869, which was considerably less than that of Rothschilds, Barings, or Browns, which have been estimated at about £6.5 million, £2.1 million, and £1 million respectively for 1870–5.[9]

Morgans lacked the international correspondent network of, for example, the Rothschilds, with their family firms in Vienna, Paris, Naples, and Frankfurt, and their able representative August Belmont in the US. And it lacked the international experience of the older and more famous firms.

One of J. S. Morgan's first moves in the campaign to transform his bank into an international house was to strengthen its agency in New York City, the firm of J. P. Morgan & Co. J. Pierpont Morgan was his son, and in the fullness of time he would eclipse both the fame and the fortune of his father. In 1864, however, he was only twenty-seven years old, and his father thought it necessary to give the firm greater stability and wider recognition, both of which would be accomplished by bringing in an older, more experienced partner who would 'command the respect of the wider business community'.[10] Junius Morgan accomplished this to his satisfaction by persuading Charles H. Dabney, one of the partners in Duncan, Sherman, to join with young Pierpont Morgan in the new firm of Dabney, Morgan & Co., which began business on 15 November 1864. The New York financial community recognized that this was the representative firm in New York of J. S. Morgan & Co., which immediately gave it some standing.[11]

J. S. Morgan & Co. needed a strong agency in New York City in order to conduct their commercial credits business, from which, like most London merchant banks, they earned a substantial proportion of their income. The two firms issued credits large and small, primarily secured ones, although for favoured customers—and with some reluctance—they issued some uncovered acceptances as well. Commissions were small, so profits depended on turnover. Small, inactive accounts were discouraged, as well as those which yielded little other business. It was the London firm, not Dabney, Morgan, which exercised ultimate authority over the allocation of credits for both houses, and it was Junius Morgan who had the final say as to who received credits, for what, and on what terms. He insisted that before a new credit was established or an existing one extended, the firm needed to know both why it was required, and what the chances were of securing the client's 'general business', provided of course that it was a 'desirable' association. According to Junius Morgan, 'safety and prudence' were to be the prime considerations at all times when considering whether to accept business.[12]

Financing trade gave merchant banks the opportunity to deal in commodities on their own account, and, indeed, the bank had been doing so ever since its establishment. The London firm continued to trade in a variety of goods, including some cotton and tobacco, but by 1864 most of the business centred on iron for American railroads and, to a lesser extent, trading in gold. The iron business continued to yield substantial profits, which (along with occasional losses) were shared equally between the London and New York firms (and sometimes with a third party). This was because railroad building in the US surged ahead after the end of the Civil War in 1865.

Both Junius and Pierpont recognized the significance of this boom early on, and both worked to gain the banking as well as the commodities business for their firms. Junius provided the initial leadership and in September 1865 he negotiated the sale of an £800,000 issue of 6% 10-year convertible sterling bonds for the Erie Railway Company, the first large American railway offering to appear on the London market, putting together an informal syndicate in London to dispose of the issue. The firm led on very few other issues, however, acting usually as a participant or co-sponsor of groups organized by other bankers. Junius Morgan would have preferred to lead such groups, but clearly did not yet possess the requisite stature; however, he welcomed the opportunity to participate as a member, since such participations could lead to other long-lasting corporate relationships. During the late 1860s, then, both Junius in London and Pierpont in New York were turning the two firms into major distributors of American railway securities.[13]

Nevertheless, 'in the decade before the American panic of 1873, traditional merchant banking (financing international trade and dealing in commodities) rather than the securities business (selling government and railway loans)' occupied most of J. S. Morgan & Co.'s time and accounted for their main source of earnings. Only once in the ten-year period did the London house's profits from its issuing and dealings in securities exceed those earned from commissions (see Appendices I and II).[14]

But in a sense, this was a short-term way of looking at things. The firms which had the best opportunities to reap the greatest profits over the long term were the first-class firms. To be considered a first-class firm a merchant banking house usually had to break into the circle of those who led on, or at least participated in, national loans, who, in short, acted as bankers to governments. Issuing or underwriting a government loan was, in fact, occasionally a loss-making activity: what made it desirable with regard to profits was that it usually led on to other business. After all, there were many other services which a bank might perform for governments—paying dividends, operating sinking funds or purchase accounts, undertaking exchange operations, making diplomatic payments, providing short-term finance by means of financial credits—all of which generated certain profits.[15] There were many opportunities for firms to share in such lending, because the period 1861–73 was a peak period for government loans. As Leland Jenks has written, 'Between the universal desire for progress and the equally universal desire for lower taxes there was a discongruity which could be bridged only by public borrowing.'[16] The great merchant bankers of the City of London issued more such loans than those of any other country.

Beginnings of an Issuing House

The first country for which J. S. Morgan & Co. organized and led an issue was Chile. Baring Brothers and then Thomson, Bonar & Co. had been Chile's London bankers, but in late 1866 the government decided to turn to Morgans. In February 1867 they brought out the 7% Chilean Loan 1866 (until the mid-twentieth century, loans were denoted by their date of issue rather than date of maturity) to redeem an earlier one; it was a successful placing, and the firm earned commission and profits of £124,500. This was rapidly followed by another, the Chilean 6% Sterling Government Loan 1867, and this time Morgans netted £360,000.[17] Further, the bank was also appointed Chile's London agent, responsible for servicing the loan and managing the sinking fund set up for its redemption. Appointments of this sort were much prized, because the agent had the use of coupon money until claimed by the holders. Since holders were notoriously lazy in claiming, such an appointment was a steady source of low-risk income. The firm's appointment as paying agent also led to other loans (the Chilean 6% referred to above, as well as the Chilean 5% Government Loan 1870). The firm continued to take an interest in Chilean business on and off for the remainder of the century, although it led on no more government loans until 1909, being supplanted in the first instance by Rothschilds (see below).[18]

The first European country for which Morgans led a bond offering was Spain, the £8 million Spanish Government 3% Loan 1869. The English loan was part of a larger offering, a loan of £10 million issued simultaneously in London, Paris, Amsterdam, Hamburg, Frankfurt, Brussels, and Antwerp. Spain had a long record of financial mismanagement, to say the least, and it had been subject to recurring and recent political troubles. The combination frightened investors and made it difficult to place the loan, and in the end J. S. Morgan & Co. lost £260,000.[19]

But the Spanish loan was the dark before the dawn. On 15 July 1870 the French Council of Ministers voted for war on Prussia, a decision followed, on the last day of August and the first of September, by the devastating defeat of the French army at Sedan and the capture of the French emperor Napoleon III. This was the signal for a bloodless revolution in Paris and the substitution of the Third Republic for the Second Empire: a provisional Republican Government of National Defence, led by Léon Gambetta, was established and the fight against Prussia continued. However, two Prussian armies were besieging Paris and the only contact the French government had with the outside world was by means of carrier pigeons and the occasional balloon. The Provisional Government therefore fled the city to Tours, where they established their headquarters. The government then sent Clément Laurier, the Director-General Delegate of the Ministry of the Interior, to London to try and borrow money to enable France to continue the war.[20]

The French representative turned first to the two leading British merchant banks, Rothschilds and Barings. But lending money to a rich and peaceful France was one thing; issuing a loan for a desperate and nearly defeated France was quite another. The Rothschilds would probably have refused on any terms, even if they had not already had to cope with the fact that two of the family banks were on opposite sides. The Barings had already underwritten a Prussian loan. The French then turned to J. S. Morgan & Co. They later testified that they considered Morgans next in rank and reputation to Rothschilds and Barings—an assessment which Brown, Shipley as well as C. J. Hambro & Son would have hotly disputed—and a firm worthy 'to entrust . . . with the signature of France'. They also felt it important that Morgan himself was an American citizen, since they planned to purchase arms and supplies from the US; as they later argued, 'It seemed to us of no small consequence to put the credit of France under the aegis of the United States.'[21]

One can understand why France might have turned to J. S. Morgan & Co. to issue a loan: having issued loans for Chile and Spain within the previous three years, the firm was already a member, if a new one, of the circle of experienced governmental bankers; besides this, Morgans had very strong links with the US, which meant that France could expect to get its orders for arms and supplies expedited through Dabney, Morgan.[22] What is less immediately obvious is why Morgan should have agreed to issue the loan, and, moreover, agreed so quickly. He subsequently explained his reasoning to George W. Smalley, the London correspondent of the *New York Tribune*:

When it first occurred to me that something might be done, I looked up the financial history of France. I found that since 1789 there had been a dozen separate governments—Monarchy, First Republic, Directory, Consulate, Empire, the Bourbons again, the Orleanists, then the Second Republic, followed by the Second (or Third) Empire, and so on. Between these successive governments there were enmities of many kinds; dynastic, personal, political. Each successor, with one exception, hated its predecessor. It was one long civil war.

But I found this also. Not one of these governments had ever repudiated or questioned the validity of any financial obligation contracted by the other. The continuing financial solidarity of France was unbroken. It was plainly a policy rooted in the minds of the people and of the governing forces of France. I saw no reason why it should be broken in this case more than any other; less, perhaps, than in many others since this money was wanted for the defense of the country. That was good enough for me. There was no gamble.[23]

Accordingly the negotiations were concluded quickly and the contract was signed on 24 October 1870. Morgan refused to be put off by the furious threats of Bismarck, who threatened to make the repudiation of the loan a condition for the conclusion of peace. The loan was for £10 million (250 million francs) at 6% interest and issued at £85 for a nominal value of £100. When it was announced, the public response was immediate and favourable, with applications for the bonds arriving not only from British investors but from those on the Continent as well. Within a week about half had been allotted, with French citizens taking about 81% of the entire issue.[24]

For some weeks public sales remained strong, but then began to weaken. Bismarck continued his ferocious campaign against the loan and this, combined with the collapse of Paris at the end of January 1871, terrified investors. The price of the bonds plunged to £55, at which point Morgan bought back a substantial amount of the issue. Those he could not resell at a profit he held—and in 1873 the French government, true to Morgan's expectation, redeemed them at 100.

Morgan's daring had been great, and the recompense was equally great. His commission had been 1½% on the first £2.5 million of bonds which he took at £80 and 3¼% on the remaining £7.5 million of bonds at £85. This amount, however, was dwarfed by the amount he made by dealing in the bonds, in particular by buying at £55 and redeeming at £100, and by 1873 J. S. Morgan & Co. had netted £1.5 million on the transaction. The risk gained its reward, both in prestige and in capital.[25]

The firm was in a good position to exploit this surge of new capital because of organizational changes which had taken place. Early in January 1871, just when the French loan began to run into difficulties, Junius Morgan was visited at his London office by Mr Anthony J. Drexel. Drexel was the most important partner in the Philadelphia firm of Drexel & Co., J. S. Morgan & Co. was Drexel's correspondent house in London,[26] and it was advice about the Drexel firms which Anthony Drexel sought. What he wanted were some ideas how he might strengthen his New York and Paris houses, Drexel, Winthrop & Co. and Drexel, Harjes et Cie. Neither of these firms had strong, energetic leaders: both resident senior partners were either too cautious or too preoccupied with daily business. Morgan had wide knowledge of both American and European business and bankers, and was known for his sound judgement, so presumably Drexel hoped that Morgan might suggest methods or men to rejuvenate his two connected houses. What is unknown is whether he was prepared for the suggestion Morgan made sometime during their talk: that his son Pierpont Morgan join Drexel's New York firm as a partner.

Drexel was certainly delighted with the idea, writing to Morgan immediately upon returning to Philadelphia that 'such a connection would be (if the matter could be arranged satisfactorily to all the parties) very acceptable to me'.[27] The main party besides himself, of course, was Pierpont Morgan. Junius wrote to his son that Drexel had called in at his office, that 'It is possible he may want to see you about a certain matter and, if he does, I hope you will go to see him'.[28] He then, apparently, sat back and awaited developments. It was a convenient occurrence for Pierpont, since he was unhappy with his own arrangements at New York and had, in fact, already notified his father that he did not intend to continue Dabney, Morgan & Co. when the partnership agreement ran out in 1871. The firm was profitable, but neither of his partners had much drive or was inclined to take risks. Therefore, when Drexel invited Pierpont along to dinner in Philadelphia in May 1871, the latter was clearly ripe for a new departure.

Drexel told Pierpont Morgan that he was dissatisfied with his firm's arrangements in New York, and he proposed that Morgan join the firm as a partner. Morgan hesitated at first, saying that he must consult his father, but in the end terms were drawn up: the New York firm would be reconstituted as Drexel, Morgan & Co. and Pierpont would be the senior resident partner, with profits and losses divided equally. Not only would this make Pierpont at thirty-four the head of a far stronger New

York firm than his current one, but he would also become a full and equal partner in Drexel & Co. of Philadelphia and a partner in Drexel, Harjes et Cie in Paris.

J. S. Morgan & Co. stood to gain immensely from the new arrangement, although it should be noted that it was not institutionally connected to the three Drexel partnerships. First, of course, it gained because its correspondent firm in New York City, now to be Drexel, Morgan & Co., was clearly going to be more powerful than its predecessor firm: this was in fact the institutional origin of J. P. Morgan & Co. Secondly, through Drexel, Harjes et Cie, whose capital at the beginning of 1871 was 750,000 francs, the London firm secured direct access to the Paris capital markets, then one of the most important on the Continent. And thirdly, it made it likely that the London firm would gain a larger participation in Drexel's Philadelphia business, no small consideration in view of the fact that Drexel & Co. was one of the US's leading banks, with active capital of some $2 million. In short, J. S. Morgan & Co. now had the kind of direct and effective representation in most of the world's principal capital markets which so benefited its main London competitors such as Barings and Rothschilds.[29]

The three Drexel partnerships actively directed business to the London firm, with all of them acting as its agents and attorneys, and with J. S. Morgan & Co. acting as their principal issuer of commercial credits, still one of the London firm's major sources of earnings. (It should be noted, however, that the London firm conducted its financing for trade independently as well as in conjunction with the Drexel firms.) The basic policies regulating the conduct of this business were determined by J. S. Morgan & Co.: Morgan himself advised the New York house on the kinds of accounts to seek and on what terms, the type of information to elicit from possible clients, what constituted acceptable collateral, and the form it should take. This continued through the 1870s and for a time into the 1880s, although it is difficult to determine exactly when the balance shifted from London to New York. One clue might be the date of the argument over whether the firms should engage in an arbitrage business in sterling and francs, as well as in bills of exchange and securities, buying them in the cheaper market and reselling them immediately in the dearer. Much of the firms' general banking business, whether for governments or private companies, was closely tied to their foreign exchange operations, a profitable part of their business. Pierpont Morgan and Drexel wanted to set up a joint account with the London firm to do an arbitrage business, but J. S. Morgan refused, saying he had neither the time nor a fancy for the business. By 1879, however, with a new and energetic London partner (see below), the elder Morgan could no longer argue that his work load was too heavy to involve the firm in this new business, and he gave in to Drexel and his son's insistence. The experiment was undertaken, and by September 1880 was deemed successful enough to justify making arbitrage a permanent part of the business.[30]

The ability to sense new opportunities was to prove to be one of Pierpont Morgan's most important assets and it was one he inherited from his father. But perhaps of equal importance is knowing when to get out of a business, and here, at an early stage in the new relationship, J. S. Morgan led the way. Ever since the foundation of the London firm in 1838 it had dealt in commodities. Indeed, dealing in the iron trade for American railroads had been an important source of profits for the firm ever since J. S. Morgan had joined it. Therefore, it was a turning-point when J. S. Morgan & Co. wrote to Drexel, Morgan & Co. in January 1873 that at the end of the year the firm intended to terminate the joint accounts set up to deal in iron rails. The reason was simply that the American output of iron rails was increasing both in quality and quantity and this meant that British exports of rails was declining. J. S. Morgan's decision to quit the trade came at the right time: not only had the volume of British rail exports dropped, but even the purely banking aspects of the trade, which the firms had emphasized since the late 1860s, had become increasingly risky. Both Drexel and Pierpont Morgan agreed.

The discussions over commodities, and the consequent withdrawal from the business, triggered off a decision of much greater importance for the strategic direction of J. S. Morgan & Co. (as well as for the American partnership), one which had, in fact, been mooted at least since the beginning of the Drexel partnerships. The firms would of course continue to finance trade and maintain their usual banking services, but the elder Morgan and Drexel believed, and the younger Morgan agreed, that the future of their businesses lay in developing an international securities business by serving the capital needs of governments and large corporations, which raised the funds they required by issuing securities for sale to investors both individual and institutional. In December 1873 they decided to develop this business. But this had a further implication: in order to have the manpower to do so, new partners would be needed.[31]

The Quest for Partners

Who chose the partners, and on what basis were they chosen? During the

1870s and 1880s the London, the New York, and the Philadelphia partnerships all added partners, and it is appropriate to link them together because all three seniors (Drexel and the two Morgans) had to agree before an appointment was made at any of the houses. There might be many criteria which a partner must satisfy before joining such a firm, and certainly for many firms kinship, the means to contribute capital, and the ability to enlarge the firm's list of clients were useful attributes. In fact, for the Drexel and Morgan partnerships the emphasis was slightly different: kinship appears to have been an important (although unmentioned) consideration in choosing the London partners during J. S. Morgan's lifetime—the new partners were all related to the old—but the paramount concern was character, with integrity being more important than any other quality. General competence in business was considered more important than technical training in banking, and no one apparently was made a partner because he could bring a list of clients along, since developing new business was largely the responsibility of the senior partners themselves.[32]

Locating these paragons was difficult and time-consuming. As Pierpont Morgan wrote to his father in October 1875, 'The longer I live the more apparent becomes the absence of brains—particularly soundly balanced brains. You would be surprised if you had devoted so much time to it as I have to see how few businessmen there are unexceptionable in character, ability, experience, and association to fit such a position. I would scarcely believe it, if I had not gone into the matter as thoroughly as I did.'[33] George Peabody had had the same problem, of course, and the London firm would, at the turn of the century, experience such acute problems in finding a decent partner that they would turn from banking and business to another field entirely in order to find one.

Meanwhile, J. S. Morgan & Co. had already by then gained two new partners (and lost an old one). The first new partner was S. Endicott Peabody, a Bostonian and a distant relative of George Peabody. He was forty-six and a partner in the banking firm of Cuyler, Peabody & Co. when he decided to accept Junius Morgan's offer of a position that was pleasant and 'fairly remunerative'. His main duty was to help Gooch to keep an eye on the London firm's growing volume of commercial credits, thereby releasing J. S. Morgan to concentrate on governmental loans and on developing business generally. Another duty was to share in the management of the firm itself, which included sorting out problems relating to the clerks. There was, for example, the episode of Mr Ernest Melton, clerk from about 1871 to 1883. From before January

1877 through to September 1883 he was in acute financial difficulty, and J. S. Morgan & Co. lent him £225 against an assignment of his life policy and a bill of sale on his furniture, as well as making repeated advances against his salary. Melton attributed much of his difficulty to the extravagance of his wife, whom he appeared wholly unable to control. Whatever the cause of his problems, he repeatedly promised Morgans to do his best to mend his ways. To this end, he submitted quarterly reports to the partners of his domestic expenditure (such as butchers' bills) and liabilities, and one of Peabody's duties appears to have been to encourage him on to the path of financial rectitude. After six years of this the case was probably deemed to be hopeless, and Melton was asked to leave the firm.[34]

Peabody's value to the firm was substantially increased when at the end of September 1873 Gooch decided to retire. Gooch had been with the firm since he had joined the elder Peabody as chief clerk in 1844, and he had been a partner since 1851. He had by 1873 accumulated a solid fortune—since the firm's reorganization in 1864 his share of the profits had been 25%[35]—and he wanted to retire and spend time with his family. (He had married late and at sixty-two was the father of two young sons, one of whom, the future historian G. P. Gooch, was born only in 1873.)

Junius Morgan apparently wanted to replace Gooch with a Bostonian, and he settled on Jacob C. Rogers, who was married to one of George Peabody's sisters and who headed his own brokerage firm in Boston (a 'first-rate' house which was worth about $150,000 in July 1871).[36] Pierpont Morgan also thought highly of Rogers, but he thought that rather than move to London, he should stay and establish a Morgan agency in Boston. Rogers had, like George Peabody, started his business life as a general merchant before going into finance, he was a highly respected member of the Boston mercantile community, and he was widely acquainted with businessmen throughout New England. Drexel, however, who was based in Philadelphia, objected to their establishing an agency in Boston, and since Pierpont Morgan would not press the suggestion against Drexel's opposition, Rogers was offered and accepted a partnership in J. S. Morgan & Co. Early in June 1873 he dissolved his brokerage firm and in October he began his duties in London.[37]

Appointed to replace Gooch, Rogers devoted himself to the firm's commercial credits and general banking business, as well as to the supervision of its internal management. He found the business congenial and the senior partner kind, but he could not abide London, and at the end of September 1878 he resigned from J. S. Morgan & Co., writing to J. S. Morgan that the state of his health required 'rest & relocation'.[38] He returned to Boston and, at the request of the two Morgans, became J. S. Morgan & Co.'s Boston agent and representative, continuing to represent the firm until his death in January 1900.[39]

His departure made the acquisition of a new partner an urgent matter, especially since Endicott Peabody had retired in December 1877; from September 1878 to January 1879 J. S. Morgan & Co. was essentially a one-man show. It is possible that his demonstrable need helped Morgan to land the partner for whom he had been angling since 1870, the American Walter H. Burns. Burns was an experienced banker, working first with New York's L. P. Morton & Co., and then acting as the resident partner with Morton, Burns & Co. in London; he then moved to Paris where he was the Paris manager of the London Banking Association and, after the organization of the United States Mortgage Co. in May 1871, its European director. During the autumn of 1870, Burns had come to London to serve as Morgan's official translator in his negotiations with the French government's representatives, and ever since, Morgan had been trying to persuade Burns to join him in London as a partner. It should also be noted that he was Morgan's son-in-law, having married his daughter Mary in January 1867.[40]

From January 1879 until December 1884 the two men were the only partners. Numbers of new subordinate staff were hired, but they still found it almost impossible to keep up with the demands of business. After much thought and discussion, the two decided to admit two new partners, both of whom were British. Robert Gordon, who was made a general partner with a 14% share in the profits, was born in Scotland, but had been a partner in the New York City mercantile house of Maitland, Phelps & Co. He became widely respected for his knowledge of government securities. Frederick William Lawrence followed the same route as Gooch had done, having served with J. S. Morgan & Co. for many years, and having moved up from a junior to a senior clerkship with the power of procuration (the right to sign the firm's name on specified documents such as bills of exchange and letters of credit). He was made a salaried partner, or 'Junior Working Partner' as the partnership agreement put it, with a salary of £3,000 per year (which grew to £5,000 per year by January 1889); only in 1898 and 1899 did he share in the firm's profits, when he received just under 0.06% (see Appendix II). Both Gordon and Lawrence remained partners until March 1900.[41]

Most of the London partnership agreements lasted for five years, and the December 1884 one was no exception. However, J. S. Morgan was now seventy-two: retirement or death would certainly come sooner rather than later, and it was decided on the occasion of this agreement to set out the terms on which the firm of J. S. Morgan & Co. would continue after his departure. The main consideration would be the wishes of his son and son-in-law. Pierpont Morgan was more than fully occupied in New York and thus could not contemplate coming to London to run the firm himself. But he certainly wanted it to continue, both for sentimental reasons and for the pragmatic consideration that the American firms would be a great deal poorer (in knowledge, contacts, and profits) without a closely allied London firm. Burns was the most likely future resident head of J. S. Morgan & Co., and he too wanted it to continue. The two brothers-in-law shared similar views on the type of business they wished to pursue and how they wished to conduct their business; they also—an important consideration—got along. Junius Morgan therefore agreed to arrange for the firm to continue beyond his retirement, death, or the expiration of the partnership agreement in December 1889, whichever came first. While he was actively working, the decision to continue the firm was his alone; thereafter the decision would be Pierpont's. If, when the time came, Pierpont and Burns agreed to continue the business, the terms of its continuance would be decided by Pierpont, while £1 million of J. S. Morgan's capital would remain in the business for up to seven years after his departure.[42]

From the time of the reorganization of the firm as J. S. Morgan & Co. in 1854 until the elder Morgan's death in 1890, then, the firm included seven partners at various times. Two of them, Gooch and Lawrence, had worked their way up the ranks within the bank, while the others were all brought in from outside. None of the entering partners contributed capital: their contributions came after they had begun to profit from their partnerships, in that each was required to leave a fixed share of the yearly earnings on deposit at the firm (on which 5% interest was paid). The benefit of this system was that the existing wealth of a candidate for a partnership was not a consideration. Rather, the partners looked for someone who was energetic but cautious, who had substantial knowledge of and experience in business, who, in short, could command the confidence of clients. The duties of partners fell into two areas, and a partner was generally recruited for one or the other: either he oversaw the firm's internal operations, which fell to the lot of the junior partners, or he dealt with clients and developed new business, the responsibility of the senior partners. The partners were chosen from amongst the relatives, friends, and business associates of the senior partners, and so long as the financing of trade constituted a substantial share of the London firm's business, numbers of the partners came from large mercantile houses (both Gordon and Rogers were men of broad mercantile experience). The other main source of outside partners was other private banks, and both Endicott Peabody and Walter Burns were experienced bankers.[43] Much time was expended over the years in locating and discussing candidates for partnerships, because such decisions were not to be taken lightly. A merchant bank lived or died on the quality of the partners, and although capital was vital for a firm to finance trade, it was almost useless if the partners lacked the judgement necessary to use it profitably but safely.

Judgement was equally necessary for a firm which engaged in loans to governments: it was not so much the size of such loans, since acceptances could also be large, but that considerations of prestige could so easily overrule the incautious. It is worth remembering just how risky a venture issuing and, in particular, investing in the obligations of a foreign government could be: it has been calculated that in the early 1880s, for example, roughly 54% of the total amount of such obligations which were listed in London were in default.[44] J. S. Morgan could hardly be unaware of the risks involved in the decision taken in December 1873 to develop the London and the Drexel partnerships into major houses of issue: after all, the French loan might have been a catastrophe. But foremost in his mind was probably the possible rewards, since J. S. Morgan & Co. had had that same year the benefits of the French government's redemption of the 1870 loan.

Banking to Governments

In the early 1870s there were two London houses which towered above all others as bankers for governments, and they were Barings and Rothschilds. Certainly Morgan gained no lasting gratitude from the French government for this daring, because the French returned to their traditional bankers—Barings and Rothschilds—for their loans of 1871 and 1872. It was Rothschilds who organized the transfer over the exchanges of the huge indemnity exacted by Germany from France.[45] J. S. Morgan & Co. participated in the 1872 loan to a minor extent (3.75 million francs), and in a sense this characterized their usual role in the issuing of governmental loans during the 1870s and 1880s: the house was much more a participant in syndicates led by others than the organizer of such syndicates themselves. They led on no other European loan during these years (although requested to do so by Italy in March 1874). This was not for lack of trying by J. S. Morgan and later by Burns.[46] This could, indeed, be seen as a record of failure by the house, but certain considerations should be kept in mind. First of all, banks tended to specialize in certain regional areas, usually the areas in which they had traded in their days as merchants, and therefore government officials would turn first to those banks with the appropriate experience, realizing that investors respected that expertise. This ties in with a second consideration, probably a more important one in this context, and that was the fact that clients and banks habitually enjoyed long-term relationships. Therefore, there would have to be pressing reasons for a government to turn to a new bank. J. S. Morgan & Co. lost out on both counts in Europe. It seems probable that European finance ministers saw the house as a recently established bank, while the older (and presumably better) the name on the prospectus, the easier to interest investors and thus the better the price of the issue for the government. Further, J. S. Morgan & Co. were probably seen as an Anglo-American bank, rather than as one with any special expertise in Europe. However, what was probably seen as a drawback here proved to be the factor which would in due course thrust the future Morgan Grenfell clearly into the front rank. It would not be too many years before governments would wish to tap American as well as British money, and it would be the bank's close links with the American money market which would enable it to occupy the place for which J. S. Morgan dreamed and schemed.

It was indeed this position as an Anglo-American bank which enabled J. S. Morgan & Co. to take a leading part in the single largest securities transaction of the 1870s, the refunding by the US Treasury of the long-term Civil War debt. This involved the sale of almost $1.4 billion of Federal bonds between August 1871 and June 1879, a substantial proportion of which were sold in London. J. S. Morgan & Co. and Drexel, Morgan & Co. played only a minor role in the 1871 loan, which was a failure because the Secretary of the Treasury refused to appoint a lead banker and insisted on an unusually low rate of commission. The second issue, which took place in the spring of 1873, was equally a failure, largely because of competition from higher-yielding securities of comparable quality and the Treasury's refusal again to allow a more attractive rate of interest. J. S. Morgan & Co. did play a leading role in this one, in that they were one of the five English banks which headed the European syndicate (Drexel, Morgan & Co. were one of the three American houses which co-managed the American syndicate).

The panic of 1873 in the US saw the downfall of Jay Cooke & Co., the pre-eminent banker to the US Treasury, and thereafter the leadership of the American government's refundings was shared by four New York firms (those of Seligman Bros., Morton, August Belmont, who was Rothschild's agent in the US, and Drexel, Morgan) and their European associates. There was much manoeuvring and jockeying for position in the repeated endeavour to be named the Treasury's banker or, failing that, to gain a larger share in the issue. No one firm was consistently on top; but according to the historian Vincent Carosso, those who came closest were the firms of N. M. Rothschild & Co. and J. S. Morgan & Co. All those involved considered the co-operation of these two firms to be indispensable to the success of the issue, and because of this, the two London seniors, more than any of their American associates, guided the course of most of the loan negotiations and determined many of the terms which went into the final contracts.[47]

J. S. Morgan & Co. refused to take part in the loan of mid-summer 1874, considering that it was not worth the effort if their houses were not to receive preference over other contenders. They in fact achieved a breakthrough of sorts in the negotiations for the August 1876 loan in that it was agreed that Rothschild would be the lead banker, but that J. S. Morgan & Co., Drexel, Morgan & Co., and the two Seligman houses would have equality in advertising the loan and in any other subsequent business for the US Treasury in which the three houses acted together. This was an outcome which was especially gratifying to Pierpont Morgan: he had been competing energetically with Belmont in Washington and New York to obtain a leading position, but he had not always received the support he would have liked from his father. J. S. Morgan believed that it was more important to retain cordial relations with Rothschilds in London, since these two houses participated in each other's non-American syndicates. The series came to an end in June 1879, and in a manner gratifying to Morgans: the Rothschilds refused to participate in this final refunding loan, and J. S. Morgan & Co. organized and headed the syndicate which sold the bonds.[48]

During the whole period of the American refunding loans and for the following decade, the partners of the London house worked hard to gain such a position that they would be included automatically in syndicates issuing government loans, if not appointed to the position of syndicate organizer themselves. The only way to achieve this position was to earn it, and this the house did, first by competing for the leadership of various offerings, and when this failed, by accepting a participation in the syndicate which was organized by the successful house. And thus, over this period, not only was J. S. Morgan & Co. included in some of the most important groups, but the size of its participations grew to be amongst the largest allocated to syndicate members, occasionally equalling those of the managing banker. Of equal importance was the fact that the price which the bank paid for the securities was usually the same as that paid by the managing banker (in the contemporary phrase, 'upon the original conditions').[49]

Morgans had reason to be especially grateful to C. J. Hambro & Son, the senior partner of which, Everard Hambro, was a close personal friend of Pierpont Morgan's. They were probably the house most responsible for Morgans' increasing involvement in the issuing of European government loans, and certainly Morgans participated in all of Hambros' loans to Norway and Sweden (which totalled some £6.5 million during the 1870s). Of course the drawback to working with friends is that it is difficult to refuse business, and Morgans felt themselves constrained to share in certain loans which they might have refused if offered by another house: a good example here was the loan issued in July 1881 by the Italian government, which lived up to its promise of being difficult to sell.[50] Nevertheless, the link between Morgans and Hambros was one which endured, with mutual benefit.

Besides the US and Europe, the other important area in which J. S. Morgan & Co. developed their government loan business was Latin America, concentrating first in Chile and later in Argentina. The only national loan which Morgans managed during the 1870s was the Chilean 5% Government Loan 1870. The firm had already managed issues for Chile in 1866 and 1867, and was named Chile's London agent. But the prestige and profits accruing to this position clearly did not compensate for the irregularities of their treatment by the Chileans. Morgan objected, for example, to the government's requirement with regard to a proposed loan in 1875 that all tenders be sent to Chile to be opened and allotted, since he believed that that was the prerogative of the managing bankers: 'No House having due regard to its position' could accept the government's condition. The treatment rankled, and nearly ten years later, in response to a Chilean request for assistance, he declined even to discuss the proposed loan: 'the circumstances connected with the treatment of ourselves by the Government in past' were such that '*I* have never forgotten'. Morgan cannot have been too surprised when in 1886 Rothschilds supplanted Morgans. They led on a November 1886 issue (the proceeds of which were to be used to convert and redeem five previous loans) and were named Chile's London agent.[51] Morgans in short, apparently preferred losing business to losing face.

Some credit for Morgans' growing involvement in Argentina, its other main area of interest in Latin America, must go to Barings, because much of their business in Latin American securities came through participation in Baring syndicates. The relationship between Morgans and Barings was of course long-standing, dating from George Peabody's time. The relationship had its peaks and troughs: in 1845 Peabody and the Barings had connived secretly to provide funds for a candidate for the governorship of Maryland,[52] while in 1857 Barings' demands on George Peabody & Co. had threatened the very existence of the firm; during the 1870s and 1880s Barings were eager to include Morgans in their syndicates, while after the Baring crisis of 1890, when Morgans threatened to supplant Barings as Argentina's lead banker, Barings fought them in a gentlemanly but dogged fashion (see below).

Argentina during the 1880s was a prime area of British investment interest, absorbing in 1889 between 40% and 50% of all British funds invested overseas. One important reason was that the country was experiencing a boom: it was stimulated by currency reform between 1881 and 1883 and then fuelled by immigration and inward investment (particularly in railroads). Another reason for the eagerness to invest was probably that noted by a writer in 1875, that Argentina was one of the three Latin American republics (the others were Chile and Brazil) 'which regularly pay their coupons'.[53] In June 1880 Morgans participated in a Hambros syndicate to buy a block of unsold Argentinian bonds dating from 1871, while in October 1883 the Argentine government named J. S. Morgan & Co. the agent for servicing that year's £5.95 million public works loan, at the same time appointing the firm one of its London banks of deposit. The breakthrough came in the following year when J. S. Morgan & Co. headed the syndicate for the Argentine Government 5% Loan 1884 (the other members were Hambros and Morton, Rose & Co., Walter Burns's old firm). The press found this loan especially noteworthy because Morgans rather than Barings were the leaders: as the London *Standard* wrote on 14 June 1884, 'the renowned house of Morgan & Co. . . . perhaps the richest private banking firm in the city' was heading the loan rather than 'the house of Baring and Brothers—a firm that has always proved such a good and steady friend to the River Plate'.[54] Barings could perhaps congratulate themselves on having missed out on this particular loan, since J. S. Morgan & Co. eventually posted a loss of £120,000 on the transaction—a loss-leader of substantial proportions.[55]

Argentina by 1884 was, in fact, in the early stages of a balance-of-payments crisis: a widening gap between imports and exports led to the drying-up of European investment in 1884 (from which Morgans had suffered), and the consequent falling-off in the supply of gold for Argentina. Early in January 1885 Dr Carlos Pellegrini, the highly respected former Finance Minister of Argentina, came to Europe to meet the country's French and English bankers. The result of the discussions was an agreement for a new loan of £8.4 million, to be secured by custom house revenues; the contract also bound the government not to issue any more loans without the consent of the lenders. They comprised four French banks and two British, Barings and J. S. Morgan & Co.: the gamble Morgans had taken with the 1884 loan had clearly paid off, and J. S. Morgan & Co. participated in most of Argentina's loans for the remainder of the decade, with participations whose size was second only to those of Barings.[56]

The Argentinian example illustrates a general shift in the ranking of London merchant banks with regard to the issuing of government loans. In 1870 Barings and Rothschilds had dominated the field, and most other banks, and most certainly J. S. Morgan & Co., trailed far behind. By 1890 and the time of the Baring crisis, as Stanley Chapman points out, although Rothschilds and Barings maintained their early lead, they were 'now closely trailed by Morgans and Hambros'.[57]

Early Corporate Finance

Much of Morgans' interest in Argentina was in the field of corporate rather than government finance, a development which of course accorded with the decision in December 1873 to move into the business of international securities. It is, in fact, probably fair to say that in general corporate finance was a more important area for J. S. Morgan & Co. than government finance: a list of loans managed or co-managed by Morgans between 1865 and 1885 contains over twice as many foreign corporate issues, in particular for railways, as for governments (including municipalities), although the total nominal value of the government issues was considerably larger.[58] These railway issues were American, and this illustrates a general point: 'US railway issues were easily the most continuous preoccupation of London and the New York investment houses' from 1865 to 1890, and although a whole clutch of London firms were involved, two firms were predominant: 'between them Barings and Morgans took 50 per cent of all the issues in the period'.[59]

J. S. Morgan himself was, of course, an experienced railway banker, with strong business and personal ties to the US's leading railway executives, but it became of increasing importance for the London house (as well as for the Drexel partnerships) that his son Pierpont soon negotiated, financed, and consolidated his way to the leading position in American railway finance. As Carosso writes,

All the Morgan and Drexel partnerships participated in the great systems building of the 1880s, but none more so than the New York firm. It was the leader among them, occupying the place once held by the London house. J. S. Morgan & Co. continued to be vitally important to the success of any large operation. Indeed, the New York firm probably would not have generated the business it did without its strong London connection. But whereas in the 1870s railroad leaders looked to London first, in the 1880s they turned first to New York. In the 1870s much of Drexel, Morgan's railroad business was as a participant in London-led accounts; in the 1880s their roles were reversed.[60]

Two of the reasons for this change are plain: age and geography. In 1880 J. S. Morgan was sixty-seven and not the man he once was: the cold, wet London winters drove him to Italy and Monte Carlo, and even when in London he was unable to shoulder the weight of responsibility which he had once carried. Further, from 1879 to 1884 Walter Burns was the only other partner, so that there was a limit to what the firm could do; besides this, the son-in-law probably never wielded the authority of the son. In the case of railway issues, geography augmented Pierpont's authority, in particular during the 1880s. The surge of railway building after the Civil War had led to a plethora of competing, uneconomic lines, and much of Pierpont's time and energy in the 1880s was spent in directing the rationalization and consolidation of some of the major lines. He and his New York and Philadelphia partners sat on railway corporation boards, and these boards often decided upon the issuing of securities, the proceeds of which would be used to finance such rationalizations.

There was possibly another reason for the shift, one which may have been connected with J. S. Morgan's advancing age and increasing ill-health, and this was his growing dislike of taking on a new enterprise or one which might require any managerial intervention by the London partners. On 31 December 1880, for example, Pierpont Morgan wrote to Burns explaining why London had not been informed in the early stages about the financing of the completion of the Northern Pacific Railroad, the issuing of $40 million of whose 6% general mortgage bonds, according to the financial press, constituted the largest transaction in railroad bonds ever made in the US. While the New York partners 'had great confidence in the undertaking (otherwise we certainly should not have looked at it) still, knowing how reluctant you might be to undertake anything connected with a new enterprise, we did not contemplate to ask it'.[61] This is not to say that the London house *never* involved itself in the management of a concern: it had done so in Argentina, and it had done so in the US in the early 1870s for the Cairo & Vincennes Railroad, where the firm's efforts to keep the property in repair and provide equipment led to the purchase of a new ten-wheeled freight locomotive which was named the *J. S. Morgan*.[62] But certainly the London house preferred to deal with the known rather than to venture into the unknown. It was not alone in this, of course: Rothschilds were notorious for acting in the same manner.

It should, however, be remembered, with regard to the Northern Pacific issues as well as with the others, that London was vitally necessary. The original issue was to have been for $10 million, and this the American investment community could have handled on its own; once the amount was fixed as $40 million, European investors were required. Once J. S. Morgan & Co. agreed to join the business, they were consulted on all matters: they vetoed a Continental offering, and were allowed to manage the loan's entire European sales, and, in short, prevailed on most points of contention between the two houses.[63] The conclusion which may be drawn from all this was that youth and initiative now resided in the New York house, which was situated in the financial capital of a country which provided the financiers with many lucrative opportunities to carry out their trade.

J. S. Morgan & Co. were prominent in financing industrial issues as well as railways, but by and large their interests were abroad rather than in the UK. Their involvement with overseas industrial firms occasionally meant that they felt constrained to carry out certain non-banking services. One example of a firm that required more than a loan was the McCormick Harvesting Machine Company, which had first come to Morgans for commercial credits. Morgans, however, soon found itself registering McCormick's patents in Britain, New Zealand, and Australia, and even arranging displays of their farm equipment at agricultural fairs. By the early 1880s McCormicks's non-financial demands had grown so onerous that the house wrote to suggest that the company appoint a resident London agent, pointing out that registering patents and selling farm machinery was 'entirely foreign to our business'.[64]

The industrial connections in the 1880s also led to early merger experience for J. S. Morgan & Co. Drexel, Morgan & Co. helped to organize, and were bankers for, the Edison Electric Light Company in New York, which had been organized to raise capital for Thomas Alva Edison's experiments with electric lamps and to develop his patents. Pierpont Morgan was an early believer in the future of the electric light, and not only was his private house the first to be entirely lit with Edison's new incandescent bulbs in the summer of 1882, but his Wall Street office was the first to be lit by current generated from the city's first central generating station, which opened in September 1882. J. S. Morgan & Co. provided Edison's English company, the Edison Electric Light Company, with many of the same services as Drexel, Morgan & Co. provided for the American company. Probably the most important of the London house's services for Edison was negotiating the merger of his English company with one of its principal competitors, a company which he had sued for patent infringement; in October 1883 J. S. Morgan & Co. announced the formation of the Edison & Swan United Electric Light Company, Ltd.[65]

This particular business had come to the London firm because of its links with the New York firm, a natural process when J. S. Morgan & Co.'s interests lay so predominantly in the US. In spite of attempts to widen the ambit of company business, in which some success was achieved with regard to government issues, nevertheless it was true that, as Robert Gordon wrote to a business associate on 3 May 1895, 'We are essentially an American firm, our business relations lying almost exclusively with the United States.'[66] In these circumstances it might easily be forgotten that there was no institutional link at all between the London and New York houses, and that Pierpont and Junius Morgan were not even partners in each other's houses. With the death of Junius Morgan on 8 April 1890, however, this was to change.

With the death of the elder Morgan, Pierpont became the senior partner in J. S. Morgan & Co., a firm which was rather more than moderately successful. Over the twenty-five years of the elder Morgan's leadership, the firm had grown to be one of the several most important London merchant banks, one whose co-operation was sought for governmental issues and whose links with the Drexel partnerships gave it access to the most dynamic economy in the world, with all that that implied for financial opportunities. Although productive of prestige, stocks and bonds were time-consuming and had not provided the firm with an equally proportionate part of its earnings, since losses were posted in six out of the twenty-five years. Only in 1884, however, had the firm needed to draw on its capital to meet a deficit (of £6,200), and it had never in any year made an overall loss on its acceptances. The firm's gross earnings, in short, had grown steadily over the years, and this was reflected in the amount of capital held by the partnership. The firm's 1889 partnership agreement defined J. S. Morgan & Co.'s capital as 'the amount standing to the credit' of its members, and by that definition capital in December 1889, four months before the elder Morgan's death, amounted to £2,386,468. The death of the elder Morgan inevitably diminished the firm's capital, but not by a crippling amount. Carosso estimates the gross value of his estate as some $12.4 million (£2,585,000), of which about $10 million (£2,085,000) represented his capital utilized by the house (he had another £451,416 bound up in personal investments). After the elder Morgan's account was closed in December 1890 and the balance transferred to a new account in his son's name, the amount posted to his credit was £1,510,000, £575,000 less than Junius Morgan had had on deposit in the firm a year earlier.[67]

The accession of Pierpont Morgan to the status of senior partner merely made manifest what had been true in fact for some time: the final authority for the London house, as for the others, now lay in New York. Burns was the resident senior in London, while Gordon, the most junior partner, continued to devote himself to overseeing the acceptance business and the internal management of the house. When in 1893 Anthony Drexel died, and his son retired from the firm, Pierpont Morgan took the opportunity to rename the New York house J. P. Morgan & Co. and to reorganize his other partnerships, and he did so primarily by centralizing control in New York. But the London house remained unaffected by the changes, since it alone was governed by a separate partnership agreement: they did not share in the other partnerships' profits and losses and neither did the others share in London's. (This arrangement proved to be a useful one for London in 1893: the panic of that year in the US caused losses of over $1 million for the New York house alone,[68] but the London house only lost £57,444 in its Profit/Loss Stocks account and was in overall profit for the year—see Appendix I.) The only link J. S. Morgan & Co. had with the other three houses—in 1890 Drexel, Morgan & Co., Drexel & Co., and Drexel, Harjes et Cie —was in sharing Pierpont Morgan as senior partner, and thus in having, in the final analysis, to defer to his authority in New York.

Morgans and Barings

Within months of Pierpont Morgan's accession to the head of J. S.

Morgan & Co., the City of London was threatened by one of the most potentially destabilizing financial crises of the nineteenth century, the Baring crisis of November 1890. The focus of the problem was Argentina, whose economic boom in the 1880s had been accompanied by speculation, price inflation, and corruption; as Sir John Clapham, the historian of the Bank of England, wrote, the story of Argentina and the crisis might 'have to include extensive and not too kindly reference to the then standard of probity among businessmen and statesmen in the Argentine'.[69] The resignation of the Argentine Cabinet in April 1890, followed by that of the President in August, when joined with the deteriorating economy, undermined the confidence of overseas investors and brought substantial losses to many of the London banks which dealt in Argentinian issues, including J. S. Morgan & Co. But the worst hit was Barings, who had been increasingly reckless in their Argentine investments. As Clapham goes on to say, 'a charge that might with justice be brought against Barings was that, in their eagerness to do business, they had not considered all these enterprises— or the expected investors in them—coolly and wisely enough'. Clapham then quotes R. G. Hawtrey's pronouncement that 'Had Messrs Baring Brothers been able to shift the burden of their South American obligations upon the investing public they would now have been standing erect.' They were not able, though they 'did not neglect all the means in their power to rid themselves in this way of liabilities'.[70] In other words, although the Argentine situation was worrying, the 1890 crisis was in no sense a general economic one: rather, it was a crisis in the affairs of a single firm, but one whose fall would inevitably bring down many others.

Throughout the second half of October 1890 there had been growing suspicions in the City that Barings were in difficulty, but it was not until 8 November that William Lidderdale, the Governor of the Bank of England, was warned by Lord Revelstoke of Barings that the house might fail. Knowledge of this was kept from the public until 15 November, and meanwhile the Bank mounted a rescue operation, secretly purchasing £1.5 million in gold from Russia and borrowing £3 million from the Banque de France, and extracting from the British government a promise to share whatever losses the Bank might sustain until a guarantee fund was set up. This guarantee fund was organized from amongst the whole banking community, and its purpose was to guarantee any losses sustained by the Bank through providing Barings with a loan. Within less than two hours the guarantee of £2,250,000 from other merchant banks was in place, with J. S. Morgan & Co. and

Drexel & Co. both pledging £100,000. The five principal joint-stock banks pledged another £3,250,000, and in the end the guarantee fund totalled £17,105,000. As Barings had proved to be solvent, if embarrassed, the fund ensured that the firm had the time to realize its assets over the next several years in order to pay off its creditors.[71]

Once the guarantee was in place, the major problem was indeed what to do about Barings' large holdings of depreciated and unsaleable Argentinian securities. The City's leading issue houses organized a committee, headed by Lord Rothschild, to investigate Argentina's financial condition, determine its ability to meet its obligations, and consider how Argentina could restore public confidence in its securities, which would allow Barings to sell its holdings and liquidate its indebtedness to the group of banks which had come to its rescue. J. S. Morgan & Co. participated actively in all of the committee's negotiations with the Argentine government. Subsequently, when in March 1891 the first agreement with the government was reached, the Bank of England made the house responsible for the 'financial management' of Barings' holdings of Argentinian securities; it also asked Morgans to serve as agent for a new funding loan. This appointment received the approbation of the financial press, *The Bankers' Magazine* of April 1891 writing that 'No English banking house stands today with the same solidity as . . . J. S. Morgan & Co.' The firm's own 'commanding position' and the fact that it had 'kept free from Argentine speculations' made J. S. Morgan & Co. the obvious choice to serve as 'practically . . . the receiver for the enormous interests involved'.[72]

A comparison between the crises of 1857 and 1890 cannot but occur. In the 1857 crisis it was G. Peabody & Co. which was in difficulty, although not because of unwise speculation, and Barings had been amongst those which had put enormous pressure on Peabody & Co.; certainly Peabody refused to have Barings as a guarantor. In the 1890 crisis the boot was on the other foot, and although *autres temps, autres moeurs*, the response of Morgans to Barings' plight was immediate and supportive.[73] Barings never again held the relative position which it had enjoyed before the crisis: it now shared a general front-rank position, rather than towering over all but Rothschilds. The new position was perhaps most immediately obvious in Argentina, because Barings now had frequently to give way to a vigorous competitor, J. S. Morgan & Co. Barings' difficulty provided Morgans' opportunity.

Over the next quarter of a century until the outbreak of the First World War, the two houses worked together in Argentina, since joint issues in an uncertain market could be safer than single-led issues, but not without occasional acrimony and one full-scale battle. In March 1891, just four months after the Baring crisis, the Argentine government named J. S. Morgan & Co. the agent for a £15.4 million 6% customs funding loan, an appointment which signalled that Morgans could claim co-equal status in the country's finances with Barings. Morgans only earned £28,700 in commissions, but more important was that much new business resulted. For the remainder of the decade it led, alone or jointly with Barings, every major Argentinian financing negotiated in London. In November 1899, however, Barings moved to reassert their old position and Morgans were not strong enough to prevent them: Barings insisted that in the prospectus for the loan then being negotiated their name should come first. J. S. Morgan & Co. retorted that if *theirs* was not first the name of Morgan would not appear at all:

Our personal feeling for them makes us most unwilling to hurt them, but we fear that our yielding will establish a bad precedent, though Revelstoke told J. P. M., Jr. in any other business but Argentina Barings would be quite willing.[74]

In the end the loan was issued under the Baring name, Everard Hambro having argued that it would be seen as courteous to acknowledge that Barings were first in Argentina and that it would not be taken as having any reference to the standing of the two firms. The Morgan name did not appear on the contract, but they still participated in order not to lose the goodwill of Argentina.[75]

By 1907, however, J. S. Morgan & Co. were in a position to insist that Barings publicly confirm Morgans' claim to equal status: they had been joint leaders on some notes, and the partners insisted they should be joint leaders on the proposed Argentine Government 5% Internal Loan 1907. Lord Revelstoke of Barings resisted, but as Jack Morgan (Pierpont Morgan's son, J. P. Morgan, Jr., who had become a partner in 1898 —see below) wrote to E. C. Grenfell (who had joined J. S. Morgan & Co. in 1900), 'The whole matter most trying & very sorry it has come up now but see no reason why we should submit to being squeezed out without saying anything or why all friction should be on our side.' In March 1907 Barings formally acknowledged J. S. Morgan & Co.'s claim to equal status for this loan.[76]

The period September 1908 to mid-January 1909 saw the climactic battle between J. S. Morgan & Co. and Barings over their positions in Argentinian finance: Barings fought desperately to retain their traditional position as the country's lead bankers, while Morgans fought equally

fiercely either to force Barings out of the lead position, or at the least to
force them to acknowledge that former supremacy had now become
equality. The crucial difference between this episode and earlier ones was
that Argentina wanted direct close access to New York money—and
here Barings, even with their links with Kidder Peabody & Co. of Boston
and Baring Magoun & Co. of New York, could not command the
position of Morgans. The Morgan plan was to use this leverage to force
Barings in London to acknowledge publicly and finally J. S. Morgan &
Co.'s enhanced position in Argentinian finance. In September 1908
Argentina opened negotiations for a £10 million gold loan with J. P.
Morgan & Co. in New York. Jack Morgan saw an opportunity to
strengthen the London house *vis-à-vis* Barings. He asked one of the New
York partners engaged in the negotiations with Argentina to emphasize
that if there were to be a contract it would have to be done on joint
account with J. S. Morgan & Co., who alone would deal with Barings.
In other words, this was to be an attempt to freeze Barings out of the
position of leader as the price for New York money. Barings were angry,
to say the least, and considered the activities of the two firms as unwar-
ranted interference with the recognized client of a friendly banker. The
London partners were anxious to confirm their equality with Barings and
urged New York to compete vigorously for the account, writing that 'If
we can only secure this business even with small profit', Barings 'would
fear our competition and would probably approach us as to working
jointly in the future'.[77]

Argentina sought to take advantage of the clash between her two
bankers and informed J. S. Morgan & Co. in December that while it
would continue the negotiations, it intended to ask Barings to bid for the
loan as well. This news quickly spread throughout the international
banking community, and there was every chance that other bankers
would take advantage of this opening and work to form groups to bid
for the loan. On the other hand, a leadership fight within an international
banking community is an uncomfortable matter: it can be dangerous to
choose sides, and the ensuing bitterness can poison relations. Neither
Morgans nor Barings wanted a permanent rupture between the two
banks, but neither wished to give in. Various bankers urged a compromise, but having gone this far Jack Morgan insisted that no solution
was possible 'unless Barings are willing to treat J.S.M. & Co. properly'.[78]
In short, as far as Morgans were concerned, Jack Morgan spoke for them
all when he wrote that 'I don't care how we fight him [Lord Revelstoke],
but am quite ready to fight him when we need to'.[79]

A week passed while both firms prepared to submit independent bids supported by separate syndicates. By 15 January 1909 Revelstoke of Barings was anxious to reach a settlement, and after the intermediation of a mutual friend he and E. C. Grenfell of Morgans met and negotiated a compromise which settled the terms of the present loans and subsequent ones as well. In short, the outcome was that J. S. Morgan & Co. now had what it had sought for so long: full equality with Barings in all Argentinian issues. Further, their joint international syndicate was so strong, according to Grenfell, that competitors would be deterred from seeking to displace the two London houses in the affections of the Argentine government.[80]

The End of the First Phase

The response of J. S. Morgan & Co. to the activities of Barings was much more determined than it had been in the 1890s, and one obvious reason for this was that, bar Pierpont Morgan himself, all of the partners were different. This was the result of decisions taken and changes implemented in the last years of the old century and the first years of the new; it is also piquant that one mooted change which did not occur would have implied a close, not to say intimate, relationship with Barings (see below).

The catalyst for the changes was the death of the resident senior, Walter Burns, and the retirement of Robert Gordon. The immediate result was that three new partners were admitted: F. W. Lawrence, the salaried partner, was made a general partner (as it was called); and Burns's son W. S. M. Burns, and Pierpont Morgan's son Jack, were both made partners. However, Burns was more interested in culture than in banking, and great things never seem to have been expected of him (one of his partners referred to him as 'quite capable' but 'young, fat and lazy'),[81] and Jack Morgan would, in due course, return to New York to work with and eventually to succeed his father. (H. Jack was as much of an Anglophile as his father, and was responsible for introducing the custom of afternoon tea into the Morgan offices at 23 Wall Street.) What was still required was a weighty appointment of a man who would take the elder Burns's place as resident senior partner. But this time the search was not on for an American: rather, Pierpont Morgan had decided to make the firm more British, and towards that end he began to search for a distinguished Englishman to fill the position.

The search took over two years, and in the end Morgan settled upon a man who was neither a banker nor a merchant but a civil servant.

Clinton Dawkins had spent all but four years of his working life in the
public service; at the time he caught Morgan's eye he was just completing
a period as Under-Secretary of State for Finance in Egypt, and was about
to take up a post as Financial Member of the Council of the Governor-
General for India. His appointment caused much press comment,
centring on the reasons for his appointment, and on the reasons why the
British government had given him early release from his position in
India. It was believed that the Bank of England and certain Cabinet
members wanted to see an Englishman as a partner in Morgans, and also
that the government thought it was important to meet Pierpont Morgan's
wishes in the matter by releasing Dawkins from his government contract.
The truth was somewhat different. In the first place, he would hardly be
the first English partner, and he would very soon be joined by others.
Furthermore, while it was true that Pierpont Morgan had requested the
government to release Dawkins early, it appears that his was not the
decisive intervention: this credit belonged, rather, to Everard Hambro,
Morgan and Robert Gordon's close friend. Hambro was a member of the
Royal Commission on the Indian Currency, and it was apparently his
efforts which persuaded the Council of the Governor-General to release
Dawkins; moreover, his house was the venue where the matter was
finally settled between Dawkins and Pierpont Morgan. It was true, as the
press reported, that J. S. Morgan & Co. wished to develop their business
in India and south-east Asia and hoped to exploit Dawkins's experience
and expertise. But probably the real reason for Dawkin's appointment
was a negative one: Pierpont Morgan's inability to find a qualified and
suitable partner from amongst the City's banking and business houses.[82]

Dawkins took up his duties in April 1900, joining the other two
resident partners, Jack Morgan and the younger Burns. On the whole his
appointment was not a success. For one thing, his usefulness was limited
by his almost total lack of banking and business experience (he had spent
four not very successful years as the South American representative of the
Peruvian Corporation); further, he was often away from the office for
long periods, in particular while he chaired the Committee on War
Office Reorganisation (for which he received a knighthood in 1904).
Such absences were bad for business: as Dawkins himself wrote to his
close friend Sir Alfred Milner, the British High Commissioner in South
Africa, although much of the work was dull as well an intermittent, 'it
is a jealous mistress. The City does not involve long hours or much
fatigue. But it means incessant presence and attention. You never know
when you may not be called upon.'[83] Dawkins chafed at this for the

simple reason that a career in the City was for him the means to an end, not an end in itself. His ultimate ambition was to enter the House of Commons, but first he wanted to acquire experience in the City and to visit the US. He also needed to earn the money to support a political career, and indeed, to support two political careers: by the time Milner returned from South Africa, Dawkins hoped to have earned enough at Morgans to finance both his own and Milner's public careers. (The two of them wished to work for the reorganization of the machinery of the Empire and the adoption of compulsory military service.)[84]

This is not to say that Dawkins did not earn his keep; besides ordinary business he was involved in the negotiations for the Boer War loans and especially in the whole affair of the International Mercantile Marine (see Chapter 4). But the fact that he was away for frequent periods meant that others had to take up the slack. Fortunately, a new salaried partner was at hand who was both willing and able to do so, and this was Edward Charles Grenfell. He was the son of Henry Riversdale Grenfell, MP and director of the Bank of England, and part of an intricate web of banking and aristocratic connections. He had read history at Trinity College, Cambridge, winning the Greaves Essay Prize in 1891. Although his memorialists remarked upon his cautious conservatism, his personality was clearly quite different in his earlier years: 'Grenfell was an amusing companion with a quick brain, a disposition . . . open and sanguine . . . a juvenile taste for absurd practical jokes, and a mature sense of humour that sometimes verged on the sardonic.'[85] He began his working life with Brown, Shipley (which also employed Montagu Norman, the future Governor of the Bank of England), and then moved to the Smith, Ellison & Co. bank at Lincoln. He was well known to the elder Burns and to Gordon, and especially to Pierpont Morgan. In April 1900, at the age of thirty, Grenfell joined J. S. Morgan & Co. Vested at once with powers both of attorney and of procuration, Grenfell's main duty was to oversee the firm's internal operations and thereby relieve the general partners of routine and enable them to develop business. Grenfell soon made himself indispensable, because he turned out to be equally effective with office management and with clients. In recognition of his value to the firm, he was made a general partner in January 1904 with a 4% share of the profits.[86]

However successful Grenfell was in absolute terms, it is probably true that for Pierpont Morgan he shone in comparison with Dawkins. By the spring of 1904 the elder Morgan was so dissatisfied with Dawkins and with the performance of the firm generally that he contemplated drastic surgery: a merger with Barings and the suppression of J. S. Morgan & Co. Barings at this point were equally dissatisfied with the performance of their New York house, Baring, Magoun & Co., and they welcomed the first tentative discussions in early spring 1904.

In April 1904 Pierpont Morgan confessed to Tom Baring that he 'guessed a mistake had been made' in appointing Dawkins,[87] and this seems to have been the point at which vague discussions began to firm up.[88] But even in the earliest days both Lord Revelstoke, the head of Barings, and Pierpont had established positions to which they would hold and which would in the end condemn the discussions to nothing. Revelstoke wrote to G. Farrer, 'his most trusted and most able lieutenant',[89] on 16 April 1904 that the more he thought it over, the more disinclined he was to form a formal connection with J. P. Morgan & Co. An agency arrangement would probably be profitable, 'but I sd be terrified at the idea of losing our independence, and of being placed in a position of being forced to follow his [Pierpont Morgan's] lead'.[90] For his part, Pierpont Morgan confessed to Barings on 28 April that he did not see 'how he could at once bring himself to wipe out J. S. Morgan & Co., though he said in strictest confidence they ought to be liquidated, and could not exist without him as partner'.[91]

What is especially interesting about that last telegram was that it was sent from a partner in Kidder, Peabody, Baring's Boston agent, to George Perkins, one of Pierpont Morgan's closest colleagues in J. P. Morgan & Co. Perkins and Robert Bacon of the New York house certainly appeared to favour the proposals being gradually developed: in their fullest form they included the absorption by J. P. Morgan & Co. of the Baring house in New York; the absorption by Morgans of Barings' associated house in Boston, Kidder, Peabody & Co., by their appointment as Morgans' agent in Boston (Rogers had died in 1900); and the suppression of J. S. Morgan & Co., with Barings to take over all of the London business but none of the partners. But Perkins and Bacon had no emotional ties to the London house as Pierpont Morgan did—and as Jack Morgan did. Revelstoke made his formal proposals to the elder Morgan in a letter dated 18 October 1904, but Morgan appears not to have given a straight yes or no. He clearly could not decide what to do about Dawkins. The following March Morgan and Revelstoke met and discussed the matter, and when Revelstoke asked why Barings' proposals were not feasible, Morgan said that 'his reason—his only reason— . . . was his fear of inflicting a mortal hurt on Dawkins by suggesting his retirement . . . '.[92] Dawkins was a very sick man and would die of heart disease within a year, but before then Barings would decide finally that nothing would come of the discussions and that they should consider other ways of dealing with their problems in New York.[93]

One interesting question is the role of Jack Morgan in all of this. Pierpont always insisted that Jack knew nothing of the matter, and that the only impediment to the proposed arrangement was the position of Dawkins. Revelstoke, however, believed rather that Jack was the obstacle, that he 'refused to lend himself to a rearrangement of which he does not approve. I expect there is little sympathy and less confidence between father and son . . . '.[94] Revelstoke, in fact, believed that Jack was the author of the move which finally killed off the proposal, which was barely twitching in any event: the appointment of Vivian Hugh Smith as a partner.[95]

In April 1905 Dawkins had had a severe heart attack and had left London for the Italian lakes in the hope that warmth would lessen his illness. Grenfell had taken over the management of much of the firm's business, but as it became clearer that Dawkins would not recover sufficiently to return to business, and since Jack Morgan was returning permanently to New York at the end of the year, it became imperative to find another partner. V. H. Smith took up his duties on 1 September 1905. The son of Hugh Colin Smith, owner of Hay's Wharf and a former Governor of the Bank of England, as well as Grenfell's cousin, he was, according to Farrer of Barings, 'a charming man, about 42 years of age, straight as a die, & from a social point of view everything that one wd desire in a partner. His experience in business, however, is extremely limited, and we sd not think he is in the least the kind of man to add the kind of strength to that firm which is required . . . He is a gt friend of Jack's & that, I imagine, is the reason for his introduction.'[96] (He clearly had something more to him that that: in spite of an addiction to horses, which triumphed over his interest in academic studies at Cambridge, he not only in due course became chairman of Morgan Grenfell, but was governor of the Royal Exchange Assurance for over forty years. He also managed to sit in the House of Lords for eighteen years without uttering a word—or at least, none for the public record.) Farrer may well have been correct in his assessment of Jack's role in the choice of Smith as a partner: certainly Smith's brother thought so.[97] But he was probably wrong in attributing the refusal of the Baring proposals to Jack alone. Pierpont Morgan also had a sentimental attachment to J. S. Morgan & Co., and would probably have intensely disliked having to preside over its liquidation. But even on practical grounds J. P. Morgan & Co. would have been foolish to get rid of their allied house in London and put themselves in the hands of a competitor: the Morgan presence there was too valuable to the American partnership's overall operations.

When Dawkins died in December 1905, Grenfell succeeded him as the resident senior, with Smith and the younger Burns under him. Both Morgans continued as partners, and each of them visited the firm at least once or twice a year, but the actual management of J. S. Morgan & Co. in the final years of its existence was left largely to Grenfell and Smith.

In December 1909 the partnership agreement expired and Pierpont Morgan used the opportunity to restructure the firm. Just as the previous agreements had done, this expiring agreement contained a clause limiting the use of Junius's name in the firm's title to Pierpont Morgan's lifetime: he was then seventy-two years old and it was imperative that new arrangements be made. On his advice, and with the agreement of Grenfell and Smith (the younger Burns retired in December 1909), a new co-partnership, called Morgan Grenfell & Co., was organized to succeed to the business of J. S. Morgan & Co. There were important structural changes as well: until 1910 the London partnership had been entirely independent of the other partnerships, with the only common tie being the two Morgans as partners, but this would now change. There were no longer to be any individual American partners, not even the Morgans: rather, J. P. Morgan & Co., combined with Drexel & Co., would now constitute a partner, contributing £1 million in capital and being entitled to 50% of the profits. Morgan Grenfell & Co. would have the same status as Morgan, Harjes et Cie had always had, which could mean a diminution in its authority and independence. For the New York house the changes meant that the structure was now in place to allow, if desired, greater control over the London house's activities, since all the American partners, and not just the two Morgans, could participate in Morgan Grenfell's business.[98]

And so J. S. Morgan & Co. came full circle. Founded by an American in London, it had established a daughter house in New York, the final authority over which remained in London as long as J. S. Morgan retained his full vigour. As he waned and Pierpont waxed, and as the American economy developed, authority began to drain away from London to New York. But even so, London retained a great deal of independence, and indeed in certain areas, such as government issues and foreign corporate finance, it led New York. Yet the disparity in resources and earnings told: in 1900 the net profits of the New York house alone were $10,891,242, while the net profits of J. S. Morgan & Co. equalled

£185,657 (about $902,293), a ratio of twelve to one. Yet the profits of neither would have been so large without the link, and this is probably what saved J. S. Morgan & Co. during the period when their all-powerful senior partner was gravely displeased. In the end Pierpont's urge to consolidate focused on his own firm, as it had already done on so many others, and the London house—now wholly British in its resident partners—was closely integrated into the American-dominated firm. Only time would tell whether this reorganization would constitute one of J. P. Morgan's successes or one of his dismal failures.

CHAPTER THREE

MORGAN GRENFELL & CO.

1910–1934

From Overseas Finance to Corporate Finance

I F creatures do not adapt to changing environments they die, and this is as true of merchant banks as of dinosaurs. Certainly the period 1910–34 was one in which the political and business landscapes were transformed, primarily by war, reconstruction, and depression. Morgan Grenfell's involvement in war and its aftermath will be treated in the following two chapters; the concern in this chapter is to look at the domestic setting of the firm.

During this period the bank changed its structure and its business activities, both as a result of external pressures. The partnership structure of J. S. Morgan & Co., and indeed the name, had changed by 1910 in anticipation of the death of the senior partner, Pierpont Morgan (who in fact died in 1913). The house changed its legal structure in 1918 in response to the imperatives of English law, while further changes in 1934 were required by American law. New directions in business were forced on it by the slow strangulation of the old: the traditional role of London merchant banks had been to finance foreign trade and to issue foreign securities, and it was these very areas of business which were devastated by the First World War. In short, the bank had to change course, and it did. It cultivated new geographical areas of business, such as India, but more importantly it looked into its own back garden and became an important player in the new game (for merchant banks) of domestic corporate finance.

The Bank and its Relationships

The year 1910 saw the beginnings of the newly organized partnership of Morgan Grenfell & Co. The senior London partner was E. C. Grenfell, tall, thin, and elegant, the very model of a London merchant banker. He had been a director of the Bank of England since 1905 and had been blooded in foreign corporate and governmental negotiations. Over the years he would continue to be the partner who dealt with governments, home and abroad, and with other bankers. His partner and cousin, Vivian Hugh Smith, provided talents of a different sort: more than Grenfell, he was the old-style *merchant* banker. Smith was the travelling partner. He made regular visits to Canada to inspect the firm's interests there and to look out for new ones, and to the Caucasus to keep an eye on the partners' investments in copper. He was also interested in engines and in industrial processes of various sorts, corresponding with engineers and going to see demonstrations of new processes. In due course he would exploit these connections in developing the house's interest in domestic business. Smith was also, unlike Grenfell, a countryman by preference, and the impression given is that had he been born an eighteenth-century landowner, he would have been in the forefront of the agricultural revolution, trying out new types of crops and new fertilizers. He was sanguine by nature: according to his cousin, 'it takes a good deal to depress him or prevent him retailing funny stories'.[1] The third important member of the firm in the earlier period was Charles F. Whigham, a Scottish chartered accountant who joined the firm in 1908 as office manager.[2] In 1912 he was made a salaried partner, while in 1918, with the reorganization of the bank into a private unlimited company, he became a general (equity) partner. He brought with him many business contacts in Scotland, but equally importantly he brought a lucid intelligence.

Under their leadership, the firm settled down to a new life. J. P. Morgan & Co. and Drexel Morgan & Co. taken together now constituted a partner and took one-half of the profits, and there is no doubt that during the shakedown period the London partners sometimes found the position rather trying. A new cable system uniting all of the firms (including Morgan Harjes et Cie in Paris) was in place by December 1910,[3] and while it undoubtedly facilitated business to the benefit of all, it also facilitated the occasional exploitation of Morgan Grenfell by the American partners. A prime example of this was provided by the negotiations over various Chinese loans. There were three groups of banks, French, German, and British, which had joined together in a consortium to encourage the Chinese government to borrow money for development. For foreign policy reasons the American President, William Howard Taft, and the Secretary of State, Philander C. Knox, wanted to secure for the US a position in China equal to those of France, Germany, and Britain, and they determined to do so through the use of American financial power. In June 1909 Knox brought together Kuhn,

Loeb & Co., the First National Bank, the National City Bank, and
J. P. Morgan & Co. as the American group, with Morgans as the leader.
The American group appointed J. S. Morgan & Co. and then Morgan
Grenfell as their representative in Europe, which meant that the London
partners, and specifically Grenfell, conducted all the negotiations for the
American group with the British, French, and German groups.[4] The
result of the first two years' work was a loan issued for the Hukuang
Railway, and the recompense for Morgan Grenfell amounted to a
one-quarter share in J. P. Morgan & Co.'s share: the total profit for the
London partners was £4,000. Smith was moved to write to Jack Morgan
that

... as remuneration for the work that has been done, I think there can be no
doubt that it is quite inadequate....

This business was taken up by J.P.M. & Co., Kuhn, Loeb & Co., the First
National and the National City at the request of the State Dept., and I
understood from you that it was important to the prestige of these firms that
they should undertake the business even if the remuneration was small. Is it
therefore reasonable that [they] should get all this work done for nothing?...

Apart from the actual time taken up I feel strongly that, if one of the partners
has the bulk of his time for two years absorbed by one bit of business, we are
considerable financial sufferers thereby. Teddy [Grenfell] has been so busy at
times with this thing for days together, that it has been impossible to attend to
other business, very often impossible even to see people, and if this is the case,
is it fair that 3 Houses of the standing of J.P.M. & Co., the First National and
the National City, who go into a particular business because it is policy to do
so, should expect a firm in London to represent them in a highly complicated
business requiring very delicate handling over a couple of years, without proper
remuneration?[5]

Since there is no evidence of any special payment, and since Grenfell
continued to negotiate on behalf of the American group, the answer must
have been 'yes'. But Smith's anger in 1911 at the willingness of the
American partners to allow the London ones to lose out financially was
as nothing to Grenfell's fury in 1913: the new President, Woodrow
Wilson, and his Secretary of State, William Jennings Bryan, believed that
what the American group were trying to do in China was immoral and
publicly censured the entire operation. The following day (20 March
1913) the American group withdrew entirely from the Chinese loan
negotiations, leaving J. P. Morgan & Co. to send their embarrassed
regrets at Wilson's actions to their European banking associates.[6]
Although Herman Harjes of the Paris firm, who had been involved in

the negotiations with Grenfell, thought that the Paris and London partners might salvage something from four years of work by securing an interest in their own national groups, Grenfell 'could not in common decency approach the English Group'. He was 'quite ashamed to have belonged to an organisation which has behaved as we have done'. The American group had caused 'unlimited trouble', first by forcing their way into the consortium and then by abruptly retiring from it.[7]

The feeling of being taken for granted and thereby suffering financial loss was wounding, but would pass; more serious for the firm was the disruption of relations with other London firms consequent upon being the agent of so much—apparently unnecessary—aggravation. These relationships could also be disturbed by a failure of the New York partners to maintain timely communications with the London partners. One of the main supports of Morgan Grenfell's importance and prosperity was that they placed the London share of American corporate issues managed by the American Morgan houses. These were frequently very profitable and consequently the opportunity to secure a share was sought after by British investors. On one occasion in June 1910 there was an issue of New York Central Railway Equipment Notes, about which there had been much discussion over the cables but no firm date of issue. Suddenly Morgan Grenfell began hearing about the issue of the notes from clients and other City firms, when J. P. Morgan & Co. had vouchsafed no information at all to Morgan Grenfell. The latter were unable to respond to press enquiries, to provide any share in the issue for their clients, and in short were left in an undignified and embarrassing position. The London partners wrote a very stiff letter to New York, which Grenfell enclosed in a private letter of his own to Charles Perkins, one of the New York partners, in which he wrote that

The fact is that we have been made to look absolutely foolish over this business in the eyes of our friends, the public & the press to whom it appears that the London agents & associates of JPM & Co, are of such small account that they receive no information at all on a question of this sort & are provided with details of a NYC issue 3 or 4 days after correspondents of other houses in NY....[8]

More than face was involved: knowledge was involved, and knowledge was (and is) power and profit. Basically, the capital of a partnership, while important in relation to the amount of foreign trade they could finance, was less important in the business of raising loans or issuing securities. Here, it was the reputation for integrity of the firm and thereby the quality of the security that was important, joined with the knowledge and contacts that provided the business. The integrity was undoubted: it was the knowledge and contacts which an incident such as the above could bring into question.

The incident was humiliating, and it was to happen again.[9] But it was presumably not intentional on the part of the American partners, and the answer seemed to be some reorganization of the New York office. This was urged by Smith in a letter to his New York partner H. P. Davison:

When I last saw you here we had a long talk about the importance of, if possible, our being kept better advised of what you were doing in New York.... I [also] talked this question over a good deal with Perkins when I was in New York, and I really think, if you have time, that something ought to be done to create an organization on your side so that we are kept more fully informed. I know it is difficult but I am quite certain that other London Houses with American affiliations are kept better informed than we are.[10]

It took some time to sort things out, and the London and Paris partners occasionally commiserated with each other over the problems involved in their relationship with New York. But they all knew that the importance of the London and Paris houses was partly dependent on this relationship; and since the European partners were concerned to foster the growth in business and importance of their respective firms, they knew it was a small price to pay.

What was the position of Morgan Grenfell relative to other London houses in the years before the First World War? In a sense there are two questions involved here, ranking and relationships, with the first much more difficult to answer than the second. It is necessary to piece together disparate bits of information, most of which are not directly comparable: bases for figures are often obscure, and even when that is not the case, the dates can differ. Beyond the figures, much of the evidence is allusive or anecdotal. Merchant banks were and can be dauntingly secretive.

In 1901, a year after joining J. S. Morgan & Co. as a partner, Clinton Dawkins set down an assessment of the house's relative standing for his close friend Sir Alfred Milner. While Dawkins's purpose—to encourage Milner to consider joining Morgans as a partner—must be kept in mind, nevertheless the picture painted in 1901 was probably broadly accurate:

Old Pierpont Morgan and the house in the U.S. occupy a position immensely more predominant than Rothschilds in Europe. In London J. S. Morgan & Co. now come undoubtedly second to Rothschilds only. Taken together the Morgan combination of the U.S. and London probably do not fall very far short of the Rothschilds in capital, are immensely more expansive and active, and are in with the great progressive undertakings of the world.

Old P. Morgan is well over 60, and no human machine can resist the work he is doing much longer. Behind him he has young Morgan, under 40 with the makings of a biggish man, and myself.

The Rothschilds have nothing now but the experience and great prestige of old Nattie. The coming generation of the Rothschilds *est à faire pleurer.*

Therefore provided we can go on and bring in one or two good men to assist the next 20 years ought to see the Rothschilds thrown into the background and the Morgan group supreme.

In London the resuscitated Barings are the only people nearly in the same rank with us. In the U.S. they are nowhere now, a mere cipher, and the U.S. is going to dominate in most ways. The Barings have nothing but Revelstoke, a man commonly reputed to be strong, but a strange mixture of occasional strength and sheer timidity. He has no nerve to fall back upon.[11]

The position of Rothschilds was a complex one. On the one hand they were frequently called upon for advice by the British Treasury, and led on the British tranche of the April 1901 issue of Consols.[12] On the other hand, even the Permanent Secretary to the Treasury was moved to castigate the Rothschilds for their 'timidity', writing that 'They won't go into anything normally with the smallest risk.'[13] What is slightly curious is that even with this reputation for cautious conservatism—words of high praise amongst 'A1' merchant bankers of the time—it was noticed that their judgement of new government issues was not what it had once been. The bedrock of the fame of the Rothschilds was their history of acting as bankers to governments, and certainly during the first decade of the twentieth century they issued loans for Brazil and Chile. But a Brazilian loan of 1913, 'although issued by Rothschilds' as Grenfell noted, was soon standing at a discount of 8%, and by March 1914 of 15%.[14] Grenfell later wrote that a whole series of Rothschild issues had been unsuccessful, and added that by 1914 'The firm greatly declined in prestige though very rich & on the death of Lord Rothschild became of no a/c.'[15]

There was, as far as one can tell, little love lost between Morgans and Rothschilds: the two firms had worked together over American government issues in J. S. Morgan's prime, but on the whole their interests were different. Rothschilds appear to have concentrated on government business, and they tended to be different governments from those which interested Morgans. By this time they were not very involved in American issues, which constituted a substantial chunk of Morgan Grenfell's business.

The position with regard to Barings was different. Barings carried a weight of history and formerly of reputation that equalled that of Rothschilds, and they and Morgans frequently moved in the same spheres. Barings' interests covered a wider area than Morgans': they had, for example, issued loans for Japan in 1902 and Russia in 1906, as well as the loans for Argentina (jointly with J. S. Morgan and then Morgan Grenfell in 1887, 1907, and 1910), and for many American railways and utilities. In addition Barings had made rather more domestic utility issues than other firms, such as that in 1900 for the United London Tramways Ltd. and in 1905 for the Mersey Docks and Harbours Board. In many areas Barings and Morgans worked together, as in Argentina and the US, sometimes standing shoulder to shoulder to keep Continental European banks out of desirable business.[16] But there had been conflict, as Dawkins had noted in a letter to Milner in February 1901: '[Revelstoke] has greatly irritated the Morgans once or twice by want of tact and by talking loosely (after they helped Barings largely in 1890), and it cost me a good deal of difficulty this summer to patch up the old alliance between the two houses which was on the point of dissolution.'[17] And of course they fought over Argentina, until the two firms came to an agreement in 1909 which stipulated that they should share all Argentinian central and provincial government business.[18] But Barings were one of the firms which Morgan Grenfell considered very good friends, and certainly Grenfell and Vivian Smith shared with Revelstoke (and Eric Hambro) a speculative venture in a Caucasian copper mine on their own account.[19] The main problem with Barings was that the firm had been very badly damaged by the 1890 crisis and it resented the fact that it no longer held its former pre-eminent position. Like Rothschilds, Barings were a house which had peaked and seemed now in a gentle relative decline, although still a first-class house, while Morgan Grenfell were clearly on the ascendent.

What about other front-rank houses, such as Hambros or Lazard Brothers, J. H. Schröder & Co. or Kleinwort, Sons & Co.? Again, it depends upon what is being measured. Some historians believe that the real measure of the importance of a merchant bank was the level of its acceptances, and here by 1913 Morgan Grenfell were very far from being amongst the leaders. It is impossible to compare directly, because 1913 numbers for most other London houses are here being compared with 1 August 1914 figures for Morgan Grenfell, but the comparison will provide an indication of magnitude. At the end of 1913, Kleinworts had £14.2 million and Schröders £11.6 million of acceptances outstanding, with Barings at £6.63 million, Brown, Shipley at £5.1 million, Hambros at £4.57 million, and Rothschilds at £3.2 million, all some way behind.[20] Morgan Grenfell had £3.3 million outstanding at the beginning of August 1914 and were therefore near the rear of the queue. However, three points must be made. Firstly, Kleinworts had made their acceptance business the vehicle of their 'dash for growth', and were repeatedly being hauled back by the suspicions of the market when it was awash with Kleinwort paper.[21] Secondly, J. S. Morgan & Co. and then Morgan Grenfell took a different approach to acceptances. The City traditionally worked on the assumption that an 'A1' firm should not have acceptances outstanding of greater than three or four times its capital; it is clear that Morgans were usually more conservative than this.[22] And thirdly, during the decade before the First World War the competition in the acceptances market was so intense that the commission rate dropped to as little as 0.25%. In the light of this Morgans decided that their capital could be used more profitably elsewhere. By 1913 Smith was concerned to build up the business once again, but only on the basis of first-class business and, in particular, with American firms recommended by the New York or Philadelphia partners.[23] By this time Morgans were more important as an issuing house than as an accepting house, although they were not unimportant as the latter: certainly they did not see Kleinworts as a threat and, indeed, referred to them somewhat disparagingly: 'Kleinworts seem to have taken the [Cuban Ports] bonds & issued them at very little profit to themselves in order to appear as an issuing house, and no doubt they have repented at leisure.'[24]

The influence of Morgan Grenfell as an issuing house did not rest solely on the number of issues it managed or co-managed. One source of strength was the house's position as a banker to governments. Besides the Argentinian loans, Morgan Grenfell managed the London tranche of Mexican bonds for which S. Bleichröder of Berlin was the syndicate leader, and led on the 1913 issue of £6 million Federal Government of Mexico 6% 10-Year Treasury Bonds; the house also managed a 1914 issue of £1 million City of Budapest 4.5% Bonds. In addition it shared in the underwriting or distribution of a large number of government issues led by other London houses. Secondly, Morgan Grenfell were one of the major distributors of American corporate issues, which gave, for example, brokers in Scotland the opportunity to share in the profits to be made in the US. In other words, the house was a very important element in a network of 'friends', primarily other first-class London houses, who shared business opportunities and forbore from poaching on each other's territory.

Whom did Morgan Grenfell consider to be their 'good friends'? Barings, of course; and Hambros, too, both in business and personal terms, were friends of very long standing, and indeed had their offices in the same building. Schröders were their 'very good friends', and when the weekly report from New York on railway car loadings arrived, it was always copied to Frank Tiarks at Schröders. Other good friends were Panmure Gordon, Robert Fleming & Co., Frederick Huth & Co., and Helbert, Wagg. Finally there were Lazards, with whom Morgan Grenfell were 'very intimate'. Indeed, the two firms set up a Canadian syndicate whose purpose was to issue Canadian industrial schemes in Paris,[25] an arrangement presumably fostered by Smith. All of these houses were reputable and conservative, and they shared information and contacts as well as business. Many of the partners knew each other socially, and marriages between their families were not uncommon.[26]

Information about bankers at this level, in particular about their manner of living, is abundant, at least relative to the amount of information available about their staffs. What is less clear is the nature of the relationships between partners and staff in their own firms. In fact, the whole area of the position of staff—who they were, their working conditions, what they were paid, what they actually did—is much more difficult to recapture at this distance in time than the lives of the partners. Evidence is sparse, since the merchant banking equivalent of the short and simple annals of the poor was seldom noted down. For Morgan Grenfell, fortunately, there is some direct evidence. Sir John Mallabar, later chairman of Harland & Wolff, began his working life in Morgan Grenfell. Smith knew his father and offered to train him, and he spent the years 1916–18 in the bank; he later wrote down some memories of the period:

22 Old Broad St. was an old building.... As you went in through the front door you were faced by an un-carpeted stone staircase leading to the two upper floors and a turning to the left which led into a small reception area with a member of the Corps of Commissionaires sitting at a high desk.... Behind this reception area and looking out into Old Broad St. there was a small interview room containing only a writing table and a few chairs, although the walls were lined with book shelves containing Stock Exchange Year Books going back into the mists of time and Times bound copies of prospectuses printed in the paper....

Facing the Reception Area there was the General Office and the Partners Office.

The General Office had ... been the garden of the old house and only occupied the ground floor, covered with a glazed roof. It was a big room and had one desk with a grille occupied by the Cashier ... in one corner. About a quarter of the room was a glassed in portion which formed the Partners Room. In it were two very large mahogany pedestal desks, one used by E. C. Grenfell and the other by Vivian Smith. Each had a fairly large Treasury inkstand (we all used dip pens in those days). Partners were in full view of staff as were staff in full view of Partners. Between the Partners Room and the General Office there was another 'compartment' with two high desks used by the Managers, who, in my day, were F. A. Ross (a Scottish Chartered Accountant) and C. R. Jeeves, each holding a half per pro signature....

Then there was the General Office containing about four or five rows of high desks. The most imposing member of the staff was Mr Minton who was in charge of correspondence. He would take general instructions from the Partners about any letters they wanted written, and which they did not want to write themselves in long hand, and Minton would then go back to his desk and compose appropriate letters written in a distinctive but easily read long hand.... Then there was Mr Firmin who took care in a general way of banking operations and Mr Stone who kept the Cash Book.... A deputy to Minton ... used the only typewriter to be seen in the General Office. No important letter was ever typed—all were written in copying ink and press copied. And all letters of any importance were always sealed with wax. At the back of the General Office there was a zinc topped table with a gas jet always burning and a supply of sealing wax and engraved seals for the purpose.

There were two or three copying presses, and a press copying machine which made the copies on a continuous roll of tissue, which was later cut into separate sheets. There were about three Smith Premier typewriters in the building, and an Addressograph machine which printed envelopes to shareholders from stencils.... We did not quite still use quill pens, but only just escaped still doing so. Willis, who founded Willis Faber, is recorded as believing business went downhill and to the devil when steel pens took the place of quills.[27]

On the first floor of the building was the cable room, where cables were coded and decoded using either Bentley's code or the firm's private code. There was also a room used by the partners' private secretary, and the dividend office, where Mallabar began work:

We [the staff of five] serviced some ten or twenty issues, either by way of coupons for interest or drawn bonds. In the latter case a partner of de Pinna & Venn would come round and supervise the draw and woe betide us if we paid a coupon on a bond after it had been drawn.

There were forms on which the owners would list their coupons (or their bonds) which would be lodged with us for some three days for examination.

Cheques payable at the London Joint Stock Bank [now The Midland Bank] ...
would then be issued in payment for the claims.

The coupons (or bonds) would then be listed ... in copying ink on the most
delightful of hand made paper.... There were three old ladies (and they were
old) inhabiting the third, or top, floor whose task it was to sort the coupons into
numerical order, after which I would cancel them with a punch operated by a
heavy wheel which could make a hole in 100 coupons in one operation....

There was a good strong room in the basement and every evening the head
of each department would take a basket of the more important papers in his
charge down to the strong room. In the morning he would retrieve them. Ross
had one key to one lock of the strong room and Jeeves had the key to the other
lock.

Financial controls appear to have been rather tight:

One of the high desks in the General Office was concerned with the post.... The
practice was that if a letter was concerned with any particular client the writer
would pencil the initials of the client (say I.M.M. for International Mercantile
Marine) on the envelope where the stamp would be fixed, and the letter would
then be entered in a letter book and stamped. At the end of the day the number
of letters the postage on which could be charged to I.M.M.—say 1s/3d [6½p]
for fifteen letters at a penny each would be noted on slips which were then
passed to the book-keepers so that the client could be charged.

Working conditions were also rather different:

Coal fires were the means of heating and telephones were not much used....
A man named Slater was in charge of stationery supplies and on joining he
provided you with the 'tools of your trade'. These consisted of about a square
foot of chamois leather used as a resting place and wiper for your pens. Three
pens—one for black, one for red and one for copying ink—black lead and blue
pencils and a penknife/scraper eraser. In addition to the three inkpots you were
also given a glass bowl containing lead shot and water with which you cleaned
your pens. Fountain pens were almost unknown in those days....

The firm had its own arrangements for getting about the City. As
Mallabar recalls, 'The firm retained a private taxi which stood all day in
Old Broad St ready for use by a Partner or any one else sent on special
errands such as I sometimes undertook taking urgent letters to the
Treasury.'[28] The City seems continually to have been on the move, since
the alternative to the use of the telephone was the private visit. The diary
of Sir Edward Holden, then chairman of the London Joint Stock Bank,
records that in April 1912 Grenfell, with another member of Morgan
Grenfell, 'called in to ask if EH be interested in an issue of Mexican
Treasury Bills'.[29] Clearly the partners took care of the business, tramping

from office to office—or riding in the staff taxi—and the rest of the house's staff supported them.

The staff at Morgan Grenfell seem to have been reasonably well paid for their work. Mallabar recalls that he started at £50 per year in 1916 and was earning £70 per year when he left in 1918. (The two managers, Ross and Jeeves, 'were reputed to earn £3000 p.a. each which seemed an enormous amount of money in those days'.[30]) Junior staff had their salaries increased each year 'in accordance with their merits and behaviour during the preceding 12 months, but both this increase, and the maximum salary to which members of the staff may attain, is entirely dependent upon themselves'.[31]

In fact, it is possible to know exactly the policy of Morgan Grenfell with regard to the payment of staff, thanks to an outraged letter written by Grenfell. William Miller had been a member of staff but had died, apparently leaving his wife in some financial distress, and consequently his son had contacted the firm with an application for aid. In response Grenfell wrote to the widow:

I was extremely surprised when your son informed me what he believed to be the position of your late husband's estate.

The members of the staff here have received salaries considerably higher than those paid for similar services in other offices, and it has been distinctly understood by them that such salaries were paid on condition that they made provision for themselves on retirement and for their families. In some other offices special provisions are made for pensions or life assurance and the scale of salary is in such cases thereby reduced. Your late husband had received for many years £550 a year, to which on occasions a bonus was added. Out of this the Partners assumed that a man of Mr Miller's position had made provision for the future.

It is therefore a matter of grave disappointment to myself and the other Partners to hear from you and your son that not only had Mr Miller made no provision towards his maintenance after retirement, but that he had not even insured his life as a support to his family.

I had understood indirectly from him that he considered his children, who were grown up, to be independent of support from him, as is I believe the case, but I had no idea that a man of his position would have lived up to the full extent of his income, knowing the conditions under which his salary was fixed.[32]

Mrs Miller wrote back to Grenfell, and either she made a convincing case or he felt in retrospect that he had been a bit harsh on her: certainly she was invited to send in a list of her debts, and these were duly discharged by Morgan Grenfell. However, the partners apparently drew the conclusion that some staff were not to be trusted to make provision for themselves, and at the end of 1912 the firm arranged for a pension and life assurance scheme for the staff.[33] The scheme (with the Scottish Amicable Life Assurance Society) was probably paid for by the staff members themselves, however, since in 1917 Grenfell wrote to a member of staff who was having to retire through ill-health that 'As you are aware, it is not the custom of the firm to allow pensions to member of the staff on their retirement, it being understood that they are expected to provide from their salaries, a sinking fund for their later years'. In this case, however, Morgan Grenfell paid the retiring staff member nearly a year's salary because of his sickness and that of his family. Only in 1937 did the firm's accounts begin showing contributions to a staff pension fund.[34]

What happened with regard to partners' salaries is a bit clearer. First of all, of course, there was the distinction between a salaried partner and a general partner, in that only the latter took a share in the partnership's profits or losses. From 1910 all the partners drew a salary. From 1910 to 1919, for example, Grenfell apparently had a salary of £10,720 plus 30% of the profits (1910), or 27.5% (1913–17), or 22% (1919). Smith had a salary of £8,680 plus a 20% share of the profits (1910–13), or 22.5% (1913–17), or 18% (1918–19). Whigham, who became a salaried partner in 1912, drew a salary which rose from £3,500 in 1912 to £5,000 until 1918; he then became a full partner and drew a salary of £6,600 plus 10% of the profits in 1918–19.[35] Enjoying a share of the profits did not, of course, mean having the right to withdraw more than an agreed amount from the house. Partners' balances derived from profits held in the business represented the major source of capital. However, partners were paid 5% interest on their capital in the business. They also drew an agreed amount each year from profits—if there were any. In the new partnership agreement drawn up in late November 1917 it was stated that Grenfell and Smith could each draw £10,000 a year from the profits and Whigham £6,000 a year,[36] in addition to their salaries.

During the 1920s a new element to partners' pay was added. For reasons which are unclear, from 1923 through 1926 the London partners received a payment from New York which varied for Grenfell from £2,792 in 1923 to £5,195 in 1925 to £233 in 1926. These payments have been his share of certain American syndicates, since the London partners were investing in the US on some scale during these years. The reasons for extra payments in the years 1928 through 1930 are quite clear, however; as Grenfell wrote,

As it fell in the boom years that MG&Co and MH&Co had fewer opportunities of making money than NY & yet rendered very useful services to NY for which no charge could be made, Mr JPM offered that 'gifts' of $40,000 [about £8,200] should be made by JPM&Co to London & Paris partners. The English Inland Revenue on enquiry made by our auditors, wrote that on the facts as stated, these gifts to London partners were probably free of tax.... It was clearly understood that the gifts were voluntary & could be discontinued. In view of slump & bad year, no such gifts were made ... for 1931.[37]

It is indeed worth remembering that being a merchant banker was not necessarily a licence to print money: in good years profits rolled in, but in bad the losses could be substantial. In the years 1910–14, for example, the partners made losses on their investments in stocks—especially North American stocks—in three years out of the five; during three of the years from 1910 to 1913 the income from commissions and interest was enough to offset the losses, but in 1913 and 1914 the losses on stocks were so great that they overwhelmed the gains made elsewhere and the partners had to debit their capital accounts. In a curious fashion, although the firm suffered over the longer term from the loss of their traditional business because of the First World War, in the more immediate term they were made much more secure by it. This was because, as described in the next chapter, they became the agents for the British government in purchasing supplies relating to the war, and the commission earned thereby completely transformed the house's financial position (see Appendix III).[38]

The First World War, and India

The outbreak of the war wreaked havoc in financial markets all over Europe, as well as in other centres such as New York City. This was of course particularly devastating for the City of London because of the large amount of acceptance credits outstanding in the names of foreign firms who were unable to remit payment. The acceptance houses refused to undertake new business from 27 July 1914, and from about 1 August bills on London were virtually unobtainable. As one historian has written,

The burden of the difficulties ... fell first on the accepting houses and, ultimately, on the discount houses and the banks. It is generally believed that there were some £350 mn. of bills outstanding at the time of crisis; of which, perhaps two-thirds represented debts payable by foreigners in London. Most of them had been accepted by merchant bankers specialising in the business, some by the big joint-stock banks. These foreign debts would be falling due at the rate of £3 mn. or more every working day, and, whatever their foreign clients might do, the acceptors were liable for their payment. In face of this threatened mass default of its foreign customers, even the strongest accepting house could not long continue payments.

The accepting houses were thus faced with imminent and terrible disaster, but the trouble would not have stopped there; if the accepting houses had been ruined, they would have dragged down the bill-brokers, and possibly even the great joint-stock banks with them.[39]

To protect themselves, the joint-stock banks began calling in their loans to the acceptance houses as well as refusing to make new loans available. Consequently the only way the acceptance houses could ensure their own liquidity was to take their bills to the Bank of England for discount, which drained the Bank of England's reserves by 16% in three days.[40]

By 31 July 1914 Government ministers became alarmed, and over the next several days discussions were held between representatives of the government, the Bank of England, the joint-stock banks, the acceptance houses, and business and commerce. A moratorium was proclaimed for Monday, 3 August; the importance of this for the merchant banks was that it postponed payment on any bill of exchange which had been accepted before 4 August. In due course it was further decided that the Bank of England would advance to the acceptors of approved bills the funds required to meet such bills at maturity. These advances would not have to be repaid until one year after peace was declared. As Whigham wrote to William Porter, one of the New York partners,

Probably this whole arrangement was as good as any that could have been devised and will no doubt be a great relief to the financial community in general, but of course as regards the Acceptance Houses it is only delaying the evil day and there will be a fearful and wonderful settling day 'One year after peace' especially for those Accepting Houses which had large Continental connections. However, sufficient unto the day.[41]

The day after the moratorium was proclaimed, Frederick Huth Jackson, the senior partner of the acceptance house Frederick Huth & Co., summoned a meeting of the representatives of the acceptance houses of London to consider the moratorium. Morgan Grenfell accepted the invitation and the group met on 5 August.[42] This informal meeting was the beginning of the Acceptance Houses Committee; membership of this committee is now overladen with such mystique that it is worth noting that Grenfell did not think it worth mentioning in his outline of the events of the war relating to finance and the partnership.

It is possible that Whigham's rather flippant tone stemmed from the relative safety of the partnership in the crisis. As Grenfell wrote to H. P. Davison, another New York partner, on 20 August 1914,

People are extremely calm here though, of course, no one knows how he stands. It is all very well for M.G. & Co. who have very few Continental acceptances and also have a big brother in New York with a sympathetic HPD [Davison] at the helm, but many of the big houses here have anything from 30 to 90 million of bills falling due of which the greater part is for German, Russian and Austrian accounts....[43]

Grenfell was referring to houses such as Kleinworts, Goschen, Konig, and Huth's; in spite of the reference to Russia, Barings were apparently quite safe. Morgan Grenfell's own acceptances were largely confined to North and South America, and while the stocks and bonds they held from those countries might be at a discount, the acceptances were all sound. As Grenfell wrote to Porter some time later,

You may remember, at the beginning of the war, the Bank of England, backed by the Government, agreed to take into cold storage such acceptances, and while it was not necessary for us to avail of the cold storage, we used it to a limited extent for a short time as the large houses, including Rothschilds, had agreed to do so, so as not to make invidious comparisons between the Houses. We did, however, pay these off very shortly, so as to be free of any accusation that we were being helped.[44]

During the period of the war attempts were made by the partners to keep regular business going, but there were official restraints. A Capital Issues Committee was set up by the Treasury to advise on applications to issue foreign loans. The rules were at first applied with some laxity: most domestic issues were allowed, along with a few colonial and foreign ones. By the summer of 1915, however, a combination of the financial demands made by the second War Loan in June and the strain on resources occasioned by industrial mobilization caused controls to become much tighter.[45] Morgan Grenfell, jointly with Barings, were able to issue £5 million of Argentine Government 6% Treasury Bonds,[46] but that was the last foreign issue of the war period. The London partners kept up their lending, and by 1917 and 1918 their stocks had largely appreciated in value above their purchase prices, but the main effort of the house was devoted to the agency for the British government.

But there was a development in the house's business that was important for the future: an opportunity arose to take over a business in India. J. S. Morgan & Co. and then Morgan Grenfell & Co. both had ambitions to develop a banking business there. One of the reasons for offering a partnership to Dawkins had been to take advantage of his Indian connections and knowledge, and it was possibly owing to him that the firm had suffered one of its more troublesome failures, that of India Development Ltd. This was an established company with large sugar, indigo, and other properties in India, as well as several manufacturing plants. J. S. Morgan & Co. began advancing funds to the company in 1902, and their commitment increased over the next few years; unfortunately, however, in May 1908 Morgans had to call in the receiver.

These difficulties did not discourage the London partners in their attempts to develop a banking business in India: rather, the lesson they learnt was the need for more effective supervision of the house's operations in India, which, in Grenfell's opinion, could be accomplished only through working with a reliable mercantile house in Calcutta. The opportunity came in September 1911, when George Yule & Co., London agency of Andrew Yule & Co. Ltd., one of India's largest and wealthiest mercantile houses, asked to establish a credit account with the London house, and Yule & Co. became the principal Indian connection for all the Morgan houses.[47]

It was a connection which was to become even more intimate. In early July 1916 Sir David Yule walked into the offices of Morgan Grenfell and proposed that Morgans take over his firm. Yule was an old friend of Smith's, and this personal relationship, together with the long-standing business relationship of the two houses, was probably responsible for Yule's proposal. He was a very wealthy man who had built up a flourishing, first-class mercantile business, but he was growing old and he had no one to whom he could turn over the responsibility for it. Many of the young men in the firm had been caught up in the war machine; his younger brother had been drowned while travelling out to India; and his only child was an eleven-year-old girl. He was afraid that the business would fall into the hands of men who would not run it on his lines, and therefore he proposed that Morgans buy it from him on reasonable terms.

Smith and Grenfell were very attracted to the business—as Smith wrote to Jack Morgan, 'The £140,000 a year commission business would make a magnificent addition to our bread and butter business here.'[48] Negotiations continued over the summer and autumn of 1916 until agreement was reached between Yule and the New York and London Morgan houses. Yule had suggested a price of £600,000, while the New York partners thought that £500,000 was a better price. In the end they

1. George Peabody, *c.*1854, by Alexander Healy
(By courtesy of National Portrait Gallery, Smithsonian Institution, Washington, DC)

HOW TO TAKE A HINT.

John Bull:—"WELL, MR. PEABODY, AFTER YOUR SECOND SPLENDID DONATION, DON'T YOU THINK
IT'S MY TURN TO DO SOMETHING FOR THE POOR?"

2. From *Fun*, 24 Feb. 1866. Peabody had placed a total of £500,000 in
the Peabody Donation Fund to be used to build model dwellings
for the poor

3. Peabody Square model dwellings by Blackfriars Road

(By courtesy of Morgan Grenfell Group)

4. Junius Spencer Morgan
(*By courtesy of Morgan Grenfell Group*)

5. J. Pierpont Morgan
(By courtesy of the Bettmann Archive)

7. E. C. Grenfell, his wife Florence, and Jack Morgan, bathing at Bridgetown, Barbados, 1921
(*By courtesy of the Hon. Laura Grenfell Phillips*)

6. J. P. (Jack) Morgan, Jr.
(*By courtesy of Morgan Grenfell Group*)

8. The changing face of 23 Great Winchester Street: Winchester House in
1820; no. 23 in 1884; and the entrance to Morgan Grenfell in 1988
(*By courtesy of Morgan Grenfell Group*)

A MORGANATIC MARRIAGE.

THE LATEST AMERICAN DO(D)GE WEDS THE ATLANTIC WITH A 'RING.'

9. A satiric view of the International Mercantile Marine
as seen by *Punch*, 30 Apr. 1902
(*By courtesy of the Mary Evans Picture Library*)

reached a compromise: £200,000 down with a further £400,000 to be paid at the rate of £50,000 a year for eight years out of the firm's profits —and if there were no profits there would be no payment. It is also notable that the official letter to Yule was written by Morgan Grenfell on behalf of J. P. Morgan & Co. As Smith explained to Davison, 'This was done on the advice of Sir Frank Crisp [a distinguished City solicitor] so as to avoid any possible question of Income Tax in the future.'[49]

Yet the arrangement nearly came unstuck. In August 1917 Grenfell wrote to Smith that 'Yule called today and left some of his Balance Sheets. I find him curiously difficult to understand as he has not got the gift of words. I do not at present see how we are to take over his business unless we find someone who understands it and can be sent out there. Certainly no-one here can attempt to look after it.' There was another problem as well: the imposition of swingeing new taxation in India, which Grenfell feared would 'make the Yule proposition look very much less attractive to us and to J.P.M. & Co...'.[50] Various telegrams between the London and New York partners make it clear that both Morgan houses seriously considered withdrawing from the agreement; it was in fact saved by Yule's agreeing to continue to run the business and by new financial arrangements. Its continuing success would, however, only be secured by finding the right man to go out to India to run it and the associated London agency. But this would have to wait until the end of the war.

In 1899 on one of his trips to the Caucasus Smith had met T. S. Catto, then secretary and office manager for the head of a shipping firm in Batoum. By the beginning of the First World War Catto was vice-president of MacAndrews & Forbes, a firm of manufacturers and merchants with headquarters in the US. His six years' residence in Russia had given him some command of the language, and therefore he was asked to join the Anglo-Russian Committee, which was in charge of purchasing supplies for Russia in the US and elsewhere, the cost of which was being met out of British advances to Russia. This meant that he soon came into contact with J. P. Morgan & Co., who were the British government's purchasing agent in the US. In due course Catto became chairman of the Allied Provisions Export Commission and the British Ministry of Food Mission in the US and Canada, and as such he visited Britain in November 1917 to confer with the government. While there he lunched a number of times with Smith, his 'closest and most intimate friend', who asked what his plans were after the end of the war. He added that he wondered whether he, Catto, could be persuaded to return to the

East, this time to India. They agreed that nothing could be decided while the war continued, but Catto's intention was to return to his position in New York. At the end of 1918 Whigham visited New York City and arranged to dine with Catto, who in the meantime had decided that he did not wish to leave New York:

I remember we then took a taxicab to go to my apartment for dinner and in the cab Mr Whigham renewed the conversation about the East, and in one sentence shook all my resolution about remaining in New York. For the first time mention was made of the name of the firm in India. It was Andrew Yule & Co. I knew it by name, but what shook me was the fact that Yule was the maiden name of my mother, that Yule was the name of my grandfather, and Andrew Yule was the name of my uncle, although in no way related to the Yules who had founded the firm in India. It seemed to me an act of Providence that I should be asked to become a partner and the governing head—so without further discussion I turned to Mr Whigham and said, 'Subject to the agreement of my wife, I accept the proposal.'[51]

The Yule organization had two parts—Andrew Yule & Co. Ltd. in Calcutta, and George Yule & Co. in London, a much smaller organization. Catto had very clear ideas about how the firm should develop, seeing the London house as the real centre which could 'become the nucleus for developments in London, India and in the USA.... In a word ... it would become the merchant department of J.P.M. & Co and M.G. & Co ... with a splendid opportunity to develop A.Y. & Co. into a great merchant firm not only in India but in other parts of the world'.[52] The London firm became Yule, Catto & Co. Ltd. in 1920. The source of the earnings, however, was Andrew Yule & Co. Ltd. in Calcutta, and all of the shares remained in Sir David Yule's hands until September 1922, when the final payment for its purchase was made. The shares were then apportioned so that Catto himself held 25%, J. P. Morgan & Co. held 37.5%, and Grenfell, Vivian Smith, R. H. V. Smith (his son), and Charles Whigham held the remaining 37.5%.[53]

Catto took up his position as managing director of Andrew Yule & Co. in 1919, a position he held until 1928, when (as he was fifty years old) he gave up the senior position to a younger man. During his years at Andrew Yule funds were put back into the company; although dividends of 10% were paid semi-annually by 1926, it was not until 1928 that, as Grenfell noted, the company at last declared dividends (of 15%) which approximated to its real earnings. But, he wrote to Morgan, 'Our holdings and yours cost us nothing & if we can choose the right men to send out in succession we shall find the business a growing one & the

[?]finest in B.[ritish] India.'⁵⁴ Although the partners as individuals held the shares in the Calcutta firm, Morgan Grenfell had a share of the London agency, Yule, Catto & Co., until 1934, when that formal link was cut with the disposal of the shareholding by sale to the individual partners. Thereafter Morgan Grenfell as such had little or no financial interest in Yule, Catto, until 1958, when the bank significantly increased their shareholding. But even in the interim relations remained close—and indeed, continue so to the present.

The year 1917 had thus seen the extension of Morgan Grenfell's interests into a merchanting and banking operation in India which would provide substantial profits for the partners. It also saw the reorganization of Morgan Grenfell itself—although in appearance rather than reality —at the behest of wartime legislation. The intent of the new legislation was to make clear to the public the origins of all partners in a firm; and therefore the writing paper of each firm had to list the name and nationality of each partner. There was no difficulty with this for Morgan Grenfell as far as nationality was concerned; carrying out these regulations, however, meant that they ran straight into another law, that which regulated the number of partners in a banking firm. When the names of all the American partners were added to those of the British partners, the sum was fourteen, while the law stated that no firm carrying out a banking business might have more than ten. The upshot was that the London and American partners decided that the partnership should be turned into a private unlimited company. As far as the London partners were concerned, this was literally a nominal change: the shareholders were called partners, and the allocation of shares meant that the distribution of ownership between J. P. Morgan & Co. and the British partners remained the same.

The registered capital of £1 million continued to be J. P. Morgan & Co.'s contribution. But the actual capital would also continue to be that amount plus the amounts standing to the credit of the British partners in the books of the firm. This was greatly in excess of £1 million. Grenfell worried whether this might make the British government think a new firm had been set up, which would threaten complicated and possibly expensive questions by the Inland Revenue. The partners and their solicitor, Sir Frank Crisp, could not decide whether the outcome would redound to the benefit of Morgan Grenfell or the Inland Revenue, and therefore they placed all the facts before the authorities. The outcome was favourable to Morgan Grenfell, thereby producing a nice combination of relief and righteousness.

What was unchanged was the relationship with the American partners. Morgan Grenfell remained a British partnership which was closely linked to, and ultimately could be controlled by, the American partnership; indeed this position of subordination is apparently underlined by the discussions as to whether the New York partners would allow the names of the British partners to appear first on the writing paper.[56] But this appearance of inferiority is misleading, and indeed questions of rank, as it were, appear never to have disturbed the close and even affectionate relationship. Because both sides broadly agreed on the business in which it would be profitable to engage, 'control' as such did not really enter into it. The British partners had the benefit of the American capital deposited in the London house, as well as the correspondent relationship, while the American partners had the benefit both of the placing power of London and the advice and expertise of the British partners. The advantages of the latter to the American partners should not be underestimated. During the negotiations over the Yule connection, for example, time and again the New York partners made it clear that they were dependent on the advice of the London partners: as the New York partners cabled to the London partners in October 1918, 'It is true that we have not been over enthusiastic about the business, nevertheless we place implicit reliance upon your own strong belief in it and we are content as heretofore to continue with you in the business...'.[57] In fact it is possible to argue, as the American historian Carosso does, that London was the dominant house: the American partners almost always agreed with the wishes and opinions of the London partners.[58] London's opinion on foreign business was of particular value to New York, and this would be especially clear during the 1920s in the negotiations over various European governmental issues.

Rebuilding their Traditional Business

But the first consideration for Morgan Grenfell in the 1920s was to rebuild their ordinary, day-to-day business. They decided to try and revive their acceptance business, which had been almost abandoned, but progress was slow. In 1925 a new department was set up, and to run it Smith found a man from Hambros, Mr Bartington. Grenfell noted that 'The man whom Vivian found is very conservative & does not run any risks beyond those incidental to commercial credits. He is also anxious to train up younger men to follow in his steps.'[59] The immediate outcome was considered very satisfactory, with an increase in acceptance commissions from £13,000 in 1924 to £25,000 in 1925.[60]

The following year the firm began seriously to try and build up acceptance business in Europe. The concentrated effort was clearly necessary: when three Morgan partners visited the President of the Banque de Bruxelles and told him that they would like to discuss acceptance credits, 'He said he was very glad to hear of this. He did not know that we did this class of business and said that it would not have struck him to ask us for a credit any more than it would strike him to ask Messrs. Rothschild.'[61] It was an organized campaign. After some discussion, it was agreed that J. P. Morgan & Co. would forbear from making direct approaches of their own; rather, the Paris and London houses would make the approaches on behalf of all three houses. They divided up Europe, with Morgan Harjes et Cie negotiating for credit business in France, Switzerland, Belgium, and Spain, while Morgan Grenfell concentrated on Holland, the Scandinavian countries, and, possibly, Germany.[62]

Germany indeed was problematical, but this was because Grenfell and Jack Morgan's antipathy had kept the houses from pursuing private German business. It was Smith who proposed breaking the embargo, writing to Grenfell in New York in late May 1926:

Mr Bartington is leaving for Holland on Monday to keep in touch with some Dutch firms with whom we are hoping to do credit and possibly banking business and the question has been raised as to whether we should not now consider doing business with German firms if the opportunity offers. We should of course only consider dealing with highest class Banks and Banking Firms and the question we wish to ask you is entirely one of principle as to whether Jack or you have any objection to doing business with Germans or whether you consider sufficient time has elapsed for us now to consider it desirable. Barings are working with Warburgs, Hambros with the Dresdner Bank and Behrens and I think probably we are the only prominent merchant banking firm who are doing nothing direct with Germany.[63]

Grenfell agreed that they could entertain German business if it was of the highest class, and Bartington and his colleague visited S. Bleichröder in Berlin and M. M. Warburg & Co. in Hamburg in addition to several Dutch banks.[64]

During 1926 the credit business did expand satisfactorily, but the commissions did not increase, largely because the big banks were 'cutting rates foolishly & unnecessarily, in some cases to $\frac{1}{8}$% for 3 months'.[65] Things were no better in 1927, partially because rates were too low and

'2 Continental gentlemen have plainly lied'.[66] The following three years, however, saw steady growth, as Morgan Grenfell moved to exploit closer connections with their opposite numbers in the commercial credits department of J. P. Morgan & Co. Acceptance commissions totalled £40,687 in 1928, £45,000 in 1929, and nearly £60,000 in 1930.

But then a combination of managerial troubles within the bank and the general economic downturn produced a decline. By 1930 the long-serving managers Ross and Jeeves had both been ill for some months and the partners found that the new managers had been 'ill-informed' about this aspect of the business. The partners had to impress on the new managers that Morgan Grenfell would only take bills eligible for discount at the Bank of England, and that the partners would look at all fresh bills daily. With the onset of the Depression, business slowed further, and acceptance commissions declined to £46,000 in 1931, to £30,000 in 1932, and to £25,000 in 1933 before rising marginally to nearly £31,000 in 1934. Thereafter they resumed their downward trend.[67]

Morgan Grenfell's other traditional business, which had likewise been devastated by the war, was the issuing of foreign loans, both government and corporate. Their attempts to rebuild this business must be seen within the general context of the new relationship of the City of London and New York: private banking in both cities had been transformed by the financial consequences of the First World War, but in opposite ways. New York now had much more capital and could aspire to replace London as the major money market, while London had less capital but had the expertise, the clients, and the market.

There were a number of reasons why New York had so much more capital to invest than London. Firstly, compared with Europe and Latin America, the supply of savings was large relative to investment opportunities, and this required 'international financial intermediation on a large scale' in order to channel it to borrowers.[68] Secondly, the US had emerged from the Great War as a creditor nation: by the end of 1919 she had invested abroad, on private account, some $6.5 billion, while her long-term liabilities had been substantially reduced through having bought back large amounts of American securities held abroad. This meant that there was an inflow instead of an outflow on account of interest, profits, and dividends which were available for reinvestment. During the 1920s, in fact, America's long-term investment rose by nearly $9 billion and 'accounted for about two-thirds of world new investment'. Britain's total overseas investments were less than half of those of the US. And thirdly, the US economy during the 1920s was basically a booming one.

London, conversely, was in a much worse state after the war. She had been forced to liquidate about 15% of her overseas investments, primarily American, and thus suffered a reduced income. Britain also suffered from a deterioration in her visible trade balance, mainly because of difficulties in her export trade.[69] But the City of London was also held back because of controls on capital exports—that is, restrictions on lending abroad—stemming from the authorities' concern with the weakness of sterling. In March 1919 Britain had been forced off the gold standard, and the primary goal of the Bank of England and the Treasury during the early 1920s was to return to it. This policy required limitations on the outflow of capital.

It was generally accepted that the City of London's pre-eminence before the war had been largely dependent on the strength and position of sterling, and on the willingness of the City to make foreign loans. In the conditions of the 1920s, it seemed that either the strength of sterling or London's command of international lending would have to be sacrificed. While the overriding concern of Montagu Norman, the Governor of the Bank of England, was to maintain and improve sterling's exchange rate, he did not wish to damage London's position as a foreign lender, and when possible he encouraged the City to remain in the market. Thus in August 1924 the Morgan cables note the heavy commercial credits being extended to Germany by other banks with Norman's approval,[70] in an attempt to capture the German market for London.[71]

In fact, the weapons with which Norman could control foreign lending and defend sterling were few and weak. A high Bank Rate would tend to discourage foreign borrowing, but it would also be deflationary domestically. Legislation to prohibit foreign lending was considered to be out of the question.[72] So, by and large, what Norman called 'personal influence', what one historian calls 'moral suasion',[73] and what Americans call 'jawboning', was his major weapon. Its success was uneven.

From 1920 to 1925 Norman imposed an 'embargo' of sorts on foreign loans as one of the policies aimed at enabling sterling to return to the gold standard. In early 1920 he asked bankers to make no short-term foreign issues—short-term being defined as having a maturity of less than twenty years. By April 1924, finding that too many issues were still being made, Norman ordered that foreign lending should be limited to reconstruction loans, which he defined as those guaranteed by the Treasury or supported by the League of Nations. In April 1925, after Britain had returned to gold, the Committee of Treasury of the Bank of England still thought that it would be necessary to 'discourage foreign issues and investment by all possible means'.[74] In October of that year the Chancellor of the Exchequer told Norman that he hoped that no loan would be floated on behalf of any country which had not settled its war debts to Britain, and this policy remained until October 1928. Nevertheless, the Chancellor announced the removal of the general embargo on foreign loans for the market at large in a public speech in Sheffield on 3 November 1925. As a result, foreign lending expanded rapidly. By this date Norman had changed his policy and was doing little to hamper foreign loans except those to Russia and Germany, on which he issued strong, but private, warnings. Finally, in 1930 he obtained the agreement of the Chancellor that official approval would be required for all foreign loans. In 1933 a strict embargo on overseas lending was imposed, with the Empire exempt.[75]

Evidence in the Morgan Grenfell cables indicates that the Governor's policy was not working very successfully. For example, in the same cable in which Morgan Grenfell refused participation in a US dollar loan for Belgium in September 1924, they added sourly that others in London would probably participate. Norman himself admitted in February 1925 that 'The demand for Foreign Issues in London cannot long be prevented by the present method of so-called persuasion.'[76] D. E. Moggridge has pointed out that Norman's controls did not prevent investors, especially big institutional investors, from subscribing to foreign issues and that the main effect was to divert commissions from London to New York firms.[77] It is also clear that Morgan Grenfell themselves were investing in the US on some scale via J. P. Morgan & Co.

One reason for borrowing in one market rather than another is the difference in the cost. Historians have differed as to whether New York or London was the cheaper market;[78] of course, it is necessary to know the date of an issue since rates fluctuated. Short-term rates tended to be kept high in London to support the sterling exchange rate. On the other hand, long-term yields on long-dated issues were usually low in London, partially because brokerage rates were lower.[79] (Consider the differences in distances involved in distributing issues, for example.) If the occasion warranted it, however, this American disadvantage might be overcome, as Paul Einzig, a contemporary financial journalist of some repute, described:

The American banker is at a disadvantage in international competition in the margin of profit he requires: overhead charges are higher in New York than in any other centre and banks there are accustomed to substantial profits on domestic banking business. They are reluctant to work for the same narrow margin as their European rivals. This does not mean that it is an easy task to defeat American bankers in a rate-cutting contest. If it comes to that, they are prepared to work without any profit or even at a loss in the field of international business, and to make up for their losses in the field of domestic business.[80]

But this sort of sacrifice could not become a regular occurrence. Even so, the cost of borrowing was not always the determining factor. For example, even after the change in relative long-term interest rates between London and New York in 1924 which made New York the cheaper centre in which to borrow, it was still necessary for the British authorities in November 1924 to impose informal controls over the flotation of new foreign issues in the London capital market in the attempt to restrict the outflow of funds as they prepared to return to the gold standard.[81]

Einzig also complained about another growing American habit—that of issuing a foreign loan in New York and then selling a substantial amount of it in London. The problem for New York was that it lacked a sizeable domestic investing public for foreign issues. He noted that half a dozen New York firms maintained branches in London for the express purpose of distributing to insurance companies and other big investors the issues for which they had taken responsibility. By issuing the loan in the first place, New York received the commission income and the US received the subsequent income from the trading contracts. The British position was further damaged, according to Einzig, because these American issues absorbed funds which would otherwise have been available for lending by British banks on their own account. Instead, they had to decline proposals and send the rejected customers to New York.[82] Certainly, in some of the Morgan loans, it was a requirement that the American distributors should not attempt to sell their shares in London.[83]

It should be noted that Morgan Grenfell, because of their relationship with J. P. Morgan & Co., suffered less than other London banks from the tendency for business to be transferred to New York. This is exemplified by the episodes of the Australian loans. When Montagu Norman decided on priorities for foreign loans, reconstruction loans for Europe and loans to the dominions and colonies were rated the most important.[84] Traditionally, of course, the dominions had always borrowed in London, but Canada and Australia now began to turn to New York for their funds. Thus the agent for Australia opened negotiations in London for the issuing of a loan in New York, but half-way through the Australians decided that they would prefer to negotiate as well as to borrow in New York and thereby save on commissions in London. Morgan Grenfell did their best to ensure that J. P. Morgan & Co. would fall heir to any such business.[85] This was reciprocal, of course, since the New York house regularly ensured that Morgan Grenfell would lead in the issuing of any London tranche of a Morgan loan. Joint issues, in fact, became the norm for many of their loans, a procedure which benefited both sides of an issuing group: London alone could not provide funds on the scale required, but its participation was appreciated by New York bankers as constituting an imprimatur of quality. American investors, according to J. P. Morgan & Co., would more readily invest in a foreign loan when they knew that London was also involved.[86]

London in the 1920s was a contracting market for overseas issues, but habit and proximity still drove many companies to borrow in London. Nevertheless, the fact that much more capital was available in New York drew more and more issuing there. But the pain for the City of London was somewhat mitigated by large issues frequently being made jointly: as Einzig remarked, 'In international loan operations of any considerable size it was difficult to form a financial group without the participation of London banks.'[87]

Notable in this general context is the extent to which Morgan Grenfell's foreign loan business held up in the 1920s and early 1930s. This was partly because of the link with J. P. Morgan & Co., now clearly after the First World War the premier investment bank in the world; but it was also because of the reputation, contacts, and expertise of the London partners. They were the London leaders in the great stabilization loans for Germany and Britain, and co-leaders (with Barings) for Belgium, which leadership largely stemmed from their role in war finance and procurement. But they were also the manager, co-manager, or syndicate member for a number of other important loans over the period, some of which grew out of new relationships in the City.

Morgans had always been close to Lazards, and in 1922 they joined with them and Rothschilds in issuing sterling bonds for two French railways, the Midi and the Orleans.[88] This was the first time Morgans had co-managed an issue with Rothschilds since the 1909 5% Chilean Government Loan. Again, they had usually been close to Barings, and the two came together in 1923 to co-manage an Argentine government loan. This was the only issue in the 1920s for Argentina, since she now raised most of her external finance in the US.[89] However, when Argentina fell into economic difficulties in the 1930s and had to convert a large part of her sterling debt, the government again turned to Barings and Morgan Grenfell for a total of eight further issues between 1934 and 1937.

Barings had been instrumental in J. S. Morgan & Co.'s move into the Argentine market in the late nineteenth century, and in the same way they encouraged Morgan Grenfell's move into Japan in the 1920s. Barings, the Hong Kong and Shanghai Bank, and the Yokohama Specie Bank had co-managed a Japanese government loan in 1902, and the Japanese government, as well as the City of Tokyo, turned to Barings again. Morgan Grenfell (and the Westminster Bank) joined Barings, Rothschilds, and Schröders for three Japanese loans: a 6% sterling bond loan in 1924 and a 5.5% loan for the City of Tokyo in 1925, both of which were issued to raise money to rebuild Tokyo after the 1923 earthquake, and a 5.5% conversion loan in 1930. The 1924 Japanese loan was a particularly profitable exercise for Morgan Grenfell.[90]

The Move into Corporate Finance

There were other foreign loans, but what is perhaps more important for the future was that they made their first issues for domestic borrowers. In 1927 Morgans were the sole managers of an issue for Anglo-American Oil Co. Ltd. of a 5.5% debenture stock and of an issue for Debenhams Ltd. of a 5% first mortgage debenture stock. The next domestic public issue did not take place until 1934, when the house issued 4% first mortgage debenture stock for Metropolitan Ground Rents. However, taking the public issues as an indication of volume of work would produce a misleading impression. From at least 1923 more and more of Morgan Grenfell's time was spent on domestic corporate finance, including merger and acquisition work. One source of clients was American companies wishing to expand overseas, such as General Motors; another was private contacts, such as Lloyd George, who needed help in raising money for his political activities; a third, in the late 1920s and 1930s, was the Bank of England in its reconstruction schemes for derelict British industry, although Morgan Grenfell saw its involvement in this as a public duty rather than as business taken on for sound commercial principles; and a fourth was business contacts, including clients who came to Morgans because of its general reputation.

Early in July 1925 officials of General Motors wrote Morgan Grenfell a letter which was read 'with great interest' by the partners, and it was agreed that the officials should call at Old Broad Street in late July. The object was the expansion of General Motors (GMC) in Britain, to be effected by the purchase of the British firm Austin Motors. In the post-war decades GMC and the Ford Motor Company engaged in keen competition, which in the 1920s spilt over from the US to other countries. However, exports of motor cars from the US to Britain were hampered, first by a tariff of $33\frac{1}{3}\%$ which had been imposed on imported motor vehicles after 1915, and secondly by a progressive tax, imposed in 1921, which taxed higher horsepower vehicles (which American cars tended to be) at a rapidly increasing rate.[91] The answer, clearly, was to expand within target countries with large domestic markets, and this GMC decided to do.

Austin Motors was in colossal financial difficulties, and Sir Herbert Austin, who was already in dispute with his board over future car designs, initiated the discussions with GMC. Morgan Grenfell acted for GMC, and by 2 September 1925 a draft agreement was signed. GMC was to subscribe for 1,500,000 ordinary shares on condition that Austin carried out a rearrangement of its capital in order to reduce the number of outstanding preference shares and pay off its outstanding debenture stock.[92] However, Sir Herbert Austin's failure to clear the arrangement with his board meant that some of the directors revolted, and a mess ensued. Whigham described the state of play by 7 September to Grenfell:

The negotiations between the General Motors and Austin continue. The essence of a really good business arrangement for both Companies is there, but the issue is a good deal confused because of the fact that Austin for some time past [h]as been planning reconstruction schemes with the result that apart altogether from the General Motors proposals various sections of shareholders have been issuing circulars and asking for support against the Directors and so on and so forth. All this will mean that there is quite a considerable risk that the projected General Motors proposals may be thrown out by the Shareholders. The whole plan involved certain reconstruction of capital which again involved the consent of the Court and special class meetings of four different classes of shareholders. Failure to get the requisite majority at any one of these class meetings throws out the whole scheme. Consequently the dissentient bodies have four different chances of gaining their way. However we are not altogether despondent and I still hope that we will get the scheme through.[93]

But they did not, and by 19 September 1925 the scheme was dead.[94] However, there was an alternative choice and early in October GMC and Morgan Grenfell opened negotiations with Vauxhall Motors. Here the situation was very different: the members of the board welcomed the opportunity presented by the talks, since Vauxhall too was short of capital for development and expansion. Discussion continued through the first half of October, but a problem familiar today cropped up: information was leaking out, and Vauxhall felt constrained to write to their shareholders on 19 October informing them of the talks and noting that their successful completion would lead to an appreciation of the share price. The letter added that 'Owing to the prevalence of unauthorised rumours in connection with such matters the Directors want the Shareholders to know the true position at the earliest opportunity and so prevent them dealing in the shares without a knowledge of the facts.' (The shares nearly doubled in price during the negotiations.)[95] On the following day an agreement was signed between Vauxhall Motors, GMC, and Morgan Grenfell: GMC deposited £210,000 with Morgan Grenfell; the existing 600,000 shares of 10 s. each would be consolidated into 300,000 £1 preference shares; for every two ordinary shares surrendered Morgan Grenfell would pay 14 s. (to be paid out of the £210,000) and hand over a new preference share; and 300,000 new ordinary shares of £1 each would be issued and bought by Morgan Grenfell for GMC, which would increase the capital from £300,000 to £600,000. The agreement was strongly backed by the Vauxhall Motors board, and at a shareholders' meeting held on 30 October the agreement was carried by a two-thirds majority.[96]

The agreement, then, provided for the injection of £300,000 of capital into Vauxhall Motors, while the British management was left in place, although GMC placed some of its own people on the board. Morgan Grenfell brokered the agreement, negotiating on behalf of GMC, but to the complete satisfaction of Vauxhall Motors; indeed, Morgan Grenfell continued to give advice through the succeeding years to both Vauxhall and GMC. The point of the exercise for Morgan Grenfell was not only the immediate commission to be made, although it was a tidy one: 4% of the total moneys involved (£510,000) came to £20,400.[97] At least as important was the setting-up of a continuing relationship in which the firm would give information and advice whenever it was required, often without remuneration, in the expectation that when an issue was required or a merger was effected, GMC or Vauxhall would turn to them. Subsequently they engaged in abortive discussions with GMC in 1929 over the possibility of GMC's setting up a holding company for all of its European possessions (it had bought Opel Motors in Germany and was contemplating taking a 30% share of Citroën); and again in 1934 there were discussions over a possible sale of a portion of GMC's equity in Vauxhall to enable some of it to be owned in Britain. No immediate business ensued; but they were the advisers of one of the strongest, richest companies in the world, which carried its own cachet, and eventually lucrative business did come their way: they arranged private placings for Vauxhall Motors in 1949, 1954, 1955, and 1957.[98]

The partners viewed their growing contacts with satisfaction, and certainly business was owed to the fact that they all cultivated a wide range of business acquaintances. However, one deal resulted from old contacts, and since it took place in a slightly shaming context, Morgan Grenfell kept their part in it quite secret. This was the episode of the *Daily Chronicle*, part of United Newspapers. In 1916 the accession of David Lloyd George to the position of Prime Minister, supplanting his Liberal colleague H. H. Asquith, had resulted in the splintering of the Liberal Party. Lloyd George remained Prime Minister until October 1922, but he was effectively a man without a party, since the bulk of the Parliamentary Liberal Party had remained faithful to Asquith and joined him on the back benches. Lloyd George therefore built up his own political fund, largely by selling honours. All parties had done this, but he did it blatantly, ennobling various war profiteers as well as more worthy recipients. With part of the proceeds of this fund he had bought a newspaper, the *Daily Chronicle*, for £1,650,000 in 1918, and over the succeeding years invested more of the fund in it. This was a very successful investment, and the fund grew accordingly.

In October 1926 Asquith finally retired as leader of the Liberal Party, and the way was open for Lloyd George to gain control of the party organization. However, part of his price for his return was the dismissal of the Asquithian chairman of the Liberal Party; and the price Lloyd George paid for this beheading was to agree to support a considerable number of Liberal Party candidates at the next general election. In order to finance this, Lloyd George decided in January 1927 to sell the *Daily Chronicle*.

Sir Thomas Catto was not quite yet a partner in Morgan Grenfell, but he had very close relations with the partners. He and Sir David Yule, representing the Calcutta Discount Company (an associate company of Andrew Yule & Co.), financed the purchase of 610,000 of the 616,504 shares of United Newspapers (1918) Ltd. from Lloyd George: to do so they established the Daily Chronicle Investment Corporation, with Lord Reading as chairman and four other board members (of whom they were two). The price of the shares was £2,900,000, and the Investment Corporation arranged to purchase the bulk from Yule and Catto, the end result of which would be a cash investment by Yule of £850,000. To raise part of the necessary funds, the Investment Corporation arranged with Higginson & Co. to issue, in the first instance, 800,000 7% first cumulative preference shares. Higginson asked Morgan Grenfell whether they would care to do the business on joint account. There was not to be a public issue, but a private placing through some country brokers and Rowe & Pitman in London. Morgan Grenfell were adamant: they 'had felt all along they did not wish to appear as handling this business for various reasons and in particular on account of E.C.G.'s position as Member for the City'.[99] However, they would be glad to assist in handling the issue as long as their name did not appear.

An open relationship would have been politically embarrassing for both Grenfell and Smith: Grenfell had been Conservative MP for the City of London since 1922 (although the City Member traditionally was not as partisan as other MPs), and his cousin was chairman of the Conservative and Unionist Association of the City of London. Besides, neither was particularly keen on Lloyd George. They appreciated his responsibility for winning the war, but they did not like him or the faint whiff of political corruption which hung around him. It was rather different for Catto, who was at least vaguely a Liberal: he later noted in his autobiography that when raised to the peerage in January 1936, he decided to sit on the Liberal benches in the House of Lords, 'partly from family convention and partly because there was more room there'.[100] In the end Morgan Grenfell subscribed for 20,000 of the 8% second preference £1 shares, burying their shame in a file.

Political contacts of a different sort led to Morgan Grenfell's involvement in the rationalization of some of the traditional heavy industries in Britain, most of which were struggling under very depressed conditions in the late 1920s. In textiles, shipbuilding, and steel a multiplicity of firms struggled to survive in conditions of over-supply. The situation was of very great concern to the Governor of the Bank, partly for its own sake and partly because the failure of some of these companies threatened to bring down many provincial banks with them. The term 'rationalization' was very much a vogue word during the 1920s—Imperial Chemical Industries was cobbled together in 1926, for example—and Norman made great efforts over several years to promote the reorganization of the iron and steel industry. This assumed even more urgency in 1929, but for a different reason: a Labour government had come to power. Clause 4 of the Labour Party's constitution called for the public ownership of the means of production, distribution, and exchange of the country's major industries, and Norman hoped that rationalization by the private sector would prevent nationalization.[101]

Morgan Grenfell (along with other members of the merchant banking aristocracy) co-operated with Norman from an early period. In his Chairman's Speech for 1928 (given in June 1929), for example, Grenfell noted that the Bank of England was endeavouring to arrange certain rationalization schemes in the cotton and heavy steel industries, and the house had agreed to take a share if it should prove advisable. Grenfell further noted that it was felt that if support was not given to such schemes, some form of nationalization by the state might be adopted. Jack Morgan had agreed that the house might take a hand in helping the American side of the Lancashire cotton industry, not, as Grenfell wrote, 'in view of profit but as a gesture to help in the general situation'.[102] But the various schemes had arisen *ad hoc*; by late 1929 Norman decided that there should be a more organized response by the City to the problems of depressed industry.

On 10 January 1930 J. H. Thomas, former leader of the railwaymen's union and now Lord Privy Seal in the Labour government, spoke at Manchester to a large gathering representing the big business interests of Lancashire. The most important part of his speech had been drafted in the Bank and cleared by the Treasury. He had, Thomas said, been discussing the problem of unemployment with those in authority, and the feeling was that the necessary reorganization and re-equipping of industry had been held back by lack of credit:

Those in the City who have been studying this matter are convinced that a number of our important industries must be fundamentally reorganised and modernised in order to be able to compete at prices which will enable them to compete with the world. Industries which propose schemes that, in the opinion of those advising the City, conform to this requirement will receive the most sympathetic consideration and the co-operation of the City in working out plans and finding the necessary finance.[103]

Three weeks later Grenfell attended, at Thomas's request, a small private meeting at his office to discuss the situation as set out in his speech. Those at the meeting, besides Thomas, Norman, and Grenfell, included Edward Peacock of Barings, Sir Robert Kindersley of Lazards, Charles Hambro, Lionel Rothschild, and five others. Thomas explained his difficulties, both with his own party and with the Opposition, and, indeed, within the Labour Cabinet. He did not want the merchant bankers to define their attitudes at the meeting: he was merely there to answer questions. The Governor immediately called on Grenfell to say something, and Grenfell stoutly averred that he approved of everything Thomas had said in his speech. The acceptance houses did not, like the joint-stock banks, have large amounts of capital, but they would certainly be prepared to study and try to devise schemes to assist industry in the

UK. Grenfell said that he spoke only for Morgan Grenfell, but he believed that those present would support the Minister. Sir Guy Granet of Higginson & Co. then spoke in support, but he was already part of Norman's Bank of England group of experts who advised on restructuring. No other banker spoke.[104]

Norman went ahead and the Bankers' Industrial Development Company Limited (BID) was set up in April 1930, but the silence of the other bankers at the January meeting was perhaps prophetic. In spite of Norman's hopes, by late 1932, as Grenfell wrote, 'The B.I.D., as it is called, has so far been unable to show any gratifying results.'[105] There were few public issues: there was the Lancashire Cotton Corporation Limited issue of £2 million 6-year 6½% first mortgage debentures, issued in March 1931, with the interest ostensibly guaranteed for the first five years by the Sun Insurance Office, but actually by the Bank of England. The BID did help to finance the steelworks built in Corby by Stewarts & Lloyds between 1932 and 1934. But many of the proposed schemes were quite impossible and rapidly earned for the BID the medical sobriquet 'Brought in Dead'. The BID was kept in being during the war, but it was finally wound up in September 1945; its functions were eventually taken over by the Finance Corporation for Industry.[106]

Grenfell never had any illusions that their involvement in the BID would be particularly profitable. As he wrote to Jack Morgan in January 1931, with regard to the financial position of the house, 'While we are not aware of any special liabilities I would mention that the Governor is apt to call upon the [Acceptance] Houses to take a share in certain industrial reorganisations which they would gladly refuse except for matters of public policy.'[107] For Grenfell, of course, there was really no choice as to whether his house became involved: he was committed both by his position as a director of the Bank of England and by his close friendship with Norman. But there was another aspect to their involvement in the BID: the partners thereby became familiar with methods useful in the rationalization of industry; and in particular they became knowledgeable about the steel industry. This would rapidly bear fruit, because from 1933 Morgan Grenfell would become closely involved in the private-sector reorganization and financing of steel.

The BID, then, was a special case and probably did not take up too much of partners' time. More important was the growing day-to-day work of corporate finance, where business came in the course of ordinary commercial contacts. A characteristic example was the British Metal Corporation, which 'was incorporated here for the purpose of carrying on the metal business in London and England generally which had previously been in the hands of the Metallgesellschaft through their subsidiary here, a firm called Merton. Vivian took a great deal of trouble and interest in the organization of the British Metal Corporation and we are still extremely intimate with them.'[108] There were many others, and the partners were continually on the look out for new business. It is very difficult to measure relative success, and certainly Barings too moved strongly into domestic corporate business; but it is worth noting that the one historian who has spent some time in comparing the records of a number of merchant banks wrote that 'In the 1920s Morgan Grenfell & Co. were probably the first merchant bank to become heavily involved both in advising and in financing industry.'[109]

*New Partners, New Premises, and a New Relationship with
J. P. Morgan & Co.*

This new domestic business was being developed at the same time as the house's traditional business in issuing foreign loans was taking a heavy toll of partners' time, particularly Grenfell's and Whigham's. Smith's time also had to be split between Morgan Grenfell and the Royal Exchange Assurance Corporation, of which he had been governor since 1914. (However, time spent there was hardly time wholly lost to Morgan Grenfell: under his leadership the Royal Exchange pursued a policy of aggressive acquisition, especially of firms in the new area of motor insurance, and Morgan Grenfell doubtless profited from the knowledge and contacts he gained in the business.) There were only so many hours in the day, and the need for more hands led the bank to decide to take on a new partner. Jack Morgan and Smith looked around, and in June 1924 Michael George Herbert joined Morgan Grenfell. Aged thirty-one and notably handsome, he was the son of Sir Michael Henry Herbert, the brother of the Earl of Pembroke and British Ambassador to the US from 1902 to 1903; his mother was an American who was related to the Astors and Vanderbilts (although with little money of her own); and his brother was Captain Sidney Herbert, Grenfell's colleague as a Conservative MP. Michael Herbert plunged straight into industrial and commercial work with great gusto, and his letters indicate that he enjoyed it and was probably good at it. (He did most of the work for General Motors, for example.) He also fell heir to the traveller's mantle of Smith, and from 1926 spent a proportion of each year in Paris or New York with the associated houses; he was particularly involved in helping to build up the acceptance credits business. But his career with Morgan Grenfell was cut tragically short: by September 1932 he had died from a long and painful illness.[110]

Useful as Herbert was, his frequent absences meant that the partners still needed more help at home. In 1928, however, another man of the requisite experience and ability became available: Sir Thomas Catto. He writes in his autobiography that

In 1928 I decided that as I was then nearing fifty the time had come to pass on the senior position in India of Andrew Yule & Co. Ltd. to a younger man, and in 1929, on reaching the age of fifty, I retired from India to return to London as Governing Director of the home firm which, originally George Yule & Co., had become Yule, Catto & Co. Ltd. in 1920. I was influenced in my decision to return home by the fact that Mr J. P. Morgan had invited me to become a partner in the well-known London private banking firm of Morgan Grenfell & Co., thus bringing me into close association with my very old friend Mr Vivian Hugh Smith and other friends like [Grenfell, Whigham, and Herbert].[111]

Catto in fact became a partner on 2 January 1928, and this necessitated another redivision of the profits, as had happened when Herbert joined the firm in 1924. But this time there would be more to go around. From 1 January 1928 Morgan Grenfell were allowed to retain 67% of the profits instead of the 50% which had obtained since 1910, apparently a voluntary surrender on the part of the American partners. If J. P. Morgan & Co. were making so much money in the US compared with the London firm that they were sending as gifts part of the American profits to the London partners, it made sense to allow the London partners to retain more of what they had earned in the first place.[112]

It was just as well that the size of the cake was increased, since it would have to accommodate two new partners by 1933. It was time for the next generation to join the house: in 1930 the son, and in 1933 the son-in-law, of Vivian Smith became partners. Born in 1898, Randal Hugh Vivian Smith (called Rufus) was the eldest of seven children. Educated at Eton and Sandhurst, he was gazetted to the 17th Lancers, fought in the First World War in France, and was invalided out of the army in 1920 as a result of a war wound. He went out to Andrew Yule & Co. in Calcutta for a year and afterwards to J. P. Morgan & Co.; he then joined Morgan Grenfell in 1923 and worked his apprenticeship (although this consisted of auditing the securities and other partner-like duties rather than sharpening the quill pens).[113] He and Michael Herbert were roughly half the age of the senior partners, and brought an injection of youthful energy.

The death of Herbert in September 1932 left the firm short-handed once again, and on 2 January 1933 Francis James Rennell Rodd became a partner. He was the eldest—and 'extremely beautiful'[114]—son of Sir Rennell Rodd, a diplomat and the British Ambassador to Italy 1908–19; he had married Vivian Smith's daughter Mary in 1928. He was also the brother-in-law of Nancy Mitford, his younger brother Peter being the womanizing wastrel she married. He was educated at Eton and Balliol College, Oxford, and after active service in the First World War he followed his father into the Diplomatic Service. However, after two years in the Foreign Office he resigned in 1924, becoming a member of the Stock Exchange for three years. He was then employed by the Bank of England from 1929, and while there was for two years manager of the Bank for International Settlements. After becoming a partner in Morgan Grenfell he finally settled down. His sister-in-law painted an unsympathetic portrait of him as the pompous Luke in her novel *Pigeon Pie*, which was published in 1940.

The number of resident British partners, then, doubled between 1924 and 1933, and it was therefore fortunate that some forethought had been given to the problem of accommodation. The partners had been dissatisfied for some time with 22 Old Broad Street and after the war had begun looking around for a freehold property to buy (they had always leased Old Broad Street). In 1923 they settled upon 23 Great Winchester Street, which, while not ideal, seemed the best available at the time. At any rate, as Grenfell noted, the property would not be in their hands until the end of 1925 and the alterations would take six to nine months; therefore, even if they did buy it and found before 1926 that a more suitable position came on the market, they could always sell it, if necessary at a slight loss.[115]

Arrangements for the move went ahead, amongst which was an increase in the number of telephones: at Old Broad Street the firm had used four exchange lines with twenty-one extensions, plus a private wire to the Midland Bank at 69 Pall Mall; in the new premises they would now require six exchange lines with forty extensions (and the private wire).[116] Information unimportant in itself, it nevertheless indicates a change in methods of doing business. Sir John Mallabar remembers that in 1916 to 1918 very little business was transacted over the telephone: rather, it was carried out by letter or visit. Now, the change in accepted procedures coupled with the increase in domestic business meant that telephones were used more and more, and memoranda of telephone conversations began to join copies of letters and cables in company files.[117]

By the beginning of 1927, then, Morgan Grenfell & Co. were settled in their new office, 'which itself', wrote Grenfell, 'contributes largely to the comfort & peace of mind of partners & staff. I do not regret the nervous strain brought on by the busses [*sic*] in O Broad St.'[118] The next few years would be busy ones, as the partners continued their work both in corporate and government finance. But the economic outlook would soon darken, with the Wall Street Crash in October 1929, followed within a few months by a miasma of depression spreading over Europe and eventually over the US. It was an unanticipated outcome of the Depression, and of the American political response to it, that the formal relationship between the London and American partners as it had been constituted in 1910 was brought to a close.

The Depression had brought widespread banking failures in the US, and a study by the Federal Reserve ascribed many of them, probably wrongly, to speculative investments by the banks in low-grade bonds. Congress concluded from this that banks must be prevented from taking such risks and must therefore make a choice: they could be either commercial banks or investment banks.[119] With the passing of the Banking Act of 1933, then, J. P. Morgan & Co. had to choose, and the partners opted to remain a bank rather than a finance house. Those who preferred to engage in finance and securities left in 1935 and set up Morgan Stanley.

The choice, furthermore, was applicable outside the US as well. The American partners were advised that it would be improper for the partners of J. P. Morgan & Co. to continue as the principal shareholders and executive officers of a British company with unlimited liability, an important part of whose business was issuing and underwriting, since they were prevented from engaging in this business in the US. The partners took legal advice in London and New York to try and ascertain whether any means could be found to maintain the close association between the two houses. The conclusion was that the only method of so doing was to convert Morgan Grenfell & Co. from a private company with unlimited liability into one with limited liability, thereby (within the context of Congressional worries) removing the high element of risk from the association for J. P. Morgan & Co. Consequently, in July 1934 Morgan Grenfell & Co. ceased to exist and was replaced by Morgan Grenfell & Co. Ltd., with J. P. Morgan & Co. holding one-third of the management shares and the London partners holding the other two-thirds. All of the London partners became directors and managing directors, while in addition—to the great pleasure of Grenfell in particular—it was found to be legally permissible for Jack Morgan to become a director and to have his name publicly announced as a member of the board. Certainly, one of the strongest links between the New York and London houses was the strong personal friendship between Grenfell and Jack Morgan, and it was only with Grenfell's death in 1941, followed two years later by Jack Morgan's, that the real separation between the two houses began.[120]

But even if there was no immediate change in either transatlantic relations or the way business was done (and there seems not to have been), nevertheless the change in organization signalled the end of an era. Traditionally, merchant bankers were finance capitalists *par excellence*: their liability was unlimited—otherwise they were not trusted—and a series of bad decisions on their part might mean not only the loss of occupation but the loss of everything. The senior partners, after all, had seen this threaten the partners in Barings in 1890.[121] But Morgan Grenfell had insisted on retaining unlimited liability in 1918, and it was only when this retention threatened to cause the loss of the formal American connection that it was surrendered. Unlimited liability meant every decision was a gamble, and this had eventually made the partners cautious and conservative in their commitments. Consequently they were quite safe during the storms of the early 1930s when others around them— such as Lazards and Brown, Shipley—found themselves in grave danger. With their homes and personal fortunes now safe from threat, would a change in attitude ensue?

CHAPTER FOUR

FINANCE AND FOREIGN POLICY

1900–1918

Wars and Rumours of War

Nervos belli, pecuniam infinitam.
(Cic. Phil. v. ii. 5)

HAD J. S. Morgan but lived, he would have seen his and his son's houses reach a pinnacle of power and prestige far beyond realistic expectation, if not beyond dreams. The fundamental reason for this was war: the preparations for war, the fighting of wars, and the reconstruction after war. As events transpired, all of this required American money, and the House of Morgan was the organization best able to direct large sums of American money to foreign borrowers and in particular to governments. In this endeavour, neither American Morgan nor British Morgan could stand alone. It was J. P. Morgan & Co.'s reputation as the premier American investment bank which attracted the borrower, particularly from 1914 on; but experience and expertise in foreign loans on the whole lay in Europe, and especially in London. During the period 1900 through 1931, many of the negotiations over foreign loans were carried out by J. S. Morgan & Co. and then Morgan Grenfell & Co. Nevertheless, without the link with J. P. Morgan & Co., Morgan Grenfell could not have aspired to the position in which they found themselves by the 1920s: their resources would have been inadequate, both in capital and in numbers of partners.

The link with J. P. Morgan & Co. was not a wholly unmixed blessing for the London partners. The American bank, it is true, had an almost unassailable standing in the US, and particularly in the financial community, as the leading bank on Wall Street. In the US the Morgan partners were a race apart: while a few were notable for their good looks ('When the angels of God took unto themselves wives among the daughters of men, the result was the Morgan partners')[1], others were held in great respect because of their sheer quality. Here J. Pierpont Morgan himself towered above all others: he was a Titan, and as such he was admired and feared. He was undeniably effective: his endeavours during the American panic of 1907 almost single-handedly saved the American financial system from a collapse of terrifying ramifications.

But there was another side to his reputation and that of his New York bank. During the last two decades of the nineteenth century, American manufacturing and transportation enterprises had been subjected to assaults by one another as various individuals attempted, by mergers and acquisitions, to consolidate their way to dominant positions in various sectors of the economy. Pierpont Morgan was one of the prime movers behind this trend, believing that competition was wasteful and that co-operation between businesses in the same sector—what he termed a community of interest—was more logical. But many Americans feared just this consolidating movement, and saw J. P. Morgan & Co. as the epitome of all that was threatening to the farmer, the small businessman, and the worker. Thus to other bankers Morgans were all that was conservative, straight, dependable, powerful, and admirable, while to many other Americans they represented the threat of monopoly capital and manipulative power.

The beginning of the twentieth century saw both the most successful of Morgan's merger operations, the end product of which was US Steel,[2] and the most resoundingly unsuccessful, the culmination of which was the International Mercantile Marine (IMM). The latter, with which J. S. Morgan & Co. were closely involved, is worth some attention. First of all, it was an international operation, involving two American and three British shipping companies. Secondly, it caused great uproar in Britain, with debates in the House of Commons, arguments amongst Cabinet ministers, and abuse heaped on Morgans by the press. This was partly because of questions of foreign policy and British prestige, and partly because of the methods used by Morgans. Thirdly, it proved to be a failure, causing heavy financial losses for both the New York and London banks, as well as costing much time and (for Pierpont Morgan) prestige. And fourthly, it ensured that relations between Morgans and the British government were for some time coloured by the knowledge that too close a relationship could bring political abuse down on the heads of the government. This can also be seen in the negotiations over the final Boer War loan in 1902—which took place during the latter period of the IMM merger—and again during the First World War, when it seemed politically dangerous for the British government to acknowledge too effusively the thanks they owed to the house of Morgan.

The IMM Merger

It is necessary then to look at the huge—and hugely unpopular—operation which resulted in the formation of the IMM. The irony for Morgans was that it was not even their own idea, and they went into it with some reluctance. The origins of the combine (or 'Shipping Trust', as it was referred to by the hostile press) lay in the attempts of two shipowners, one American and the other British, separately to capture a dominant place in the North Atlantic shipping market. Clement A. Griscom, owner of the International Navigation Company (NJ), wanted to merge his own unprofitable line with the Baltimore-based Atlantic Transport Co., owned by Bernard Baker; this was to be the focus of an American-controlled shipping group which Griscom hoped would dominate the North Atlantic shipping routes. In June 1899, however, he learnt that Baker was negotiating the sale of his line to John Ellerman of Frederick Leyland & Co., a British company which was the largest freight line in the North Atlantic. Ellerman had access to capital in Britain (he was essentially a financier rather than a shipping man), and to lure Baker away from him Griscom had to offer access to capital as well: he went to see Pierpont Morgan.

In December 1900 an agreement was reached: Atlantic Transport would be merged with the International Navigation Company, Atlantic Transport would be allowed to order six new ships with funds advanced by J. P. Morgan & Co., and two other companies, whose names were not at first specified, would be added to the merger. These were Leyland & Co., controlled by Ellerman, and the White Star Line (the Oceanic Steam Navigation Company, in due course the owner of the *Titanic*). At this point Morgans were involved only as bankers who would advance the funds for the ships and arrange the sale of the preferred stock.[3] In fact, Pierpont Morgan was not very keen on involving himself in the operation, writing to his London partners that 'I do not think favourably of entertaining shipbuilding business.'[4] But once the first commitment was made, the banks were ineluctably sucked in, and by April 1901, when the two merged American companies had completed the acquisition of Leyland & Co., the London and New York banks had together invested about $11 million in the proposed shipping combine.[5]

Over the next months, much time and effort was expended in trying to persuade the other shareholders of the White Star Line, and particularly Bruce Ismay, the son of the founder, to allow their shares to be bought by the combine. William Pirrie, the head of Harland & Wolff, the Belfast shipbuilders, acted as agent for both Morgans and Griscom in the negotiations. As the owner of the second largest block of White Star shares (after Ismay), Pirrie had a considerable interest in the outcome. His support was bought with the promise that his firm would have any British shipbuilding contracts from the new combine. An agreement was finally reached on 4 February 1902. This included the provisions described above, with the addition that the Dominion Line, a small British company running freight to Canada and New England, would also be bought. In the same period the combine also came to a traffic agreement with the two major German lines, the Hamburg–America Line and the North German Lloyd, in order to prevent a rate war.[6]

There was, of course, another large British shipping line, and that was the Cunard Company, the White Star's great competitor. Pierpont Morgan wanted to come to some agreement with Cunard in order to further a 'community of interest', but he discovered that the stock was too widely dispersed to be easily purchased, and that there were no options floating around London.[7] It would have had to be a hostile bid if pressed. The British government was first warned about the (secret) agreement of 4 February by the chairman of Cunard (the second Lord Inverclyde), and Cunard in due course used the supposed threat to British interests posed by the combine to extract generous subsidies from the British government.[8]

Meanwhile, Morgans put together a $50 million underwriting syndicate to support the issuing of the bonds needed to raise the combine's initial cash requirements. There was no difficulty in securing participation —many of those who had profited from membership in the recently completed US Steel syndicate rushed to join—and $36 million was raised in New York and $14 million in London. The syndicate had to be confirmed in their commitment by 30 April 1902, and this would be done by a public announcement of the formation of the combine. The announcement was delayed while Morgans tried to come to some agreement with Cunard, and waited to see if Congress passed a bill to provide subsidies for American-registered ships (which could affect the organization of the new combine). Neither transpired, and the announcement, accompanied by some managed news stories in New York and London, was finally made on 19 April 1902.[9]

This was the signal for open opposition by newspapers and politicians.

Part of the press criticized the organization of the combine on financial grounds, but the supposed threat to British prestige and national security came in for even more discussion. Here the newspapers were joined by certain Cabinet members and a number of back-bench MPs. The financial press in particular looked at the total capitalization of the new combine, which was set at $50 million in bonds, $60 million in preferred stock and $60 million in common stock; they then compared this total with the much smaller figure arrived at by adding together the capital stocks of the component companies, and came to the conclusion that much of the stock of the new combine was pure water. But financial writers looked only at the stated capital of these companies, without adding surplus and reserves (for the White Star Line its reserves, repairs and renewals fund, and surplus came to more than twice its stated capital). Equally important, this was not how bankers assessed it; rather, they valued the worth of the combine not by capital but by future earning power:[10] this had been the procedure with US Steel and the market had supported it.

The general press and the politicians were probably more concerned with what appeared to be an American grab for domination of the North Atlantic freight business, since the threatened loss of British dominance to the Americans was believed to have grave implications for national security. The White Star Line ran some very fast ships, and in time of war the Royal Navy could commandeer any British-registered ship for war duty, in this case to act as armed cruisers. But even the slower ships could be used to transport vital supplies, a question critical for a country which depended on imported food to live. If Leyland & Co. and the White Star Line were absorbed into an American-dominated combine, might not these ships be transferred to American registration?

Morgans, and particularly Pierpont Morgan, were amazed at the hostile response of British politicians to the American moves, but they had neglected to take into account the current British sensitivity to questions of naval dominance. Germany had, in 1898, passed the First Navy Law, the text of which made it clear that Germany planned to build a navy which would match and in due course exceed that of Britain. Threatened with loss of naval dominance from the east, the British now apparently had to cope with a rival from the west as well. Not everyone in Westminster was equally exercised—the Prime Minister, the Marquess of Salisbury, was not desperately worried, for example, nor was the Marquess of Lansdowne, the Secretary of State for

Foreign Affairs—but the Cabinet had to respond to the fears of its supporters.[11]

Therefore, although some members of the Cabinet had known about the agreement since at least 26 March 1902, the public announcement of the formation of the combine, and the consequent uproar, forced the government into action against Morgans. On 5 May, Clinton Dawkins, who was to take the brunt of the government's anger over the subsequent two months, met with the First Lord of the Admiralty, Lord Selborne, who told Dawkins that 'he and certain ministers led by [Joseph] Chamberlain [the Secretary of State for the Colonies] were determined to take active measures [to] prevent English lines passing under American control. He was quite satisfied control would be exercised in [a] friendly manner by [Morgans] but there would be no guarantee about ... successors who might eventually transfer ships to some foreign registry possibly not American [i.e. German] or replace English by foreign crews.'[12]

Dawkins, as the resident senior partner of J. S. Morgan & Co., led on all of the negotiations between Morgans for the combine and the British government (except when Pierpont Morgan himself was in London), and this placed him in an unenviable position. He was, after all, both British and a former high government official, and was himself deeply concerned about the position of the Empire and British military and naval strength. He shared some of the government's fears, and had done what he could, as he wrote to his close friend Mitner on 9 May 1902:

... from a national point of view of course the American control, when in course of time it passes out of Morgan's hands, *may* be used against us....

Personally, I warned Selborne in confidence weeks ago and advised him to extend his cruiser contracts with the White Star—which he did—as all ships carry their contracts into the new concern. But he did not do more and Chamberlain did not awake to the importance of the subject until all arrangements were completed & in the papers. It is a disagreeable business in many ways. But I think I did everything I could to advise them in time, more than perhaps I ought to have done as a partner....[13]

But Dawkins loyally argued the Morgan case throughout the difficult weeks that followed. On the same day as his letter to Milner was written, the press published the text of the 4 February agreement, which stimulated back-benchers to press ministers to do something. There were three debates in the House of Commons during May on the issue, and ministers reflected this pressure in their discussions with Dawkins and, from 13

May, Pierpont Morgan himself, who returned to London from his cure at Aix. As Dawkins wrote,

... Chamberlain has taken the question up very hotly, partly I think out of resentment at the reticence practised by the ship-owners towards the Govt., partly out of chagrin at the Germans having secured a better arrangement on paper and taunting our Govt. with sleepiness and ineptitude, partly from a desire to appear the chief protector of any menaced British interest.

I had an interview with him.... Finally I told him he had better see [Pierpont] Morgan, got them to dinner and fixed up an interview.

At the dinner Morgan offered to bind the combine not to transfer any of the British ships in the combine to any foreign register for fifty years, but instead of accepting this and other concessions offered by Morgan, Chamberlain tried to tie the combine down even more firmly. Morgan spoke 'impressively' of his feeling that 'nothing would do more to establish a good understanding and feelings between the two countries than community of business interests', but Chamberlain merely repeated his threats, 'leaving Morgan very sore and astonished and inclined to withdraw all his offers'.[14]

Pierpont Morgan in fact genuinely felt misunderstood. He told an English acquaintance when they happened to meet in Paris that 'He expected to have been received with open arms on his arrival—as the man who had done our country a good turn. Instead of this, he had been everywhere cold-shouldered, having been suspected of filching our mercantile ships away from us.'[15] Dawkins conveyed this to one of the New York partners, adding that 'It seems to be that whenever you run up against a Government on either side of the Atlantic you are sure to have trouble and to meet with unreasonableness and impulsiveness.'[16]

In the midst of the fight to convince the British government that national security interests were not at stake, the New York partners nearly contrived to destroy all the work of Dawkins and Pierpont Morgan. The New York partners thought that the combine, which was thus far nameless, 'should have name indicating American control'.[17] Dawkins and Jack Morgan cabled back in exasperation that

we strongly deprecate any indications of American control being inserted as would necessarily stir up again very strong public feeling here which now beginning subside.... We understand feeling in Government still extremely strong and any increase in it might very easily produce some hasty and regrettable actions on their part [such as forbidding the sale of the ships to the combine, or at least removing the subsidy to the White Star ships]. The only chance prevent this in our opinion is to suppress as much as possible the national aspect of the matter and emphasise the commercial advantages only.[18]

Pierpont Morgan decided several weeks later that the name should be the International Mercantile Marine.[19]

The crisis began to be resolved when Pierpont Morgan and Dawkins drew up a memorandum for the Cabinet setting out the concessions that the IMM were willing to make to meet the objections of the govern-ment. They offered to contract for fifty years that no British ships built or to be built by the IMM would be transferred to a foreign registry without the written consent of the President of the Board of Trade; that the British ships in the IMM should always carry a fixed proportion of Royal Navy men; that they should be available as cruisers and transports at thirty hours' notice; and that a percentage of IMM ships should always be built in British yards.[20] The Cabinet did not consider the memoran-dum until 7 August, however, and meantime Dawkins and Pierpont Morgan continued their lobbying. Morgan dined with the King on 11 June—as Dawkins put it, he 'hoiked my old man over from Venice to dine with Edward Rex'[21]—and it was clearly a success, one observer noting that the 'dinner went off very well ... & ... Mr Morgan had a good deal of talk with the King'.[22]

When the Cabinet met on 7 August 1902, they considered, along with Dawkins's memorandum, the report of the three-man Cabinet commit-tee deputed to consider the matter (the members were Chamberlain, Selborne, and Gerald Balfour, the President of the Board of Trade). This committee thought it important to 'avoid unnecessary friction with the Morgan Combination, and in particular to abstain from action likely to stir up national animosities...'.[23] A. J. Balfour, the new Prime Minister, met with Dawkins and Morgan on 8 August and mutual assurances were exchanged. The following week the Cabinet met again and decided that because Morgan's informal assurances would not necessarily bind his successors, what was needed was a formal agreement. In the end, what can only be described as a treaty between the British government and the IMM was drawn up by Dawkins and the two Balfours. This was subsequently approved by the Cabinet and thence by the IMM, and announced by Gerald Balfour in a speech at Sheffield on 30 September 1902. Finally, on 1 August 1903, the Anglo-IMM treaty, as it were, was laid before Parliament.[24]

The IMM was incorporated in October 1902, and voting control was vested in a five-man voting trust on which American financial interests had three representatives (two of whom were Pierpont Morgan and another Morgan partner, Charles Steele); the two British representatives were William Pirrie of Harland & Wolff and Bruce Ismay of the White Star Line. There was also a British board on which Dawkins was forced to sit, much against his will, by the express wish of the Prime Minister and the American and British directors. It was this British board which was to conduct the real management of the IMM, and the whole exercise took up a good deal of Dawkins's time and declining stores of energy. The merger was a failure nearly from the outset. It was burdened with very high costs, which stemmed from the high prices paid for the component companies, and it was found to be nearly impossible to make organizational economies. Further, the early years of the merger saw a growing trade imbalance, in that American exports to Europe far out-stripped her imports, and this meant that those ships which had to keep to fixed schedules often sailed with half-filled holds. The syndicate participants felt the cold wind even more quickly, and eventually had to take up 100% of the issue, since no favourable market for the bonds ever appeared. It has been estimated that J. P. Morgan & Co. lost between $1 million and $1.5 million. As for J. S. Morgan & Co., when in March 1906 it valued its holdings of IMM securities, it placed on them a value of £351,364, an amount suggesting a loss of something over £90,000 on its own underwriting participation of nearly £450,000.[25] Worse, it hung on the London firm like a vampire, sucking time and energy out of the partners (in particular Grenfell) for the next thirty years. It had also rendered negotiations over the final Boer War loan, which took place at the same time as the political outcry over the merger, rather more fraught than perhaps they might otherwise have been.

The Boer War Loans

Since October 1899 Britain had been locked in combat with the two Boer republics in South Africa, the Transvaal and the Orange Free State, over British attempts to annex them. It had been assumed that the war would be over by Christmas, but the grievous defeats suffered by the British Army in December 1899 ensured that its duration would be rather longer. During the first months of the war, it had been financed by means of Treasury bills, but this could be only a temporary expedient, and by early 1900 the British government needed to borrow. However, the Chancellor of the Exchequer was uncertain whether they should issue a new short- or medium-dated stock (referred to as Exchequer bonds), or a further tranche of the irredeemable stock, Consols.

In 1900 London was still the major international financial centre, a position not seriously challenged until the 1920s. Yet a harbinger of change might have been noted in January 1900, when the Chancellor found it desirable officially and directly to tap the New York money market. It was, in fact, the first time since the Seven Years War (1756–63) that the British government had looked abroad for funds. This seemed, therefore, a reversal of the natural order of things, and as such, was rather resented in the City. One firm used by the Chancellor, Sir Michael Hicks Beach (later Lord St Aldwyn), was J. S. Morgan & Co., and through it J. P. Morgan & Co.

The question of how the government should borrow, whether by issuing Consols or shorter and dated stocks, was a recurring question during the war. Consols originated in 1751, when Henry Pelham at the Exchequer grouped together a number of funds into the 'three per cent consolidated annuities'. Over the following century and a half these became the safest and amongst the most marketable investments possible. Certainly the Bank of England in February 1900 urged an addition to Consols. As R. S. Sayers has written,

This was to be the Bank's standard advice throughout the war and it was based on belief that, because of the interest of bankers in this stock for liquidity purposes and perhaps the special air of sanctity with which tradition had endowed it, Consols could always be marketed on finer terms than any new stock the Treasury might invent.[26]

Certainly, when the Joint Permanent Secretary to the Treasury, Sir Edward Hamilton, talked to bankers such as Rothschilds, they argued that if the government wished to ensure success in raising funds, they would have to issue Consols, on the grounds that that was what the banks and the public wanted: if ever the holder of Consols wanted cash he would easily find a market, but the same could not be said about any other stock.

However, the concern of the Treasury was not so much with the current marketability of the stock as with its future. As Hamilton wrote in his diary, 'we . . . would prefer raising the money by a special stock with a short currency, in order to avoid adding to the permanent debt of the country and creating more of a stock which had got out of hand and was likely to get so again as Consols'.[27] Indeed, they hoped that in due course the Transvaal, the main gold-producing region of southern

Africa, would contribute to the cost of the war,[28] and this contribution would pay off a medium-dated stock. Otherwise, the Treasury would certainly not want to saddle a future Chancellor with the need to find a large sum so soon, and all at one date. For this reason, then, the government in early 1900 inclined towards making a medium-dated issue. But financing the war was only part of the problem: it was also necessary to replace the Treasury's gold stock—supplies of gold from the Rand had nearly stopped with the onset of war—and to relieve the mounting pressure on the London money market.[29] New York could provide new gold, and thereby solve part of the Treasury's problem.

Negotiations with Morgans—but very tentative and secret ones—began in late January 1900. The exchange was initiated by the London partners, and it is probable that the idea came from Dawkins. The British High Commissioner in South Africa was his close friend Sir Alfred Milner, and Dawkins was in any case an expert in imperial finance. He contacted Joseph Chamberlain, the Secretary of State for the Colonies, who was mildly encouraging, and Chamberlain passed on his suggestion that part of a proposed loan be placed in the US to the Chancellor, who met with Jack Morgan (and possibly Robert Gordon) on 16 February 1900. Here the Chancellor laid out his thoughts. He had not yet finally decided, but he thought it probable that he would need to arrange a loan of perhaps £30 million. If so, he thought it might be advantageous for Britain to place part of it in the US: firstly, it would be an international demonstration of popular American support for Britain's position *vis-à-vis* the Boers (Britain had been showered with abuse by virtually every advanced nation bar the US for her role in South Africa); and secondly, it would be an opportunity for Britain to obtain gold. He thought the rate of interest would be $2\frac{3}{4}\%$. Finally, the Chancellor asked whether Morgans would object to working with Rothschilds and others; the partners of course did not object, as long as the American end of things was wholly in their hands, and to this the Chancellor agreed.[30]

Morgans were important to the Treasury only for the American market, and as far as it is possible to ascertain from the evidence were seldom consulted by them on other matters. For general financial advice the Permanent Secretary and the Chancellor tended to consult the Rothschilds (Alfred or Natty), Revelstoke of Barings, and—in particular —Sir Ernest Cassel. The last named was born a German Jew, a self-made man who had risen to a position of great importance in both financial and social circles (he was the financial adviser to and close friend of King Edward VII, and his granddaughter Edwina later married Lord

Mountbatten). As Hamilton wrote in his diary, they were 'representative men' of the City ... 'whom I now regard as my first counsellors'.[31]
Rothschild argued for safety in the proposed loan and for the interests of
City firms, sentiments with which Morgans would undoubtedly have
wholly agreed. (The Bank of England certainly understood its constitu-
ency, arguing that it was necessary to pay attention to market conditions
rather than to depend on a political appeal. As the Governor wrote of
the bankers, 'Their patriotism is a mere matter of price—make that
attractive enough and there will be no danger of the loan not being
subscribed.'[32]) Cassel, on the other hand, tended in his private talks with
Hamilton, sometimes over dinner, to encourage more populist methods.
In the case of this loan, the £30 million National War Loan of 1900
(maturing in 1910), Cassel's advice in due course would cause some
embarrassment to J. P. Morgan & Co.[33]

Morgans had assumed that the loan would be underwritten, and that
as an important underwriter they would be assured of part of the issue;
therefore, favoured American investors could count on being able to
invest in the issue through J. P. Morgan & Co. But the Chancellor
changed his mind and decided that the loan would not be underwritten,
on the grounds that the Treasury feared attacks from British investors.[34]
What this meant was that it was clearly going to be a desirable investment, and British investors would be cross if the Americans were able to
buy too large a proportion of it. (This fear of political repercussions
stemming from too obvious a dependence on the American market
meant that the need for gold was lost from sight.) The anticipated success
also convinced the Treasury that there was no need to pay underwriting
fees. The Chancellor had consulted with the Rothschilds and Cassel and
they had assured him that they would gladly assist the government by
helping to guarantee the success of the loan. The Permanent Secretary
therefore wanted to take a chance and appeal to the general public to
support the loan.[35]

The implications of this decision were to upset Morgans once again.
The New York partners applied for a total of £12 million worth of the
bonds, a total arrived at after Jack Morgan and Gordon had talked with
the Chancellor, who had been apprised of the amount J. P. Morgan &
Co. felt they could dispose of in New York. The partners realized that
their application would probably be scaled down, but they were shocked
at the extent: they received only 6% of the amount for which they had
applied, or £720,000, with a subsequent allocation of £35,500 for 'the
small applicants' on their list (Morgans in fact required £400,000 to meet

all of the small applications, defined by them as those subscribing for less than £10,000).[36]

This difference in scale was perhaps the crux of the matter. Morgans had assumed that this was to be the usual type of government issue, which would be taken up by a relatively few substantial investors; if so, the ability of the New York firm to place issues in the US would be rewarded by their receiving their requested allotment. But the goal of the Treasury was very different: they had decided to go for a popular issue. Advertisements were placed in 408 newspapers, and the result was almost 40,000 applications. The outcome, therefore, was the opposite from that which J. P. Morgan & Co. had hoped for and expected. As Hamilton wrote in his diary:

The Loan, which the Stock Exchange with their love for slang have nicknamed 'Khaki', was closed on Wednesday evening. It was subscribed more than 11 times over; & the number of applicants has exceeded 40,000, of whom nearly $\frac{1}{4}$ have applied for £100 only. So we have got the small fry in, which was just what was wanted.[37]

In allotting the issue, all applications for £400 or less were allotted in full, while those for £5,000 and more received only 6%[38]—so J. P. Morgan & Co. were hardly the only disappointed applicants.

In the end, therefore, the pickings were very slim, and the only immediate achievement for Morgans after all the negotiations and cable correspondence between the London and New York banks was the prestige accruing from the fact that the Bank of England had named J. P. Morgan & Co. its sole American agent for the loan.

Yet the relationship had been established, and when within four months the need arose for further funds, the British government turned again to Morgans. On 24 July 1900 the Permanent Secretary to the Treasury trotted along to the Bank of England and found himself paying 4% on nine- or twelve-month Treasury bills. This confirmed to him that the British government should look for other means to raise funds. One possibility, which the Chancellor preferred, was to issue more of the Khaki loan. But to do so would force the price down, to the dismay of the multitude of small investors whom the Chancellor had lured into his net the previous March. The Bank as usual preferred Consols, but the Chancellor would not hear of it. Hamilton later that day consulted Rothschilds and Cassel, and they agreed with him that it was best to issue Exchequer bonds,[39] medium-dated stock.

Hamilton then asked Dawkins to come and see him on 26 July 1900 in order to tell him that the government 'have temporarily stuck fast and ... to see whether we can get a considerable portion of their new issue placed in the US'.[40] The partners cabled to J. P. Morgan that afternoon, informing him that the Chancellor wanted to issue about £11.5 million $2\frac{3}{4}\%$ 3-year bonds at $98\frac{1}{2}$ and wanted Morgan's co-operation:

If you saw your way take any amount say 2 to 5,000,000 or more would make you absolutely firm offer probably of whole application. Regret was expressed at inconvenience you had previously been put to on behalf of C of E.... We think if we could take about 5,000,000 would place us very strong position with government in future.[41]

Morgan was not very encouraging:

Would gladly do all our power assist C of E but the fact is the parties who participated in previous effort assist English Government are not very well pleased at treatment received, then again nearly everyone out of town at moment, again with previous issue at $1\frac{3}{4}$ dis^t see nothing tempting present terms.

He advised that the London partners keep contact with the Treasury, but to let the Chancellor know that any participation such as was being suggested would be very difficult.[42]

It was presumably this distinct lack of enthusiasm which led the Chancellor to look elsewhere. Dawkins conveyed Morgan's reply on 27 July, and on the 28th found Barings on his doorstep. The Chancellor had asked Barings to see J. S. Morgan & Co. to ascertain whether the two houses might work in conjunction. With what was clearly some trepidation, the London partners cabled the proposal to Pierpont Morgan, asking whether he would mind sharing control of the New York end of the proposed loan.[43]

Morgan's response was wholly predictable:

Am dumbfounded with action C of E, we have been engaged several days negotiation with him under strict injunction to keep secret absolutely everyone, now, without any notice from him, we are approached by others stating so done under instructions from him. Cannot possibly understand, disgusted with the whole business and inclined to withdraw unless would place C.E.D. awkward position.[44]

The London partners rushed to mollify Morgan, assuring him that if he wished to forget the whole thing Dawkins would not find it awkward. They reminded him that Morgans had been contacted first, and this had been meant by the Chancellor to emphasize the government's recognition of their former services. They also pointed out that the joint pressure of Morgans and Barings would probably force the Chancellor to offer better terms for the proposed loan. (The Chancellor in any case was 'notoriously stupid and most unbusinesslike but he will probably retire soon...'.) J. S. Morgan & Co. could never expect to run the London end alone and were thus quite happy to share the business. Most important, 'in view of probable future business seems a great pity lose our hold when it will be impossible recover later on'.[45] These arguments were compelling and Pierpont agreed to work with Barings.[46]

There is a small but interesting point here which is worth noting, because it illuminates the position of J. S. Morgan & Co. in the official mind. When the London partners cabled to Pierpont Morgan on 28 July 1900, they had explained that the reason why the Chancellor had called in Barings was that he was evidently afraid for political reasons of not giving an 'English Banking House interest in business'. That is, in spite of the fact that the London house had been in business for over half a century, and had for most of that period dominated the Morgan London–New York axis, the predominant reputation of Pierpont Morgan apparently ensured that J. S. Morgan & Co. was perceived as only a branch of the New York house, with no independent standing as a British house. Certainly the Permanent Secretary of the Treasury referred to Dawkins in his diary as the 'manager of the great American house of Morgan here'.[47]

For the British government, then, J. S. Morgan & Co. were useful in providing access to American money, but the Treasury at least found the whole situation regrettable. As Hamilton wrote:

I don't much like the idea. It looks so much as if we had ... to go cap in hand to America to enable us to carry on the war. On the other hand, there are threats of tight terms here; and the only way of preventing excessive tightness is to get gold. So there are direct advantages to be attained by our negotiating with our Anglo-American friends.[48]

Accordingly, Hamilton saw Dawkins and Revelstoke on 31 July 1900, and the proposal was that J. P. Morgan & Co. should make a firm offer on 1 August for from £3 million to £5 million. They protested the following day that this gave them no opportunity to test the market and the Chancellor would have to wait a day. Meanwhile, Hamilton saw Dawkins and Revelstoke again, along with the Bank of England officials, Charles Goschen (the senior partner in the City firm of Frühling & Goschen as well as a director of the Bank of England), and Everard

Hambro, all of whom seem to have agreed that access to the American money market was vital at that juncture. This apparently convinced the Chancellor, who determined to close with the offer of Barings and Morgans to subscribe to £4 million or £5 million.[49] There was a problem over the commission—the Chancellor wanted to pay $\frac{1}{8}$% while Morgans held out for $\frac{1}{4}$%—but this was settled by the Treasury's paying $\frac{1}{8}$% and insisting that the Bank of England pay the other $\frac{1}{8}$% as the price for getting gold. (The Chancellor asked that the extra commission be kept absolutely secret.)[50]

There was one other contretemps, for which the Bank was responsible. In the end the Chancellor had agreed that Morgans in the US would subscribe firm for £6 million, and this should have been made clear in the prospectus; but 'the Bank of England are averse to this', noted Hamilton, 'and think we can arrange the matter by closing the list as soon as the sum required (10 millions) had been applied for'. What happened, of course, as Dawkins later wrote to Milner, was that things 'went hopelessly wrong ... owing to the colossal stupidity of the Bank. After Hamilton and I had agreed on a prospectus stating that subscriptions were invited for X millions of which X had already been subscribed the Bank struck this out, and [the Chancellor] weakly consented thereby exposing the Govt to violent abuse for issuing a prospectus withholding a material fact.' As the London partners later wrote to the New York partners, 'Public very much chagrined at large amount placed US as no statement that effect was in prospectus and subscription closed so promptly froze out whole Stock Exchange.' J. P. Morgan & Co. lost out as well: they had anticipated having £7 million to distribute in the US, but they were assured of only £6 million, and as the New York partners wrote to the London partners on 8 August, 'We have been obliged allot entire amount at our disposal leaving us no bonds and merely paltry $\frac{1}{4}$% to pay expenses'. In the end, in fact, they received only £5,643,000.[51]

An unquantifiable but undoubted cost for Morgans was the anger of the City of London. There must have been anger at the decision of the Chancellor to go outside the home market for funds, which raised some question as to the financial strength of the City. But beyond that, the choice of the house of Morgan caused intense jealousy in the City, and in the words of the senior clerk at Rothschilds, there was 'a hell of a row'.[52]

By early 1901 the government's need for further funds was undeniable and worrying. As Hamilton wrote, 'The more I look into financial prospects the less I like them. Indeed I view our future with great anxiety.'[53] Dawkins did as well, writing to Milner that 'We are really getting into an intolerable situation; securing shortnesses of gold and temporary arrangements with the American market which only means that we increase our growing indebtedness to that country which it is impossible to liquidate without further scarcities of gold.'[54] Hamilton too worried about British financial dependence on the US, but in larger terms: 'Our commercial supremacy has to go sooner or later; of that I feel no doubt; but we don't want to accelerate its departure across the Atlantic.'[55]

This feeling on the part of the Permanent Secretary to the Treasury may well have contributed to the outcome of the next set of negotiations with Morgans; it certainly contributed to his satisfaction with that outcome. On 19 January 1901 Dawkins and Revelstoke saw the Chancellor, who was considering whether he ought to issue £11 million 3% 5-year Exchequer bonds in February, and wanted to know whether Morgans would take a firm amount and try to ship gold. Morgans and Baring Magoun & Co., Barings' New York house, together answered that they would do what they could to help, although they would prefer a 3-year bond. Negotiations then lapsed for some days, since Queen Victoria was dying.[56] Dawkins, however, assumed it would go through, writing that 'I think it will end in our placing a large amount ... in the USA. We will not be popular here, but it is the only way of getting a good price *and* of helping the gold situation here *and* of so keeping up the Govt credit that [the Chancellor] may secure good terms for the large loan that he will issue in the early summer.'[57]

Dawkins and Revelstoke saw the Chancellor again on 5 February, but, Dawkins wrote, the Chancellor 'cannot make up his mind'.[58] But, as Hamilton wrote, the Chancellor had

a very difficult decision to take. We are told on the one hand that the City is so stuffed with Bonds & Bills that we shant get our eleven millions subscribed here, and on the other hand that it will be most unpopular if he places any part of the Loan in America. On the whole, I believe it will be best for him to run his risk here. The difficulty about getting good advice is that I don't believe it is possible to obtain really disinterested advice from City men.[59]

On 8 February 1901 the Chancellor went along to the Bank, and the decision was taken to issue the whole of the loan in Britain, putting it up to open tender without a minimum. (Hamilton wrote that Dawkins and Revelstoke were quite nice about the government's declining their offer.) On 11 February Hamilton learnt that the bonds had been subscribed more than twice over, and it was with relief that he could write that 'I am glad we have kept clear of America on this occasion.'[60]

But it was impossible to do so the next time. The failure of peace negotiations in February meant that the war would continue for some time, and thus substantial funding would be required. On 25 March 1901 Hamilton and the Chancellor met with Bank officials, and it was decided that the government needed to borrow £60 million, 'in order to make it reasonably certain not to have to borrow again for the War in the course of the next twelve months'. The Chancellor wanted the issue to be by tender, but the Bank preferred a fixed price, to which Hamilton felt they would have to agree, 'for we must try and get the general public to subscribe and tender acts as a bar to that'.[61] By 2 April the Treasury and the Bank had decided on an issue of Consols.[62]

On 11 April 1901 Pierpont Morgan arrived in Britain. On the 16th he and Dawkins came to pay their respects to the Chancellor and, wrote Hamilton, he was 'quite open to a deal in connection with the new loan'. (Hamilton also confided to the privacy of his diary his opinion that Morgan 'impresses one at once as a strong man; but the appearance of his nose, poor man, is a terrible drawback to his company'.)[63] They met several times, and when on 18 April the Chancellor hesitated about the loan, Hamilton

told him I was certain the longer he put it off the more would Consols be 'beared' against us. He must strike suddenly & close with the best offer instantly. He left it with me. After seeing Cassel & Dawkins as well as Natty Rothschild and Daniell [the Government Broker], I came to terms for the Government just before the hour of the Budget. I believe $94\frac{1}{2}$ is on the whole good; and that as 30 millions have been placed the other 30 will be … quickly subscribed for. In the City there is always a 'sheep-like' tendency to follow on a lead.[64]

On 19 April 1901, then, Pierpont Morgan could cable his New York partners that the British government 'have accepted finally our terms'. J. P. Morgan & Co. and Baring Magoun & Co. would together head an American syndicate to take £10 million firm on a placing; but 'Chancellor of the Exchequer fears criticism exclusive arrangement with us. Asks us consent English syndicate being formed. Have consented and Rothschilds form a Syndicate here for £20 millions on the same terms, except they will get only $\frac{1}{8}$% [commission] instead of our $\frac{1}{4}$%.'[65] What is not entirely clear with regard to the last point was the position of Barings: they headed the British syndicate jointly with Rothschilds, and in consequence was their commission only $\frac{1}{8}$%?

In the US, demand for the issue, 'rated one of the best investment securities available, greatly exceeded the amount the American group held for public sales'.[66] In Britain Consols had fallen by 19 April, and Hamilton congratulated himself that 'the terms accepted ... are turning out good. The City people won't get fat upon the Loan.'[67]

The fact that some in the City did feel overloaded with Consols would mean prickly negotiations for Hamilton when the time came in the spring of 1902 for the last Boer War loan. By mid-December 1901 the City assumed that the British government would have to issue a new loan, but they also knew that the Treasury wanted to avoid another issue of Consols and instead go for a 3% Transvaal loan guaranteed by the British government. This would be taken to mean that the end of the war was in sight and gold shipments from South Africa would soon resume, and Consols consequently would go up. By the beginning of January 1902, however, the London partners had decided that the Government would probably be obliged to issue more Consols unless there was a real change for the better in the war before March; the conclusion they drew was that they had better all sell their Consols without delay, before the rest of the market decided to do the same.[68]

By mid-March 1902 the Chancellor was taking soundings about a new loan. He saw Lord Rothschild on 18 March, who was 'violent' for a Transvaal loan. Then the Chancellor sent the Permanent Secretary to see Dawkins, who 'went as strong for Consols as the Jew had gone against them'. Dawkins afterwards discovered why Rothschild had argued so urgently for a Transvaal loan: 'He took a lot out of the last Consol issue & has still got them on his hand, at a loss. We took the same amount, but are out at a slight profit.' Dawkins planned to let the Chancellor know just why Rothschild was arguing as he was, and, as he wrote to his friend Milner, 'It is a pity he [the Chancellor] himself knows nothing of the City, or he [would] be less bothered by threats that he will lose his friends & that people will not "come in". Friends don't exist in this kind of thing, and the very big houses *dare not* be left out.'[69]

The Chancellor and the Permanent Secretary continued to take soundings, in particular from Revelstoke and Cassel; their conclusion was that it would not be possible to issue a loan while the war was still on, and therefore it would indeed have to be Consols. By 10 April 1902 Dawkins could warn New York that the Chancellor would probably issue a loan of from £30 to £40 million of Consols. Pierpont Morgan himself had by this time arrived in London to complete the negotiations for the IMM, and he joined Dawkins in his visits to the Treasury.

Meanwhile, the New York partners had reported that there was not much enthusiasm over the prospect of British Consols, and this information presumably enabled Dawkins and Morgan to persuade the Chancellor that the Consols would have to be issued at an agreeable price.[70] Hamilton was not very pleased at the need to work with Morgan—'I would rather do without him this year. American assistance is not appreciated much in the City'[71]—but in the end he agreed that the Chancellor had made a good bargain. Morgans would take £5 million for America at 93½.[72]

The man who was *not* happy was Lord Rothschild, and he knew that Morgans were to blame. Hamilton had seen Rothschild just after having seen Pierpont Morgan on 14 April 1902, and when Hamilton had told Rothschild the price he had looked very unhappy. But, as Hamilton noted, 'when he finds that Morgan has come in, he will be bound to follow the American lead'.[73] That the arrangement was a good one for Morgans is clear from a cable sent by the London partners to the New York partners on 15 April:

JPM's idea is as follows. That in all probability peace is not far distant and he thinks it desirable to make some profit on this probably the last chance we shall have therefore thinks we had better keep, that is JPMC & JSMC as much of their share of the 5 m as you can do so conveniently.[74]

Morgans presumed that the London firm would share in the London tranche, which would increase their share of the issue, and this gave Rothschild his chance for revenge. Dawkins wrote to the Permanent Secretary on 15 April that

Mr Morgan wished to take a participation in the London syndicate for his London house . . . as he did last year upon the personal invitation of Lord Rothschild in that case.

Upon my seeing Lord Rothschild . . . he stated this was impossible, as the Chancellor of the Exchequer had given instructions on the distribution of the £11,000,000 which must prevent him meeting Mr Morgan's wishes.[75]

The instructions which had been given to Rothschilds had of course not included any such prohibition. They had in all £16 million of Consols to distribute, £11 million after the £5 million to Morgans and Barings in the US, and of this, £2 million went to the Bank of England and £2 million to Cassel. As the Permanent Secretary wrote on 15 April 1902, 'the remainder will be left to the Rothschilds to dispose of, though we have stipulated that the Joint Stock Banks should be invited to cooperate'.[76]

That same day, he both received the letter from Dawkins and met Pierpont Morgan at dinner, when the latter complained of the Rothschild refusal. The Permanent Secretary contacted Dawkins and offered a participation, but Dawkins refused: there was no point, now that it had gone to a premium. The loan was a success, being over-subscribed many times (the Chancellor, of course, drew the conclusion that he had given it away too cheaply).[77] Dawkins, when writing to his friend Milner, took some credit for the success:

> The battle of Consols vs Transvaal loan was waged up to the 11th hour, Natty [Rothschild] on the side of Transvaal and I unus contra Urbem totem on the other. I think I clinched the matter by introducing Pierpont M. at the psychological moment who took £5,000,000 Consols at a price Natty said they would *not* go at, and offered to take as many more as wanted. Consequence, a grateful Beach [the Chancellor], Natty following the lead sullenly, an issue over subscribed and 2 p.c. on his £5,000,000 in Pierpont's pockets.[78]

This was the last of the Boer War loans, an episode which was a watershed in the affairs of both the New York and London Morgan houses. The New York house gained immense prestige from having been the sole or joint agent for the British government for the loans in the US. As Carosso notes, 'Recognition as a leading lender to Europe's principal creditor nation also made his firms especially attractive to other European governments and businesses, some of which sought to give their loans added cachet by having Morgan issue them.'[79] The London house, of course, shared in this. Just as the standing of stockbrokers today is a function less of their size than of their placing power, the ability of J. S. Morgan & Co. to provide access to the American market meant that they were now viewed as the London end of an immensely strong Anglo-American banking link, not as J. P. Morgan's smaller branch.

But the emphasis must still be on their position as an Anglo-American house (in spite of the firm's substantial involvement in Latin America), and certainly when J. S. Morgan & Co. tried to become involved in other areas their relationship with government could be less fruitful. This was particularly the case in countries where British imperial interests were threatened. The Edwardian period was in many respects the high noon of the British Empire, but those responsible for British foreign and colonial relations were acutely conscious of growing challenges from other European countries to Britain's position: she was a sated power and thus had everything to lose, in comparison with, for example, Germany, which appeared to have everything to gain from changes overseas. Areas of special concern to Britain included the Ottoman (Turkish) Empire, where Russia was a continuing and Germany a recent threat; Persia and India, where Russia threatened; and the Chinese Empire, where Russia, France, Germany, and Japan were all attempting to carve out exclusive spheres of interest. The Foreign Office therefore tried to utilize all peaceful weapons available to conserve British positions, and the period saw a number of Foreign Office attempts to 'guide' London finance in ways which would support British political and diplomatic interests.[80] These were not traditional areas of interest for J. S. Morgan & Co., and when they did attempt to develop business there the British government sometimes asked them to step aside.

One example was the episode of the Berlin–Baghdad Railway. In 1899 the Anatolische Eisenbahngesellschaft, which owned a railway running from Eskişehir to Konia, managed to wring out of the Ottoman government a concession to extend it to Baghdad. The Deutsche Bank wanted to internationalize its financing by inviting British and French banks to participate. London banks showed some initial reserve, but in June 1901 J. S. Morgan & Co. agreed to take it up jointly with Sir Ernest Cassel if the time was right and the railway promised to purchase some of the building materials in Britain. By March 1902, if not earlier, the British government were interested in the project. They were primarily interested in stopping it, since its continuance to the Persian Gulf would threaten British interests in the area; failing that, they wanted London to have an equal participation in the project.[81] Thus they backed the efforts of London bankers, which included Barings as well as Cassel and Morgans, the Foreign Secretary expressing 'satisfaction that for once "politics and finance could go hand in hand".'[82]

With the encouragement of the Foreign Office, negotiations with the Deutsche Bank continued, and by April 1903 had come to a successful conclusion. Then the London press got wind of what was happening, probably from information supplied by the Russian Embassy in Paris, and things rapidly came unstuck. It turned out that Lansdowne had not consulted the whole Cabinet over the matter; an uproar in the newspapers encouraged a split in the Cabinet; and without united government support the London bankers were not willing to go ahead with the project.[83] They were exceedingly angry with the government. As Revelstoke complained to Hamilton, he had been asked by the Foreign Secretary to take the matter up, and now, because of the changed attitude of the government, he and his associates would have to give up the venture and had been made to 'look small'.[84]

In 1908 J. S. Morgan & Co. again suffered because they considered working with a German bank. This time it was the Dresdner Bank, who asked them to join in competing for a proposed £1.3 million loan to Turkey. However, British relations with Germany were even more tense than they had been in 1903, and Turkey was an area where German economic penetration alarmed the Foreign Office, since Germany was clearly aiming to supplant Britain as the Ottoman Empire's main foreign protector. Accordingly, the Foreign Office backed a financial group consisting of Cassel, Revelstoke, and Sir Alexander Henderson (a stock-broker and railway financier) in bidding for the loan. At an interview on 20 November 1908 with Smith and Grenfell, Charles Hardinge, the Permanent Under-Secretary of State at the Foreign Office, advised them that while the Foreign Office 'could not prevent them from competing for the loan if they wished to do so . . . competition could do no good except to the Turks, and that in Cassel's combination the British and French groups would have a predominant position which they [Morgans] would not have [in a Dresdner-Bank-led group]. Consequently in British interests it would be preferable that they should not succeed.' Hardinge reported to Sir Edward Grey, now Foreign Secretary, that 'they were very nice & said that in that case they would reject the overtures of the Dresdner Bank'.[85] In the circumstances, of course, there was little else the London partners could have done, and in any case, it was a firm rule for the Morgan banks that foreign loans had to be approved by the issuing house's government.[86]

On the whole it was better for the firm to confine itself primarily to Latin American, European, or American business, and between 1900 and 1910 J. S. Morgan & Co. helped to underwrite national loans for the governments of Argentina, Portugal, Italy, Sweden, Finland, and Greece, as well as participating, mostly through Hambros, in selling the bonds of several Scandinavian cities. The London firm also led the Morgan banks in expanding operations in Africa and Australasia, where they were a participating underwriter in groups headed by Cassel, Stern Brothers, Panmure Gordon & Co., Marks Bulteel & Co. (the Bulteels were related to the Grenfells), and Berlin's Mendelssohn & Co. Most of these, indeed, were conducted entirely on J. S. Morgan & Co.'s own account—rarely did any other Morgan house join in these operations.[87]

The First World War

But the time was nigh for the greatest joint venture in Morgan history:

financing and supplying the governments of the Entente powers during the First World War. J. P. Morgan & Co. acted as purchasing and financial agent for the British and French governments in the US, as well as purchasing agent for Russia, Italy, Serbia, Romania, and Greece (all of which were allies). Morgan Grenfell & Co. (as J. S. Morgan & Co. had become in 1910) took care of the negotiations at the London end and thus shared fully in the work (and received 25% of the commission income generated by the arrangements). The transatlantic link, in short, was crucial both to Morgan Grenfell and to the British government. It was crucial for Morgan Grenfell because it ensured its rise to the very top rank amongst London merchant banks; and it was crucial for the British government because the link would ensure that Britain (as well as the Allies, who were all to a greater or lesser extent supplied and financed by Britain) had the supplies and money needed to fight the war.

The concern of the British government in July 1914 was not with any putative European crisis: rather, it was with Ireland and what seemed to be the threat of a civil war. The assassination on 28 June 1914 of the Austrian Archduke Franz Ferdinand and his wife in Sarajevo, the capital of Bosnia (now part of Yugoslavia), seemed an event devastating to the Austro-Hungarian Empire—he was, after all, the heir to the throne —but not to Britain. The crisis seemed containable, and meanwhile it hardly impinged on the consciousness of most people, who were enjoying a now legendary hot, golden summer. Therefore when the July crisis accelerated into the August crisis, it took many by surprise, in particular when Britain found herself at war on 4 August 1914.

Britain, in common with the other belligerents, was unprepared for both the scale and the duration of the war. British war planning had been based on the assumption that she would utilize her superior naval power and concentrate on supplying her allies with *matériel* while blockading the Central Powers (Germany and Austro-Hungary) and slowly starving them of resources. She would not provide a mass army of her own; rather, Britain's Continental allies were expected to provide the bulk of the land forces with Britain contributing an expeditionary force of six divisions (150,000 men). But very soon after war began, the Secretary of State for War, Lord Kitchener, succeeded in persuading the Cabinet that it was vital that Britain should after all raise a mass army. In addition, the British army was unprepared for the change in tactics necessitated by trench warfare (as opposed to a war of mobility on the Boer War pattern) and in particular for the enormous expenditure in shells. The result of these strategic and tactical problems was to be a transformation first of

War Office purchasing procedures, then of British financial machinery, and ultimately of Britain's standing as the supreme financial world power.

The normal system of buying by the Contracts Department of the War Office in peacetime had been by competitive tender, confined in general to a limited number of approved British suppliers. It soon proved impossible to restrict orders for munitions to known firms, since the need was so great. But even with the expansion of the War Office approval list there were not enough firms to meet all the orders, and very early on the government had to turn to the US for further industrial capacity, especially in rifles and shells, and for supplies of food.[88]

The British War Office sent a representative out to the US in September 1914, and he was quickly followed by others, both from Britain and from the other belligerents, which led to confusion and the competitive bidding-up of prices. By the end of October 1914 the British Ambassador to the US, Sir Cecil Spring Rice, had come to the conclusion that what was needed was a single agent to be responsible for purchasing in the US, and he was probably the first to propose to the Foreign Office that this responsible agent be J. P. Morgan & Co. Spring Rice already had personal links with Morgans—he had been best man at Jack Morgan's wedding —but he had also talked over the suggestion with two British Treasury representatives temporarily in the US, Sir George Paish and Basil Blackett, and they not only strongly approved of the idea, but argued for it themselves once they had returned to London.[89] It took some weeks for the idea to be accepted by the departments who might be expected to utilize such a purchasing agent: for one thing, the War Office and Admiralty preferred to continue as they had always done, negotiating themselves in London with representatives of American firms, rather than leaving it to others in the US, and for another, many officials preferred not to have to pay commissions to a private firm. But the probable scale of purchasing was such that the British government needed an agent who already had expertise and contacts in the US; the war would not wait while Britain built up her own organization. Thus the Prime Minister, H. H. Asquith, backed the idea, as did the Chancellor of the Exchequer, David Lloyd George. Finally, in January 1915, the Commercial Agency Agreement was signed by the War Office and the Admiralty on the one side and by J. P. Morgan & Co. and Morgan Grenfell & Co. on the other.[90]

The Commercial Agency Agreement committed Morgans to securing the most favourable terms for British purchases and to stimulating productive capacity when necessary. For this Morgans would receive a 2% commission on the net price of all goods purchased up to £10 million and 1% upon excess of that. (These were adjusted in various ways during the war.) In view of the fact that a later charge against the firm by members of the US Congress as well as some historians was that Morgans had made entirely too much money out of their position as British agent, it is interesting to note that Lord Kitchener, for example, had thought that no more than $50 million worth of orders would be placed in the US. In the event total payments made by Morgans on behalf of the British government alone during the war rose to $18,000 million, in addition to $6,000 million for the French. According to one report, purchasing commissions totalled $30 million altogether, with an added unknown sum in banking commissions.[91]

While negotiations were going on in London, Thomas Lamont, one of the senior New York partners, approached E. R. Stettinius, the President of the Diamond Match Company, to ask him to take charge of the purchasing for the British government. Morgans were only too aware that they did not contain within their own organization the technical expertise necessary to purchase, intelligently, items such as shells, shrapnel, and other *matériel*. In fact, the intention was never that the firm itself should engage in the purchasing. Rather, they established a brokerage arrangement with Stettinius, whereby he set up and ran the necessary organization, and was paid on a commission basis. The organization, called the Export Department, was situated on the firm's premises at 23 Wall Street in order that it could avail itself of the firm's influence and financial acumen. By May 1915 it was apparent that pressures on the Export Department had been underestimated and the staff was greatly expanded. By June 1915 Morgans had decided that the brokerage arrangement was not a satisfactory way to organize the matter. One possible reason for this was that Stettinius's commission threatened to exceed the income of any Morgan partner: in 1914 his net income had been reported as $97,173.49, while in 1915 his net income was $858,856.84, of which $500,000 was commission from the Commercial Agency. At any rate, Morgans decided to pay the expenses of the department themselves, and absorption was completed when in January 1916 Stettinius became a Morgan partner.[92]

One question which arose early on for the British government was, how were they to communicate with J. P. Morgan & Co.? This, of course, was where Morgan Grenfell came in. Charles Whigham became Stettinius's opposite number in London. Space for his staff, the Supply

George Peabody (1795-1869), an American born merchant, gave more than £1 million for the benefit of the working classes of London. A statue of him in Threadneedle Street commemorates his philanthropy.

MR. PEABODY AT GUILDHALL

Yesterday Mr. George Peabody, the eminent benefactor of the deserving poor of London, attended at Guildhall, accompanied by the Lord Mayor and the Lady Mayoress, at the request of the managing committee, to distribute the prizes gained by the successful competitors at the Working Classes Industrial Exhibition, which has been held there for some weeks.

Mr. PEABODY, who was greeted with acclamations, said:-

My Lord Mayor, Ladies, and Gentlemen, — I beg to acknowledge with heartfelt gratitude the kind expressions which the Lord Mayor has just used towards me. I assure you there is no man who feels such language with more sensibility or gratitude than I do, and I can assure you I am extremely thankful and complimented by the kind manner in which you have received the flattering remarks which have just emanated from my friend the Lord Mayor.

Contrary to my expectations, I am able, on the eve of my departure from these shores, to discharge a duty which your kindness has called me to fulfil. Though a stranger to you, and of another country, you were pleased to intimate to me that my presence among you this day would give you gratification (cheers), and on my part I am bound to say that while I have been constrained to decline many invitations recently addressed to me,

I have reserved to myself with peculiar satisfaction the opportunity of meeting the working men of London, whose representatives you are, in the midst of the scene of their honourable rivalry and the display of their most meritorious achievements. (Cheers).

Such successfu competition as that which meets its due reward this day must be productive of the highest advantage to the people at large, and all classes of the community derive a benefit from the elevating tendency of the persistent industry and skill displayed in the construction of these works of art which are now about to receive the token of public commendation. Springing as I do from the people, and owning with you the Anglo-Saxon stock, I unfeignedly rejoice in this fresh evidence of the advancement of the industrial classes in the dignity of labour and in those habits of self-reliance and honest independence which ennoble any people, and afford the surest guarantee of the true prosperity and moral greatness of any country. (Cheers)

It is true that these prizes which I am about to distribute are the just reward of your own personal efforts, but I hope you will allow me to remind you that in receiving your certificate of undoubted merit you will accept it also as an acknowlegment made by you in this century which will be productive of good and redound to the advantage of future generations, who must profit by your laudable exertions in the field of scientific research, and in the open workshop of a nation's constructive skill. (Cheers). Should the Great Disposer of all event give to me the happiness of returning to this country, I hope to see the complete success of projects designed by me for the permanent welfare of the deserving poor of this metropolis (loud cheers), and I may then enjoy further opportunities of intercourse with those in whose welfare and happiness I have so great an interest. (Renewed and prolonged cheers.)

In the enlarged dancefloor laid at Riverside for Rambert's season. In the rest of the programme, however, the lack of space became more apparent. Merce Cunningham's *Doubles* lost more than it gained. As with a wide cinema screen in a small hall, the wider stage distorts

graphy looked like up-market showbiz dancing, blatantly — albeit effectively — designed to send the audience home happy, although I suspect not humming Steve Reich's tunes.

JOHN PERCIVAL

Department, was limited, and it was 'obtained by leasing part of Gresham House, the adjoining building [to the firm's premises at 22 Old Broad St], and knocking a hole in the wall between the two buildings ... and off the passage leading from one building to the other' was Whigham's office. Once the orders were negotiated in the US 'the rest of the paper work was done at 22 Old Broad St.... All this record keeping was done on very large sheets of paper by means of dip pens.'[93] Whigham himself spent his mornings decoding and reading the cables from New York; his afternoons were taken up with visiting the various governmental departments, in particular the War Office, where he delivered responses from Morgans in New York and collected requests for information and for orders to be placed; and in the evenings he wrote cables, and encoded them if they were secret, to be sent to Morgans in New York each night.

The 'amazing elaborate code' used by Morgans had been created by Whigham and Stettinius, and its possession was, according to Grenfell, an 'extraordinary' privilege, which had been given to them in a 'fit of broadmindedness' by Lloyd George. It *was* extraordinary, in view of the strict censorship of all outgoing cables, that Morgan Grenfell should have been allowed to use a private code. Such a code was denied even to the War Office and the Admiralty, who had to send their messages through the Foreign Office and via the embassy in Washington and the consulate in New York. This caused frequent delays, and consequently the War Office, for example, sometimes asked Whigham to send official War Office messages through their private channels in order to expedite them.[94]

Morgans continued as purchasing agent for the British government until August 1917, when British war missions already resident in the US took over the administrative responsibility. However, the Morgan partners continued to give financial advice. Until September 1915, Morgans' duties with regard to finance had been merely to disburse funds sent over from London, whether directly as dollars, or as pounds or gold which they sold in New York for dollars. Because they had to buy and sell foreign exchange, however, they noticed when in December 1914 the pound weakened against the dollar in New York for the first time since the war had begun. Over the spring and summer of 1915 Grenfell repeatedly warned the Treasury and members of the British Cabinet that something would have to be done. Although the pound was also weak on other neutral exchanges, the fight to keep confidence in sterling soon centred in New York. Because of its supplies of food and raw materials, such as wheat, cotton, petroleum, and copper, and because of its actual and potential manufacturing capacity, the US became the greatest foreign source of supply for Britain during the war. Already in 1915 the volume of imports from America was 68% greater than in 1913 (and by October 1916 Britain would be spending 40% of its war expenditure in North America). Thus one of the main duties of Morgans was to try and keep up the rate of exchange.[95]

Grenfell had been a director of the Bank of England since 1905, and he acted as the liaison between the Treasury, the Bank, and J. P. Morgan & Co. over financial matters. Every morning Grenfell would call at the Treasury, carrying the latest exchange quotation from New York, where he would discuss with Sir John Bradbury or Sir Robert Chalmers, two of the three Joint Permanent Secretaries to the Treasury, the instructions to be sent to New York; then he would dash back to the office and, with the help of trusted subordinates, encode the Treasury's messages to be sent out to New York, just as Whigham was doing for the War Office. Throughout the spring and summer of 1915 Grenfell tried to convince the government to do something about the growing threat to the pound, such as cutting down the spending in the US of the War Office and especially of the new Ministry of Munitions.[96] In this he was backed by the Treasury officials, but the Chancellor, now Reginald McKenna, did not have the weight in Cabinet to enforce cuts, especially against the opposition of the Minister of Munitions, Lloyd George. Both Morgans and the Treasury officials were working with weak material here, since McKenna was not yet on top of his job; as Grenfell noted in a cable to New York, 'We left the Chancellor somewhat chastened, but he has a lot to learn, and we none of us can afford the time to teach him...'.[97] However, a foreign exchange crisis in August 1915 convinced the Cabinet that changes would have to be made: but rather than cut down on spending, they decided to try new methods of raising dollars, and this change meant new and important tasks for Morgans. In September 1915 the British and French governments sent the Anglo-French Loan Mission out to the US to try to issue an unsecured loan in dollars, which Morgans arranged, and in 1916 the British government, through Morgans in New York, issued three collateral loans. They also sold British-owned American securities in the American market.[98] Neither the British government nor the Bank of England had the international machinery or the expertise to do this easily, and the house of Morgan was now clearly the British government's American banker.

As such, Morgans also carried out the other duty of a banker to his client, and this was to loan money themselves to the government.

Morgans advanced funds to Britain at 2% interest in the form of a demand loan, and although part of this was carried by other banks, the New York partners themselves carried a large part of it: for example, when in July 1917 the demand loan amounted to approximately $400 million, the Morgan partners alone carried $165 million. By 25 April 1917, this demand loan amounted to $436.8 million,[99] a substantial amount even for a Morgan-led syndicate, and the need to eliminate it would precipitate a crisis in Anglo-American relations in the summer of 1917.

During the First World War the power of the Treasury over the spending departments was weak, and it had in particular lost control early on over the biggest-spending ministry of them all, the Ministry of Munitions. By November 1916 the tactic of issuing collateral loans in New York was reaping diminishing returns. The British government wanted to issue another unsecured loan in the US, analogous to the 1915 Anglo-French loan of $500 million, but after sounding out the New York market Morgans had to report that it would be impossible to do so before January 1917 at the earliest. Morgans felt that something had to be done to raise funds before then, and they persuaded the British government to authorize the issue of short-term, unsecured Treasury bills, denominated in dollars, which were meant to be taken up by the American banks and repeatedly renewed. Unfortunately, one of the more aggressive New York Morgan partners, H. P. Davison, went up to Washington to acquaint the Federal Reserve Board with this intention. He made it very clear that Morgans were not asking the permission of the Board, but merely doing the polite thing by giving them advance notice. Furthermore, Davison said that Morgans intended to issue the Treasury bills without limit, possibly to an amount as high as $1 billion, and as fast as the market could absorb them. The Board took fright. They were afraid that this move by Morgans would clog the banks with paper which appeared liquid but which was in fact long-term; further, in response to Davison's warning that if Treasury bills could not be issued the Allies might have to cut down on their purchasing, the Board called his bluff and replied that the US economy was already too involved with war trade. In the end the Board and the President issued a warning to investors to be careful about investing in foreign paper, and Britain suddenly had on her hands a full-scale exchange crisis.[100]

As far as the British government was concerned, the crisis was the fault of Morgans. Morgans had actively campaigned for the Republican candidate for President and against the Democratic President Woodrow

Wilson during the autumn of 1916, in spite of their acknowledged position as British agent. They had been cavalier in their treatment of the Federal Reserve Board, and when the Board had reacted, Morgans had been publicly defiant, until instructed to act otherwise by the British. The Foreign Office minuted that the conduct of Morgans had been 'overbearing and ill-advised' and that of Davison in particular had been 'injudicious'. The British ambassador in Washington complained that he had not been consulted by Davison, and the Foreign Office minuted that they had 'more than once pointed out ... that Morgans cannot be regarded as a substitute for the proper diplomatic authorities in conducting negotiations likely to affect our relations with the United States'.[101] The Treasury defended Morgans, but clearly also harboured doubts, and decided to send out its own representative to take over the responsibility for finance in the US.[102] This was Hardman Lever, the Financial Secretary to the Treasury, and he remained in the US, with an office in Morgans, until July 1919.

Once the US entered the war in April 1917, things necessarily changed. First of all, the American government itself began to make loans to the British government (the genesis of the war debts), and although this did not entirely eliminate the British need for private funds—Britain raised $800 million privately during the period between 1917 and 1919, when the American government loaned her $4000 million[103]—it meant that financial negotiations now took place between the two governments without the use of a private banking firm as intermediary. Secondly, the American government began to look more favourably on the House of Morgan as elements in the government found their contacts and advice to be irreplaceable. Unfortunately, one government official who never really became reconciled to Morgans was the Secretary of the Treasury, William Gibbs McAdoo,[104] and the British government sometimes suffered because of the association with Morgans.

One possible example of this was the crisis over the demand loan in the summer of 1917. This demand loan was the money loaned at 2% interest by the Morgans and their syndicate of 367 banks to the British government, a loan which had shot up in the spring of 1917 to over $400 million. The British government had received what they thought was a promise from the Secretary of the Treasury in June 1917 that as soon as the First Liberty Loan (the American War Loan) was issued, some of the money would be used to repay this demand loan. Unfortunately, what the British took as a promise the Americans meant only as an expression of good will, and the politicians had written nothing down. (Neither had

Lord Cunliffe, the Governor of the Bank of England.)[105] The date for repayment in the minds of the British Treasury and of Morgans was 2 July. When this date arrived, Davison again strode into the American Treasury and in effect demanded to know where the money was. The effect of this intervention on the American Treasury was quite devastating,[106] with McAdoo announcing that 'I do not propose to allow NY bankers and their allies to use the British Government as a club to beat the US Treasury with.'[107] Morgans panicked and threatened to begin selling the deposited collateral immediately, since pressure was being put on them by the banks, but soon recovered their composure; the problem of the overdraft was then sorted out. The sale of the collateral (there was approximately $700 million worth to secure an overdraft of $400 million) was begun quietly on 10 August 1917, and the British floated $150 million worth of 90-day Treasury bills, which were later taken up by the participants as payment.[108]

For the rest of the war, Morgans left Anglo-American financial negotiations in the US to the respective Treasury officials. The firm continued to disburse funds, but this was a matter of routine, not policy. In Britain, Morgan Grenfell, and in particular Whigham and Grenfell, continued their direct war work. Whigham, in fact, was dragooned into government service and was eventually sent to the US as Deputy Director-General of War Supplies, responsible for purchasing munitions and supplies.[109] Grenfell continued his liaison work with the Treasury and the Bank, which was necessary but nerve-wracking. The Governor was not only megalomaniacal, he more and more refused to talk to many people, and Grenfell found himself to be one of the few people to whom the Governor would speak at any length (they were distantly related). Grenfell thought the whole problem stemmed from problems with Cunliffe's teeth, and that if only he would take off the time to go to the dentist, everything would be all right.[110] Whatever the facts of the case, Grenfell had his hands full during the war, lobbying the British government on behalf of Morgans in the US, consulting the New York firm on behalf of the government, and acting as go-between for the Governor of the Bank and the Treasury officials, almost as though they had been hostile sovereign powers.

On 11 November 1918 the war ended. The Morgan banks were proud both of the role they had played in helping to defeat the Central Powers, and of the international position they had achieved in the four years of war. Morgan Grenfell were now without any doubt in the first rank of London merchant banks; more than that, the London and New York firms together constituted the most important investment banking group in the world. This can be readily demonstrated by their activities during the 1920s and early 1930s, when they were called upon by governments to lead the private banks in the reconstruction of Europe.

CHAPTER FIVE

FINANCE AND FOREIGN POLICY

1921–1931

Reconstruction, Reparations, and Débâcle

THE 1920s was a decade of money, with questions about raising it, lending it, and spending it occupying the forefront of politics. Finance was at the centre of the geopolitical stage because of the course and outcome of the First World War. First, Europe had to be reconstructed and currencies had to be stabilized; and secondly, there were war debts owed by the victors to each other which had to be funded, and reparations to be paid by the losers to the winners. This all required money, which was only really obtainable on any scale from the US. But there was no question of public money being provided; rather, the American government wanted private money to step forward and lend. Even less could the British government contemplate using public money to rebuild Europe, and it too gave every encouragement to the private banker and investor to shoulder the task.

The financial world to which treasuries and central banks were turning so hopefully was in an uncertain state, with the guideposts of the past destroyed by war. The most obvious casualty was the stability of the major European currencies: sterling had officially gone off the gold standard in March 1919, although it had required direct dollar support since the summer of 1917, while the franc and the lira had required support by the pound and dollar during most of the war. Thus currencies fluctuated. Another obvious change was in creditor/debtor relationships, and in particular the decline of France and Britain and the rise of the US. And the third change was the rise of an internationally important money market in New York City, which, while full of investors innocent of knowledge about foreign issues, was nevertheless awash with money and labouring under few restrictions.

The task, then, was to extract money from Americans to lend to Europeans, and this required banks with strong organizations on both sides of the Atlantic. Various banking houses besides Morgans had houses in both London and New York, Barings and Lazards being two examples. But the House of Morgan, its pre-war reputation even more enhanced by its wartime activities, towered above all. It is true that many firms were eager to manage an issue for a government, but it is also true that, rightly or wrongly, certain governments were known to believe that without the involvement of the House of Morgan an issue would not succeed. This chapter, then, will look at Morgan's activities in the reconstruction of Europe, where they were called upon to give advice to individual governments of a strictly financial or economic nature, in particular on the stabilization of currencies; it will also look at their involvement with reparations, when, as in the discussions of the Dawes and Young Plans, they acted as financial diplomats. It is not the intention to describe all the various episodes in detail, but rather to make a number of general points about the activities and intentions of Morgans.

Stabilization of Currencies

First of all, Morgans were motivated to a considerable extent by an altruistic concern for their government clients. This can be seen in their discussions about and activities in aid of Britain's return in 1925 to the gold standard. Most (although not all) influential officials, politicians, and bankers in Britain united in believing that Britain should at some point return to gold, although there was a good deal of disagreement over just when it should happen. Montagu Norman, who had become Governor of the Bank of England in 1920, saw the return to gold as the culmination of Britain's post-war efforts to restore its position as a major centre of international trade and finance. But it seems clear that at least as influential in driving Britain back on to gold was fear of the consequences if she did not. Both Germany and Hungary were due to return to gold in the summer of 1924; Australia and South Africa were threatening to do so without Britain; Holland and Switzerland wished to do so; and Sweden got tired of waiting and went back on to gold in March 1924 without Britain. In other words, as Benjamin Strong, the Governor of the Federal Reserve Bank of New York, pointed out to Norman, Britain was getting pretty far back in the queue.

Conditions in late 1924 seemed propitious to Strong for the stabilization of sterling, although several directors of the Bank as well as Sir Otto Niemeyer of the Treasury were doubtful. In the autumn of 1924 money had flowed to Europe and the exchanges were strong. The return and threatened return to gold of so many countries alarmed British officials, who did not wish Britain to lag behind. The wartime power to embargo gold was due to run out at the end of 1925, so a decision would have to be made. Speculators believed that Britain would return to gold, and this in fact helped push the currency up to parity (the pre-March 1919 exchange rate of $4.86 to £1) in the spring of 1925. In short, events appeared to drive the decision along.[1]

Strong seems to have been responsible for bringing Morgans into the matter. He thought that there should be private credits extended to the British government and the Bank of England, as well as a Federal Reserve Bank of New York credit to the Bank, both credits to be available to defend the pound; once this was accepted by the British—and Niemeyer was never really reconciled to it—they would of course turn to their financial agents in the US.[2] The upshot of discussions was a plan for Anglo-American co-operation at both private and central bank level.[3] A credit of $200 million would be extended by the Federal Reserve Bank of New York to the Bank of England, while a credit of $100 million would be extended by J. P. Morgan & Co. to the British government: the point was not to use the funds to push sterling up to parity, but rather for the arrangement to act as a warning to speculators that the parity would be maintained. In the event, neither credit was ever drawn on over the two-year period of their existence.

The negotiations over the credits were reasonably straightforward, with decisions having to be taken over their amount, form, and duration. There was, however, some quibbling over the commission charged, which Niemeyer for one thought ought to be eliminated (he feared trouble with Parliament). Thomas Lamont (the New York partner who was second only to Jack Morgan himself) in fact had eventually to write a memorandum for Norman to show to Niemeyer justifying a commission, and in the end Morgans agreed to halve interest and commission on the $100 million credit for the second year if the British government wished to cancel it before it was due to run out. They did not, and Morgans received over the two-year period $500,000 (almost £103,000) in commission as a management fee plus their share of the $2 million commitment fee.[4]

The question of Belgian stabilization illustrates a recurring problem in the relationship between private bankers and governments: that is, to what extent ought a bank to impose its own requirements as the price for a loan? The plan to stabilize originated within Belgium, and Morgans were mildly encouraging.[5] But the crucial pre-conditions, before the necessary stabilization loan and credit could be extended, were that

Belgium should balance her budget and fund her floating debt. The Belgian government's freedom to do this was limited by internal political considerations, and it seemed that no matter what proposals they made the Morgan partners were not satisfied.[6] The stumbling-block was Russell Leffingwell, one of the New York partners, who did not believe that the balance sheet as proposed told the whole story.[7] Finally, the London partners learnt that the Belgian finance minister was slashing the budget more than he believed to be politically or economically wise, purely to convince Morgans to co-manage a public bond issue for the Belgian government. At this point Morgans realized that they were getting excessively involved in political matters and chose to terminate the negotiations.[8] Stabilization was deferred for a year until conditions were more satisfactory, and finally carried through in the autumn of 1926, when J. P. Morgan & Co. in New York and Morgan Grenfell & Co. in London co-managed with Barings the bond issue for the government which accompanied the central bank credit extended to the Belgian central bank.[9]

The question of Italian stabilization shows Morgans in yet another light—that of helping to further central bank co-operation, a project dear to the hearts of Strong and Norman.[10] Morgan Grenfell often acted as intermediary between the governors of the central banks of France, Belgium, the US, and Britain, but their role is highlighted in the Italian case because, unusually for Morgans, they found themselves at odds with Norman and the Bank of England. Italy, which was under the control of Benito Mussolini and the Fascists, had consolidated its floating debt in November 1926, and this led Morgans to consider that the time was ripe for Italy to return to gold. However, Morgans also considered it vital that a central bank credit be arranged, and here Norman was a stone wall. For Norman the growth of central bank co-operation was a prime consideration, but in order for a central bank to enter the magic circle, it had to be independent of its government. Unfortunately, when Count Giuseppe Volpi, the Italian finance minister, was in London in December 1925, he had shocked Norman by stating in effect that he intended to control the policies of the Banca d'Italia.[11] Now Morgans thought it very likely that Norman had misunderstood Volpi—not difficult to imagine, since the Italian and the Englishman were conversing in French—and in fact, Bonaldo Stringher, the Governor of the Banca d'Italia, had proved himself an excellent Governor, as Benjamin Strong testified. But Norman refused to meet Stringher, so that the New York partners were moved to write testily that 'We think the Italian situation is of too great importance to Europe and to us to drop it because the conversations which Montagu Norman had with Volpi last winter did not give Montagu Norman satisfaction.'[12] After repeated urgings from Morgans, and possibly from Strong, Norman decided that 'in Italy no one is independent' and agreed to meet Stringher.[13] Finally, on 20 December 1926, after eight days of meetings in London, which began with discussions between Stringher, Norman, and Morgans and into which Barings, Rothschilds, and Hambros (with whom Morgan Grenfell had a standing arrangement to do Italian business) were later brought, a credit was agreed;[14] on 22 December 1926 the Stabilization Decree was issued in Rome.

For Morgans themselves, the work they did towards the stabilization of currencies was amongst their most important, seeing the help they gave to countries wishing to return to financial rectitude as the completion of their war work. As Jack Morgan and another partner wrote in October 1925, '[we] feel it is of such great importance to the United States and the world in general to add to the number of gold basis countries that we should make every effort...'.[15] But as Morgan wrote to Grenfell in July 1924, 'We must however be very sure not to let our desire to help the politicians to straighten out the tangled affairs of Europe lead us away from the fundamentals...'.[16] And by fundamentals, Morgans meant their duty to ensure that any issue which they sponsored rested on so strong a foundation that 'small private investors' would not be led astray.[17]

Reconstruction and Reparations

Morgans' involvement in reconstruction and reparations brought them unambiguously into the sphere of international diplomacy during a period which lacked both an International Monetary Fund and a World Bank. It was, for example, the co-operation of J. P. Morgan & Co., Morgan Grenfell & Co., the Bank of England, and the Federal Reserve Bank of New York which made possible the loan of 1923 which set Austria on the road to reconstruction and prosperity (at least until 1931). The British government and the Bank of England inherited from the war period an interest in stabilizing Austria, because the Bank had assumed liability for the acceptances of the Anglo-Austrian Bank of Vienna. After the war this was reorganized as a British bank, and in due course it helped to restore Britain's financial position on the Continent, at the same time stimulating British interest in Austrian reconstruction. As early as July 1919 British officials were discussing various schemes to assist Austria, but the unstable conditions in the country, which· Austrian financial officials either would or could not remedy, discouraged private investors, and the British government itself was too weak to do much on its own.[18]

If private financing was vital, it must come in part from American investors, and there were repeated attempts to organize a loan with American participation. In one attempt in late November 1921, the British government approached Jack Morgan, who was in London, and asked him to consider a proposal for a private loan to the Austrian government. It was to be floated on the London and New York markets, with the Gobelin tapestries as collateral. The answer was discouraging, the New York partners remarking that it 'would create rather a pawn-broking impression' for them to issue such a loan, even if it were possible. Such a loan would not find a market.[19] In May 1922 negotiations began again in London between representatives of the Austrian Ministry of Finance, the Anglo-Austrian Bank, the Bank of England, Morgan Grenfell & Co., and J. P. Morgan & Co. The group of interested British banks and Morgans sent G. M. Young, a director of the Anglo-Austrian Bank, to Austria to report on the situation. This report was so discouraging that in June the prospect of a loan was again abandoned; one Austrian historian has blamed the failure on 'the [Austrian] government's amateur handling of financial affairs'.[20]

By early 1923, however, various reforms had been put into effect in Austria and yet another attempt was made to raise a private loan. On 15 January there was a meeting of private bankers at the Bank of England to consider a League of Nations plan for a long-term loan of 650 million gold crowns (approximately £28 million or $130 million). It would be guaranteed by the governments of Britain and of several European countries and backed by Austrian customs receipts and revenue from the state tobacco monopoly. The British government agreed to guarantee 20% of the issue. Whigham and Smith of Morgan Grenfell cabled to Morgan the assessment of Sir Otto Niemeyer of the Treasury (who was also the British member of the League of Nations Financial Committee) that the plan had either to go forward or to break down, with all of the consequences that the latter would entail. For themselves, if the other British banks went ahead, Morgan Grenfell would find it virtually impossible to stand out. The New York response was firm: there was no possibility of placing any Austrian bond in the US. All that J. P. Morgan & Co. could do was to take some of the burden off Morgan Grenfell if they felt constrained to take more of the proposed issue than was convenient for them.[21]

Fortunately for Austria, conditions apparently changed over the next few months. The American government refused to join the other countries in guaranteeing a public issue, or even openly to support it, but in due course J. P. Morgan & Co. ceased to find this refusal an impediment. On 10 March 1923 Lamont wrote to Grenfell that Morgans were more than usually interested in the Austrian situation, and in April, when the matter was taken up again, J. P. Morgan & Co. became involved; by 10 May they agreed to head a syndicate in New York with Morgan Grenfell leading another syndicate in London. The loan was issued on 11 June 1923, and within minutes the loan was 'heavily oversubscribed' in London and 'vastly oversubscribed' in New York, the latter syndicate receiving subscriptions totalling $125 million by 10.15 a.m.—five times greater than the sum for which the syndicate was committed.[22]

The results of the issuing of the Dawes (reparations) Loan for Germany were equally outstanding, but if the political and financial negotiations extended over a shorter period, they were much more time-consuming and intense than those over Austria. The central problem was the Franco-German balance of power, but the immediate crux was how to force Germany to pay the reparations required by the First World War peace settlement, the Treaty of Versailles. France had occupied the Ruhr in order to force Germany to pay; France wanted to drain Germany of funds to weaken her economy, but she also required German reparations to help rebuild the areas occupied by Germany during the war. (She could not realize external assets to help pay for rebuilding, because a substantial proportion had been devastated by the Russian and East European defaults.) Germany, however, had allowed the destruction of her currency through inflation in protest at the French occupation and the reparations burden. The interrelated problems then were the reconstruction of the German monetary system, the withdrawal of France from the Ruhr, and the raising of a foreign loan both to back the new German mark and to rebuild the economy so that Germany could pay reparations.[23]

Theoretically, the private bankers would be involved only in the raising of a loan, but in practice they were in the thick of the political discussion as well. Negotiations over the matter had begun in January 1923, but although they were repeatedly consulted privately, it was only in the summer of 1924 that Morgan partners, in particular Lamont and Grenfell, became continuously involved in political as well as financial discussions. The major problem was whether or not France would be able to retain the right to impose physical sanctions on Germany if the latter again defaulted on reparations (it had been partly German default which had driven France to occupy the Ruhr in the first place). Morgans felt very strongly that if France retained this right, there could be no German loan, since the bondholders would hardly want Germany under the threat of an invasion which would probably lead to a default on the bonds.[24] By the third week of July 1924 the situation was very tense: Morgans realized that if they continued to insist on France's losing her right to physical sanctions, the French government would probably fall; the London conference discussing the implementation of the Dawes Report would break up and the British government, which was 'very shaky', might fall as well;[25] but if they did not continue to insist on it, there would be no loan. Newspapers were starting to blame 'the bankers' for putting the terms of the loan before political requirements, and the New York partners left at home decided that Lamont and Grenfell should withdraw from talks until the politicians could clarify the situation. Morgans were not alone in their stance, and Montagu Norman was probably even stiffer than they were in his requirements. The British government, too, backed the suppression of the French rights, to which the French finally agreed.[26]

Once the political decisions were taken, however, the Morgan role became even more important, if in a different way. That is, a public issue could be agreed, but would bankers underwrite it? Jack Morgan and Lamont spent over two weeks at the end of September and the beginning of October 1924 travelling around the Continent in order to persuade bankers to take up their share of the loan. France, for example, was scheduled to take £3 million of the total, but the French bankers simply did not want to loan money to Germany: as the two wrote to New York, 'In France, Italy and Belgium it has not as you suggest been a question of how much the Governments wanted them [the bankers] to take but rather how much the Governments could force the reluctant and short-sighted Bankers to take.'[27] In order to force the French government to coerce the French bankers, Morgans told the French Minister of Finance that a $100 million long-term loan, which the French government wanted Morgans to issue in New York, would not be floated unless the French bankers co-operated.[28] The problems in France were replicated to a greater or lesser extent in most of the other European countries, and, as Morgan and Lamont wrote, 'Sweden is literally the only country that we have not had to bleed and die for.'[29] Even British bankers were reluctant, leading Norman to summon together representatives of the banks and issuing houses and allocate to each the amount necessary to make up London's share.[30] (The result here was that Morgan Grenfell did not get as much as they would have liked. Morgan Harjes et Cie were also dissatisfied, since they received none of the French share and were reduced to asking for $200,000 of J. P. Morgan & Co.'s allocation in the US.)[31] The loan was finally issued in New York on 14 October and in London and Europe on 15 October 1924. For J. P. Morgan & Co. it was the largest over-subscription they had ever received, with subscriptions totalling $750 million for an issue of $110 million. In London it was over-subscribed by a factor of ten, and in most of the Continental markets as well it was over-subscribed, rapidly going to a premium in all markets.[32]

Thus, in the discussion over the Dawes Plan, the 'alliance' of Morgans, the Bank of England, and the British government worked to deny to France the retention of her right to impose physical sanctions on Germany if Germany defaulted on reparations. Looking at it the other way, the Germans found to their delight that the conditions which Morgans felt it necessary to impose on France in exchange for floating the German reparations bonds went beyond what Germany felt she herself could achieve. Morgans were anguished to find themselves in this position, since their political sympathies in general were with France rather than with Germany. But in the final analysis, their duty was to float successfully and with a clear conscience the German reparation bonds, and consequently they found that the line between finance and politics was one which they had continually to straddle.[33]

The Morgan partners found themselves in this position once again near the end of the decade during the negotiations over the Young Plan and the Bank for International Settlements. In this case, however, they had to work against rather than with the British government. The Young Plan grew out of the situation arising from the Dawes settlement, in that the temporary arrangements set up by the Dawes Plan, by restoring confidence, had encouraged a vast outpouring of American and other money. This money had flowed mainly into Germany, and the resulting extravagance and inflation, as well as the growing debt burden, caused S. Parker Gilbert, the Agent-General for Reparations, to call for a change in the arrangements by which Germany would make reparations payments. The Dawes Plan provided for protection for Germany in the transfer of funds: Gilbert felt that until Germany had the entire responsibility for making the payments, her financial authorities would not exercise the necessary self-discipline.

There were other factors involved. Germany wanted the Allied occupiers out of the Rhineland. France regarded this occupation as security for German reparation payments, of continuing importance to her as she had signed (but not yet ratified) an agreement with the US to repay her war debt. On the more technical side, the Dawes Committee had fixed a schedule of annuities on an interim basis; it would be the duty of the Young Committee to determine Germany's total reparation liability and to propose a definite replacement for the schedule for making reparations payments to which the Allies had forced Germany to agree in 1921 (the London Schedule of Payments).[34]

The whole episode of the Young Plan fell into a number of parts. At the meeting of the Council of the League of Nations in Geneva in September 1928, Germany brought up the question of the occupation of the Rhineland, and this in turn caused France to refer to the question of reparations. The outcome was an agreement to appoint a six-power committee of financial experts to make a report, by this time a hallowed response to a political problem with financial implications. The duty of this committee would be to devise a final reparations plan; the chairman was to be the American industrialist Owen D. Young, who had been a member of the Dawes Committee. The other American representatives on the Young Committee of experts were Morgan and Lamont, and their membership ensured that Morgans were intimately involved in the negotiations as principals, rather than unofficially as with the Dawes negotiations.[35]

The Committee met during the first half of 1929, presenting its Report on 7 June 1929. Then came the first Hague Conference, which was almost wholly taken up with virulent British objections to the Report and the consequent renegotiations; the outcome was a British victory,[36] which was enshrined in the protocol of 31 August 1929. In January 1930 came the second Hague Conference, which formally cancelled the reparations clauses of the Versailles Treaty, regulated non-German reparations, provided for the evacuation of the Rhineland, and brought into force the modified Young Plan.[37] The final step was the issuing of the reparation bonds, the so-called Young Loan, in June 1930.

The Young Report had called for a Bank for International Settlements (BIS) to be established at Basle, which was to act as an organization to receive and distribute reparation payments and as a forum for international co-operation amongst the central banks. The Morgan partners, and especially Morgan, Lamont, and Grenfell, were closely involved with the discussion over the new bank: it was the question of the BIS's organization and standing which involved them in acrimonious debate with the politicians, and especially with the British. The Treasury wanted an organization which would be limited to reparation duties; they wanted it to be under the control of the national governments; and at one point they wished it to be located in London.[38] The Governor wanted an organization which would be a politically neutral central bank for the central banks; however, over the period of discussion, he seems to have lost faith in the concept and to have accepted that it would act only as a private meeting-place for central bankers to discuss common problems. His disillusionment may have had less to do with the attitude of the Treasury than with the fact that the direction and management would be largely American and French.[39] Morgans, along with most other American and British private bankers, wanted an organization that was a bank rather than merely a reparations organization, and one that was politically neutral and would deal only with central banks and governments.[40] The bankers in particular insisted on political neutrality: without that, no American participation, public or private, would be possible.[41]

This last argument, of course, was the commanding one, and it forced the British—and the French—to give way on the BIS's neutrality. It is an interesting episode, because now, unlike during the Dawes negotiations, Morgans were constrained to put pressure on their erstwhile allies, in particular on the British. The fact that the British government was Labour was not the crucial question: after all, so had been the government during the summer of Dawes. However, Morgans suffered from what Jack Morgan called the Chancellor's 'extraordinary negotiating methods', of which the prime ingredient was obstinacy (the Chancellor was Philip Snowden); and the Treasury fought hard to try to impose their ideas on the organization of the bank.[42]

In the end the British government gave way. The BIS was located in Basle, it was to act both as a reparations organization and as an organization for central banks, and it was to be politically neutral. But the BIS was not to be a threat to the policy-making prerogatives of either the Treasury or the Bank as had been feared. Rather, coming into being as it did at the onset of the Depression and conflict, it began its life of useful obscurity, a convenient meeting-place for central bankers but with limited funds, and hence powers, of its own.[43]

The 1931 Crisis

The climax to the House of Morgan's involvement in high politics and diplomacy, and in particular its relationship with the British government, came with the 1931 crisis, which began with suspension by major banks in Austria and Germany and the consequent imposition of exchange controls, and moved thence to Britain. Here, in spite of the endeavours of the House of Morgan, the Bank of England, and the three political parties, the Labour government destroyed itself and the pound again went off the gold standard. It was a harrowing experience, and the end result for Morgans was wholly undeserved abuse.

The 1931 crisis began in May with the failure of the most important bank in Austria, the Credit Anstalt; the Austrian government then imposed strict controls over all gold and foreign exchange transactions, which trapped £300 million of short-term loans in Austria. The crisis next moved to Hungary, which in July imposed the same strict controls. The run then spread to Germany, which had very large short-term debts to foreigners and heavy investments in Austria. To try to re-establish confidence, Reichsbank President Hans Luther flew to Paris and London on 9 July in an attempt to gain a new large credit.

This flight struck a real blow to Morgan confidence in Germany. On 5 June 1931 the German government had declared that the country was too poor to pay reparations, and the German approach to getting new credits, which was to plead that the alternative was total collapse in Germany, left them aghast. This was hardly the way to convince private investors to subscribe. In this case Morgans were especially angered, since they had, through the Dawes and Young negotiations, involved themselves deeply but unwillingly in arranging for and marketing the reparations bonds, and the contempt they felt for the Germans—Jack Morgan called them a second-rate people[44]—boiled over. They were particularly angry that German nationals were in large measure being allowed to take their funds out while foreign creditors and banks were being asked to continue their credits, and in sum, J. P. Morgan & Co. believed that

by this time the rest of the world is thoroughly tired of the incapacity which the Germans have shown to deal with their own problems and that the Germans themselves might as well understand here and now that they are not going to be babied any longer and that if they get future credits it will be only because they deserve them.[45]

The London response to the German problem was more complex. The London partners, of course, shared the antipathy to Germany, but they were closer to the fire. Firstly, Germany was one of Britain's major trading partners, and for industrial, commercial, and financial reasons it was important that the German financial system be rescued. And secondly, there was very real fear that if the German crisis were not contained, it would spread to neighbouring countries. By 11 July 1931 there had been established a Joint Committee of the Acceptance Houses and the British Banking Association to determine what united action they should take with regard to the withdrawal of German credits. On 15 and 16 July New York banks, too, met to decide what they should do, and their decision, which was largely the same as that of the London banks, was to honour existing lines of credits so as not to cripple commercial life. But there was a crucial difference in these two decisions: because of the centralization of the British financial system in London, this Joint Committee could speak for all the important institutions, while in New York only the major New York institutions had agreed to maintain their assets. In fact, smaller banks elsewhere in the US closed out their credits.

The two national groups had, in fact, different objects in view. American banks held over 40% of Germany's long-term external debt, and because of fears as to the difficulty of satisfying American banking inspectors about this, they wanted at least to limit their short-term exposure in order to improve their balance sheets. In other words, the Americans wanted progressively to liquidate their German indebtedness. British bankers, on the other hand, fully realized that it was impossible to liquidate German short-term debt entirely; rather, what the British wanted was a system whereby confidence could be restored, so that new money could be put into Germany, thereby enabling the City of London to retain their acceptance business.[46] But the arrangements did not work, and even though the position of frozen British credits was not as bad as it might have been (£64.7 million[47] or about $300 million, compared with the American total of $1 billion), nevertheless it was enough to put the pound in danger.

In July 1931 the crisis spread to London, where the pound was subject to both international and domestic strains. Firstly, there was a growing balance-of-payments deficit; secondly, the report of the Macmillan Committee on Finance and Industry made clear the extent of London's short-term foreign lending, in particular to Germany; thirdly, because of the exchange controls in central Europe, those wishing to increase their liquidity turned to London and sold currency for gold; and fourthly, there were growing fears about the stability of British government finances, much aggravated by the revelation in the report of the May Committee on National Expenditure of a prospective large budget deficit.[48]

On 13 July, the same day that Germany declared that all banks would be shut for two days, the Macmillan Report was published; on the 15th sterling fell sharply in Paris. Over the subsequent week the Bank of England lost over £20 million of gold from its reserves, £5 million on 23 July alone, and sterling weakened. The Bank Rate went up to $3\frac{1}{2}$% and the Governor met the Chancellor on 24 July to obtain his agreement for the Bank to investigate whether they could obtain central bank credits in Paris and possibly New York, and whether it would be possible for the government to borrow £20 to £25 million from commercial bankers in New York and Paris, to be held abroad as a reserve with which to defend the pound. Jack Morgan arrived in London on 26 July and Norman spoke to him about the proposed loan. Morgan advised Norman that before the British government could borrow in New York the government 'would have to show at least some plan of restoration of financial stability and should at least have expressed the intention to reduce the expenditures to come within their means'.[49] The gold drain slowed down for a couple of days, but then picked up again, and on 29 July 1931 the Bank of England put up the Bank Rate to $4\frac{1}{2}$%. On the following day the Bank arranged two three-month, renewable £25 million credits, one with the Federal Reserve Bank of New York and one with the Banque de France, both of which were announced on 1 August 1931.[50]

Meanwhile, on 31 July the May Report on National Expenditure had been published, and this had revealed a prospective £120 million budget deficit (subsequently revised upwards to £170 million). It should be remembered that this was a time when budget deficits were unthinkable —or at least unthinkable for a government with any pretence to fiscal integrity. The deficit seemed largely attributable to overspending by the Unemployment Insurance Fund, and there was thus much pressure on the Labour government to cut the dole paid to the unemployed as the price for political, and possibly financial, support. Certainly, when the pound fell sharply in Paris on 5 August, the Bank decided that the government had to realize, as the Bank saw it, the need to cut its coat to fit its cloth. Therefore the Bank did not use any of the credit to support the pound, considering it 'necessary to lose gold and to raise the discount rate again, in order to make the ... Government understand the seriousness of their position'. Fighting a domestic battle, the Bank failed to anticipate the foreign reaction to their manœuvres, and its action was 'misinterpreted all over the world as a fundamental weakness in the London position'.[51]

On the following day the Bank lost another £2.5 million in gold, and this renewed run on the pound convinced the Bank that the problem was one of lack of confidence in the ability of the Labour government to control public expenditure. Therefore, on behalf of the Committee of Treasury of the Bank, Sir Ernest Harvey, the Deputy Governor (the Governor was away in Canada), wrote to the Chancellor warning him that foreigners expected a 'readjustment of the budgetary position', that the time the government had to act was very short, and that if they did not, the reserves would be in danger.[52] By 12 August the Bank had lost £14 million of the £50 million American and French central bank credit.

The Bank now increased the pressure on the government, and in this Grenfell played his part. A director of the Bank, he was fully aware of events (and kept his partners and J. P. Morgan & Co. apprised), but he did not take part in the discussions with ministers. This was not because of his position with Morgans, but because of his position in politics as a Conservative MP. Since the whole stance of the Bank was that it was politically neutral and concerned only for the pound, Grenfell left discussions with the government to others. What he did do after 11 August was to help the Bank to organize the leaders of the opposition parties to help put pressure on the Cabinet, although other bank directors took the lead. On 13 August, for example, Grenfell had discussions with Conservative Party leaders Stanley Baldwin and Neville Chamberlain, with Sir Samuel Hoare on 18 August, and then with Chamberlain and Hoare several times from 20 to 23 August. Grenfell and other Bank directors and officials kept the Conservative and Liberal opposition leaders informed of the exchange position and of the views of Morgans and the Federal Reserve Bank of New York. However, this was done with the knowledge of the Prime Minister, Ramsay MacDonald, who was equally concerned about the position of the pound but unable to convince a substantial minority of his Cabinet that budget cuts were necessary.

It became clear to the Treasury that the government would have to raise a loan to supplement the central bank credits, and therefore Mac-Donald asked the Deputy Governor to sound out the Governor of the Federal Reserve Bank of New York, George Harrison. But the statutes governing the Federal Reserve banks prohibited their lending to foreign governments, and therefore the British government would have to turn to private bankers. The New York Morgan partners had already returned a discouraging reply on 8 August to an earlier enquiry,[53] but as Grenfell wrote on 19 August to Morgan at his estate in Scotland, the Prime Minister continued to believe that a loan 'could be placed in New York if satisfactory promises of good behaviour were made here'.[54] Grenfell determined therefore to send the following cable to Morgans in New York, first clearing it with Jack Morgan and showing it to the Deputy Governor, so that everyone would know where they all stood:

Have intimated to authorities here that there is no likelihood of bankers being able to place British Loan five or ten years in New York unless Government makes satisfactory announcement as regards balancing Budget. If such a statement were to be made which appeared to you and us indicative of real reform in finance and one permitting you to paint a satisfactory picture would you think it possible to make such an operation for say $250,000,000. This is purely a private message for you in order that I may give an opinion if asked by authorities.[55]

The Cabinet Economy Committee had in fact met several times over the previous week to work out cuts in expenditure, but on the morning of 20 August the Conservative and Liberal opposition leaders, to whom MacDonald and Snowden had shown the Cabinet proposals, pronounced them inadequate. This was serious; but the devastating blow was administered by the General Council of the Trades Union Congress (TUC) late on the same day when they declared their opposition to most of the proposed cuts. The TUC opposition galvanized a substantial minority of the Cabinet into arguing that, while the budget needed to be balanced, this should not be achieved entirely at the expense of the working class. Rather than the dole being cut, taxes should be raised. (The standard rate of income tax was 4s. 6d. (22½p) in the pound.)[56]

One who intended to fight the TUC's verdict was the Prime Minister, and he elicited from the Deputy Governor the statement that in his view it was 'essential, particularly from the point of view of the foreign interests concerned, that very substantial economies should be effected on Unemployment Insurance. In no other way could foreign confidence be restored.' MacDonald appealed to the Cabinet on 21 August to make the cuts, but the most they would agree to was to continue to consider economies.[57]

On the same day, the New York partners replied to Grenfell's cable, and they were pretty discouraging: there had been rumours of the rapid disappearance of the central bank credits (and in fact by 21 August 1931 the Bank had used up £33 million of the £50 million credits) and therefore market sentiment was bad; and besides, most of the leading bankers were away on holiday. In other words, it would be very difficult to arrange quickly and successfully a long-term, public loan for the British government.[58] Grenfell showed the cable to the Deputy Governor, and when that afternoon the Prime Minister and the Chancellor told the Bank of the Cabinet's agreed £56 million economy programme, the Bank officials told the politicians that the Bank could hold out for only four more days, that the Bank now needed a short-term credit before a long-term loan (as Morgans had suggested in their cable), and that the economy programme 'would not do'. On 22 August MacDonald told the Cabinet of the previous day's discussions with the Bank directors and the Opposition leaders, and proposed a new scheme of £68.5 million in economies, including a 10% cut in the rates of unemployment insurance payments. Without committing themselves to the scheme, the Cabinet authorized MacDonald and the Chancellor to consult the Opposition leaders, who said they would not oppose the scheme if the bankers were satisfied; MacDonald got Cabinet permission to put the scheme before the Bank directors, who were to discuss it with Harrison of the Federal Reserve Bank. The Deputy Governor then telephoned Harrison, who, after expressing disappointment at the total amount of the economies, said that the government would have to work through Morgans.[59]

Grenfell in fact had already telephoned the New York partners on 21 August to warn them that an official approach was imminent. Their reply on Saturday, 22 August 1931, was stern:

Certainly we wish to avoid undue discouragement. At the same time we think you will realise that the public here generally including the banks and banking houses have for a long time looked with great apprehension upon the continued neglect of the present Government to establish sound fiscal policies and it is going to take a great deal more than simply the joint declaration of three Party Leaders to convince the investment and banking public here that real amendment has been undertaken and that the Government is in a position to command heavy foreign credit favours.

The partners, however, thought that an agreement of the party leaders on a satisfactory programme might be adequate for a private credit transaction between Morgans and the British government, but not for a large public loan (the government were mooting $500 million, half in France and half in the US). In any event, most of the New York partners would gather on Sunday, 23 August, at one of their houses on Long Island to hold themselves ready for any communications from London.[60]

Late in the evening of 22 August, Grenfell sent the day's final telegram to the New York partners to put them in the picture. After setting out the Prime Minister's proposed economy plan (which Harvey of the Bank of England was revealing to Harrison of the Federal Reserve Bank of New York on the same day), he added the following:

If as result of what you and Harrison tell us we report that this is not sufficient to form a basis for a successful loan operation by removing anxiety abroad we understand Prime Minister will resign and advise the King to send for leaders of three parties and recommend formation of National Government to carry through whatever may be necessary to make situation satisfactory. We have seen leaders of other two parties and our impression is that they will co-operate.[61]

Thus the New York Morgan partners were aware that on their response might depend the survival of the Labour government.

On the morning of Sunday, 23 August, the Prime Minister sent his official request to J. P. Morgan & Co. In the early afternoon Grenfell sent another cable to the New York partners explaining that the reason the cable was coming through the Bank of England (via Morgan Grenfell & Co.) was that if the Prime Minister 'were to tell his Cabinet that he had already exposed his plan to foreign bankers and asked for a loan his Cabinet would be much incensed and he would get nothing through'. There was a Cabinet scheduled for 7 p.m. that evening and the Prime Minister hoped for a reply from New York by that time.[62]

At 6.15 p.m. that evening George Whitney, one of the New York partners, rang Grenfell at the Bank of England and told him they were still discussing the matter. He rang again at 7.15 p.m. and alerted him that he would telephone again in an hour and simultaneously send a long cable message. At 8.15 p.m. Whitney again telephoned Grenfell at the Bank and sent a long message which was taken down in shorthand in the presence of the Deputy Governor. As soon as the message was finished 'the Deputy-Governor, who had been rung up three times by the P.M., took the message down to him at the Cabinet meeting. The P.M. seemed very flustered, came out, looked at it and rushed back and read the whole thing to the Cabinet.... The Cabinet continued to sit and it was clear that there were very violent discussions.'[63]

It should be realized just what was being asked of Morgans. The Prime Minister wanted to know whether American financial assistance would be available if the Cabinet decided to adopt a scheme to which it was not yet committed, and to which the opposition parties would give support if Morgans thought it good enough. Morgans could not get much of an answer from the Bank on whether the Bank thought the scheme was adequate. So, knowing what might happen to the Labour government if their answer was unfavourable, 'both Morgans and I [Harrison] thought that was not a fair question to put to us; that while we were certain that a very definite budgetary program must be put through if they [the British government] were to float a loan here, nevertheless it was impossible for us at this distance to determine whether the program was adequate enough'.[64] In the circumstances, Morgans could only answer part of the question: there was no way they could decide upon a possible long-term loan until Parliament had convened and acted upon the budgetary proposals, but if the Cabinet wanted a short-term credit they could let them have an answer in twenty-four hours. The telephone message and confirming cable ended with the following interrogatory statement:

Are we right in assuming that the programme under consideration will have the sincere approval and support of the Bank of England and the City generally and thus go a long way towards restoring internal confidence in Great Britain. Of course our ability to do anything depends on the response of public opinion particularly in Great Britain to the Government's announcement of the pro-gramme.[65]

In other words, Morgans were asking only for assurances that those more in a position to know the situation supported the government's programme, and since the Bank had already taken soundings amongst various City bankers they knew that the City would do so. But the Prime Minister seems to have used the message as ammunition within the Cabinet and implied that the bankers were demanding the cuts which he and the Chancellor were demanding. His attempt to bounce the Cabinet did not work and a large minority of the Cabinet refused to accept the proposed 10% cut in the rate of unemployment benefit and decided to resign.

About 10 o'clock the P.M. came out very tired and flustered and said he was completely beat and that although prepared to go on if there were three or four dissentients he found so many that he must throw his hand in. He then went off to Buckingham Palace and exposed his case to the King, saying he must resign and somebody else must be found to take office. It would appear that the King adopted a calm and soothing attitude and, after listening carefully, told the P.M. to sleep on it and not to take a hasty decision when he was so tired.[66]

In the event, the following day a National Government was formed, made up of the three parties (although with few Labour members), and led by MacDonald as Prime Minister and Snowden as Chancellor. Their function was to get the new economy programme through Parliament and then resign to enable a general election to be held, although in fact the coalition went to the country as a government, rather than as three separate parties, and received a mandate to remain together. Meanwhile, those members of the Labour Cabinet who had resigned had met together and decided that the Labour government had been the victims of a 'bankers' ramp'. They did not agree on just which bankers had done the ramping—Morgans' name had not appeared in the cable of 23 August, and the Cabinet supposed the reply had come from the Federal Reserve Bank of New York. Others blamed the Bank of England, a supposition rather closer to the mark. On 25 August 1931 the *Daily Herald* published a story accusing American bankers of having demanded a cut in the dole as the condition for a credit,[67] and from that time on the story that 'brutal foreign bankers had laid down terms as regards the dole', as Grenfell characterized it,[68] had a secure place in Labour Party mythology.

But while governments come and go, the need for money is inexorable, and the fall of the government did not remove the need for a credit to support the pound. In fact, a leading article in *The Times* on the morning of 24 August 1931, the day the government finally resigned, implied that the credits extended by the Banque de France and the Federal Reserve Bank of New York were almost exhausted. In fact, this was nearly true—four-fifths of the dollars and three-fifths of the francs were gone; the result was a massive drain. That day the Prime Minister and the Bank of England asked Grenfell to contact J. P. Morgan & Co. and ask them to consider giving a short-term advance of $100 to $150 million secured by Treasury bills (the Bank of England was to attempt to raise a similar amount in Paris).[69]

The following day the New York partners telephoned Grenfell and reported that they were certain they could raise $150 million in New York and might possibly go as high as $200 million, assuming that the Prime Minister's statement on behalf of the new government had a 'stimulating effect in the City of London'.[70] Morgans suggested the rate should be $4\frac{1}{2}$%, with an opening commission of 1% plus $\frac{1}{4}$%, and emphasized that the arrangements should be made quickly, since the New York partners had a continuing fear that further bad news might make it more difficult to arrange the credit on decent terms. On 27 August Jack Morgan, who was now in London, went to the Chancellor to agree the formal letter from Morgans to Snowden as Chancellor. Negotiations with the Treasury had been touchy, since the government felt that a rate of $4\frac{1}{2}\%$ was too high; as justification, Jack Morgan sent to the Chancellor, with the formal letter, a copy of part of a cable from the New York partners:

In reference to the proposed interest rate in America we may emphasise further that there is not a single institution in our whole banking community which actually desires the British Treasury Notes on any terms either as to commission or interest. If they go into the matter it will be because of their becoming convinced that it is important and necessary for the whole banking community here to co-operate in the support of sterling.

The cable went on to note that because the British bills were not eligible for rediscount in the American market, the funds would be simply frozen. And as President Herbert Hoover pointed out to Lamont when Lamont cleared the proposed operation with him, 'both the Administration at Washington and ... the ... banking group would undoubtedly be criticised by the Interior and Western Press on the ground that we were permitting domestic banks to fail with heavy losses to depositors in order to utilise available assets in helping out the British banking and Govt situation'. Under the circumstances, although perhaps Morgans could have crowded the interest rate down to $4\frac{1}{4}\%$, it would have been foolish to try and do so.[71] (The New York partners shortly thereafter wrote to the London partners that 'by almost main strength and constant endeavour, together with conversations with our newspaper friends...', they had 'worked the total amount in the market up to $200,000,000.... As it was the amount of declinations from possible participants whom we invited was immeasurably greater than in any other similar operation that we have ever conducted.') On 28 August Jack Morgan signed the letter to the Treasury committing J. P. Morgan & Co. to organizing a syndicate to loan the government $200 million.[72]

Unfortunately, the existence of the American (and French) credits was not enough to save the pound. Although the news that £80 million had been borrowed served temporarily to check the run, nevertheless 'pressure of an unprecedented kind was continuous' inside the Bank of England, with the Committee of Treasury meeting frequently (many of the meetings of which Grenfell attended by invitation). On 2 September the Bank had reserves of £219 million, which included the credits; on 9 September there were £204 million, on 16 September there were only £148 million, and from then on the Bank knew it was only a matter of a short time before the formal steps to go off gold must be taken.[73] The roots of the problem remained the same: 'the illiquidity of the world's financial centre and the collapse—principally due to the view taken of British Government finance—of confidence among the creditors'. The immediate crisis was encouraged by reaction to the government's announcement of across-the-board cuts of government employees: this led to 'mutiny in the British [i.e. Royal] Navy' and, worse, the backing down of the government. According to the historian of the Bank of England, it was the news of the so-called mutiny and then the suggestion that the government did not have the courage to stick to its guns, plus the fear of an early general election with an uncertain outcome, that prompted the final drain on the reserves. On 16 September the Bank lost £3.5 million, on 17 September £10 million, and on 18 September £18.75 million, and that night the decision was taken.[74] On 21 September 1931 Britain again left the gold standard.

And with this abrupt change in Britain's international position came the end of this phase in the history of Morgan Grenfell. The bank was at the apogee of its international influence and, happily, it was a position from which it was never to be dislodged by competitors. It could retire from the field unbeaten because the nature of the game changed: no longer would private banks be utilized in quite the same manner. National and international institutions would be established, and they, as well as governments themselves (and their central banks), would replace private bankers as the most important lenders to other governments for state purposes.

For Morgan Grenfell & Co. the result of the generation's work was that their reputation as a merchant bank was now second to none. From this time, presumably, dates the caricature of the bank as so blue-blooded and select that they disdained to sully their hands with non-governmental business. This was, of course, wholly untrue. Morgan Grenfell, their usual international business devastated by war, had begun during the same period to build up their reputation in the next field in which they would, in due course, be acknowledged as the best in London: domestic corporate finance.

CHAPTER SIX

MORGAN GRENFELL & CO. LTD.

1934–1961

The Old Order Changeth

THE middle years of the century were a period of drift. The previous hundred years had seen the London partnerships moving steadily upwards, gaining experience, and increasing profits, influence, and power. Now, while still profitable and influential, the bank nevertheless remained on a plateau for some years. There were causes outside the bank's control, in particular depression and war. But there was also an ageing partnership, increasingly conservative and increasingly disinclined to put in the long hours and hard effort needed to build up business. This was not a state of affairs peculiar to Morgan Grenfell: during the decade of the 1950s in particular, the whole City of London was notoriously inbred and complacent, a situation which was not helped by the exchange controls maintained by the government until 1958, when sterling returned to *de facto* external convertibility on current account. (Capital account exchange controls, i.e. restrictions on investment abroad, persisted until 1979.) But newer and younger influences were at work within Morgan Grenfell, which by the early 1960s began to change the course of the bank. The symbolic turning-point was 1961: not only did profits begin to move off the plateau on which they had rested since the end of the war, but more important, Kenneth C. P. Barrington crossed over the only too visible line which had always separated directors and managers —gentlemen and players in the then-current parlance—and became a managing director. Whether or not all the directors realized that they were signalling a profound change in the bank's culture is unknown: but it was this change which was to help rescue the bank from its gentle relative decline and set it on the upward path, which in due course made it again a real force in the City.

From 17 June 1934 Morgan Grenfell & Co. was a limited company, entirely separate from the American and French Morgan houses. However, it seems clear that legally separated though they might be, emotionally the London partners—now termed managing directors— still felt themselves part of the House of Morgan: Grenfell noted in his Chairman's Speech for 1935, given on 5 May 1936, that 'An event of outstanding importance in the group of Firms was the formation in September of the independent firm of Morgan, Stanley & Co. to do financial and issue business in New York. . . .'.[1] Indeed, it would be difficult to tell from a reading of the firm's correspondence that any such separation had taken place, and this would continue as long as directors remained on both sides who had been through the Great War together.

E. C. Grenfell had been a partner since 1904 and the senior resident partner since 1910. He had carried a great burden during the First World War and in the 1920s, when he had been continually active in all of the governmental work in which Morgan Grenfell were then engaged. But by about 1926 he began to have health problems, which eventually forced him to take nearly a year off; thereafter he gradually withdrew from the more routine work, a withdrawal which was mirrored by a decrease in his salary and in the percentage of profits to which he was entitled. He still took part in work with important clients, such as the negotiations with The United Steel Companies in 1933 and 1934, but with his elevation to the peerage as Lord St Just in the 1935 Birthday Honours, his involvement declined. He had developed serious heart problems, and although he still spent some time in 23 Great Winchester Street and maintained his correspondence with Jack Morgan, he spent more and more time on his estate in Kent. He finally died on 26 November 1941.

His death did not come as a surprise and in fact was considered a welcome release; the death which did come as an appalling shock was Whigham's in 1938. Apparently no one had realized he was ill. One of his pleasures had been hunting, a pleasure he shared with Vivian Smith; he died of a heart attack on 12 February 1938 after a day spent riding with the Bicester, and was discovered lying on the ground with his horse keeping watch over him. Whigham had been a general partner since 1918, and had played a very important part in the growth of Morgan Grenfell's domestic corporate business.

With the death of Whigham and the withdrawal of Grenfell it was clear that more directors were needed. Vivian Smith—created Baron Bicester in 1938—was in his prime, but he sat on a number of other boards, as well as being in the middle of his fifty-year career as a director of (and since 1914 governor of) the Royal Exchange Assurance Company. There was T. S. Catto, created Baron Catto in the New Year's Honours in January 1936, and the two younger partners, Rufus Smith and Francis Rodd. But it needed more than these to maintain and develop the business. This was still a time when directors did more than make the strategic decisions and bring in the clients: they also worked out the details of an issue and went through the accounts of whatever company had come to them for help. They were not entirely without technical assistance, but directors of that time did much of the work which in the years after the war was done increasingly by managers.

On 1 January 1939 the firm appointed two more managing directors, Wilfred William Hill Hill-Wood and William Edward, 2nd Viscount Harcourt. Hill-Wood (widely known as Willie) was born in 1901 and educated at Eton and Trinity College, Cambridge, where he won a cricketing blue. After touring Australia and New Zealand with the MCC he joined Morgan Grenfell. This interest in cricket was considered a great asset by the staff: he engaged the interest of Jack Morgan in building and equipping for Morgan Grenfell a sports ground with a fine pavilion and facilities for both cricket and tennis at West Wickham in Kent, next to Langley Park Golf Course. (The pavilion suffered a direct hit by a bomb during the Second World War and the ground was never again used by Morgans; in due course Kent County Council compulsorily purchased it in order to build a school on the site.) Hill-Wood's close friendship with Jack Morgan, whom he visited frequently at his shooting lodge at Gannochy,[2] helped to maintain the old association with the New York firm. When he was appointed he was groomed for a directorship by working as manager for a year. In due course Hill-Wood would direct Morgan Grenfell's investment management department, which, in the days before the growth of pension funds, concentrated on a limited number of private clients.

The other new managing director, the 2nd Viscount Harcourt, known as Bill, had inherited the title in 1922 while still at Eton. The grandson of Walter Burns and thus the great-grandson of J. S. Morgan, Harcourt was the last member of the founding families to work in the bank. After coming down from Oxford, he joined Morgan Grenfell and worked his way around the various departments in the time-honoured manner of those destined to become managing directors. He also spent two months working in New York at J. P. Morgan & Co. and Morgan Stanley & Co. before settling down in London. However, his work at the bank had frequently to be shared with public duties: for example, he was Economic

Minister in Washington and head of HM Treasury Delegation in the US from 1954 to 1957, during which period he was also the UK Executive Director of the World Bank and of the IMF.

In the inter-war years, when Harcourt first began working at the bank, his primary duty, together with Rufus Smith and Francis Rodd, was to support the older managing directors in their work for clients, whether they were governments or companies. When clients came to see a senior director, one of the younger men might sit in on the discussion, helping and learning.

A lot of time was spent in maintaining contacts with companies, since the relationship between a merchant bank and its client was meant to be a long-standing one: when the basis traditionally was the acceptance credit, it behoved the merchant bank to know in some detail about the strengths and weaknesses of the issuing firm. This intimate knowledge meant that no one was better placed to give financial advice. This became of increasing importance during the century, as the habit grew of making fixed-interest and equity issues. By the late 1950s Morgan Grenfell had as clients a number of the largest companies in the UK:

in heavy electricals it had a stronger connection than any other bank, while in the motor industry it was concerned with two major tyre producers. It was strongly represented in bread and flour, in advising the largest millers. It had two or three quite large brewery clients, a couple of paper makers, one large textile group, the largest of the furniture makers, two of the principal store groups, and a joint connection . . . with a major British oil company.[3]

The client list also included half a dozen of the leading American-owned companies in Britain, and several of the largest steel companies. Rather than try to look at all of Morgans' work for clients over the period, the steel industry will be used as an example. Here, Morgans' most important client was The United Steel Companies, with whom the firm had maintained a nearly continuous relationship since 1929.

Morgan Grenfell and Steel 1929–1939

The United Steel Companies originated in 1917 and 1918 through the amalgamation of several companies under the leadership of Mr Harry Steel, since 1915 the chairman and managing director of Steel, Peech and Tozer Ltd.[4] This particular amalgamation involved an exchange of equity and debenture capital between the new company and the four constituent businesses, which was followed by two further acquisitions in 1918.[5] The

1920s, however, were a difficult decade for United Steel: it carried a heavy burden of debt, and the post-war depression, which hit steel-making as it had hit shipbuilding and textiles, ensured that various projects turned sour. Its management was hardly inspired, and indeed a severe financial crisis sparked off a palace coup in late 1927, when Walter Benton Jones became chairman.[6]

On 5 June 1929 J. Ivan Spens, chief accountant and a director of The United Steel Companies, came to Morgan Grenfell for help. United Steel was in very bad shape and owed about £3 million to its bankers; an offer had been made to the shareholders by Clarence Hatry of Austin Friars Trust Ltd. to buy a substantial proportion of their shares for cash, and they were inclined to accept. But Spens clearly had his doubts about Hatry, and he suggested to Whigham and Grenfell that if Morgan Grenfell & Co. would interest themselves in United Steel, Hatry might be willing to retire from the business. It is not clear whether or not the partners were inclined to help United Steel, but if so, they were clearly discouraged from doing so by the Governor of the Bank of England when they spoke to him later that day. The Governor spoke out very strongly against Hatry and his plans, with the result that the following day, when Spens called in at Morgan Grenfell, the partners told him that they were unable to help.[7]

The United Steel shareholders were duly bought out by Hatry, but this precipitated one of the largest frauds the City had ever seen. Hatry's goal was to reorganize the heavy steel industry by means of merger and rationalization, as he had already done with light steel. His biographer has written that as part of his strategy, Hatry took over United Steel and United Strip and Bar Mills Ltd., the shares of which were then controlled by a holding company, The Steel Industries of Great Britain, Ltd. He next planned to float the new company on the London Stock Exchange. Unfortunately, Hatry ran into difficulties, caused partly by the Depression and partly by the implacable hostility of the Governor. Hatry continued to be short of funds and, desperate to rescue his scheme, he turned to fraud, obtaining funds from banks 'on the security of forged corporation scrip certificates (for [the cities of] Gloucester, Swindon and Wakefield), which need never be presented for registration and could be redeemed when the steel combine was floated'. He eventually confessed in September 1929 and his companies went into liquidation.[8] It would be Morgan Grenfell's task, in due course, to help extricate United Steel from the ruins of Steel Industries of Great Britain.

Between 1928 and 1932 the board of United Steel executed a turn-

around in the company's fortunes by means of rationalization, centralization, infusions of new management, and schemes to increase produc-
tivity.[9] In the five years from 1929 to 1933 the company's share of the
UK steel business rose from 8% to 16%, accompanied by a progressive
improvement in earnings. The improved financial position and, in
particular, the absence of Hatry meant that when United Steel again
approached Morgan Grenfell in November 1933 for advice and assistance, the partners were much more welcoming than they had been in
1929. Benton Jones and Spens, still the chairman and chief accountant of
United Steel, wanted the bank's help in two separate (but connected)
deals: an issue of a £3 million debenture stock in order to repay existing
debts and provide about £500,000 of new money; and the liquidation of
The Steel Industries of Great Britain Ltd. (Hatry's company), of which
Benton Jones was also chairman. This would involve buying from the
existing shareholders for cash the shares of United Steel Companies and
then floating them on the market. There were also various complicated
legal claims on the company arising out of the Hatry débâcle which had
to be settled.[10]

The partners' first move was to consult the Governor of the Bank,
who felt that United Steel's position with regard to The Steel Industries
Ltd. ought to be cleared up. After consulting with Edward Peacock of
Barings and Nigel Campbell of Helbert, Wagg (in their capacities as a
director of the Bank and a director of the BID respectively),[11] the partners
met on 7 November with the chairman, the managing director, and a
director of United Steel. It was at this meeting that opposing ideas
emerged:

Benton Jones suggested that the proposed new Debenture issue was a matter
quite apart from, and could be proceeded independently of, the liquidation of
Steel Industries of Great Britain Ltd. E.C.G. pointed out that it would be
undesirable to proceed with the Debenture issue until the liquidation of Steel
Industries of Great Britain Ltd. and all disputes arising therefrom had been
completed as the latter operation from its nature was likely to revive the Hatry
taint and be detrimental to the Debenture issue.

Grenfell then departed for the House of Commons while the others
continued the discussion, from which it appeared that their ideas were not
necessarily quite so far apart as had first appeared. The Board of Steel
Industries wanted an assurance that there would be a debenture issue,
because it would help in their liquidation proceedings if the shareholders
knew that the debt would be eliminated; on the other hand Morgan
Grenfell insisted that they could not be expected to promise to make a

debenture issue where the offer would remain open for more than a very limited period, since the market price was liable to change. In the end it was decided that Morgan Grenfell would study the problems and plan the debenture issue, but would not go ahead until the legal problems had been solved and United Steel separated from Steel Industries.[12]

Over the next few months United Steel with Morgans' advice worked to extricate itself from its legal problems. By late April 1934, matters were far enough advanced to contemplate the liquidation of Steel Industries Ltd. and the sale of United Steel shares to the public. On 4 May 1934 Grenfell informed the Governor that Morgans proposed to form a small syndicate and make a bid for the shares of United Steel, which were held by Steel Industries. On 7 May representatives of the nine members of the syndicate gathered at 23 Great Winchester Street to work out the details of the bid, and again on 24 May to give their final approval to the documents. The contract letter, dated 25 May, obliged the syndicate to purchase 4.5 million shares of United Steel from Steel Industries of Great Britain Ltd. at a price of 20s. (£1) a share; the syndicate also took an option until 15 January 1935 at 23s. on the remaining 2,077,223 shares, which were also owned by Steel Industries. Four days later, the syndicate offered the shares to the public at a price of 21s. 6d. (£1·07½): within five minutes the list was closed.[13]

By late September the members of the syndicate had to decide whether or not to exercise their option. Morgan Grenfell thought it was necessary to decide before 4 October: that was the date of United Steel's annual general meeting, at which a dividend of 5.5% would be declared. If the syndicate exercised their option before that date they would receive the dividend, which was equal to 10.2d. per share net (4½p). Since United Steel shares were trading at 24s. 6d. per share, it was presumably not too difficult to decide to exercise the option; however, there was the very real danger that when these shares flooded the market the price would fall. It was therefore decided to organize a pool for part of the issue, which Morgans would manage.

Morgans organized the pool on behalf of the syndicate on 2 October, exercised the option on 3 October, and oversaw the issuing of the shares on 9 October 1934. Their price on 9 October was 24s. 6d., and the pool swung into action. It had been agreed that a specific number of shares owned by each member of the syndicate would be put under control of Morgans for six months; for example, Morgan Grenfell themselves were responsible for purchasing 276,962 shares, of which they pooled 51,962 and withheld the remaining 225,000 from the market. They were authorized to sell at their discretion the shares held in the pool, with the object of maintaining an orderly market—that is, keeping up the share price. It clearly worked, since by the end of November the price was 25s. 9d. (£1·28¾). The arrangement expired on 19 March 1935, and the shares which the syndicate members had withheld could now be sold freely.[14]

Once the partial extrication of United Steel from Steel Industries had taken place, negotiations for the proposed debenture issue could go ahead. The decision was taken to issue £2.5 million of 4% debenture stock, secured on nearly all the company's wholly owned properties as well as on the entire issued share capital of its two principal subsidiaries. The list was opened on 9 October and closed five minutes later, with the issue heavily over-subscribed.[15]

Meanwhile, suits arising from the Hatry fraud continued, and by April 1935 United Steel had a choice: they could continue the fight or they could settle and emerge with perhaps £150,000 from their claims. Benton Jones and Spens came to Morgans for advice, and Catto advised them that if the settlement cleared up all outstanding claims they should accept, because otherwise litigation—and costs—would continue to mount. They accepted the advice. Later in the year United Steel came to Morgans for advice on a different matter: they wanted to make a friendly bid for the Lancashire Steel Corporation. Benton Jones argued that since these two companies were 'the largest in the Midlands', they should merge; Vivian Smith and Whigham agreed and together they formulated a case to persuade Lancashire Steel. However, Lancashire Steel turned down the suggestion; and hostile bids being at that time virtually unknown, there the matter rested. Both of these sets of discussions exemplified the kind of problems on which firms would increasingly turn to their merchant banker for advice, rather than to their solicitor or accountant as in an earlier period. In these two cases, advice was given on the basis of a long-term client–banker relationship, and in neither case did Morgans charge a fee. Payment would come when an issue was next made.[16]

On 28 April 1936 Whigham called on the Governor of the Bank to inform him that 'our friends The United Steel Companies' contemplated raising further capital, by selling about 2.2 million shares at a price of about 25s. (£1·25) a share. There had been an increase in steel production in the previous two or three years and United Steel wanted to increase their capital expenditure, possibly expanding capacity. The Governor remarked that it seemed to be a very satisfactory business, and Morgans felt free to go ahead and sponsor the issue. It was decided to increase the capital of United Steel by a half, to £10 million, by authorizing the issue of a further 3,350,000 £1 shares; 2,200,000 of these new shares were to be offered to the shareholders in the form of a rights issue at 25s. a share. The issue was not underwritten by a syndicate, but Morgan Grenfell undertook to purchase at 26s. any shares not taken up.

As it happened, Morgan Grenfell were left with only 65,437 shares. Since the existing shares were trading at 32s., it was expected that the rights would be fully subscribed. However, they ran into the problem of dilution of shareholders' earnings. Market reaction was adverse, and by 23 May 1936 they had fallen to 29s. 6d. Nevertheless, the *Financial Times* for one noted that the money would be well used, and that the fall in the price of United Steel's shares was overdone.[17]

In November 1938 Morgen Grenfell arranged the last pre-war issue for United Steel, an issue of $4\frac{1}{2}\%$ 10-year notes, which piqued the City: no one could quite work out what it was for, although as the *Investors Chronicle* noted on 26 November, 'The name of John Summers has been mentioned in this connection.' In fact, the issue was part of a rescue package arranged by the Bank of England for John Summers & Sons Ltd., in which the Bank's partners were United Steel and Morgan Grenfell. John Summers was an important firm in the sheet steel trade, and it needed £3·6 million to complete a strip mill. Unfortunately, the concurrent and very public difficulties of another steel firm, Richard Thomas and Co., made it impossible to raise such a sum from the public. In these circumstances the Committee of Treasury at the Bank agreed with the Governor that the Bank could loan the firm up to £2 million of the funds necessary. The Governor then presumably contacted Morgan Grenfell, who arranged matters with both Summers and United Steel.

United Steel had already had talks with John Summers over the question of the production of wide-strip sheet steel. The two companies had examined the possibility that United Steel's subsidiary at Appleby-Frodingham might provide slabs to Summers, but it turned out that the home-produced ores of the Midlands made steel that was not suitable for wide strip. Nevertheless, United Steel was amenable to the suggestion made by the Bank and Morgan Grenfell that it put £1.2 million into a joint venture to help finance the completion of Summers' strip mill. It was for this reason (and to replace funds invested in the Sheffield Coal Company and in its Shireoaks Collieries) that United Steel made its 1938 issue. Their investment in John Summers gave them control of one-sixth of the share capital, which was later judged to have been a valuable investment. In the end, United Steel contributed their £1.2 million, the Bank through the BID contributed £1 million, and John Summers raised £2 million through a debenture issue sponsored by Morgan Grenfell and Helbert, Wagg.[18]

The November 1938 capital-raising exercise was made up of two simultaneous issues. One part was a rights issue of 882,180 £1 shares, offered at the rate of one new share for every ten already held; these shares began trading at a 4s. (20p) premium. The other part was the mystifying issue of £1.5 million 4½% 10-year notes. The notes were placed privately. Indeed, they were very readily taken up, since Morgan Grenfell's name ensured their quality; by the time first dealings began they were trading at a premium of between 1½ and 1¾ percentage points.[19]

The period since 1929, then, had seen Morgan Grenfell establish a commanding position in the steel industry, for not only did they provide advice and assistance for United Steel and John Summers, they also advised Colvilles, for whom in 1936 they had raised £3.1 million by an issue of ordinary shares.[20] Their growing experience in the industry meant that they could command the loyalty of their clients. This would prove very useful after the Second World War, when merchant banks had to try to pick up the pieces of their businesses. By 1953 Morgan Grenfell would be the obvious choice as the merchant bank for the majority of the great steelmasters.

The Second World War

War broke out in September 1939 and business came to an abrupt halt. An earlier history of the bank describes it as going into semi-hibernation with the departure of staff.[21] In fact, profits had already been declining sharply since 1938, and the war period was not as unprofitable as the earlier history appears to imply.

The week before the declaration of war saw Morgan Grenfell reorganizing itself in preparation. Letters written that week had three copies made—one for the London files, one for safekeeping near Bath, and one for Haresfoot near Berkhamstead. Haresfoot, one of the Smith family houses, was owned by Hugh Adeane Vivian Smith, Bicester's third son, and those staff (including fifteen to twenty women) who dealt with routine affairs were evacuated there upon the outbreak of the war. The remainder of the staff stayed in London, taking it in turns to sleep in 23 Great Winchester Street to watch for fires. The bank was damaged during the blitz, when it caught part of the blast from the bomb which destroyed the nearby church of Austin Friars.[22]

For the first months of the war, men engaged in reserved occupations were not allowed to join the forces. Bank clerks were one such group, and thus a number of Morgan Grenfell staff were available to the bank until 1941. Eventually fifty men and three women, out of a staff in September 1939 of one hundred men and thirty-two women, were engaged in national service of one type or another; out of this number six men were killed.[23]

Directors, not being in a reserved occupation, were involved in war work fairly early on. Harcourt, for example, went off to war with the 63rd Oxford Yeomanry Auxiliary Territorial Regiment Royal Artillery; he later served at General Alexander's sometime headquarters in Bari, 'at the control end' of supplies and help for the Partisans in Yugoslavia.[24] He was awarded an MBE in 1943 and was 'granted the honorary rank of Lieutenant-Colonel on being disembodied [sic]'.[25] Francis Rodd, who in 1941 succeeded his father as Lord Rennell of Rodd, joined the Ministry of Economic Warfare and in due course returned to Africa and the Middle East, where he had spent part of his time in the Great War. In the summer of 1942 he was appointed to the local (acting) rank of major-general, at forty-six apparently one of the youngest men to be so appointed. He served in the Civil Affairs Administration in the Middle East, East Africa, and Italy, where one of his tasks as a foreign exchange expert was the financial reorganization of the former Italian colony of Eritrea. In due course he was made a Commander of the Bath and KBE.[26] He returned to Morgans in 1944.

Hill-Wood had a less dangerous and more amusing assignment: he joined the postal Censorship Department and was sent out to the US, where he acted as financial adviser for the western area. This meant that he and his colleagues, in co-operation with the United States Office of Censorship, worked to deny to the Fascist powers financial aid from Latin America, by enforcing the Trading with the Enemy legislation and blacklisting companies and persons in Latin America who had dealings with the enemy and freezing their funds. One of Hill-Wood's colleagues in censorship was an employee of Rothschilds, and he wrote a description of Hill-Wood and Charles des Graz, Sotheby's chief expert on old books, who lived and worked together:

Charles and Willie had decided at the outset that Washington was a place which they were quite prepared to visit as often as necessary but not to live in. They accordingly established their office in New York, where much more was going on than just the business of government and diplomacy, as in the capital, and where they could live fuller lives. . . . They were inseparable, at any rate until the evening when their active social lives began, and when they came down to Washington it was always together . . . Willie small and ruddy and cheerful, with curly ginger hair and the figure of a quondam athlete proper to a member of a famous family of cricketers. Their . . . figures became familiar in the corridors of the Embassy not only to me but to many others who if they had had any idea what the two of them were up to would doubtless have strongly disapproved.[27]

One partner lost by Morgan Grenfell to war work ended by leaving permanently. In April 1940 Catto was appointed as Director-General of Equipment and Stores at the Ministry of Supply; then in July he was appointed to the new post of Financial Adviser to the Treasury. The idea was that he would have a roving commission and act in close contact with the Chancellor of the Exchequer, Sir Kingsley Wood, in smoothing out day-to-day difficulties; this was all part of the Treasury's attempts to utilize 'practical business men' in solving the problems arising in the Treasury's area of responsibility.[28] In 1944 Catto was appointed Governor of the Bank of England, and it fell to him to guide the Bank through its nationalization in 1946.

This left as directors only Bicester and Rufus Smith to continue the business of the firm. Business had been contracting even before the war —in March 1939 the firm had reduced its capital by £500,000—and in December 1942 it was reduced by a further £500,000, making it £1.5 million.[29] The second reduction in capital slightly worried the Bank of England, who pointed out to Morgans that while their capital was then ample, more might be needed later. Besides, comparisons would be drawn with competitors in the amount of capital and reserves (Morgans were currently lying third, behind Barings and Kleinworts), and there might well be some loss of prestige.[30] Certainly, the first two and a half years of the war were pretty bad for Morgans. The capital markets were confined to government financing for the duration of the war, and the wartime restrictions were accentuated by the loss of their Continental connections in France, Belgium, Holland, Denmark, and Norway, following the German invasions.[31]

But matters then began to improve, and by the end of 1942 the balance sheet was transformed. One cause was the bonds account, which improved by 3,400%, from a profit of £3,456 in 1941 to a profit of £121,701 in 1942. Another cause, and of a more enduring importance, was a revival in private transactions. Morgan Grenfell carried through the purchase and partial resale of £3.5 million of shares of F. W. Woolworth & Co. Limited which were held in the US, receiving permission from the Treasury to transfer them to Britain. Even apart from the appreciation in the value of the shares retained by the firm, there was a commission of £26,542, contributing to the profit that year of £284,268 (compared with £39,706 in 1941).[32]

The following year saw profits more than double, the result of two large transactions and a healthy income from investments. One of the transactions was the absorption by Morgan Grenfell of Cull & Co., which was described by Rufus Smith in a letter dated 10 October 1944 to a Morgan et Cie partner in Paris:

What happened was this: About $1\frac{1}{2}$ years ago the three remaining partners came in to see us and said that as they were all elderly men they wished to retire from business and wondered whether we would be willing to take over their company and run it as a subsidiary. After long discussions and for many reasons we said we were not prepared to do this but if they were willing to liquidate Cull and Co. and influence their connections in our direction, we would be only too happy to co-operate. At first they did not much care for the idea but after thinking it over they again came in and said they would be pleased to fall in with our suggestions. It was therefore arranged, as the easiest way of accomplishing the matter, that we should buy all the shares of Cull and Co., the capital being entirely covered by cash, and thereafter put the company into voluntary liquidation. This of course took time to carry through but the company was actually finally wound up last week. . . .

By taking over the business we acquired some valuable connections, the chief of which are the Chester Beatty group, Central Mining and British Celanese. We also took over quite a number of deposits.[33]

To this transaction was attributed an increase in profits for the year of £241,020.

At the same time as the negotiations with Cull and Co. were going on, Morgans were also engaged in another very profitable operation. The house purchased, mainly from the executors of the late Lord Wakefield, about $99\frac{1}{2}$% of the issued share capital of C. C. Wakefield & Co., for which they paid £1,904,842. Most of the shares were placed privately, but only after Morgans received the gross dividend; their total profit in the end was £215,941.[34]

The remainder of the war saw the firm continue to earn healthy profits, which can be ascribed both to a growing income from investments and to the growing number of private transactions carried out for an increasingly wide circle of clients. Some of the work was done by the directors not involved in the war, but much of it was done by the manager, George Erskine. He was a Scot and had taken a degree from Edinburgh University before joining the staff of the Bank of Scotland in 1913, where he remained until he joined Morgan Grenfell in 1929. When Morgan Grenfell became a limited company in 1934, Erskine became the company secretary, and then manager. He, too, was involved in war work, having become deputy chairman of the NAAFI (the Navy, Army and Air Force Institute, which provided canteen facilities and provisions) in 1941. He retained this job until 1952, and was knighted for this work in the 1948 New Year's Honours List. But even with his NAAFI duties he was probably the most energetic of those left at 23 Great Winchester Street, and this was recognized by his being made a director of Morgan Grenfell on 1 January 1945.

Morgan Grenfell would continue to benefit from Erskine's freedom from family responsibilities (he was unmarried) and indefatigable sociability. He was a tremendous 'goer-out and getter of business; he always went to City cocktail parties and dinners'.[35] He also had an innovative financial mind: he was responsible for inventing 'floating charge' loans, where—unlike the earlier United Steel debentures, for example— companies could provide all of their assets as security for loans rather than specify certain factories or pieces of land. This had the advantage that a company could sell any of its assets without worrying whether it was encumbered by a debenture which would then need to be repaid immediately. This innovation, plus the fact that he was actually in place at the end of the war, meant that Erskine built up an extremely good business, and by the early 1950s it has been estimated that the bank was responsible for over 50% of the public issues of fixed interest debt for industrial companies made in the City.[36]

Steel 1945–1950

Morgans also benefited from a wave of new issues immediately after the war, and, indeed, made the first such public issue. They owed this to their previous work for John Summers & Sons, who turned to them as soon as the capital market was opened up again to non-government issues. In December 1945 Morgans and Helbert, Wagg jointly managed an issue of 1.8 million $4\frac{1}{2}$% preference shares.[37] They were to make another four issues for John Summers, in 1947, 1950, 1954, and 1957.

Their main steel client in the pre-war period, however, had been United Steel. Even before the war was over the company turned to

Morgans, this time for help in reducing the burden of the $4\frac{1}{2}\%$ 10-year notes issued in November 1938. The Trust Deed limited United Steel to a debt of £3.6 million, roughly the amount already incurred by the sale of the $4\frac{1}{2}\%$ notes plus the debenture stock issued in 1938. Thus the company wanted to pay off the notes early, which was permitted by the Trust Deed at a price of 101. Spens, who was still a director of United Steel, came to see Rufus Smith and Rennell (back from the war) on 30 October 1944, and they discussed how to deal with the financial needs of the company. They wanted to convert the £1·5 million $4\frac{1}{2}\%$ 10-year notes into $4\frac{1}{2}\%$ preference shares, and to issue a further £1.5 million preference shares for cash. United Steel had an option to purchase the John Summers & Sons stock still owned by the Bank of England (of which the Bank was anxious to rid itself), and for this they would require a further £1 million; they wanted to keep the remaining £500,000 as cash.

The following day Bicester, Rufus Smith, and Rennell met with their brokers to discuss the price at which the shares might be issued; the information was later conveyed to Spens, along with the news that Morgans' commission would need to be $2\frac{1}{4}\%$ (or $1\frac{1}{2}\%$ after expenses). The permission of the Capital Issues Committee of the Treasury was obtained and the $4\frac{1}{2}\%$ preference shares were offered to holders of the ordinary shares on 10 August 1945. Approximately 90% were subscribed by the public, and Morgans took up the remainder. The $4\frac{1}{2}\%$ 10-year notes were then duly redeemed at 101 on 15 December 1945.[38]

United Steel were thus rid of the notes, but they also wanted to redeem over £2 million of the 4% debenture stock. This was for two main reasons. Firstly, the notes and debentures had been partly secured on their collieries, which the company were required to sell to the new National Coal Board, and thus they had to release the charge. Secondly, the Trust Deed imposed restrictions on other borrowing; paying off the debentures and lifting the restrictions would enable United Steel to raise additional loans to finance the modernization and extension of its plant (in spite of the fears of its chairman that the Labour government might indeed carry out its pledge to nationalize the industry). Thus in May 1946 holders of the debenture stock were given notice of repayment at 102 on 30 September and offered conversion into new $4\frac{1}{2}\%$ cumulative preference shares. The whole of the issue was underwritten by Morgans for a commission of 6d. ($2\frac{1}{2}$p) a share, resulting in a net profit of £15,708.[39]

In November 1946 the chairman of United Steel, still Walter Benton

Jones, outlined at the annual general meeting the company's development plans for the period to 1953, much of the cost of which would be met from the company's current resources and the compensation to be received from the National Coal Board. However, when Benton Jones and Spens called on Erskine on 28 November 1946, they made it clear that the company would wish to make a further public issue in due course. Benton Jones explained that they would need about £20 million for capital expenditure over the following five years, £15 million of which could be provided by the company itself. There was therefore no immediate urgency, but at the same time he wanted to plan the capital-raising well in advance so that it could be timed to meet shareholders' willingness to supply funds. After some discussion, it was agreed that the answer was to make a further issue of 4½% preference shares. United Steel was to make an application as soon as possible to the Capital Issues Committee, and plans would be drawn up to make an issue early in 1947. Treasury permission was received, and on 11 January 1947 the announcement was made of the issue of £1.7 million 4½% preference shares at a price of 24s. (£1·20). Morgans again received an underwriting commission of 6d. a share, or £14,692.[40]

On 12 June 1950 Rufus Smith lunched with Benton Jones and Spens at United Steel and the three of them discussed further finance for the company. Benton Jones and Spens wanted to borrow about £5 million, probably in October, and it was arranged that the company's accountants and Morgan Grenfell would begin work on preparing the necessary documents. But all came to naught, as Erskine wrote in a memorandum on 13 October 1950:

On the 21st September Sir Walter Benton Jones came in to express his very sincere regret to R.H.V.S., at the trouble which had been caused to us in preparing documents for the proposed 4% debenture stock of the United Steel Companies. He explained that with the entry into force of the Iron and Steel Bill the company would be unable to proceed with the scheme. [He] . . . had been aware for a week that the government had decided to vest Steel companies, but had been under pledge of secrecy until this day. [He] . . . was obviously very much upset at the decision and very pained by what he had to say.[41]

The Denationalization of Steel

Of all the nationalization decisions taken by the 1945 Labour government, that concerning iron and steel was the most contentious. Even the Labour government found it difficult to come to a decision to nationalize the steel industry, since it was hard to come up with a non-ideological and widely accepted argument in its favour: unlike the railways or the coal-mines it was not loss-making; unlike the coal-mines it was not suffering from the owners' unwillingness to invest; unlike the electricity industry there was no natural monopoly. Moreover, the steel unions did not want the industry nationalized. It came down to a question of political faith: for a substantial section of the Labour Party, to be a good Socialist meant supporting the nationalization of iron and steel in order that 'the people', as represented by the state, would control the 'commanding heights' of the economy. Thus the industry became a political football, and the whole post-war history of the industry and of the process of nationalization (and denationalization) must be seen in this context.

When iron and steel were nationalized the result was different from coal, the railways, gas, or electricity, when

the physical and other assets were transferred to the statutory Board who were to run the industries, and the old companies were dissolved. Under this 1949 Act the Iron and Steel Corporation was to take over and hold the shares of ninety-seven companies and so become the holding company of an enormous group of wholly owned subsidiary companies comprising the heavy steel industry. It would exercise powers of control through the ordinary machinery of the Companies Act available to a shareholder with a controlling interest.[42]

The vesting date, when the new corporation took legal control of the companies, would be 1 January 1951.

The Conservative Party had pledged during the debates on the bill that they would resell the iron and steel industry to the private sector when they returned to power. When the results of the general election on 23 February 1950 gave the Labour Party an overall majority of only five, there was a widespread assumption that there would soon be another election, with the likelihood of a Conservative victory. It was therefore an unpleasant shock to the steel industry to be told on 18 July 1950 by George Strauss, the Minister of Supply, that regardless of its small majority, the government was determined to put the Act into operation and would vest the ownership of the individual nationalized companies in the new Iron and Steel Corporation on schedule. Furthermore, the government now wanted a list of names from the industry from which to select members of the new corporation.

Sir Ellis Hunter was the president of the British Iron and Steel Federation (BISF) and Sir Andrew Duncan was chairman of its Executive Committee. Under their leadership, the BISF's Executive Committee decided, on the dubious basis that Labour had not received the votes of 'a clear majority of our people' (the Labour Party had won more seats, but the Conservative Party had received more votes), not to co-operate with the government, and they declined to provide any names. However, once the members of the corporation had been appointed in October 1950, Hunter and Duncan realized that only another general election —with a Conservative victory—would prevent the formal takeover of the companies by the corporation. Therefore, they decided on a two-pronged strategy. Firstly, they would dig up any valid reason or pretext for delaying vesting which could be put to the Ministry of Supply in good faith. And secondly, in response to the Conservative Party's pledge to 'unscramble' steel if they won the next general election, they would ascertain whether it could be done.[43]

On 27 October 1950 Hunter called in at Barings to talk to Sir Edward Peacock, at this time one of the most influential men in the City. Hunter told Peacock that he, Duncan, and Sir Archibald Forbes, President of the Federation of British Industry (FBI), had discussed the Conservative pledge to denationalize iron and steel; indeed, it had been Duncan who had convinced Winston Churchill, the Conservative Opposition leader, to make the parliamentary pledge. But if the industry was to be returned to private ownership, the three men thought that it should go through traditional channels and with the consent of both sides of industry and both major political parties. By traditional channels, they meant that the securities should be sold in the usual way, and this would require the active co-operation of the City. The purpose of Hunter's visit was quite simply to begin the process of discovering whether this was possible.

On 4 December 1950 Hunter, this time accompanied by Duncan, returned to Barings. He met with Peacock and four of his fellow directors, and with Bicester and Sir George Erskine, the latter now a managing director of Morgan Grenfell, which was by now considered the major 'steel house' amongst the City issuing houses. The lunch was somewhat disappointing for Hunter and Duncan: Peacock thought that denationalization would be possible only if the Conservatives were quickly returned to office and Labour pledged not to renationalize. Bicester injected a note of realism, noting that it was impractical to expect Labour to make such a statement. Duncan then revealed that the Conservative Party's Central Office had already set up a working party on steel denationalization which wanted to contact the City, but the merchant bankers almost noticeably flinched at the thought of talking to the political working party.[44]

What the bankers did was to constitute their own Working Committee to see what could be done. Over the next several months this committee, made up of Forbes of the FBI, Erskine of Morgans, Lord Ashburton of Barings, Sir John Morison, senior partner of the accountants Thomson McLintock, T. S. Overy, founder and senior partner of the solicitors Allen & Overy, and J. Ivan Spens, an accountant who sat on the board of the United Steel Companies, met in the utmost secrecy —neither the Bank of England nor the other issuing houses knew what was happening. By 21 March 1951 they had agreed a memorandum setting out in general terms how the operation might be conducted. Again, the memorandum was supposed to remain secret, but late in March Peacock secretly loaned a copy to the Governor of the Bank of England, C. F. Cobbold.[45]

The memorandum made it clear that there were a number of important problems. The committee took as the underlying principle the need for ownership to revert to the private sector in order to reintroduce competition and encourage efficient management. But they felt that there were other important factors involved, such as the need for a capital reconstruction of the industry so that it could more easily find finance for investment, the ability of the market to absorb the substantial issues involved, the need to carry through the denationalization as speedily as possible, and the position of those who had held steel shares when the industry was nationalized, as well as the expected political difficulties.[46]

The response both of the Governor and of senior Bank officials such as Sir Kenneth Peppiatt was horror at 'the prospect of the industry becoming a shuttlecock in the political game'. As the chief cashier and chief accountant wrote on 27 April:

If, however, on coming to power the Opposition decide upon 'unscrambling', it would in our view be essential that such an operation should be conceived in the simplest possible terms, namely a straightforward offer of the shares for subscription by the public for cash. That in itself would be so huge an operation as to tax the Companies' (and issuing Houses') resources and to introduce complications such as reconstruction of capital, priorities to former shareholders and tendering of Steel Stock would present very great if not indeed insuperable difficulties.[47]

There the matter rested for some months, and apparently nothing could change the Bank's collective view that 'unscrambling in the sense of attempting to re-market the shares is not a practical proposition. It would still seem more fruitful to approach the problem with the object of securing decentralisation of control and management—not sharehold-ing.'[48]

But politics, of course, has its own priorities, and both civil servants —who tended to share the Bank's reservations—and the Bank itself were forced by events to begin planning. On 25 October 1951 the Conservative Party won the general election, and on the 29th the Governor of the Bank wrote to Sir Edward Bridges, the Permanent Secretary to the Treasury and Head of the Civil Service. Bridges had asked Cobbold for a note on some of the financial points which would be raised if the new Conservative government decided to denationalize the industry. Cobbold sent him a memorandum; but he also sent him a top-secret note:

The major difficulty which I have always seen in these proposals is a political one and is not referred to in the memorandum. It is whether there is any means of assuring potential investors or reinvestors that they do not run the risk of another Nationalisation Act, perhaps on less favourable terms, in the event of a change of Government. Uncertainty on this point would seem to me a great obstacle, particularly bearing in mind the large figures involved. . . .[49]

The Chancellor of the Exchequer, R. A. Butler, in due course called in the Governor to talk. The Governor did not feel he could give the Chancellor any advice until he had been able to get hold of some more facts, and this, he felt, was only possible by 'getting together some people in the City'. He felt driven to re-emphasize to the Chancellor how difficult a task it would be, 'especially if the Opposition made clear their determination to undo anything which might now be done as soon as they had the chance'.[50]

And of course, the Opposition did so. In the King's Speech on 6 November 1951 the government announced that the Iron and Steel Act would be annulled and the steel industry reorganized; in the debate on the Address on 12 November George Strauss, who had been Minister of Supply in the Labour government between 1947 and 1951, pledged that a future Labour government would renationalize iron and steel and that the total compensation already paid out would not be increased.[51] Although hardly a surprising statement, it was alarming to those who found themselves responsible for actually carrying out the government's plans.

Bicester and Peacock, present and past directors respectively of the Bank of England as well as managing directors of their houses, together with the Governor, had already taken the lead in formulating the City's

10. E. C. Grenfell, 1st Baron St Just, by Fred May, in
the National Portrait Gallery, London
(*By courtesy of Morgan Grenfell Group*)

11. C. F. Whigham and
E. C. Grenfell at Sandwich,
Kent, 1915
(*By courtesy of the
Hon. Laura Grenfell Phillips*)

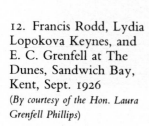

12. Francis Rodd, Lydia
Lopokova Keynes, and
E. C. Grenfell at The
Dunes, Sandwich Bay,
Kent, Sept. 1926
(*By courtesy of the Hon. Laura
Grenfell Phillips*)

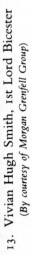

14. Thomas Sivewright Catto, 1st Baron Catto
(By courtesy of Morgan Grenfell Group)

13. Vivian Hugh Smith, 1st Lord Bicester
(By courtesy of Morgan Grenfell Group)

15. Morgan Grenfell cricket team, 1926. Left to right, back row: H. Lees; Gardiner; F. N. H. Pexton; K. Davison; John Izard; W. Halman; S. T. Warren; front row: Parsley; H. T. Mullins; A. T. Scott; S. A. Barrett; A. C. Hunt; in foreground: Brown (scorer)

(By courtesy of John Izard)

16. William Edward, 2nd Viscount Harcourt
(By courtesy of Morgan Grenfell Group)

17. Sir John Stevens
(By courtesy of Lady Stevens)

18. The building of the Channel Tunnel
(By courtesy of Eurotunnel)

19. Lord Catto, D. E. Bernard, D. A. Pease, Sir George Erskine, and
W. W. Hill Hill-Wood in the Partners' Room, mid-1960s
(*By courtesy of Morgan Grenfell Group*)

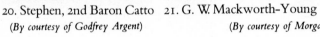

20. Stephen, 2nd Baron Catto   21. G. W. Mackworth-Young   22. Christopher Reeves
(*By courtesy of Godfrey Argent*)   (*By courtesy of Morgan Grenfell Group*)

23. Queen's Awards for Industry (1975) and for Export
Achievement (1982 and 1986)

(*By courtesy of Morgan Grenfell Group*)

24. Sir Peter Carey

25. John Craven

(*By courtesy of Morgan Grenfell Group*)

response to the proposed denationalization. They had convened a small committee to investigate the question, and this committee also worried about the political fight which was brewing. Peacock came in to talk to the Governor on 12 November 1951, and they provisionally agreed that the Bank should form a small working party to examine the financial aspects of denationalization. On 19 November Peacock and Forbes came in to tell the Governor of their worries about the direction of the debate in the House of Commons, and they agreed that the Governor should alert the Chancellor to the City's anxieties. The Governor then spoke to both Bridges and the Chancellor, and followed up the discussion with the latter by sending him a short memorandum. He told the Chancellor (as he had agreed with Peacock) that he had been approached informally by representatives of leading City interests who were giving a great deal of thought to the problem of steel and who were apprehensive about the difficulties of financing an operation of the size contemplated if steel continued to be the focus of political controversy.[52] The following day the Governor met with Bicester and Peacock and they agreed on the formation of a small private group to advise him and the Deputy Governor about any recommendations that the Bank should make to the Chancellor; they also agreed that the Governor would discuss these recommendations with Bicester and Peacock before he discussed them with the Chancellor. The three of them agreed that the members of this working party should be H. C. B. Mynors, Executive Director of the Bank, and Hugh Kindersley, a director of Lazards and the Bank, both representing the Governors; Erskine of Morgan Grenfell, John Phillimore of Barings, Forbes of the FBI, and Sir John Morison, who would eventually be head of the Iron and Steel Realisation Agency.[53]

Political controversy over steel would continue to be a severe problem, both without and within the government. The question of the Labour Party's reaction was, of course, a continuing but—with the government's majority—a medium- and long-term concern; the more immediate problem was trying to get the Conservative government to agree on a bill. The government was not united on the desirability of denationalization (they were arguing over road transport as well as over steel), let alone on the way it should be carried out or on the extent of government supervision which should be retained. The Minister of Supply, Duncan Sandys, believed in the policy, but he had to push his proposals through the Steel Committee, the Cabinet committee set up to consider the denationalization issue, and bulldoze though he might, it was too senior to be levelled easily. In the event, the Cabinet decided on 24

April 1952 to drop steel denationalization for that session, a decision which upset both the Conservative back-benches and the management in the industry.[54]

Finally, in July 1952 a White Paper was published. The following month Sandys wrote to the Governor that 'we should, I think, be clearing our minds on the arrangements to be made for disposing of the nationalised companies', adding that there should be at least embryo plans in being when Parliament reassembled two months later. The Governor had a word with Sandys and they agreed that the Governor should do a little exploring in the City and the Bank and let him know the result in September.[55] On 16 September 1952 the Governor and Sandys met with the Chancellor, and after some discussion they decided that a leading accountant, such as Sir John Morison, should be invited to assist the Treasury and the Ministry of Supply with the whole denationalization operation. No promises could be made, but implicit in the choice—as the Governor later confirmed privately to Morison—was the assumption that he would in due course head the Steel Agency set up to 'own' the steel companies on their way back to the private sector.[56]

Thereafter there were two streams wending their way towards the sea: the public political stream, concerned with the Iron and Steel Bill and its passage, and the private City stream, concerned with actually making the politicians' plans work without wrecking the industry or scaring off the investor. In the public arena a lot of hard work went into drafting the bill, almost as much as went into pacifying politicians. (Even Churchill was not convinced that Sandys was going about things the right way, remarking to his crony Beaverbrook in September that the sale of the steel companies was impossible and that the best solution was to leave control to private enterprise, but ownership to the government.[57]) But the manœuvring paid off in the end, because once the bill was introduced it met with very little difficulty. The Iron and Steel Act, which became law on 6 May 1953, had only thirty-six clauses and two main points: (1) it dissolved the Iron and Steel Corporation and transferred the shares in the nationalized companies to an Iron and Steel Holding and Realisation Agency, whose sole function was to return them to private ownership; and (2) it established a supervisory Iron and Steel Board which would, in conjunction with the Ministry of Supply, exercise 'very considerable powers' with regard to prices, raw materials, capital investment, and research.[58]

Meanwhile, the City began to gear up for action. Morison prepared detailed memoranda on two steel companies, one of which was United

Steel, and the Governor agreed that Morison should try out his ideas on the Bank's working party, whose members included Erskine. There had been a vague suggestion floating around that the Bank should perhaps make the issues, but no one really liked the idea. By 25 February 1953 Morison pointed out that some of the issuing houses, such as Morgans, had started working on their clients' figures, and he thought that the responsibility should be put squarely on them. The Governor thought that this would be very tricky, especially with regard to Hugh Kindersley; it is unclear why, unless it was a question of prestige: Lazards was likely to lead on far fewer issues than, for example, Morgans, if the houses made the issues instead of the Bank.[59]

At about the same time Benton Jones of United Steel called on Morison, who told him that the steel companies should go ahead with the preparation of schemes for the sale of their shares to the public as quickly as possible, and that United Steel should contact Morgan Grenfell. On 27 February Peddie of United Steel wrote to Erskine to inform him of all this, and to say that Benton Jones and Spens proposed to call on Morgans, meanwhile enclosing two memoranda setting out the company's position. Erskine replied, agreeing to a preliminary meeting on 9 or 10 March 1953. Early the following month Erskine wrote again, this time enclosing a memorandum setting out Morgan's preliminary views as to the minimum basis upon which negotiations with the Realisation Agency should commence. A major point was that the price would have to be set so that the government would not raise less in aggregate from the sale of the shares than the amount they had paid for them on nationalization plus the retained profits ploughed back into the companies while they were under state ownership. Over the next two months Morgans and United Steel worked to reconcile the requirements of the government and the financial needs of the company.[60]

Meanwhile, Morison continued taking soundings amongst the companies and the institutions, and it was while talking to the Prudential Assurance Company that he received the first real inkling of danger. As Mynors of the Bank noted after talking to Morison,

Morison's lunch with Ray and Brown [of the Prudential] was friendly but depressing. They emphasise that they have never underwritten more than they would take firm: they are scared stiff of the political risk: and they are afraid of being faced with a fait accompli and told to pay the bill.[61]

The institutions, and in particular the insurance companies, would prove to be the main stumbling-block to a successful flotation.

The Bank of England's working party continued to think about the problems involved. In mid-March 1953 Morison had a talk with Erskine,

who is right off the idea that the Bank must make the issues. Clearly he is getting interested in the problem as he gets down to brass tacks, while the political atmosphere is somewhat cleared. He thinks the issues should be made by the House that has the connection, but that there should be a syndicate of the six or seven big Houses inside which the work would in fact be allotted to the one most concerned.[62]

Three days later Peacock and Rufus Smith of Morgans called in to give the Governor their 'first reactions' on the subject of selling steel securities. They accepted the need for a consortium of issuing houses, which the Governor had suggested in a note of 18 March (taking Erskine's point), but they felt that the Realisation Agency should make the offer and the consortium should underwrite it, rather than the consortium buying the shares and reselling them to the public. They thought that the Bank of England should be the receiving bankers, perhaps subcontracting some of the work to the joint stock banks (the clearing banks). Finally, they emphasized that the crucial element was the attitude of the insurance companies.[63]

On 25 March 1953 the Governor felt ready to make his recommendations to the Chancellor. He advised that a group of issuing houses should have initial discussions with Morison about their acting on the Agency's behalf in marketing steel securities to the public. This group should comprise houses which had in the recent past acted for the principal companies whose shares would have to be sold: (1) the house having the closest connection with each particular company should take the lead in each case; (2) if, in the case of any smaller company, a house outside the group had particular connections, that house should be included in the group for that particular business; and (3) the group should use the services of the leading brokers in this class of business. In short, the Governor wrote, 'I think it most important that the operation should be handled so far as possible on ordinary market lines and by the people who have most experience in this line of business',[64] advice which was accepted.

While the Governor was engaged in consultations in the City,[65] the Chancellor conferred with the Minister of Supply. On 1 April 1953 Sandys replied to Butler that while there would be political danger in the government's appearing to approach private buyers for the steel companies' shares before the bill reached the statute book, it would be quite a different matter if the City began making preparations on its own account. His view was that 'it is very necessary for the Issuing Houses to get moving as quickly as possible . . . [but] the operation should, as far as possible, be represented at this stage as a City rather than a Government initiative'. A copy of this letter was handed to the Governor on the following day, and he fully concurred.[66]

The City was now to steam ahead with preparations. On 8 April 1953 the Governor sent memoranda to a list of the eight issuing houses which were to constitute the consortium, and on 9 April the Governor, the Deputy Governor, and the Chief Cashier met with representatives of the houses: Morgan Grenfell; Barings; Rothschilds; Schröders; Lazards; Hambros; Helbert, Wagg; and Robert Benson, Lonsdale. The Governor made the point that 'the sale of shares in iron and steel companies was a Government policy decision and it had to be made a success; there was need for the full City machinery to be used for this purpose, if only in the interests of the City itself'.[67] David Colville of Rothschilds found this argument unacceptable and he made this clear, probably at the meeting and certainly in a memorandum later sent to the other representatives:

This whole matter is far too political. Nationalisation was a spiteful act, carried through without a mandate, and denationalisation is being effected to redeem a party pledge. The City is much best [*sic*] kept out of politics.

What the Bank of England is in fact doing is to use its influence in the City, acting as the nationalised agent of a Government controlled by a political party, to obtain the support of private enterprise to help implement the election promises of that party. In effect, private enterprise is being suborned by a nationalised institution for political ends and the Bank is, moreover, seeking to throw the whole political onus and possible loss on the City, without taking either risk or responsibility.[68]

Colville would probably not have received much support at the meeting for these views. As far as can be ascertained, the more general view there and elsewhere was that it was important for the steel companies to be returned to private ownership. But everyone agreed that the operation would be very complex and difficult, although the Governor thought things were immeasurably better than they might have been the previous summer. But he did feel he ought to convey to the Chancellor the feelings of the issuing houses, writing on 14 April 1953 that 'One or two judges with many years of experience have told me that it looks like the most difficult task with which they have ever been faced.'[69]

It was probably inevitable that Morgan Grenfell would now take the lead. By this time they were the major 'steel house' amongst the accepting and issuing houses; Bicester and Erskine had a great deal of technical knowledge about steel, as did one of the younger members of Morgans, J. E. H. Collins. 'All the great steelmasters were constantly in and out' of Morgan Grenfell's offices and Collins made repeated and extended visits to their works.[70] Bicester and Erskine had worked on a number of issues for several of the steel companies in the 1930s and 1940s, and it was presumably because of his expertise (and energy) that Erskine had been asked by the Bank early on to form part of its secret working party. The decision that the issue for each company would be led by the house which was its usual merchant banker was a further reason for Morgans' lead. Morgans had on their clients list six steel companies, including five of the largest: United Steel, John Summers, South Durham, Colvilles, Dorman Long, and Stewarts & Lloyds (the last named jointly with Helbert, Wagg). As Bicester put it to the Governor, Morgans were getting 'an almost embarrassing lot of this business'; the Governor thought that they would be wise to bring in another house in one or two cases.[71]

On 13 April 1953 the representatives of the eight issuing houses met at 23 Great Winchester Street for their first discussions, with Rufus Smith taking the chair. They formed a subcommittee of five from amongst their number, with Erskine as chairman, to draw up plans for the first issue,[72] and members worked doggedly to sort out the legal and technical problems involved. At the same time Morgan Grenfell were working with United Steel on its sale, as well as on the reorganization of its capital. The Iron and Steel Act became law on 6 May 1953, and on 13 July 1953 the shareholdings of the Iron and Steel Corporation were formally transferred to the Realisation Agency to be returned to private ownership. (The Minister of Supply would later write to Sir Archibald Forbes, then of the Iron and Steel Board, that 'I need hardly say how glad I am that you are now relieving me of this awkward child.')[73]

The unscrambling of the steel industry began with the private sale of Templeborough Rolling Mills to its former owners.[74] When reporting this on 8 August 1953 *The Economist* made two accurate predictions of how the first public issue in the autumn would be organized: that preferential treatment would be given to investors who had held steel shares on vesting day (1 January 1951); and that investors would have the option of paying for shares with cash or by tendering a wide list of gilt-edged stocks. (*The Economist* argued that a number of institutional investors had purchased steel shares before nationalization as a cheap back door into gilt-edged stocks, for which steel shares had been exchanged.)

Back in early April Morgan Grenfell had assumed that the reorganization of United Steel's capital structure, the issue of new securities, and the sale to the public would all take place on 1 October 1953; in the event they were only three weeks out. The summer and early autumn saw some hard bargaining, in particular between Morgans and United Steel on the one hand and Morison and the Realisation Agency on the other. It had been decided that the first public issue was to be United Steel, and the Agency was clearly determined to make it a financial success for the government. While in public ownership United Steel was deemed to have received loans of £8 million from the government for investment; these loans would have to be repaid to the Agency. United Steel also required a further £8 million to finance further investment in the period to 1957. The first decision was to sell to the Agency United Steel's holding in John Summers at the 'takeover' price of 34s. per share, or £5 million. Then came the hard part: how to arrange the capital structure of the firm in a manner which 'would best suit the Company's interests and meet, in so far as it is necessary to meet, Sir John Morison's demand for a substantial profit on the transaction'. Agreement was finally reached on 16 September 1953.[75]

Nevertheless, Morison and the Treasury continued to worry that the government had not driven a hard enough bargain. Morison confided his uncertainty to Erskine, who replied on 13 October 1953:

You mentioned to me that the Treasury are a little apprehensive in case there is a runaway market in United Steel shares after dealings begin on the Stock Exchange resulting in a substantial premium over the issue price. We, ourselves, do not believe that there is much likelihood of this happening. In fact, we are more concerned in the opposite direction in case there may be an absence of sufficient buying orders to maintain the price at a premium over the issue price.[76]

Morgans had good reason to worry. In the previous July the Prudential had warned Erskine and Rufus Smith that the insurance companies *in toto* should not take more than 50% of the steel issues for fear of attack by the Labour Party that they were taking control of the industry, and that the Prudential itself would not take more than one-fifth of that 50%. Further, on the same day as Erskine wrote to Morison, the Sun Insurance Office wrote to Morgan Grenfell that they would accept the underwriting offer of 250,000 shares, but warned that they would probably be sellers if they had to take them up, as they would wish to have only 75,000–100,000 shares as a permanent holding.[72]

Morgans did most of the work of organizing the offer for sale. They had to cope with the *Daily Mail*'s version of investigative journalism, which involved sending a journalist to Brown Knight and Truscott Ltd., the printers of the prospectus, to try to find out how many copies they were printing; as it happened, the worker the journalist asked did not know, and the works overseer knew that he should not divulge anything to anyone.[78] Morgans did not, however, retaliate against the *Daily Mail* by excluding them from the extensive list of newspapers which received commissions for printing the prospectus. A number of newspapers thought that the list should have been even longer: the *Dundee Courier* was not the only paper which wrote to complain about being left out. In due course Morgans analysed how many shares were bought on application forms placed in each newspaper, and the winner by a long way was the *Daily Telegraph*.[79]

Finally, on 23 October 1953, the prospectus for the first steel denationalization issue was published. It was an offer for sale of 14 million £1 ordinary shares of United Steel Companies at 25s. per share.[80] The result was about 52,400 individual applications for a total of approximately 40,389,000 shares. In the sense that the issue was heavily over-subscribed the operation was a triumph for Morgan Grenfell and the consortium. But as Bicester noted in his speech to his shareholders, 'It was a disappointment to the Consortium that in subsequent market dealings the shares fell below the issue price due mainly to an absence of buying orders from institutional investors, very few of whom 'made up' their comparatively small allotments.'[81] The fear of suffering a substantial loss if steel were renationalized by a future Labour government had been too great. Morgans and the consortium had been warned.

In order to avoid criticism the consortium had been asked to keep expenses as low as possible.[82] They received a commission of 6d. per share, which came to £350,000; they were left with £50,952·11.2 after the expenses, which was divided amongst the eight members of the consortium. Morgan Grenfell's share came to just £6,369·1.5, although they also received a fee of £10,000 from United Steel for their help with the reorganization of the company's capital.[83]

The denationalization of United Steel was, of course, the first of many. The year 1954 saw a number of other steel issues, as Bicester described them for his shareholders:

In the early months of 1954 progress was rendered extremely difficult by the lack of response to the Lancashire Steel Corporation Limited's offer made in January and the shares of that Company and The United Steel Companies Ltd both fell to substantial discounts under the issuing prices. The turning point was, however, reached in June when the shares of Stewarts & Lloyds were successfully sold back to the public and thereafter each subsequent issue met with increased success culminating in the first few days of 1955 with the overwhelming response to the Colvilles Ltd offer of 10,000,000 Ordinary Shares of £1 each at 26/- per share when 150,000 applications were received for a total of approximately 130,000,000 shares.

The Offers for Sales of shares in the large Steel Companies continued to be handled by the Consortium of Bankers; the Company [Morgan Grenfell] acted as joint leading house for each of the offers made in 1954 except in the case of Lancashire Steel where the Consortium was led by Schröders.

The offers were for Stewarts & Lloyds, John Summers & Sons, and Dorman Long.[84]

It had been decided early on to concentrate in the first instance on the denationalization of six of the largest steel companies; this stage was completed in January 1955 when Morgans led the consortium in sponsoring the offer for sale of Colvilles. The issuing houses then decided that the machinery of the consortium was unnecessarily elaborate in the case of the smaller steel companies and it was dissolved. It was decided that each issuing house should separately underwrite the offers for sale of the companies for whom they were accustomed to act, and Barings, Lazards, and Hambros each sponsored issues, with Hambros sponsoring two. In view of the progress made with the sales of equity capital the Realisation Agency also decided to make a start with the prior charge capital. In May 1955 Morgan Grenfell underwrote the offer for sale of 10 million of equal amounts of preference shares and debenture stock of the English Steel Corporation.[85]

In 1957 Morgans were part of the consortium which organized the denationalization of The Steel Company of Wales, which was at the time the largest equity issue ever made in the City (40 million £1 ordinary shares at par). But 1957 was also notable in that the bank resumed its former relationship with a number of steel firms, underwriting an issue of 6 million ordinary shares for United Steel, and further issues for Colvilles and the South Durham Iron and Steel Company the following year. Morgans acted for United Steel again in 1961, when they made a rights issue, and in 1963 when United Steel joined Acme Steel of Chicago in acquiring Gerrard Industries, one of its customers, which made tensional steel strappings and wire-tying machines.[86]

But unknowingly at the time, the 1963 transaction was the last time Morgans acted for United Steel, and the relationship which had lasted for thirty years came to an end. United Steel did not go elsewhere for advice, but they engaged in no further transactions before 1967, when the Labour government carried through the operation which the industry and City had feared in 1953. The 1967 Act to renationalize the steel industry followed the pattern of the 1949 Act, in that the shares of the individual companies were held by a government holding company. But two years later the government took powers to transfer the assets of the companies to the new British Steel Corporation and to wind up the companies. Thus in the end a public corporation owned and worked the plants directly, in the manner of the gas, electricity, and railway industries.[87]

For many in the City, this was a dispiriting end to the saga of steel denationalization, and that is perhaps one reason why it has been almost entirely forgotten, both by the City and by Morgan Grenfell. Yet, expressed in a later terminology, this was the first great privatization; the Act to denationalize road haulage received the royal assent a month before the Iron and Steel Act, but its return to private ownership was not through the medium of the Stock Exchange.[88] There was no precedent for the scale of steel denationalization, and Morgan Grenfell, and in particular Erskine, had to blaze a trail through hitherto uncharted territory.

The Ending of an Era

Erskine, indeed, is remembered as 'the only director who was doing anything' during the early 1950s: the usual directorial hours were eleven to four, and things were run by the general manager.[89] This is perhaps less surprising when the age of the managing directors is considered: Bicester died on 17 February 1956 aged 89, and his son Rufus, then aged 58, succeeded him as chairman; on this date Rennell was 60; Hill-Wood was 55; Erskine himself was 59; and the youngest, Harcourt, was 47 (but he was away on secondment to Washington from 1954 to 1957). In short, the hot blood of youth was conspicuously absent. But this was the case elsewhere, too, as a contemporary observer makes clear:

Banks like Hambros, Baring's, Lazard's, Samuel's, Morgan Grenfell's and others were largely run by the families and associates of the founders. . . . Many of the chief personalities were by then distinctly old men, *vieillards* as the French understand it, in their early eighties or late seventies. But because age was a good deal more fashionable then than now, so were many of the opposite numbers in industry and politics. . . .

Most of the merchant bankers in key positions had been young men at the turn of the century. For example, in 1951, Lord Bicester, the first baron and chairman of Morgan Grenfell, was eighty-four. . . . At Baring's the second senior director, Sir Edward Peacock, was eighty, while the senior director . . . the Hon. Arthur Villiers, was nearly seventy. Lord Kindersley, the first baron and chairman of Lazard's, was eighty, while his colleague, Lord Brand, also the first baron, was seventy-three. Mr Alfred Wagg, one of the creators of Helbert Wagg as a bank . . . was seventy-four.[90]

From this point of view, what *The Times* called the 'inertia of the earlier post-war years'[91] is entirely understandable.

The atmosphere in Morgans in the early 1950s—profitable, with an extensive and distinguished list of clients, but staid and dull—dismayed two of the younger members of the bank, Stephen Catto and J. E. H. Collins (known as Tim); but partly because they were who they were, they were able in due course to effect some changes. Catto was the elder son of Lord Catto; after Eton, Cambridge, and service in the Royal Air Force Voluntary Reserve between 1943 and 1947, he came to Morgan Grenfell in 1948 at the age of twenty-five. He had planned to work in Yule, Catto and came to Morgans for training. He began in the cashier's office, where he helped to write up the accounts by hand; when the time for decision came, he elected to remain in the bank.[92] Tim Collins had had a good war, joining the Royal Navy in 1941 and occupying his time in aiding the partisans in Yugoslavia by 'smuggling people in and out'; he was made an MBE in 1944 and awarded the Distinguished Service Cross in 1945. In 1946 he married the daughter of Rufus Smith; aged twenty-three, he then chose to join Morgan Grenfell rather than his father's fur business in Birmingham. He was immediately sent to Glyn, Mills for two years' training. Upon his return to Morgans he joined Catto on 'the usual round of the office doing all sorts of menial jobs',[93] a method of training future partners and directors which had not changed since the 1920s, when the sons of partners and of their friends and associates began to join the bank.

This round continued until November 1954, when both Catto and Collins were sent abroad for a year. Catto went for six months to an associated firm in Australia and then for another six months to J. P. Morgan & Co. in New York; Collins reversed the process, spending his first six months at J. P. Morgan & Co. and then six months with an associated firm in Canada. When they returned to London at the end of 1955, they felt that Morgan Grenfell was pretty dull, particularly in comparison with J. P. Morgan & Co. They were given senior executive positions, but found it difficult to make any changes, since influence lay largely with the directors. By the end of 1956 they were restless: Morgan Grenfell 'was rather in the trough into which any institution falls when one generation is near to its end and a new generation has not arisen'.[94]

But then their opportunity came. While in Canada, Collins had made a number of 'useful' friends, and at the end of 1956 he was invited to become a director of the Hudson's Bay Company. At that time only directors could be directors of other companies, so Catto and Collins together suggested that they both be made directors. There was some reluctance on the grounds that men in their early thirties were too young:[95] clearly it had been forgotten that Grenfell had become the senior resident partner at 34, Rufus Smith a partner at 32, and Harcourt a director at 30. But in the end the older men agreed, and Catto and Collins both became managing directors on 1 July 1957.

They set about trying to extend Morgan Grenfell's business, and in particular they wanted to develop the banking business. In 1958 the authorities released all advances from restrictions and a period of explosive growth followed. Advances by accepting houses increased by almost 450% between 1958 and 1963,[96] and the younger directors wanted Morgans to have their share. Under their impetus both lending and deposits increased sharply between 1957 and 1962; unfortunately, banking profits did not always rise in line. In 1957 income from interest (and discount) on advances totalled £274,068, while interest paid on deposits totalled £194,085, leaving £79,983. In 1961 both shot up, with interest received totalling £457,102 and interest paid totalling £332,700 —an income of £124,402. The following year both interest received and interest paid surged ahead: interest received nearly doubled to £836,007, while interest paid more than doubled to £778,506. But the result was an income which had plunged to less than half the previous year's, to £57,501.[97] Clearly, much remained to be learnt.

Morgan Grenfell lacked sufficient staff trained in banking because it continued to concentrate on investment and corporate finance. Arranging and underwriting issues for companies and giving them advice and assistance was a very lucrative, if somewhat erratic, business, and most of the energy of the directors and managers during the 1950s was concentrated on this work. Indeed, the New Issues Department (as it was called) provided the scope for the development of a manager's expertise to such an extent that a player became a gentleman. This was very much an augury, and not only for Morgan Grenfell. All over the City in this period the old generation began to give way to the new, and the new, more often than not, was unrelated to the old. New types of business were growing, and new types of people were required.

Kenneth Barrington, who was certainly a gentleman if not a director, worked his way up the hierarchy in Morgans, a hierarchy which in effect had a fork in it, so that a man went either to the left and became a manager or to the right and became a director; the jump was rarely made from manager to director. Indeed, the memory within Morgans is that Barrington was the first to make the leap (although Erskine had done the same, since he had acted as company secretary for ten years before becoming a managing director).[98] Barrington began in the accounts department before the war, and upon his return from active service the bank sent him away to do his accountancy articles, with a view to his returning to take over as company secretary and chief accountant. It was in his chief accountant's office that much of the planning of new issues was done in the early 1950s.[99] He worked closely with Erskine on the denationalization of steel, and he and K. F. Chadwick, another manager, acted as joint secretaries to the issuing houses' Sub-Committee on Steel.[100] He is given much of the credit for building up the corporate finance business during the 1950s,[101] and this is supported by the anecdote told about his election to a managing directorship:

There was a meeting scheduled with a major client and when he arrived he was met by two partners who suggested that they begin. The client asked 'Isn't Mr Barrington coming to the meeting?' and the partners said 'Yes, but there's no need to wait for him.' And the client said 'Well, actually, I'd rather wait until Mr Barrington is here.' And they all thought about that and decided that if clients were going to ask for Mr Barrington he'd better be a partner rather than a manager.[102]

The fact that in this story the directors are still called partners gives a clue to the atmosphere within the bank. Barrington's accession heralded a profound change in both the atmosphere and the way of doing things, which together constituted a new corporate culture. The year of his directorship, 1961, was a turning-point: the nature of Morgan Grenfell's business changed, the type of people joining at the executive and directorial level of the bank changed, and, finally, the scale of activity and profits began to rise. The year 1961 signalled the end of drift: the problems which the bank was to face in the next quarter-century stemmed rather from rapid growth.

CHAPTER SEVEN

DOMESTIC RESURGENCE
1961–1981

AFTER the years of drift came the years of acceleration. In 1961 Morgan Grenfell was poised on the brink of profound and continuing change. The partnership culture would give way to one more in tune with a fast-developing bank; the structure of the bank itself would change; investment management would be brought back to life from a state resembling suspended animation; corporate finance would enter a period of relative decline in comparison with a growing and invigorated banking division, although it would be increasingly profitable by the end of this period; and the bank would expand its operations overseas, having by 1981 an international presence and reputation. This would all require new and different types of people—staff numbers would double, and then double again—and new infusions of capital. Not surprisingly, some of these developments were more successful than others. Joint ventures overseas were not notably successful, and an imaginative attempt to provide venture capital for film-making lured the bank into financial deep water. But Morgan Grenfell saved itself by its own efforts, and indeed went from strength to strength. By May 1981, the date of its final separation from Morgan Guaranty (the product of a merger between J. P. Morgan & Co. and the Guaranty Trust Company in 1959), it was clearly one of the top merchant banks in London, with a reputation for energy and innovation second to none.

A Changing Corporate Culture

In 1961 Morgan Grenfell still retained its traditional atmosphere. In spite of its having been a limited company since 1934, the directors were still referred to as partners, and the traditional yawning gulf remained between the directors and the rest of the bank; nevertheless, it was a 'most relaxed and happy place'.[1] Certain restrictions remained in force: men were still not allowed to smoke in the office during banking hours, nor could they be seen by the clients drinking tea at their desks; such activities could only take place downstairs. The men, however, could at least wear their own clothes—the women (always referred to as ladies) had to wear overalls. The wearing of such overalls had been required before the war, but had tapered off thereafter. Those women who had worked in the bank before 1945 continued to wear them (they were green), but new staff members joining the firm after the war did not, presumably because of clothes rationing. However, one day about 1949, Lord Harcourt visited the offices of the Legal and General Assurance Company, and much admired the (to him) smart overalls the female employees wore. Decisions were taken, and in about 1950 each female employee of Morgan Grenfell was measured for, and in due course received, two pairs of buttoned and belted, burgundy-coloured overalls. Thereafter, no female employee was allowed into the banking hall without her overalls on. By the 1960s the style and colour had changed, becoming either blue or green nylon wrapover overalls which tied at the back, akin to those of a greengrocer. But their life was coming to an end, fading out sometime in the mid to late 1960s.[2]

By choice, their death should be dated autumn 1967, since this date marked a fundamental change in the bank, both in structure and personnel. Until then the bank was essentially run by the general manager, Wilfred Drew, and the managers under him. The directors decided strategy and took the decisions, but the managers executed the decisions and ran the bank, hiring the staff and dealing with administration. Directors and managers had separate dining-rooms,[3] and, in short, the arrangements appear to have resembled the army. Virtually everyone started at the bottom, but clearly there were differences: there were the officer-cadets, such as Stephen Catto and Tim Collins, there were the non-commissioned officers who climbed the hierarchy to become managers, and there were the other ranks. It took a combination of extraordinary talent and energy to cross the line, and only four had succeeded in the hundred and twenty years or so since Morgan Grenfell had been founded.

Morgan Grenfell were not alone in making changes in the 1960s. A number of merchant banks in the City moved from partnerships as a decision-making form to a functional organization: the new era of freedom in international trade meant new business opportunities, and these often involved repetitive financial transactions which could be more usefully organized by department; in addition, financial markets were evolving into new and often complicated forms, and these required increasingly specialized skills. Indeed, Morgans (and Lazards) were rather behind many of the others in making such organizational changes.[4]

During 1965 the bank employed Associated Industrial Consultants to prepare a report on the organization of the office, and they recommended changes in management systems, departmental responsibilities, and deployment of staff, and the introduction of modern equipment. Consequently, in 1966 departments were grouped under the headings of Banking, Investments, Issues, and Administration, with each group being responsible to a separate manager; data-processing equipment was installed in January 1967.[5]

But these changes, while functionally useful, did nothing about the gap between the officers and the non-commissioned officers. This gap was eliminated by changes introduced in 1967, probably because of the results of recruitment policies in effect since 1962. In April of that year Charles Rawlinson, an experienced chartered accountant, joined the bank, the first of a growing number of professionally qualified recruits. Such men would naturally expect to have the opportunity to rise to the top of any organization for which they worked, and if prevented from doing so by outmoded restrictions, would eventually leave. If the bank was to attract and keep the qualified staff it required for its new ventures, it would have to give them the opportunity to become directors. Indeed, in September 1964 this was recognized, and D. E. Bernard and E. P. Chappell, who had joined Morgans from Oxford, and D. A. Pease, also an Oxford graduate, who came to Morgans from the investment house John Govett and Partners, all became managing directors. But it was also eventually recognized that the path which they had followed should be open to everyone and openly so. Thus in 1967 the titles of general manager and manager were abolished, and the new title—and category—of assistant director was established. All the managers were appointed assistant directors, and it became clear that there was only one stream in the bank: anyone who was good enough could become an assistant director, and all assistant directors were eligible to become directors. Coincidentally or not, various changes in personnel also took place: Bicester, Hill-Wood, Rennell, and Erskine all retired as managing directors or directors, and Drew retired as general manager. Lord Harcourt now became chairman, and George Law, a former partner with the City (and the bank's) solicitors Slaughter and May, became a managing director, as did Sidney Eburne and David Berriman, former managers respectively of the Investment and Banking Departments. The remaining managers, K. F. Chadwick, A. S. Chapman, and E. S. Pavitt, became assistant directors, as did W. H. Martin, John Sparrow, and Charles Rawlinson.[6]

There was one other new recruit in 1967, Sir John Stevens, who joined as a managing director on 1 October 1967: there is general agreement that he was one of the most important directors in the history of the bank, and that he drove developments over the subsequent six years. Trained as a solicitor, he had seen war service in Belgium and France (coming out at Dunkirk), and with the Special Operations Executive in Greece and Italy. He then joined the Bank of England as an adviser in 1946, served with the International Monetary Fund in Washington from 1954 to 1956, was an executive director of the Bank of England from 1957 to 1964, and then Economic Minister in Washington from 1965 to 1967. Harcourt, too, had been in Washington from 1954 to 1957 (also as Economic Minister), and they continued a friendship which had been cemented by the war.

Harcourt was responsible for actually inviting Stevens to join Morgan Grenfell. Well aware that management changes would have to be made, he apparently felt unable to effect these on his own. Further, there was a big age-gap between the older partners and the younger men, and Harcourt deemed Stevens a suitable person to fill the gap. Stevens had been one of three candidates mooted to become Governor of the Bank of England in 1966 after Lord Cromer, but he had lost out to Sir Leslie O'Brien, and he may well have felt that there was nothing further for him at the Bank. Whatever the facts of the matter, the outcome gave satisfaction to both the Bank and Morgans. Stevens kept his close association with the Bank; he became a non-executive director while at Morgans and called at the Bank daily, continually talking things over with the Governor. Morgans for their part had acquired one of the most distinguished men in City life as future chief executive and chairman.[7]

One attraction of Stevens for Morgans was that he was a banker, and above all an international banker, since Morgans still wished to increase the banking side of their business. By 1963 the growth in their money market activity had meant that the balance sheet had grown to a record £86 million, an increase of £34 million over the previous year. Visits were made to banks on the Continent to foster relationships, and profits on foreign exchange transactions were beginning to rise, even if from the rather low figure of £15,000 in 1962 to the only slightly more impressive figure of £25,000 in 1963. Acceptance credits were extended, and there was a small Treasury operation which consisted of borrowing and matching loans against deposits. Managers 'did the money', arranging the distribution of the firm's surplus cash, primarily by placing it in the discount market overnight. Partners from the discount houses, dressed in their top hats, called on Morgans each day to discuss the rate the discount houses were paying for money. Morgans would already have an idea of their own position—whether money was required and should be 'called off the street', or whether they were long on money and could place more funds with the houses. Morgans had also begun cautiously using the inter-bank market. Cautiously, because the older directors disliked 'borrowing' funds from another bank, although they were quite willing to lend them. But by about 1965 the bank decided that a real effort had to be made to develop the banking business further.[8]

It was the financial consequences of this drive for growth which caused growing concern in the Bank of England. The Bank was concerned about Morgans' weak and old-fashioned management and a lack of leadership at the very top. It was also more and more concerned about the adequacy of the bank's capital, since they were, in the eyes of the authorities, very highly geared. Gearing was defined as the ratio between deposits (or money borrowed by the bank) minus reserves, and the capital base, which consisted of shareholders' capital plus reserves minus fixed assets such as buildings. Deposits were re-lent or invested, so the real concern was, what multiplier of Morgans' capital was being lent? The gearing ratio in 1960 was 5.5, in 1961 it was 6.4, in 1962 it was 12.9, in 1963 it was 41.2, in 1964 it was 51.4, in 1965 it was 78, and in 1966 it was 75.[9] The Bank kept urging Morgans to do something about this, but these figures support the Bank's contention that Morgans took little notice. (The occasions for these strictures were the yearly visits by Morgans' chairman, Bicester, to the Governor, when the two of them would discuss the previous year's balance sheet.)[10] One answer in May 1967 was to have a rights issue, which raised the capital to £4 million. But, in general, Morgans argued that because they were only doing first-class business, lending in particular to other banks, there was very little risk, and therefore they were justified in having a higher gearing on this capital. Certainly the feeling was that the Bank accepted this argument.[11]

Because of the secretiveness of merchant banks during that period it is difficult to get a clear pictures of the habits of other banks and how their gearing compared with Morgans'. Some work has been done on the published accounts of a few merchant banks, however. In 1968, for example, according to the published accounts, Morgans' gearing was 20.7, while that of Lazards was 16.9, of Warburgs 6.1, of Hambros 15.6, of Hill Samuels 11.6, of Kleinworts 12.6, and of Schröders 17.2. On the other hand, with regard to advances as a percentage of deposits in 1968, Morgans' was the lowest at 27, while Lazards' was 56.4, Warburgs' was 63.9, Hambros' was 37.7, Hill Samuels' was 45.2, Kleinworts' was 56.3, and Schröders' was 45.7. Morgans, in other words, were very prudent; a substantial proportion of deposits was held in liquid form, such as gilts and overnight money in bank accounts.[12]

Whatever other merchant banks were doing at the time, Morgans' approach certainly led to a growth in profits, which increased by $16\frac{1}{2}\%$ in 1966, by 64% in 1967, and by 41% in 1968 (Appendix IV). Most of this was due to decisions taken before Stevens joined the bank, and included the purchase in September 1964 of The United Leasing Corporation Limited, the basis of Morgans' continuing business in leasing. (It was through this company that David Berriman and John Sparrow joined Morgan Grenfell.) Nevertheless, Stevens recognized that the foundation of Morgan Grenfell's financial strength, their overwhelming dominance of the fixed interest market, was under threat: the British government was borrowing most of the long-term money available and there was little left with which to finance industry through the medium of fixed-interest loans. This, together with accelerating inflation, was causing interest rates to rise. Stevens therefore decided Morgans must change and develop, or die.[13]

Two Financial Disasters

Yet, before he had a chance to do much, Morgans got itself into a quagmire of appalling proportions: the bank was involved in providing venture capital, and became involved in the business of financing films. In the summer of 1967, one of the senior directors at Morgans had the producer Dimitri de Grunwald to lunch in the bank. De Grunwald had devised a novel way of financing films, and he came to Morgans for backing. The most popular method during the 1960s was for one major distributor to provide the finance for a film in return for the right to distribute it throughout the world. The guarantee could then be discounted at a commercial bank and the proceeds used to produce the film. This meant in practice, however, that the distributor (as distributor and usually, in addition, as cinema owner) received the lion's share of the profits; further, most of the big distributors were American and thus the return on most films remained in the US. De Grunwald proposed to set up an International Film Consortium of many distributors, each of whom would guarantee a small proportion of the total cost of the film in return for controlling the distribution in his own territory. Morgan Grenfell agreed to back him.[14]

In theory the scheme was a good one. It involved going to distributors and saying that a film on a specific subject with specific actors was going to be made, and obtaining the distributor's agreement that he provide a certain percentage of the cost. When enough distributors to cover the cost of the film had been signed up, the film-making could go ahead. In July 1968 the announcement was made that distributors in thirty-three countries were members of the Consortium, and Morgans between 1968 and 1970 advanced £3 million to finance ten films. The money was lent to a Bahamas-based company called Films International, 45% of which was owned by Morgans and its associates, and which was administered by the Trust Corporation of the Bahamas, of which Morgans were a major shareholder. Films International then lent the money to the individual producers to make the films. London Screenplays was the management company which developed the screenplays and then transferred them to each of the film production companies; it was financed on an overdraft from Morgans. De Grunwald was the chief executive of London Screenplays, and he and its financial director, Antony Z. Landi, owned 55% of the shares, while Morgans owned 45%.

In April 1969 Morgans set up a syndicate which included three other banks to share in the advance of $11 million to finance six films; they were the First Wisconsin National Bank of Milwaukee, Williams & Glyn's Bank Limited, and Roywest Banking Corporation Limited, with First Wisconsin taking $\frac{2}{11}$ and the others $\frac{3}{11}$ interest each. Later in the year, in order to ensure US distribution, Morgans signed an agreement with the Winthrop Lawrence Corporation whereby it would distribute all London Screenplays' films in the US; the corporation was part of the interests of Lammot Du Pont Copeland, Jr., son of the DuPont chairman, who had been introduced to Morgans by de Grunwald. He and Winthrop Lawrence jointly guaranteed, essentially, half the risk. Finally, London Screenplays took out insurance against cost overruns with a completion guarantor called Film Finances.[15]

The venture initially went well. The first film with which Morgans were involved was a Western called *Shalako*, starring Sean Connery and Brigitte Bardot, whose earnings, over many years, succeeded in covering its costs. But things gradually started to go very wrong. First of all, the whole basis of Morgans' providing film finance was that money would only be made available against firm guarantees by distributors. As it turned out,

The organisation used to obtain such guarantees (outside the U.S. and U.K.) was Cinexport S.A., a company based in Paris . . . [which] exaggerated the extent to which guarantees had been or were being obtained. Apart from the first film made, 'Shalako', few of the others had a significant part of their cost covered by guarantees when production commenced. Nevertheless, Morgan Grenfell advanced money in respect of such films.[16]

It is true that film makers are often over-enthusiastic about the potential of new film products, and that business people sometimes fail to detect this. Even so, to advance money was not necessarily such a ridiculous thing for Morgans to do as it might seem. When a producer arranged a film, the stars had to be booked in advance and given a precise shooting schedule: it was not generally acceptable merely to indicate that when the money was available, shooting would commence. Therefore, money started flowing out before all of the guarantees were in position: should Morgans have called a halt and sacrificed face, the shooting schedule, the stars, and perhaps the film, losing the $700,000 already invested? Or should they have believed those responsible for obtaining the guarantees when they told Morgans that the guarantees were nearly all in place, and continued to advance funds? Morgans did the latter, and were soon savaged by a film called *Murphy's War*. Everything went wrong: it was being shot in the Amazon Basin with expensive film stars, and first the boat broke down, and then a star broke his ankle; the result was that there was an eventual cost overrun of $1.2 million.[17]

But the real blow came with the bankruptcy in November 1970 of the Winthrop Lawrence Corporation, basically the bankruptcy of Du Pont Copeland, Jr., who had become involved in extensive and unwise land speculation. At a stroke this removed American distribution and the guarantee for half the risk, and as a result Morgans' position 'was changed from that of making advances which were partly secured by guarantees to one where the cover in respect of most of the films became very low'.[18] It also meant that $3,047,000 expected during 1970 by way of discounted promissory notes was not received.[19]

Morgans immediately set about establishing other distribution arrangements in the US, but the receipts for Morgans and the other banks in the syndicate would now depend on the commercial success of the films, rather than on distributors' guarantees. Unfortunately, two of the six films were not commercial successes, as Morgans admitted in a memorandum of 12 February 1971 to the other three banks. (In fact, in the end none of the films was a commercial success.) They recognized their responsibility as the organizer of the syndicate, and proposed a plan whereby the loans.would be deemed to be interest-free from 31 December 1970, but that the proceeds from all the films—not just those for which the syndicate had provided advances—should go first to the other three banks. Receipts would eventually flow in, and it was hoped that the plan would minimize the chances of the banks' losing any of the principal of their loans. The other banks, however, were not impressed, and made a counter-proposal: Morgans should immediately repay to the other members of the syndicate 'all the amounts advanced by the other banks under the six Agreements to Films International together with interest outstanding to the date of repayment'. The banks would then re-lend the same amount to Morgans for twelve months. Indeed, one of the three banks, First Wisconsin, threatened to sue Morgans for negligence for not exercising stronger control over the costs. The upshot was that Morgans refused the offer of a loan from the three banks, repaid them in full on 28 April 1971, and took all of the loans on to their own books.[20]

By May 1971, only $7 million (£2.90 million) of the $23 million (£9.58 million) advanced had been recovered; it was estimated that a further $11 million (£4.58 million) was probably collectable. Morgan Grenfell set up a network of film distribution companies under the management of Michael Flint and John Smith, the intention of which was to maximize the receipts. The advances were optimistically shown on the books as good loans, but Morgans never recovered as much as they had hoped, and in the end their losses were substantial.[21]

Films International was not Morgans' only worry in the spring of 1971: they were also caught in the bankruptcy of Rolls-Royce. In March 1968 Rolls-Royce had contracted with the Lockheed Aircraft Corporation in the US to supply 450 engines for the new wide-bodied civil aircraft which Lockheed was building, the Tri-Star. The engine, called the RB211, utilized new materials as well as the most advanced technology. Under the contract with Lockheed, Rolls-Royce promised to begin delivery in 1971 at a fixed price of £354,000 per engine. Morgans were one of thirteen members of a syndicate, managed by Lazards, which was providing Rolls-Royce with a revolving acceptance credit of £20 million. On 29 April 1970 this facility had been extended for a further year, at which point Lazards had assured both Morgans and Barings that the company was a safe proposition to which to lend for another year. Unfortunately, the cost of developing Rolls-Royce's RB211 engine had nearly doubled, and the company would suffer a loss on every engine it sold. On 17 September 1970 Rolls-Royce warned the Ministry of Technology and the Bank of England of probable difficulties.[22]

The initial response of the Ministry was to produce a financial plan which called for large sums to be made available by the City and the government, but on 23 September Lord Poole, the chairman of Lazards, told the Deputy Governor of the Bank that this plan was not viable. On 28 September Poole asked the Governor if all the lenders could be warned about the situation, but the Governor refused, since he wanted first to talk again to the government. On 12 October a meeting at the Bank was held to brief the two clearers and the insurance company involved—the Midland, Lloyds, and the Prudential Assurance Company; and finally, on 14 October 1970, the members of the syndicate were called to the Bank and informed of Rolls-Royce's difficulties. The company had estimated that the total costs of developing the engine would be £65.5 million, but it now emerged that the more likely cost would be £137.5 million; because it was a fixed price contract, the cost of manufacturing the engine would mean a loss to the company of £60 million. Rolls-Royce's auditors were insisting that provision be made for this loss, and this would eliminate all of its reserves and produce a deficit of £20 million. The government was insisting that the £60 million would have to be found in the City, but the attitude of the clearers and the insurance company was entirely negative, although discussions with the government were continuing.[23] These produced a new plan, but the accepting houses in the syndicate found it quite unsatisfactory, largely because their advances would appear to rank below those of the clearers for repayment. However, at a meeting at the Bank of England on 10 November 1970 attended by the Deputy Governor,

it was made very clear that if we [the syndicate] were prepared to contemplate withdrawing our facilities or seek a date for repayment or in any way disturb the arrangement which had been made by the Clearers and the Government, then we would have to stand the consequences which were likely to be far more onerous to us than to the other lenders. It was eventually agreed by all the Acceptance Houses, after a considerable debate, that they had no choice but to continue their participation in the Acceptance for as long as was necessary.[24]

But this attempt to keep Rolls-Royce from going under was doomed to failure: on 3 February 1971 the chairman of Lazards informed the syndicate that Rolls-Royce had decided that the money made available to them by the government and the clearers would not be sufficient to complete the RB211 contract, and that they proposed to appoint a receiver. At a meeting later that day at the Bank of England, the Governor and Lord Poole bluntly informed the members of the syndicate that it was highly unlikely that the acceptance houses would get any of their money back.[25] Negotiations were put in train, but the outlook was very bad, and Morgans that year made a provision of £1.125 million against the Rolls-Royce loss. However, this story eventually had a happy ending: by June 1973 it was clear that Morgans would be repaid the principal (£1.5 million) in full, plus interest at 5% up to the time of the liquidation.[26]

Nevertheless, in the spring of 1971 Morgans had been hit, virtually simultaneously, by two financial disasters, Films International and Rolls-Royce, and over the year steps were taken to contain the damage. Provision was made for bad debts, to the order of nearly £3 million in 1970 and over £5 million in 1971. In 1970 the losses wiped out the contingencies (inner) reserve; an exercise was undertaken to revalue various assets, such as the bank's buildings, and this enabled the reserve to be increased to half the 1969 level. Indeed, by December 1971 the reserve was slightly higher than in 1969.[27] In November 1971 Morgans borrowed £3 million for five years from the National Westminster Bank, and this was treated as loan capital (in January 1976 it was extended for a further seven years).[28] But in order to ensure that lack of financial controls would not again be a problem, the bank set up a credit committee. This was a director-level, formal committee, whose purposes were to ensure that credit decisions were properly researched, to formalize the keeping of proper records of the decisions made, and to ensure that everyone was aware of the obligations entered into by the bank. At the same time, Stevens invited David Keys, then at the Bank of England, to join Morgans: 'very experienced and tough and unsentimental', Keys's role was to ensure that no important commitment of funds was made without proper research.[29] Indeed, the bank became so risk-averse that they were caught neither by the property crash and secondary banking crisis in 1974, when in fact they were a net provider of funds, nor by the collapse in shipping later in the decade.[30]

Finally, a restructuring of the bank's capital seemed required. It was decided that the best way to do this was to superimpose a new company over the existing company: the obligations of the old company, Morgan Grenfell & Co., would be left with the bank, while the capital would be paid up into the new company, Morgan Grenfell Holdings Limited. This would enable the best possible gloss to be put on the accounts, and it had tax advantages. On 24 November 1971 the new company was incorporated, and on 31 December, at an Extraordinary General Meeting, the offer by the new company to acquire the whole of the issued share capital of Morgan Grenfell & Co. Limited was accepted. At the meeting of the bank board on the same day, Harcourt and Collins resigned as chairman and vice-chairman respectively; Harcourt then became chairman of Morgan Grenfell Holdings, and Stevens became chairman and chief executive of Morgan Grenfell & Co., still the name of the bank (now the wholly owned subsidiary of Holdings). The existing managing directors (who included Charles Rawlinson, Christopher Reeves, and John Sparrow, all of whom had become managing directors on 1 January 1970, and Guy Weston, who had become a managing director in June 1971) became directors of Holdings. At the same time, the managing directors became executive directors of the bank; they were joined as executive directors by David Bendall, Henry Gorell Barnes, Blaise Hardman, Eric Pavitt, and Bryan Pennington. On the whole, Morgan Grenfell & Co., and Morgan Grenfell Holdings Limited were virtually the same organization, although as other activities developed, the bank in practice, as well as in theory, became but one of several subsidiaries of the holding company, although the dominant one.[31]

The role of the Bank of England in all of this was less than has been supposed in Morgan Grenfell. Certainly the Bank was concerned: but because Stevens had been employed to turn Morgans around, and because the Bank had such confidence in him, the Bank assumed that things would work out. The memory in Morgans was that the Bank was doing its best to force Morgans to merge with another house; but there is apparently no evidence for this in the files of the Bank of England, and, indeed, the then Governor 'do[es] not remember that the troubles of Morgan Grenfell at that time were so great that the danger of a link up with another House was present in [his] mind'.[32] In other words, the Bank was not acting as a marriage broker: rather, it was saying *nihil obstat*.[33]

There were a number of discussions with other institutions, but even without Morgans' difficulties, this would not have been a matter of overwhelming surprise in the City. Mergers had been fashionable for a decade amongst financial institutions, including the accepting houses, and conversations were frequent and recurring. Morgans had been 'flirting' with Barings for twenty years about merging—they were 'our sort of people'—but it was apparently all gentlemen's club talk.[34] There was also discussion about the possibility of doing something with Lloyds Bank, or with other British institutions.[35] In 1972 Kenneth Keith, then head of Hill Samuel (itself the product of mergers in 1959 between Philip Hill, Higginson, and Erlangers, in 1965 between Philip Hill and M. Samuel, and in 1969 between Hill, Samuel and Noble Lowndes), approached Lord Shawcross, who telephoned John Meyer of Morgan Guaranty in

New York to say that Keith had suggested that Morgan Guaranty should use their influence to engineer a merger between Hill Samuel and Morgan Grenfell so that Hill Samuel could take over the management.[36] One set of discussions which were serious, however, were those with Robert Fleming and Co. in 1973.

There was great concern within Morgans about the fund management side of the bank, which had for years been run by Hill-Wood (until his retirement in 1967). Although Morgans had some prestigious clients, such as part of the Ford pension fund, the business was not profitable, and Stevens nearly sold it off. Flemings, conversely, were very strong as an investment management house, with five times the amount under management that Morgans had, while they were weak in corporate finance, one of Morgans' strengths. In the end the possibility of a merger foundered because of personality clashes, although Flemings' explanation for rejecting the proposal was that they preferred to keep their own character. When the full merger did not come off, there was talk about hiving off Morgans' fund management section and selling it to Flemings, but in the end it was decided to retain it and make it profitable.[37]

Development of Investment Management

Pease and Eburne were put in charge, with instructions to make it profitable and make it grow. The problem was that it had originated as a service to clients, rather than as a profit centre; there was of course a difference between performance for clients and profitability for the bank, and the prevailing view was that there was very little one could do about profitability. In 1975 Eburne took early retirement to move into the public sector: the Crown Agents were in grave difficulties, and Morgans had been invited to advise them. A senior person was needed actually to take up residence and sort things out, and in fact Eburne became its head. Pease left the Investment Division but maintained contact with several of the private clients, and Sparrow took over full responsibility for investment management in March 1975, with a remit to make it profitable or to shut it down. The first thing he did was to insist that fees be raised; this caused more than a little apprehension in the division that there would be a mass exodus of clients. Finally, one adviser suggested a rise to one client, who not only did not object, but admitted that he had been wondering for some time why Morgans had not raised their fees long before. This response, of course, encouraged the others in the division, and the general rise in fees and consequent rise in profitability

apparently unleashed an acute but previously suppressed business sense.
The economic environment changed as well—the *Financial Times* Share
Index reached its low on the day Sparrow was asked to take over
investments, and then a bull market began—and that year the Investment Division made its first ever profit.

As head of the Investment Division, Sparrow was assisted by Patrick
Dawnay and, in particular, by Henry Gorell Barnes. Gorell Barnes had
been head of the Investment Research Department under Pease and
Eburne, and was notable for analysing the business he was conducting as
a business. The decision was taken to concentrate on managing funds for
corporations, and consequently Sparrow decided to sell Morgans' unit
trusts to Gartmore Fund Management. Another important decision was
to exploit the opportunity to manage funds for non-residents, particularly for Americans who wanted to invest funds overseas, and who
presumably would turn to London for advice and skills. In 1974 the
Employee Retirement Income Security Act (ERISA) became law,
thereby permitting US pension funds to invest abroad, and Morgans
decided at the beginning of 1976 to set up a vehicle to offer investment
services to such clients. Sparrow and Christopher Whittington spent a
measurable amount of time during the year negotiating with the US
authorities over their requirements for such a company, and finally,
in November 1976, Morgan Grenfell Investment Services came into
existence.

In March 1977 Gorell Barnes succeeded Sparrow as head of the
Investment Division, while Chappell became chairman of Morgan
Grenfell Investment Services (Gorell Barnes became chairman in 1981).
Gorell Barnes built up a team to market Morgans' services throughout
the US, thus putting Morgan Grenfell ahead of the competition. This
marketing drive also had the complementary effect of making Morgan
Grenfell, as an entity separate from the American Morgan firms, con-
siderably better known.[38]

Although the US was the first object of Gorell Barnes's attentions, it
was only one piece of the jigsaw he was attempting to construct. His
ambitions for Morgan Grenfell were international, and this really took
two courses. First of all, he and his team introduced the international
equity product, i.e. managing foreign assets on behalf of US pension
funds. Until the late 1970s these funds had very little invested outside the
US; but Gorell Barnes correctly anticipated the change in legislation
(ERISA) which encouraged US pension funds to look beyond US
equities for investment purposes, and he invested resources over several

years to develop this argument. Several people in the New York office spent all of their time travelling around the US, advising such funds of the range of services which Morgans could provide. The result was that Morgan Grenfell were two years ahead of their competitors when ERISA was passed.

The first US pension fund business came only in 1979, but it rapidly developed, until by the late 1980s Morgan Grenfell were by far the largest non-US-based manager of international assets for such funds. Indeed, this substantially increased the international funds under Morgans' management, and these were then invested in the Japanese and European markets; this allowed an investment infrastructure and depth of knowledge about these markets to be developed which provided the basis for future activities.

A less significant but not unimportant development by Gorell Barnes and his team was the exploitation of the 'captive insurance' market. Rather than pay premiums to insurance companies to insure themselves against product failure or other disasters, large companies themselves began to put aside funds to cover contingencies. Unlike pension fund money, which is equity-orientated, captive or self-insurance money is fixed-income orientated, and in the late 1970s and early 1980s Morgan Grenfell became very rapidly the leading manager of such funds, developing skills and knowledge in international fixed-income funds which led to other developments later.[39]

In Britain, Gorell Barnes increased Morgans' pension fund management business, and by the end of the 1970s Morgans had a 'massive' investment management business. Indeed, by 1984 Morgans had a larger amount under management for UK pension funds than any of the other accepting houses—including Flemings.[40]

Gorell Barnes, one of the architects of modern asset management, represented the new generation of professional investment directors. He re-orientated Morgans away from retail and private client work to institutional money management on behalf of pension funds and insurance companies; at the same time he took the finite resources available and redirected them away from domestic and towards international business. He inspired his colleagues, and his sudden death on 12 November 1983, from a heart attack while shooting, stunned them, as well as many others in the City, in particular since he was only forty-four. Within the bank, his death was seen as a watershed: it symbolized the end of an era in which Gorell Barnes had built up the Investment Division to a level where it was now a fully-fledged part of the bank.[41]

The Growth of Banking: Foreign Exchange, Export and Project Finance

The success of the Banking Division—Stevens's area of expertise—was more immediate, with profits from two main areas, foreign exchange in particular and export or project finance. Indeed, by 1973 these profits (plus the freezing of dividends) had allowed the balance sheet to become so healthy that the Bank of England had ceased to worry over-much about Morgans.[42] Foreign exchange had traditionally been dominated by the accepting houses; indeed, until 1914, 'the market consisted of the accepting houses, plus a few foreign bill brokers who met on the floor of the Royal Exchange'.[43] Improvements in the speed of overseas communications encouraged many other banks and foreign exchange brokers to enter the market after the Second World War, but the accepting houses had a head start. Morgan Grenfell, however, seems not to have put the resources into foreign exchange dealing which would have enabled it to be amongst the leaders, and during the 1960s the foreign exchange department had to be built up from a low base. Stevens developed the foreign exchange dealing operations as well as that for foreign currency dealings. There was an increase of foreign exchange dealings in Eurocurrencies in the later 1960s, but the explosion came in mid-1972. From the end of the Second World War until 1971 the exchange rates of the world's major currencies had been pegged to the dollar, which in turn was pegged to gold at $35 per ounce. In August 1971 the dollar was allowed to float. The unpegging of the dollar of course caused turbulence on all the foreign exchanges. Britain found it increasingly difficult to maintain the rate of the pound and on 25 June 1972, after a week of severe pressure, the pound was allowed to float. Foreign exchange profits could then be made by taking positions in currencies, not just by buying and selling for clients.

Once Stevens had turned his attention to the bank's foreign exchange department, the change in profits had been immediately apparent: in 1967 the profit of the exchange department was £45,627, in 1968 it had doubled to £89,946, and in 1969 more than doubled again, to £203,774. At that point Geoffrey Munn, Patrick McAfee, and E. A. Bradman were invited to join the firm, Munn to develop the foreign exchange business, McAfee to develop a Eurocurrency loan and deposit book, and Bradman (as chief accountant) partly to sort out the foreign exchange books. Bradman discovered that (as often happens) management systems had not kept pace with business developments: there were outstanding unreconciled accounts with Morgan Guaranty Trust Company running to thirty-six pages, and even though Australia had switched from sterling to dollars some years before, the Australian dollar books were still being kept in sterling. By May 1970, however, the books were sorted out, and thereafter kept pace with the trading.[44]

Trading, indeed, increased to such an extent that the major shareholder, Morgan Guaranty, became seriously alarmed (among other things, Morgan Grenfell were making the market in London for Italian lire).[45] In December 1972 Lewis Preston, executive vice-president of Morgan Guaranty, wrote to Stevens that

For some time now several of us have been concerned about the high level of trading done by Morgan Grenfell's Foreign Exchange Department. . . . We have now looked at the forward exposure and are alarmed at both its high level and its rate of growth. . . . While the foreign exchange book is generally in balance as to currencies and maturities, the total exposure of £2,300,000,000 is completely out of line in relation to your capital, total assets, or any other standard. . . . From the standpoint of profitability we think the firm's forward exchange earnings do not justify the exposure. We understand that MG's income from foreign exchange trading in 1972 will be in the £550–560,000 area. . . . It seems clear to us that this level of profits for foreign exchange is not really worth the credit risk taken.[46]

Bradman and McAfee prepared some notes, on the basis of which Stevens wrote an explanatory letter to Preston. First of all, the gross figure of £2,300 million was misleading: Morgan Grenfell used the strict Bank of England definition of forward contract, which was 'any unmatured contract'. Therefore the figure quoted included all unmatured spot deals, as well as short-dated swaps; excluding the former would reduce the total figure by about £500 million. Secondly, the computer presented the figures for accounting purposes by converting to sterling *both sides* of any forward contract which did not involve sterling, and eliminating the double-counting would reduce the total figure by £701 million. And thirdly, there was included in the total figure £15 million of interdepartmental forward contracts, representing swaps done between Morgan Grenfell's foreign exchange and treasury departments. Therefore, the true figure for forward exposure was about £1,050 million. Stevens further revealed that the foreign exchange trading profit for 1972 was in fact rather larger than Morgan Guaranty's figure, namely £690,000. He also added pointedly that 'the Bank of England not only controls our positions against sterling, but also requires a weekly return on totals of all our outstanding contracts. I do not think they would be slow to tell us if they considered we were overtrading.' And finally, virtually all Morgan Grenfell's dealings were with other first-name banks.

Stevens added at the end of the letter that they were concerned at the continual increase and were taking internal steps to reverse direction.[47] This may have been written partly to mollify Preston, but he did indeed institute a review of Morgans' exchange practices to consider to what extent they should pull back. Munn was concerned that while limits on outstandings in foreign exchange business with individual counterparties were desirable, too stringent limits would create considerable problems. They might have to turn down perfectly good business and thereby harm relations with other banks and with clients, and the staff might lose interest if expansion, and possibly profitability, were restricted. Stevens agreed with the first point, but emphasized that 'what fusses me is that we may be in a situation in which we are overtrading without profit —that is, that the size of our profits does not go up and down with the size of your book. . . . Meanwhile, you will damp down activities selectively, as Blaise Hardman suggests, and I will keep my ears open at the Bank of England.'[48] The Bank does not seem to have objected to Morgans' habits, which indeed were not speculative, and profits continued to increase: they were nearly £1.4 million in 1975 and nearly £4.7 million in 1981.[49]

It was in export and project finance, however, that Morgan Grenfell led the field. An early example dates from 1958 when, after two years of negotiation, agreement was reached for a medium-term (ten-year) syndicated cash advance of £2.75 million for Heavy Electricals Private Limited of Bhopal, India, to finance their purchases of machine tools and other goods through Associated Electrical Industries Ltd. in the UK. But Morgans' continuing and active involvement dates from 1968, when it financed a project for Guest Keen and Nettlefolds in Zaïre. Project finance involved the arrangement, possibly from a variety of sources, of the funds necessary to appraise, finance, and construct a large capital project; the security for the loan was often the output of the project itself. When, as was frequently the case, the project was sited overseas, a complex and subtle approach to both finance and diplomacy could be required. Early in the 1970s Morgans began seriously to build up their expertise and contacts, with Stevens recruiting people from the Foreign Office and elsewhere who combined linguistic ability with close knowledge of foreign countries. (One prominent example was Robert Owen, who had a great influence on the development and execution of project finance.) This linguistic and cultural expertise was combined with the financial and deal-making skills of other members of the banking department. The result was a series of prestigious and profitable deals, with Morgans in some years taking a 25% market share of buyer credits, and external recognition, such as when Angus Dunn and Martin Knight wrote a standard work on export finance.

The key to the eagerness of Morgans—as well as of other banks—to become involved in export finance was the subsidies and guarantees for up to 85% of the export value provided by the Export Credits Guarantee Department (ECGD) of the British government. The ECGD guaranteed the loan, so that the exporter and his banker were both assured of payment if the buyer defaulted, whether for commercial reasons or as a result of political upheaval. Further, the ECGD subsidized the rate of interest on the export business financed under the medium-term credit facility; this meant that borrowers were, in the early 1970s, only having to pay $4\frac{1}{2}\%$–$5\frac{1}{2}\%$—very cheap money. The Treasury via the ECGD provided a subsidy or 'interest make-up' equal to the difference between the rate payable to the banks by the overseas buyer and the rate at which the banks were able to obtain funds in the London Interbank Market, plus a profit margin fixed by the ECGD. The whole field was very competitive because it was lucrative.

The British government, as well as other governments, backed export drives in response to the increase in the price of oil. But the price increase meant that the oil-exporting countries had massive surpluses, which were recycled through Western commercial banks, and thus the banks had a great deal of money to lend. Therefore, commercial loans could be easily arranged to go alongside the export credits.[50] But Morgans moved a step beyond organizing such deals: Stevens and Reeves decided that rather than continue to allow the clearing banks to lend the export credits to the overseas buyer, they would take them on to their own balance sheet. Thus, utilizing their deposits, Morgans began to compete with the clearers and lend the money themselves, thus putting on their book loans which had very good margins and were guaranteed by the government.

For many years the dominant position in export finance had been held by Lazards, and most of the big contractors were their clients. Morgans presumably could match Lazards' ECGD expertise, but to wean away these clients something more was needed. Morgans decided that what they could offer was 'country' expertise, using the staff recruited with Foreign Office and World Bank experience and an expanding network of offices. In most of the countries attracting such big projects, the acquiescence if not the actual co-operation of the home government was required. Stevens recruited David Suratgar from the World Bank to build up contacts and relationships with governments, and over the years Morgans took on a financial advisory role to the governments, central banks, or state enterprises of, for example, Pakistan, Chile, Jamaica, Turkey, Barbados, and Trinidad and Tobago. Governments in Africa found their services particularly helpful, and Morgans advised the Sudan, Tanzania, Uganda, Zambia, Botswana, and Zimbabwe. When various governments ran into financial difficulties at the end of the 1970s, Suratgar created a unit within the bank to advise on debt restructuring, and in general to provide borrowing and project finance advice to the international public sector.

Africa was only one of the regions which became of growing importance to Morgans in the 1970s. Stevens was the first to see the possibilities in two other relatively untapped geographical areas—the Soviet bloc and the Middle East. While at the Bank of England, Stevens, who spoke fluent Russian, had been largely instrumental in developing the Bank's links with their opposite numbers in Gosbank, and while at Morgans he was chairman of the East European Trade Council. Morgans became, and continued to be, the dominant export finance house for the USSR, as well as for other East European countries; in November 1977 a representative office was opened in Moscow, in conjunction with Moscow Narodny Bank and the Bank of Scotland. In September 1972, for example, they arranged the first bond issue for a communist country, the US$50 million $8\frac{1}{2}\%$ Bonds 1987 for Hungary, and signed a fiscal agency agreement with the National Bank of Hungary.[51]

Morgans were also prominent in export and project finance for the Middle East, a key area because of the wealth generated by the oil-producing countries. This is an area of the world where personal relationships are extremely important in the development of business, and David Douglas-Home was the principal contact between Morgans and the ruler of Dubai, the first Middle Eastern country for which Morgans acted. In 1969 Morgans financed the Rashid Hospital, and thereafter the bank arranged finance for all of Dubai's major infrastructure projects, beginning with the US$375 million Dubai Aluminium project in 1973. In Oman, where McAfee was the main contact with the Sultan's government, Morgans have since 1973 been the leading banker in financing virtually all of the major Omani projects. Indeed, by the mid-1980s Morgans were dealing with all of the countries of the Gulf Cooperation Council.

One of Morgan Grenfell's biggest projects was not in the Middle East, however, but in Brazil: this was the $2 billion Aço Minas steel complex. The contractor for the complex was Davy Corporation, with whom Morgans repeatedly worked, and they asked Morgans to put together a financial package which would be acceptable to the Brazilian government. A multicurrency package was required, both to facilitate purchases of supplies for the project and to enable Morgans to tap three major money markets—necessary in order to finance the largest project which had, up to then, been attempted. Chase Manhattan Bank led the American syndicate, the Dresdner Bank led the German one, and Morgans led the British. The commercial credits were put together with export credits guaranteed by the ECGD, and the contract was signed in June 1976.[52]

One of the most complex of multinational and multicurrency projects with which Morgans were involved was the Channel Tunnel. Such a scheme was briefly considered by Napoleon in 1802, while in 1872 Rothschilds sponsored an issue of shares in the Channel Tunnel Company, and one and a half miles of tunnel were actually built. However, despite Queen Victoria's support, this project was abandoned; and later schemes met the same fate, either for technical reasons or for fear of rendering the UK defenceless against invasion. It was not until an American group called Technical Studies Inc. was formed in 1957 to study the feasibility of a tunnel and subsequently interested others, that the idea of a Channel tunnel was seriously resuscitated. Morgan Grenfell, represented by Lord Harcourt, formed part of a British group which helped to finance the studies through a syndicate made up of British, French, and American interests called the Channel Tunnel Study Group. When the Heath government came to an agreement with the French to support the construction of a tunnel, Harcourt became chairman of the British Channel Tunnel Company Limited. However, when a Labour government came to power in 1974, the Tunnel project was one of those which they thought merited reconsideration. By late 1974, with the rapid increase in the rate of inflation, the government became acutely worried about the rising costs: money would have to be spent on a railway between London and the Tunnel, for example, and the eventual cost of government loan guarantees was unknown. Therefore, in January 1975, in spite of the fact that most of the land needed had been acquired and a quarter-mile of service tunnel from the UK side already built, the Government withdrew its support. In March, the Department of the Environment informed Harcourt that the obligation of the British and

French Governments to the British Channel Tunnel Company would be discharged by the purchase of all the shares of the British company by the British government.[53]

It was believed at the time of cancellation that the project could be reopened in five or ten years' time when economic circumstances would have improved, and when the Conservative government came to power in 1979, the new Minister for Transport, Norman Fowler, tried to encourage a bid to build a tunnel on a private basis. A consortium of contractors, made up of Balfour Beatty, Taylor Woodrow, and Edmund Nuttall, decided to try to put together a plan, and they brought in Morgan Grenfell as their financial adviser. Morgans put together a classic project-financing arrangement, but it foundered because the government refused to provide any guarantee of fall-back financing and, at that time, no one thought it would be possible to raise £1 billion of equity from the private sector (this was before the big privatisation issues), so by 1982 this attempt had also been abandoned.

The Department of Transport, however, in a bid to sustain a flicker of life, commissioned a group of five commercial banks to do a further feasibility study on financing for a tunnel. In 1984, the Channel Tunnel Group (CTG)—an amalgam of the contractors and banks in the UK who had studied the tunnel project—was put together, with the aim of revitalizing the whole idea in co-operation with their opposite number in France, France Manche. The turning point was the enthusiastic statement in support of a tunnel on 30 November 1984 by Margaret Thatcher, the UK Prime Minister. Thereafter, the British government machine was at least benevolently neutral, and in April 1985 the British and French Governments issued a joint 'Invitation to Promoters' to submit bids for the private financing and construction of a fixed link across the Channel.[54]

Morgan Grenfell and Robert Fleming were already the financial advisers to the CTG, and early in 1985 they decided that the equity could in principle be raised without public sector backing. Morgans' representative from 1979 to 1983 had been Angus Dunn; he then went off to Morgan Grenfell Asia and Singapore and was succeeded by John Franklin. The financial adviser's role now divided into two parts: firstly, Morgans had to help draw up a financial plan which would enable the CTG to win the mandate to build the tunnel from the British and French governments, and secondly, they then had to help raise a total of £6 billion in loans and equity finance. Morgans and Flemings put together a 'Preliminary Information Memorandum' in September 1985 to inform the institutions about the economics of the project; in response, many of them sent letters in which they stated that they would in principle subscribe to an equity issue if asked to do so. By now there were four principal groups preparing submissions for the government. The schemes proposed included a 'drive-through' tunnel and a bridge as well as CTG's twin-rail-only tunnel. It was a combination of its technical feasibility, environmental impact, and the financial strength (backed up by the visible support obtained by Morgans and Flemings) that led the government to award the mandate to CTG and its French partner, France Manche, on 20 January 1986. The Anglo-French treaty was signed by Mrs Thatcher and President Mitterrand of France on 12 February, and the concession agreement was signed on 14 March 1986. With the coming into force of the concession agreement the two partners merged into a single organisation, Eurotunnel, and Lord Pennock of Morgan Grenfell became the first UK co-chairman.

Eurotunnel's financial advisers now concentrated on actually raising the required funds. By January 1986 Morgans had two teams working on the project: a project finance team advised Eurotunnel on the structuring and negotiation of the approximately £5 billion of multicurrency loans to be raised, while a corporate finance team advised on the equity issues; Franklin was the overall co-ordinator. The first tranche of funds came from the so-called Equity Nought and Equity One in the summer and early autumn of 1986, when the ten contractors and five banks who had jointly prepared the submission to the government provided £46 million as initial equity.

The overall financing programme now called for a further injection of equity from a private placing of shares with financial institutions, followed by the obtaining of the commitment of a syndicate of commercial banks for the loan finance and, finally, a public issue of shares for the balance of the equity. Simultaneously, Eurotunnel would negotiate contracts for the construction of the tunnel and with the two national railway companies who would be the largest customers once operations began. Each of these steps, as well as the completion of the political processes in the UK and France, would have to be completed before Eurotunnel could authorize the start of the tunnel-boring from the coasts of England and France. In addition to advising Eurotunnel on each of these elements, Morgans and Flemings had also to design an equity structure that would meet the often conflicting regulatory requirements in the UK and France as well as provide an attractive investment which would suit market requirements in both countries.

During the summer of 1986 the conflicts between the interests of the various founder shareholders spilled into the public arena. At the same time a publicity campaign mounted by anti-Tunnel interests (in particular by Flexilink, a group of Channel ferry operators) began to take shape, concentrating on lobbying Parliament, which was then debating the legislation intended to provide the authority to proceed with a tunnel. The marketing of the private equity placing (known as Equity Two) had already been delayed from early summer, and was held up until the construction contract and preliminary commitment for loan finance could be put into place. Equity Two was eventually launched in October 1986 but, following the delays and publicity campaign, a number of institutions which had earlier provided letters of support now felt that the risks were too great, and declined to invest. As a result, the placing to raise £206 million succeeded only because the Bank of England intervened to encourage institutional support. Morgans and Flemings picked up the balance.

A number of key management changes were made in the aftermath of Equity Two, including the appointment of a new UK co-chairman. Lord Pennock remained as a Director of Eurotunnel, and Rory Macnamara was seconded from Morgans' corporate finance department to co-ordinate the final stages of the equity programmes as part of the Eurotunnel management. Morgans and Flemings were now joined by S. G. Warburg as UK financial advisers and a joint team was formed from corporate finance staff drawn from each of the houses.

Almost every aspect of the planned public share issue (Equity Three) was unique to Eurotunnel. It was to be the first time that any company was simultaneously floated in London and Paris, and the equity was to be sold to investors in 'units' of indissolubly twinned Anglo-French shares. Working with Banque Indosuez, the lead adviser in France, Morgans and the other UK houses had to reconcile the technical problems (sometimes by encouraging changes in the law in the UK or France), design marketing programmes, and plan the logistics of producing the largest volume of documentation ever assembled and distributed in connection with a share issue.

As the equity programme developed through the spring and summer of 1987, the final pieces of the jigsaw began to fall into place. Following the re-election of a Conservative government in June, the parliamentary processes in the UK and France were finally completed and the treaty between the two countries was ratified at the end of July. In August, a group of fifty banks underwrote a £5 billion loan, which was then successfully syndicated amongst 198 participants. Public perception of the project began to become more positive, and early soundings amongst potential investors were encouraging for the scheduled launch of Equity Three in mid-November.

The stock-market crash on 19 October 1987 cast doubt over the possibilities for completing the final step, but on the advice of the issuing houses it was decided to go ahead, and on 27 November 1987 the £770 million issue of shares in Eurotunnel was completed. Although the sub-underwriters had to take up 20% of the issue, given the state of the market it was as successful as could have been hoped, with over 300,000 private investors becoming shareholders. Eurotunnel, the biggest private infrastructure project of the twentieth century, was now secure in its funding: the rest was up to the engineers.[55]

Eurotunnel was a somewhat unusual project for Morgans, in that much of their work in project and export finance was found in areas other than the Western industrialized nations. Morgans were prominent in this field in the Soviet Union and Eastern Europe, in the Middle East and Africa, and the result was a series of projects—for Iran and Hungary in 1972, Abu Dhabi in 1973, Bulgaria in 1974, the USSR in 1975, and Romania and Poland in 1976, to give some examples. Morgans' pre-eminence in this field was recognized when they were awarded the Queen's Award for Industry for export achievement in 1975, the first merchant bank to receive this award, and one which the bank was to receive again in 1982 and 1986.[56]

Morgan Grenfell's success, compared with the other merchant banks, can be attributed to the fact that export finance profits were ploughed back into the business. This took the form of hiring people with the necessary linguistic skills and knowledge of foreign cultures, and establishing an international network of representative offices larger than any of their competitors' in the 1970s. Morgans then had in the bank a group of people who understood foreign cultures as well as foreign markets, and who therefore could meet international clients on their own grounds.

In 1975 Christopher Reeves became deputy chief executive, and Blaise Hardman took over from him as head of the Banking Division. At that stage banking consisted of all the international activities, together with the Treasury and foreign exchange business, deposit-taking, and commercial lending and leasing. The balance sheet continued to grow rapidly through the rest of the decade and there was a healthy growth in banking profits. Indeed, the fact that banking was much more profitable than corporate finance during most of this period was sometimes productive of tensions within the bank, since the majority of directors continued to be corporate finance men, some of whom were unhappy about the diversion of resources to and concentration on the development of banking. Bicester, for example, had held to the old merchant banking adage that you lend your name, not your money, and it was only after his retirement in 1967 that the banking side of Morgans really began to grow.[57] Others may well have still felt that way.

The Growth of Corporate Finance

In 1961 Morgan Grenfell had been predominantly a corporate finance house in the old meaning of the term. Mergers and acquisitions were still a comparatively rare, although growing, phenomenon, while the service which industrial clients mainly wanted was help in raising money. Until the 'cult of the equity' took over in the 1970s, the major instrument was the issue of fixed-interest stock, where Morgans were far and away the most important merchant bank. This supremacy was perhaps symbolized by the events of 24 February 1961, when Morgans under Collins managed or co-managed the sale of the debenture stocks and preference shares of the seven major denationalized steel companies (the *Financial Times* of that day was thick with prospectuses). But the rise in the level of inflation and interest rates during the 1960s slowly strangled this activity. At the same time, the market for corporate advice was erratic and uncertain. Morgans had their long list of traditional clients, but newer companies, perhaps headed by energetic and thrusting chief executives or chairmen, tended to turn to other banks such as Warburgs, who had a reputation for innovation and daring. A further drawback for Morgans was probably the fact that in 1961 they had 'lost the ICI/Courtaulds takeover bid, and thereafter were labelled, in many people's minds, as a House which, more often than not, lost its bid battles'.[58] But Morgans invested in people, and over the two decades the corporate finance department grew in reputation and gradually produced a larger share of the bank's profits. By 1981 it was poised to leap into the position which it thereafter held, that of a dominating—if not the predominating— player in the field.

In 1961 the embryo corporate finance department, called the issues department, consisted of five people, Barrington, Bernard, Chappell, Pavitt, and Donald Wells, who were joined by Rawlinson the following year. They all sat in the building which had once been the offices of the private bank Cull & Co., bought by Morgans in 1943 (the building was demolished in 1987), aided by one secretary, Miss Ann Uwins. Besides issuing fixed-interest stock, typically sold to institutions, the group worked on the occasional takeover—indeed, in 1961 this work took up a good deal of their time. Besides the disappointing ICI/Courtaulds fight, they handled a very big merger and acquisition operation, the takeover by American Ford of UK Ford; the work came to Morgans because of the friendship between Sir Patrick Hennessy, chairman of the Ford Motor Co. Ltd., and Erskine, and was entirely arranged over the Whitsun holiday by Erskine, Barrington, and Collins. This takeover, worth £220 million, was the largest yet seen in the UK; Morgans screwed up their courage and asked Ford UK for a fee of £50,000.[59]

By 1968 Barrington wanted to create a larger and more coherent department, and invited George Law, whose experience as a solicitor had been in international commercial and financial work, to join as a managing director. After Law's arrival there were four directors doing corporate finance, supported by the first batch of assistant directors. A probable reason for Barrington's wish to strengthen corporate finance in the bank was that in 1967, for the first time, profits from merger and acquisition work exceeded profits from making issues. In 1968, in fact, the profits from the forty-six corporate finance transactions (described then as advice and assistance) were more than twice those earned by the ten new issue operations (described as underwritings and placings): £563,998 as compared with £232,461.[60] But 1968 was also a notable year for another reason: advising in a takeover struggle when American Tobacco bid for Gallaher, Morgans showed innovation and daring which the City had not yet come to expect from such a traditional institution. They won—and brought down on their heads the wrath both of the Panel on Takeovers and Mergers and of the Governor of the Bank of England.

In May 1968 Imperial Tobacco decided to dispose of the 38% it held in its rival Gallaher; they were advised by Robert Fleming and Morgan Grenfell, and Morgans and stockbrokers Cazenove and Co., who had worked closely together since the turn of the century, placed the bulk of the shares with the institutions. In the last week of June an American tobacco company, Philip Morris, made a bid for Gallaher, which was followed soon after by another by American Tobacco. American Tobacco were a client of Morgan Stanley in New York, and on their advice had come to Morgan Grenfell. The reference from the American cousin made Morgan Grenfell particularly keen to win, and Barrington and Law threw themselves into the fray. American Tobacco announced an offer to acquire half the ordinary share capital of Gallaher at 35s. a share, on the basis that if more than half the share capital was tendered for acceptance, acceptances would be scaled down *pro rata*. The offer of 35s. was rather above the market price, as well as above Philip Morris's offer of 25s. Immediately after the announcement Morgans instructed Cazenoves to purchase up to 35% of the ordinary shares in the market at 35s. per share; because of their recent placing of Gallaher shares, Morgans and Cazenoves knew where most of them resided, and Cazenoves approached the placees and offered to buy back the shares. Consequently, within two hours Cazenoves had purchased 35%, and purchased nearly another 5% while the buying programme was being stopped; the favoured institutions therefore were able to sell 100% of their shares, whereas acceptors of the partial offer were not. The takeover code said that if a partial bid was made, it should be made *pro rata* to each shareholder.[61]

The result was uproar in the City, an appeal to the takeover code, and a reference to the takeover panel. The code had been drawn up in 1959 under the auspices of Cobbold when Governor: after Warburgs had defied the City during the Great Aluminium War in 1958, engaging in previously unknown strategems such as utilizing the press and appealing to shareholders over the heads of the board, Cobbold had felt that things were becoming a bit unruly, and a voluntary takeover code was instituted. As takeovers became more and more common during the 1960s, many encouraged by the Wilson government, the government nevertheless fretted that perhaps something akin to the American Securities and Exchange Commission should be instituted; and it was partly to assuage the government's fears that O'Brien as Governor had invented the takeover panel as a body to ensure adherence to the code. He had had great difficulty in finding anyone to head it, and had only just managed to dragoon Sir Humphrey Mynors, a former Deputy Governor, to take on the chairmanship; it was largely staffed with people from the Bank's discount office. Further, it had only been in place since 27 March 1968, and thus had had very little time to settle in before the contretemps with Morgans began.[62]

The panel announced in the third week in July that the bid had broken one of the basic principles of the code, that all shareholders should be treated alike. However, it was more difficult to say that a rule had been broken, since the rules were not very specific, and the following week the panel announced that while it accepted Morgans' explanations, the code had been broken and the matter was being referred to the Council of the Stock Exchange and the Issuing Houses Association. Morgans and Cazenoves, meanwhile, protested furiously and publicly: as far as they were concerned, they had acted in good faith, and they felt that this had not been acknowledged by the panel in its decision and announcements. Harcourt in particular was toweringly angry, feeling that his integrity had been impugned. The Governor then felt driven to write an open and strongly worded letter to the Issuing Houses Association, pointing out that it was in no one's interest that the questioning of the panel's rulings and its authority should continue, and requesting that the Association and the Stock Exchange Council propose sanctions against future wilful infringement. In due course the furore died down, and a working party of five was set up to revise the code, one member of which was Barrington. The code was tightened up and its rules clarified.[63]

Morgans suffered no lasting damage from the uproar, with even the usually censorious *Economist* allowing that the controversy 'could have been due to the lack of experience of merger techniques'.[64] Indeed, those involved at the time believe that it was very important for Morgans' image as a corporate finance house: it showed them in a new light, because people had not thought that anyone at Morgans was capable of employing aggressive tactics in the same way as Warburgs and other houses. Equally important was the fact that Morgans (and American Tobacco) won, with a cost to the latter of a fee of £104,000 payable to Morgans.[65]

Thereafter the issues department did not lack work, but this was at least partly a reflection of the fact that the 1960s' fashion for mergers and rationalization was coming to a peak: the market had been rising, and it has been estimated that in 1973 there were as many if not more takeover bids than in 1985. There was tremendous pressure on the corporate finance directors and assistant directors, particularly in 1972 and 1973.[66] In the latter half of 1972, in fact, Morgans were involved in a takeover battle which was to prove a turning-point: the agreed bid by P&O for Bovis. As the *Investors Review* later wrote, 'Morgan Grenfell made merchant banking history'.[67]

In April 1972 the chairman of the Peninsular and Oriental Steam Navigation Company, Ford Geddes, concluded from the preliminary figures for the financial year that the year's profit figure might be even lower than the previous year's already low figure; indeed, the predicted earnings, when published in the accounts, would contrast with the rising value of their property holdings. There was thus the danger that P&O might become the object of a bid. At the same time, the house-building and construction group Bovis Limited was looking for a union with a larger company. The crucial part of the jigsaw was added in May 1972, when the chairman of Lazards, Lord Poole, joined the board of P&O, along with Mr A. D. Marris, another Lazards director. As it happened, Lazards also advised Bovis; Poole and Marris saw a way to help both of their clients, and late in June Geddes and Frank Sanderson, the chairman of Bovis, met for talks. On 10 August 1972 the results were published: an agreed bid by P&O for Bovis, valuing Bovis at £130 million, with a connected agreement which, by making Sanderson the joint deputy chairman of the whole group and chairman of an executive committee, opened the way for Sanderson to inherit the chair of P&O: 'P&O would acquire the shares of Bovis, and Sanderson would acquire P&O.'[68]

In the *Sunday Telegraph* of 13 August there was a one-sentence reference to the fact that Lord Inchcape was none too happy, but apparently this hint passed unnoticed. Inchcape was one of the longest-serving non-executive directors on P&O's board; he had been out of sympathy with the executive directors for some time, and he had opposed the bid at the crucial board meeting, when it had passed with a nine to seven majority. However, he only made his feelings clear after opposition had appeared from other quarters. On 24 August the *Investors Review* published an analysis of the bid, ending with advice to P&O shareholders to stop the deal, and this stimulated Inchcape to air his views against the merger in the *Sunday Times* of 27 August. In this interview he revealed the boardroom split in P&O, his perception of how the votes of the two Lazards men had swung the consensus in favour of the deal, and his own view of the deal as in 'the worst interests of P&O share-holders'.[69]

Morgan Grenfell were investment advisers to clients owning £439,677 deferred stock of P&O (about $\frac{2}{3}$%), part of which was registered in the name of Morgan Nominees Limited; Morgans them-selves did not beneficially own any preferred or deferred stock. Possibly stimulated by the Inchcape interview and the *Investors Review* analysis, the investment department of Morgans did their own sums on the offer and decided that it did not provide a good enough deal for P&O shareholders: Bovis profits were inflated and not sustainable, because they owed a great deal to the recent increase in land values, and because house-building was on the downward sweep of the cycle; conversely, the outlook for P&O was steadily improving because of anticipated shipping profits and fuller utilization of property assets. In sum, P&O shareholders would, they decided, be giving £100 million to Bovis shareholders.

Therefore, on 13 September 1972, Morgans announced that they proposed to contact major shareholders in P&O on the bank's own behalf
to examine the merger proposals with them. To the City, the idea that
Morgans could be working without a client to pay was unbelievable.
But Morgans were working for a rather good client: themselves. They
had decided that the merger proposals were very bad, and Morgans'
'decision to oppose the merger . . . was a deliberate attempt by us, on
a slightly high risk basis, to try and make Morgan Grenfell a name which
people would start to think about'. Catto and Law were allocated to the
operation.[70]

The following day, when the P&O board met to authorize the formal
offer documents for Bovis, two of the executive directors refused to sign
the document, and announced publicly that they were opposing the bid.
(Within a week a third executive director would make his dissent public.)
One result was for P&O's shares to be temporarily suspended. On 19
September the P&O board met the press, and the result was disastrous.
By the morning of 25 September, when Morgans convened a meeting
of institutional shareholders who held approximately 25% of the issued
preferred and deferred stock of P&O, the question of the bid was clearly
an open one. Morgans wanted to know whether a significant body of
P&O shareholders shared their doubts: the answer was that they did, and
Morgans were appointed by the meeting to act as their spokesman and
present a list of fifteen questions to the board of P&O. The list was
handed over to Lazards that afternoon.[71]

A further meeting of institutional shareholders was held on 28 September, at which Morgans told them that, while Lazards had told Morgans
that further information would be given, they would not say when, or
whether all of the questions would be answered. The meeting authorized
Morgans to ask the P&O board to postpone its decision, to enable the
information to be provided, and, failing that, to ask the takeover panel
to obtain a postponement of the Extraordinary General Meeting (EGM)
of P&O scheduled for 12 October. Both the P&O board and the panel
rejected the appeal.[72]

Meanwhile, on 3 October 1972, the same day the first Morgan
Grenfell letter to P&O shareholders went out, reports appeared in the
press of the existence of another bidder, and P&O shares were again
temporarily suspended. Then on 4 October the new bid was revealed:
Lord Inchcape, as head of the Inchcape Group, was offering to buy P&O
for £230 million, a considerably higher valuation than that under the
Bovis arrangement. The first response of the P&O board was to adjourn

the EGM scheduled for 12 October. On 6 October Bovis offered new terms to the P&O board, which would reduce the benefits Bovis would obtain from the merger (they were revised again in the third week in October); the implication was that the initial terms had indeed been too generous to Bovis, as the dissidents, including Morgans, had claimed. Catto and Law told the press on 24 October that the new terms were 'a good deal cleaner and better', in Law's words, than the previous offer, but that Morgans would probably continue to oppose the bid because they were still not good enough. Meanwhile the P&O board had rejected the Inchcape bid on Friday, 13 October.[73]

The pace now quickened, and P&O shareholders were the recipients of a snowstorm of letters and circulars: on 31 October the circular setting out the arguments against the bid of Alexander Marshall, one of the dissident executive directors of P&O, was posted; on 1 November P&O and Bovis's second offer document was posted, followed on 6 November by another P&O circular and by the Inchcape circular; and on 7 November the second Morgan Grenfell letter to P&O shareholders was posted. In addition, there was a barrage of publicity. Jessel Securities, the largest shareholders in P&O, fly-posted the City with stickers 'telling Bovis No', while the advertising agencies for P&O and Bovis ran a sustained campaign. It was estimated that over £$\frac{1}{4}$ million was spent on press advertising during the hundred days of the fight.[74]

On 9 November 1972, the day of the adjourned EGM of P&O shareholders, Sir Donald Anderson, P&O's past chairman, published his opposition to any deal; subsequent investigation showed that this intervention had a decisive effect on many of the small shareholders in P&O. At the EGM that day, the voting structure was changed, with the approval of Morgans as well as the institutions: before, every £100 of stock was allowed one vote, with a maximum of twenty votes per stockholder; now, the basis became one share one vote. This vastly increased the power of institutional shareholders, who tended to take an active interest in companies, at the expense of the small shareholders, who were inclined to be passive. There was a final intervention that weekend, when Sir Donald Anderson announced that if both the Bovis and Inchcape bids were rejected, Lord Inchcape had agreed to have his name put forward as chairman of P&O. Thus P&O could remain independent, but with new management.[75]

Friday, 17 November 1972, was the date of the EGM, and a proxy race began. Proxies had to be filed by 3 p.m. on Wednesday, 15 November; Morgans filed some at the beginning of the week, and

Lazards issued confident statements that the poll was going well. What Lazards did not know was that Morgan Grenfell still had proxies representing some 10m. votes which it had not yet filed. On Tuesday, with some 14m. votes counted, P&O was claiming a 2–1 majority. Just before the 3 p.m. deadline on Wednesday, Morgan Grenfell slapped in the remainder of its 10,000 proxies, representing some 10m. votes. It was only as these were processed on Thursday that Geddes and Sanderson began to realise something had gone drastically wrong. MG's proxies meant that the institutional votes which had been counted were broadly split, as had been expected. But they also showed that the small shareholders had rebelled.

Late that Thursday night, the final verdict emerged as a 5–2 rejection of the deal.[76]

At the EGM on 17 November, Geddes and the P&O board admitted defeat, and Geddes said that he and the deputy chairman would resign. The reaction was wild applause. Lord Poole also announced his intention of resigning, and announced that Lazards would waive their fee, a statement received with jeers by the assembled shareholders. But after the blood-letting, the company had to carry on. The new managing director was the dissident executive director Alexander Marshall, and on 10 January 1973 Lord Inchcape became chairman of P&O. It is worth noting as well that in March 1974 P&O took over Bovis—at a price which was only a fifth of the 1972 offer.[77]

Morgan Grenfell approved of the 1974 offer, but to their chagrin they had to do so as outsiders. On 9 October 1972, in a meeting between Catto and Law on the one hand and Geddes and his deputy chairman on the other, Morgans had proposed among other management changes the replacement of P&O's financial advisers (Lazards and Williams and Glyn) by Morgan Grenfell—according to Catto a 'delicate point'.[78] The same suggestion had been made to the institutional investors, both orally and in the letter Morgans sent to shareholders on 8 November. Certainly, the appointment appears to have been widely expected in the City. It therefore came as something of a blow to Morgans when J. Schröder Wagg were appointed instead. The ostensible reason was that the P&O board were considering the still-pending bid by the Inchcape Group for P&O, and since Morgans had come out for the continued independence of P&O, they had disqualified themselves as neutral advisers. Another reason given was that the P&O board believed that merchant bankers should be the servants of companies, not the masters, and they felt Morgans would demand too much of a say in P&O's affairs; they therefore appointed Schröder Wagg to advise them, but as skilled tacticians without a place on the board (as Lazards had had). Morgans themselves were inclined to believe that personality clashes provided as important a reason as any.[79]

Nevertheless, Morgans gained immensely in prestige through their leadership of the institutional opposition to the bid. At the beginning of the fight they were referred to as a 'prestigious merchant bank . . . with a somewhat faltering image of late', while by the end they were referred to as 'newly-respected'. Morgans themselves agree that it gave the bank a much higher profile: public awareness of the name was much greater, since they were for three months continually in the press, and that was not unimportant; but crucially, the institutional investors gained a great deal of respect for the bank, both for what Morgans did and for the way they did it, and this was true whichever side the institutions backed. Again, as in 1968, in a difficult and contested battle, they had won.[80]

This emphasis on the need to win was inescapable, because the costs of losing, particularly losing disastrously, could be very high. One cost could be damaging publicity, and certainly Lazards suffered. Under the headline 'Lazard legend lost in P&O's pool of tears', the journalist Kenneth Fleet wrote in the *Daily Telegraph* that

The hope must now be that its sorry involvement with P&O will precipitate the thorough overhaul that Lazards of all the remaining barnacle-bottomed four-funnellers left in the City so manifestly needs. Its record in corporate finance is wretched. In the new issue market it has yet to be penetrated by modern thinking. In investment stockbrokers find it inept.

The unfortunate thing is that Lazards hitherto would not accept that it did anything badly and seemed to resent professional help, even when forced to seek it.[81]

Lazards recovered from the set-back, but obviously a related and long-lasting cost could be loss of business, since no company would wish to entrust its affairs to a bank deemed to be unable to carry out its wishes successfully:

In the mid-1960s Robert Fleming, one of the smaller merchant banks not normally involved in takeover business, strayed into the field. The international merger it tried to put together was an unpleasant failure. For the next twenty years it did not handle a single major takeover.[82]

The corporate finance directors in Morgans were overwhelmed with work, right up until the end of 1973 and the beginning of 1974—and then the flow of profitable issue and takeover work stopped. This had nothing to do with Morgan Grenfell, but it demonstrated once again the extent to which corporate finance work—and profits—are at the mercy of outside events, since companies became concerned less with growth than with sheer survival. What happened, of course, was the property market crash and secondary banking crisis; the *Financial Times* 30 Share Index fell from about 350 at the end of 1973 to 146 in January 1975. Banks became very cautious indeed about lending, clients' share prices were falling, and so the latter had neither cash nor paper to be acquisitive. Very little business just walked in the door; rather, Morgans had to try somehow to generate it as best they could, by creating ideas and going out and selling them.[83] But they had the advantage that lack of involvement in the crisis of 1974 allowed them to consolidate their position, while their competitors were rocked backwards. Indeed, Morgans moved to improve it, by radically restructuring the corporate finance department and by deliberately recruiting the brightest young corporate finance men they could find. This was done during 1974 and 1975, and was designed to ensure that when market conditions improved and issue and takeover business again picked up, Morgans would have 'the best equipped corporate finance department in the City' ready to take advantage of the opportunities which would then be available. Certainly, many of those who were to help make Morgans a power in corporate finance during the 1980s joined the bank at this time. By the latter years of the decade, with the economy improving and the political climate changing, business picked up. New techniques helped contribute to a massive increase in the earnings of corporate finance, notably the underwriting of cash alternatives on takeovers and the sub-underwriting of the risk with institutional investors, which enabled Morgans to charge an underwriting commission as well as an advisory fee.[84] The contribution of corporate finance began greatly to transform Morgan Grenfell's profitability.

By 1981, then, Morgans had transformed their London-centred activities. In 1961 the activity of the bank was largely concentrated on issuing fixed-interest securities, in which they dominated the market—in some years 70% to 80% of all the money raised in the London market was channelled through Morgans.[85] But this business declined, and the other aspect of corporate finance, giving advice and assistance, eventually replaced it in importance. At the same time, what had been only an embryonic banking business in 1961 was rapidly built up, so that during most of the period it made the major contribution to profits. The most rapidly growing parts of banking were foreign exchange and export finance, both of which supported and drew.support from the concurrent growth of Morgan Grenfell overseas.

CHAPTER EIGHT

INTERNATIONAL DEVELOPMENTS AND THE BREAK-UP OF THE MORGAN FAMILY

1961–1981

A MAJOR reason for Sir John Stevens's historic importance in the development of Morgan Grenfell was that he propelled the bank overseas. When he joined in 1967, Morgans had already attempted five forays abroad, but four were joint ventures with mixed results, and in only one of them did Morgan Grenfell play an active role. Stevens emphasized the need to divert significant resources into overseas developments as part of his drive to increase the banking side of Morgans, and until 1979 international activities were treated as part of the Banking Division. He fathered the first Morgan-Grenfell-only office abroad, which was set up in 1969 in Munich, and although the bank devoted fewer resources to Europe during the period than did, for example, Warburgs, it expanded widely elsewhere, initially in the Far East. Stevens was notably a great generator of ideas, some of which were more successful than others. G. W. Mackworth-Young, who succeeded him as chief executive in 1974, developed Stevens's international theme and, in conjunction with Christopher Reeves, his own eventual successor, ensured that Morgan Grenfell had a working international organization that seemed, for the future as then anticipated, well planned and well structured. By 1981 Morgans were established in Europe, the Near and Far East, Africa, and North and South America. Most importantly for the future, they were established in two cities which would thereafter become major foci, Tokyo and New York.

Morgan Grenfell were not alone in the renewed attention paid to opportunities overseas. Morgan Guaranty and the securities house Morgan Stanley (which had spun off from J. P. Morgan & Co. in 1935) also increased the resources devoted to foreign business. The two American houses were in part following their clients, who were moving into Europe and elsewhere, both to borrow on the Eurodollar market and to set up or take over businesses. The three cousin houses tried several times to set up joint ventures; but the repeated failure of such attempts to work together, when combined with the growing competition between Morgan Guaranty and Morgan Grenfell in their home markets and overseas, led in 1981 to the decision by Morgan Guaranty to sell its shareholding in Morgan Grenfell. Thus ended a family association which had lasted for over a hundred years.

Early Overseas Ventures: Australia, Canada, and the Bahamas

Morgan Grenfell's first venture overseas pre-dated Stevens by nearly two decades: Australia in 1949. Discussions were held with Lazards and Consolidated Zinc about undertaking business in the Australian markets; the result was the Anglo-Australian Corporation Pty. Ltd., with the Aus £300,000 issued share capital divided amongst the three partners. It was the first issuing house in Australia, and high hopes were entertained for it, but never met. A major problem was that an Englishman, Sir Eric Speed, was sent out from London to run it — not, perhaps, the best approach in Australia. In 1959 it joined with Sir Ian Potter's Australian United Corporation (AUC) in setting up the United Discount Company of Australia and Australian United Acceptances Ltd. to participate in the new money market. In 1961 Consolidated Zinc sold its share of Anglo-Australian to Lazard Frères of New York and Morgan Guaranty International Finance Corporation. By 1962 Potter decided that he wanted to become more involved in international banking, and approached Morgans and Lazards with a view to a merger of the Australian businesses. As Ian Potter & Co. he ran the most successful stockbroking business in Australia, and the intention was that he would move out of this to run the combined business. Accordingly, in February 1963 the interests of Anglo-Australian and Australian United were merged. The subscription of an additional £1 million in capital brought the holdings of Morgans and Lazards up to 35%, split two to one between the New York and London houses, leaving Morgan Grenfell with about 6%. A further 10% of the capital was held by the Bank of New South Wales. Unfortunately, profits did not improve for Morgans, probably because Potter did not in fact leave his stockbroking firm, and indeed took most of the profits through the brokers, leaving the underwriters in Australian United with very little. Other institutions came in, but eventually they all decided that it was ridiculous to have such small holdings, with none of them running it. Thus in 1977 Morgan Guaranty bought out the others.[1]

Morgan Grenfell now reorganized their position in Australia. There had been a representative office in Sydney since 1973, and this was now upgraded to a full (if small) merchant banking operation in October 1977, although Guy Weston and Julien Prevett did not go out until the following April. Then, with the money received from the sale of the AUC shareholding, Morgan Grenfell Australia joined with the Australian Mutual Provident Society, the largest institution in Australia, to form AMP–Morgan Grenfell, of which Morgans owned 25%. Morgans wanted to operate in the Australian money market, but were prevented from doing so by Australian regulations; by forming AMP–MG (which then acquired 100% of the share capital of AMP Discount Corporation Limited and of AMP Acceptances Limited), they gained an entrée into the market. By 1983, however, the market was changing, and Morgan Grenfell Australia sold its share of AMP–MG back to AMP; and at the end of 1985, when the regulations were changed, Morgan Grenfell Australia set up its own money desk.[2]

By the end of 1987 the emphasis was changing towards 'big ticket' corporate finance and establishing institutional stock exchange business. The number of offices had also increased through the 1980s, with representation in Adelaide, Melbourne, Perth, and New Zealand, in addition to the head office in Sydney, employing over two hundred people. However, Morgans were increasingly dissatisfied with the performance of the Australian operation, especially with the slender returns from the high cost base and the lack of integration of the various activities with their counterparts elsewhere in the group. Consideration was given to closing down the operation altogether; but it was decided that the Australian operation, if properly managed, would generate good flows of business to London and within the Pacific Basin — and besides, the cost of closing it altogether would be quite large.

In early 1988 the money market operations were cut back; the Perth office was closed; the New Zealand operation was sold to its management; the underwriting team was cut back and merged with securities; and the Australian domestic asset management business was streamed directly to London. Following this, in mid-1988 a full-scale review was carried out exploring a spread of alternatives from total closure to an Australian integrated merchant bank/broking house. Coincident with the withdrawal from stockbroking in London, though, the securities side (still predominantly private-client oriented) was sold. The domestic asset management business was also sold, whilst retaining (and developing) funds for Australian clients directly handled by London; and the offices in Melbourne and Adelaide were closed.

The intention was to refocus the Australian business on corporate and project finance for major corporations, with a continuing emphasis on cross-border business. The small treasury and foreign exchange business would continue, all run with much tighter management control from London.[3]

Morgans' experience in Canada also began with very high hopes which were gradually deflated. Sometime in 1951 or early 1952, Morgan Grenfell discussed with J. P. Morgan & Co. ways of undertaking a financing and issuing business in Canada, either by setting up from scratch or by taking over a Canadian company. It was suggested that they should talk to Peacock at Barings, who as a Canadian had experience of and an interest in Canada which might be valuable. Meanwhile, I. C. R. Atkin of J. P. Morgan & Co. was consulted by W. C. Harris, owner of a finance and issuing house in Toronto, who wanted advice on expanding his business. Atkins asked whether Harris might be interested in a joint Morgan Grenfell/Baring proposal; he was, and discussion soon led to agreement. On 1 October 1952 Harris and Partners Ltd., the successor to W. C. Harris Co., opened for business; Peacock was chairman, and Hill-Wood one of the four other board members.

Things began well, with the expansion of the business in the following year, and by 1955 net profits were Can$241,640. But the remainder of the decade was difficult, and it was not until 1960 that they had another good year. That same year Harris and Partners opened a London office, and this was perhaps symptomatic of a growing independence on the part of the Canadians. In 1961 there was a major reorganization: Harris wanted to give his 'boys' a bigger part of the business, and the Bank of Canada was encouraging foreign businesses to turn over control to Canadians. This was, in fact, what happened. From 1961 Morgans' shareholding drifted down from 25% to 20% to 15%. Results continued to be mixed, with one of the better years, 1967, yielding £58,000 in dividends based on net profits of Can$631,328. But eventually Harris and Partners merged with Dominion Securities, which left Morgan Grenfell with only 10%; feeling that there was little point in having such a small shareholding, Morgans sold out.[4]

Morgan Grenfell's move into the Bahamas had its origins in a journey by Bicester across the Atlantic, during which he became friendly with the president of the Royal Bank of Canada. The Royal Bank were planning to go into the Bahamas, and asked Morgans to join them. The Trust Corporation of the Bahamas, which had been in existence for some years, was essentially the personal investment vehicle of A. V. Davies, the chairman of Alcoa. In September 1957, Morgans bought 5,000 £20 shares at a price of £28 per share, a total investment of $140,000, and Rennell joined the Board. The Royal Bank of Canada and the Montreal Trust Company bought shares at the same time. Catto meanwhile was on the London Committee of the Hong Kong and Shanghai Banking Corporation, and when that bank wished to become a shareholder in 1958, a hundred shares were found for them. At the same time an increase in the holdings of Morgans and the two Canadian banks brought their holding of the issued share capital to over 50%. The intention of Morgans was to turn the Trust Corporation into a vehicle for the institutional rather than the private investor, and to that end Morgan Guaranty was encouraged to take 2,000 shares in 1960. This brought the institutional shareholding to 72%, and the following year Davies finally retired as chairman, a departure which was perhaps speeded up by the lack of profitability of the Corporation under his leadership (average earnings on shareholders' funds were 4.8%). Business expanded only gradually, and the Corporation trundled along until 1965. Then the Royal Bank of Canada and the Westminster Bank came together to form the RoyWest Bank Corporation Ltd. to carry on a specialized banking business in the Caribbean area and to acquire the Trust Corporation; Catto joined the RoyWest board. Again, Morgan Grenfell's holding was reduced, and this encouraged them to agree when RoyWest in due course suggested that it buy out the other shareholders.[5]

It would be too much to claim that all of these investments formed part of a grand strategic design. In January 1962, nevertheless, in a letter to the Bank of England, Morgans provided some justification for these disparate ventures:

You will appreciate that our own business here in London is predominantly in the underwriting of public issues and the general securities business. Our policy in recent years has been to make trade investments in overseas territories in order to provide our own clients here in Britain with access to financial advice in many of the overseas countries where they operate, and also to take an active part in the financial life of these overseas countries, thus helping to increase the two way trade in commercial and financial business and so also increase the foreign exchange earnings. These trade investments are in Canada, Australia, India, and the Bahamas. . . .[6]

'India' referred to Morgans' shareholdings in Andrew Yule & Co.

Expansion in Europe

The reason for the letter was to notify the Bank of Morgans' desire to expand into a new area—France. Planned as a joint venture with Morgan Guaranty, discussions had been taking place since November 1960, when Collins had met with Julian Allen, Morgan Guaranty's Vice President for European Offices. The idea was to establish an investment bank—a *banque d'affaires*—in Paris. As J. P. Morgan & Co., Morgan Guaranty had once had the Paris partnership of Morgan Harjes and then Morgan et Cie; but this had been incorporated in 1945, and as Morgan Guaranty Paris it was not allowed to participate in underwriting, formerly the Paris office's most profitable business. Therefore, Morgan Guaranty now wanted to establish a new organization, in which its international subsidiary Morgan Guaranty International Finance Corporation would have a large minority interest but the majority shareholding would be held by European banks.

Morgan Grenfell were quite keen on the idea, but first there was a hurdle to be vaulted: the Bank of England. Harcourt and Catto visited the Bank in October 1961 to sound them out, and were very cordially received. In normal circumstances Morgans would have received their agreement, since the proposed investment in the European Economic Community was the type of thing the Bank wanted to see; but current exchange control regulations would not permit the investment, so Morgan Grenfell would have to bide their time until conditions changed. In January 1962 Morgans tried again, asking permission to subscribe for a 30% interest in a new French *banque d'affaires*, Morgan et Cie, SA. It would have an issued share capital of Fr.f.5 million, and the other shareholders would be Morgan Guaranty International Finance Corporation with 40%, and two Dutch banks, Hope & Co. of Amsterdam and R. Mees & Zoonen of Rotterdam, each with 15%. The hope was that the new bank would take an active part in the European underwriting market, as well as carrying out general securities business and giving financial advice on French and other Continental affairs to the clients of the shareholders. This time the Bank's response was more helpful: permission was granted as long as the money required was found by borrowing outside the Scheduled Territories (essentially the sterling area) on terms which would not require repayment until exchange controls permitted funds to be remitted from the UK. The funds were loaned to

Morgan Grenfell by Morgan Guaranty at the 'prime rate, of $4\frac{1}{2}$%, although in the end Morgan Guaranty International held 70% of the shares while Morgan Grenfell had 15% (and Bank Mees en Hope, who had merged their business, held the other 15%).[7]

By 1963 Morgan et Cie were open for business. According to Morgan Guaranty, 'the new company should attempt to improve methods of distributing stocks in Europe, patterned, where applicable, on American practice. It would be desirable to introduce into the company some first-quality young American investment banking talent.'[8] New York seconded two men, Norbert Leroy as general manager and Jack Kath, and they immediately went into action. As a friendly German article put it, 'two middle-aged men have been travelling throughout the Federal Republic since 1961, have been snooping around the German industry and high finance, and have been annoying a lot of banks'.[9] They also annoyed the British, as Harcourt made clear at a board meeting: 'I again voiced my extreme disquiet at the conduct of Norbert Leroy and more particularly Jack Kath, in their handling of the underwriting business particularly in their approaches to brokers in London and discussions with various people in the London market, not only without consultation with us, but before even informing us that there was any tentative business to be done.'[10] Morgan Grenfell had not put in any of their own men, and would regret it. It seems clear that the two men either did not recognize, or chose not to recognize, national demarcation lines. This was less of a problem in Britain, which tolerated foreign financial institutions and was used to having its currency utilized by foreigners, than it was to prove in, for example, Switzerland and Germany.

There was, for instance, the episode of the first Swiss franc issue made outside Switzerland. Morgan Grenfell were involved in this, although it is not clear if Dallas Bernard or the Americans originated the idea: Swiss francs abounded, and if an issue were made in the currency, they could easily be converted into whichever other currency was desired. It was therefore arranged that a loan would be floated in London on behalf of the City of Copenhagen. As soon as it was announced, there was an explosion from the National Bank of Switzerland: Morgans had not asked their permission, and would not have received it if they had. (Well into the 1970s the Swiss fought against allowing their franc to become an international currency: they were afraid they would lose control of their money supply and would then become a prey to inflation. Besides that, they felt that issuing in Swiss francs belonged by right to Swiss banks.) But it was too late and the issue went ahead. The Swiss government reportedly told Washington that if there were any more such flotations, Switzerland would convert an equivalent amount of her dollar reserves into gold. In London Morgans' Eurocurrency dealings were hampered for a time, and Morgan Grenfell's ability to do business in Switzerland and their relations with Swiss banks were both affected for a number of years.[11]

German banks were not far behind the Swiss in their desire to control all the financial business in their own country. Morgan et Cie's first underwriting was on behalf of a German mail-order house; it was an immediate success, but at the price of incurring the anger of the German banks and, particularly, of Deutsche Bank. Morgan et Cie apparently looked for German entrepreneurs who were long on dynamism but short on capital, the very type who found it difficult to get help from the German banks. One such was the founder of the mail-order house Friedrich Schwab & Co. KG. Schwab's partner sat on the board of the Deutsche Bank, and he first discussed his requirements with them: however, the offer from the Deutsche Bank would have reduced Schwab's shareholding in his own company, and would have given the bank and his partner a higher share of the profits than Schwab. Schwab rejected the bank's offer, and insisted that he would accept that of Morgan et Cie. The reaction of Deutsche Bank was to refuse to sell the Schwab stock; immediately all other German banks except one also refused to place any of the issue. For Morgan et Cie the whole operation was in grave danger of becoming a disaster.

An urgent call went out to Morgan Grenfell that Morgan et Cie —which most people regarded as Morgan Guaranty's other office in Paris —needed help, and on the Sunday Collins went over to Paris. He then went on to Frankfurt, where he saw Schwab, and returned to London on Monday night. The following morning Morgan Grenfell called together a meeting of nearly all the merchant banks, explained that Morgans were in trouble, and would they please rally around. They did (except for Warburgs, presumably because of their close German connections), and a London syndicate and pool were set up to carry the Schwab stock for as long as necessary. Of the $13 million, Morgans and the syndicate were stuck for nine months with around $9 million. It was eventually bought by Singer Manufacturing Company, which became a partner in Schwab (the chairman, Donald P. Kircher, sat on the Morgan Guaranty board). Morgan Guaranty in New York were extremely grateful to Morgan Grenfell for the rescue operation, which saved not only the issue but their face.[12]

This was the only major set-back, however, and in the three and a half years of Morgan et Cie's independent existence they participated in and sometimes co-managed over a hundred issues in various currencies, including a score of Eurodollar issues. There was a surge of such issues in the autumn of 1965, after the imposition by the US government of the voluntary foreign credit restraint programme in early 1965, which was intended to limit the outflow of capital from the US in order to help the American balance-of-payments deficit. Morgan Stanley & Co. did not have a European office, and wished to take part in the business. There were negotiations about their buying shares in Morgan et Cie in 1963 and again in March 1966, but nothing transpired.

Later in the year, however, Morgan Guaranty received a blow which forced Morgan et Cie into the arms of Morgan Stanley. The US authorities ruled, for a number of legal reasons, that Morgan et Cie could not take part in various proposed operations; one obstacle was the Trust Indenture Act of 1939, which prevented Morgan et Cie from underwriting the securities of a company for which Morgan Guaranty Trust acted as a trustee—no small problem, since the Morgan Guaranty trust department acted for a substantial number of American companies. Negotiations with Morgan Stanley received new life, and in due course a new company was set up in Paris, called Morgan et Cie International SA (MECI). This was to be two-thirds owned by Morgan Stanley and one-third by Morgan et Cie: Morgan Grenfell's share in the new company would thus be 5%. MECI developed into a powerful Eurobond issuing house, but Morgan Grenfell had little say in the company. In 1974 Morgan Grenfell itself opened a representative office in Paris, and in 1980 this was upgraded to a wholly owned subsidiary, Morgan Grenfell France SA.[13]

During the same period as Morgans were developing business in France, they were also expanding into Ireland. During 1964 and 1965 Morgans, with J. Schröder Wagg, opened a number of acceptance credits and arranged two issues for Irish companies. Their success led to cordial relations with the Bank of Ireland, who asked Morgans to assist and advise them on a very big operation: the joint purchase, with the Commercial Bank of Scotland (later the Royal Bank of Scotland), of the National Bank Ltd. This was a London clearing bank with branches in Scotland, Northern Ireland, and the Republic of Ireland; the agreement was that after it had been purchased by the two banks, it would be divided, with the UK parts taken by the Commercial Bank of Scotland and the Irish part by the Bank of Ireland. Splitting a bank is a very complex business, and this operation involved court proceedings in Dublin, Belfast, Edinburgh, and London, and Acts of Parliament in London, Belfast, and Dublin. The scheme was completed in April 1966.

One conclusion drawn by the Bank of Ireland was that there was no adequate merchant banking capacity in Ireland, and so the Bank itself should set up a merchant banking subsidiary. They turned again to Morgan Grenfell and Schröders, and in September 1966 the Investment Bank of Ireland (IBI) was born, in which the Bank of Ireland held 60% of the shares and Morgans and Schröders 20% each; Charles Rawlinson was seconded to Dublin as the first managing director. About 1970 Schröders decided to retire from the IBI, and the shareholding then became 75 : 25. It had always been envisaged that at some point it was probable that the Bank of Ireland would want the IBI to become a wholly owned subsidiary, and the separation in March 1977 was thus a friendly one, with Morgans selling their shares at an agreeable profit.[14]

When John Stevens joined Morgans in 1967, then, he found that Morgans' international operation consisted of small shareholdings, some more profitable than others, in a series of joint ventures in Australia, Canada, the Bahamas, France, and Ireland. He believed that Morgans must develop a more significant international presence than these holdings represented, and in particular he felt strongly that the bank must secure a position on the European continent, where the Common Market was contributing to impressive economic growth. Stevens's decision was that Morgans should first set up in Germany, partly because it was the strongest European economy and partly because it seemed to be the most liberal, since it had no exchange controls. In July 1969, then, Morgan Grenfell (Overseas) Limited was incorporated.

The obvious place for a representative office would have been Frankfurt, the financial centre, but Morgans opted for Munich. This was insisted upon by the man chosen by Stevens to set up the office, Kenneth Grandville, a former Diplomatic Service officer, who became Morgans' European representative. Grandville came from an Austrian family, and argued for Munich as handy for Switzerland and Austria as well as Germany; the one advantage was that it appealed to Bavarian nationalism, and a few good accounts, such as that of BMW, resulted. Grandville died soon after taking up his post, and his successor had to be found from outside Morgans, since there was no one then available within the bank who could speak German.

The aims in setting up the Munich office had been three: to look after British clients who wanted to invest or operate in Germany; to obtain

German clients; and to maintain contact with German institutions. But over the 1970s, it was found that exchange rate movements had militated against development of the first two aims, and as for the third, most German institutions set up offices in London. By 1978 it was clear that the main business Morgans were doing in Germany was project finance, and since this could be adequately supported from London, the Munich office was closed.[15]

No further foreign outposts were established between 1969 and 1972, presumably because management attention was concentrated on domestic developments. In 1972, however, there were two moves mooted, one non-controversial and long-lasting, the other controversial and, in the end, aborted. The first was the setting-up in July 1972 of offices in Jersey and Guernsey, which have concentrated on the provision of company secretarial, accounting, and management services and on investment management.[16] Morgan Grenfell (Jersey) Limited and Morgan Grenfell (Guernsey) Limited have been so successful that together, as Morgan Grenfell (C.I.) Ltd, they constitute one of the main revenue-generators of the Channel Islands. The second was the beginning of serious discussions amongst the 'Morgan family' about future collaboration, including the merging of their non-US and Canadian interests.

'Triangle' and its Aftermath

On 16 and 17 January 1972, Stevens, Barrington, Chappell, and Reeves met with four partners from Morgan Stanley. The meeting was secret —in particular from Morgan Guaranty—and the purpose was to consider possible areas of co-operation, which might even include some form of share exchange. A week later, the Morgan Stanley partners had what was later termed the 'planning Friday', in which they discussed long-term strategy, and made the unanimous decision that the Morgan family had a unique opportunity to provide international financial services to meet the needs of worldwide business. By mid-February Stevens's assessment was that 'our talks with Morgan Stanley will continue to lumber for some time at the end of which we may be faced with a situation that requires rapid thinking and decisions', which was roughly what happened.[17]

By early March the idea had emerged of a firm to be called 'Morgan International', which would pool the expertise of the Morgan family, although some members of Morgan Stanley continued 'to evangelise on the virtues of an MECI Limited mostly owned by Morgan Stanley and run by Morgan Grenfell which will astonish the world'.[18] Although various ideas would be mooted over the following fifteen months, discussion would return to the idea of a Morgan International, and Morgan Stanley would never shake loose the conviction that whatever resulted from the talks, they should, if possible, control it.

It was only in August 1972 that Morgan Guaranty really joined in the talks. Stevens and Chappell went to New York and met with Pat Patterson, Walter Page, and Lew Preston of Morgan Guaranty:

The meeting was very friendly. We got the impression that the full scope of our talks with MS was only beginning to dawn on them, and that they had imagined previously that they were being asked to bless some bilateral MG/MS arrangement rather than contribute to a general Morgan family exercise. They showed considerable interest in the larger operation. . . . .[19]

The name for the discussions now became 'Triangle'.

Over the subsequent months there were visits back and forth, and Morgan Stanley and Morgan Guaranty men pored over Morgan Grenfell's books, trying to fathom just how a merchant bank did business. Ideas were proposed and discarded, although one to which Morgan Stanley stubbornly clung was that it could take a 50% shareholding in Morgan Grenfell, and even the insistence of the Bank of England that it would not countenance the idea failed to convince.[20] Then, as Stevens had predicted a year earlier, pressure was suddenly put on Morgan Grenfell. On 16 March 1973 Stevens 'spoke to Lew Preston on the telephone. He told me that it looked as if MGT and Morgan Stanley were going to agree to set up Morgan International and, in his view, it would be a great pity if MG were not associated. When I reminded him that we had had nothing in writing setting out their ideas he promised that he would send a copy of the proposed plan.'[21] The 'Proposal for Discussion', dated 20 April 1973, arrived at Morgan Grenfell on 1 May, and the following afternoon the Holdings Board met to consider it.

It was proposed that the three firms establish a new company, Morgan International, to conduct various activities outside the US and Canada. Morgan Grenfell would continue its UK capital markets business and Morgan et Cie International would continue its international issues business. Morgan International would be owned 45% each by Morgan Guaranty and Morgan Stanley and 10% by Morgan Grenfell, and would increasingly be the focal point for the international non-commercial banking business of the three. Morgan Grenfell would continue as a UK firm, but instead of the 31.67% shareholding by Morgan Guaranty, there would be substituted a 50% shareholding by Morgan International. MECI would continue as a *banque d'affaires*, coming under the 100% ownership of Morgan International.[22]

There is very little contemporary evidence that any member of the Holdings Board backed the plan as it stood, regardless of whatever feeling there might have been on the general advisability of some sort of joint venture with the two American cousins. The written reaction of David Bendall, who had joined the bank in 1971 from the Foreign Office to help Stevens develop the international side, was perhaps more trenchant than most, probably fuelled by his Europeanist outlook. He pointed out that Morgan Grenfell were being asked to surrender not only currently profitable business, such as Eurobonds and project finance, but also future business in Europe, Asia, and so on. In return they would receive only 10% (and for UK shareholders, a net 5%) of MI's equity and profits. On the other hand, Morgan Guaranty and Morgan Stanley were giving up very little. Morgan Stanley, for example, were not willing to surrender their profitable Eurobond business in MECI, and the two in effect were only surrendering future possibilities. Further, MI would clearly be American-dominated, and it was inconceivable that a British bank should develop its relations and business with other European countries under an American flag. In sum,

this is a breath-takingly onesided deal, favourable to MGT in particular, since they would have a very cheap entry to international investment banking. Meanwhile, MG will be bottled up for good in the UK. Europe is not the *foreign* market for MG but our future domestic market.[23]

The scheme, in short, had caused 'considerable ill-feeling' in Morgan Grenfell; indeed, a number of the corporate finance directors threatened to resign *en bloc* if the proposals were implemented. It transpired that the shape of the proposal resulted from the failure of the two American firms to agree. Morgan Guaranty, who were already building up an investment business in London, were primarily concerned about its rationalization, while Morgan Stanley were more concerned with underwriting and thus maintaining the position of MECI. For its part Morgan Grenfell thought that 'London was really the capital market of the EEC and that we regarded ourselves as an operation which should be used to lead the Morgan attack on business in this area'. It was clear that the next series of meetings, to be held on 20 through 22 June 1973 at the Grotto Bay Hotel in Bermuda—usually a venue for honeymooners—would bring matters to a head.[24]

The Morgan Grenfell team was made up of Stevens, Reeves, Peter Phillips, Gorell Barnes, Sparrow, and Bendall, the last-named three being rooted opponents of the whole scheme. Stevens by that time did not know what he wanted from the talks, if anything, but thought that something might be salvaged. The opening statement by Morgan Stanley made manifest what would become the fundamental reason for the failure of the talks — their refusal to put either their US issuing business or their Eurobond business into the Morgan International pot: what were they proposing to contribute? Stevens made an opening statement for Morgan Grenfell, and the two American firms

were somewhat taken aback by our opening remarks in which we repeated that the Proposal was unacceptable, both to MG's Board and the Bank of England, that the concept of cooperation rather than union was far more practicable, and also outlined the areas of growth for MG which we saw as being likely over the next few years. In spite of the fact that the former had been communicated to them on several occasions in the past, this appeared to be the first time that they, and particularly Pat Patterson, appreciated the firmness of our views. It was necessary to reiterate that it would not be possible to increase the American involvement in MG both because we did not wish such a thing to happen and also because it was not possible if we wished to remain a member of the BBA [British Bankers' Association] and an Accepting House.

Stevens then turned things over to Bendall. His argument was that since Britain was about to join the EEC, it would benefit all three houses if Morgan Grenfell had the flagship position in Europe, because they would have a better position compared with American banks. He added that Europeans did not like Anglo-Saxons, but they disliked the British less than the Americans. The meeting came to a rather rapid close after his statement, with the Americans asking for a recess; during this period the representatives of the two American firms plus Stevens—but not Bendall, by special American request—had a meeting, during which Stevens discovered just how badly the American had taken Bendall's remarks: the Americans' decision was that there was no need for further meetings. Apparently he had shocked them badly, since they had never, they said, found themselves unpopular in Europe. In general terms the Americans had every reason to be shocked: Stevens had presumably not warned them that he had been unable to sell the concept of Triangle to his own colleagues, and therefore Morgan Grenfell's statement came, apparently, as a complete surprise. In an informal meeting between Stevens, Bendall, Patterson, and Preston, Preston reacted rather excitedly with a threat to sell out all MGT's shares in MG. [Patterson] was much calmer and suggested a further meeting on the following morning since lack of prior consultation had produced embarrassment to them and closer regular consultation should be established. We [Morgan Grenfell] raised again the fact that their present shareholding was not sacrosanct and they drew our attention to the problem of the name.

However, Morgan Guaranty the following month underlined its desire to retain the one-third shareholding.

In order to salvage something from the fiasco, it was agreed that there would be quarterly summit meetings in either London or New York.[25] It had been possible for both Morgan Stanley and Morgan Guaranty to meet Morgan Grenfell in Bermuda, since they were discussing non-US business; the 1919 Edge Act permitted a commercial banker and a securities house to combine for business outside the US, whereas the 1933 Banking Act prevented it inside the US. However, at the summit meetings, which lasted until 1981, business throughout the world was discussed, and Morgan Grenfell therefore met with either the one or the other, but not the two together.

The discussions with the American cousins had of course stimulated within Morgan Grenfell the consideration of alternatives. Indeed, by mid-April 1973 a proposed 'Triangle 2' had been drawn up, which involved Morgan Grenfell, Mitsubishi, and Suez, the last a favourite of Stevens. In December 1969 Stevens had been appointed one of the UK directors of Compagnie Financière de Suez, and one of his duties was to advise them on future planning. They wanted to expand in London, perhaps by acquiring a merchant bank or by developing their own subsidiary; he advised them that any bank which they could acquire would probably not have a very good business, and a subsidiary would take years to become viable. He suggested that instead they should look for alliances, and he offered one with Morgan Grenfell. By late 1973 a co-operation agreement was worked out, which was to include an exchange of shares (the latter never carried out, largely because of the total imbalance in size).[26] But before it could be implemented Morgans were struck a stunning blow: the unexpected death of Sir John Stevens on 27 October 1973 at the age of fifty-nine.

During 1973 Harcourt, the chairman of MG Holdings, had gradually withdrawn from the day-to-day work of the bank, increasingly turning things over to Stevens. Stevens in his turn had arranged for G. W. Mackworth-Young to join the bank to be groomed as his own eventual successor. Mackworth-Young was the second senior partner at the stockbrokers Rowe & Pitman; he was, in fact, their corporate finance partner, one of his major attractions for Stevens. Because Stevens was a banker and a foreign exchange man by background, his relationship with the corporate finance people could sometimes be touchy: some corporate finance directors believed that he did not understand the nature of corporate finance (and investment) business, because they were client-oriented rather than transaction-oriented, and indeed he sometimes gave the impression that both corporate finance and investment management were dispensable. Stevens was presumably aware of the consequent unhappy divisions within the bank, and the recruitment of Mackworth-Young was intended to help heal the breach (corporate finance had worked with Mackworth-Young for years and he had their confidence). Unfortunately, between Mackworth-Young's agreement to join and his arrival on 1 January 1974, Stevens died, and all the arrangements fell into disarray. Instead, Collins became non-executive chairman of MG Holdings, Catto chairman of the bank, and Rawlinson became finance director, the first time the bank had had one. There was no chief executive as such, but an executive committee of the board of the bank was established, comprising Catto as chairman and Mackworth-Young as vice-chairman, together with Bernard, Chappell, Eburne, Reeves, and Rawlinson, who were responsible for day-to-day management.

Mackworth-Young spent 1974 finding out how Morgans worked and learning about his colleagues; then on 1 January 1975 he became the chief executive, with Reeves as his deputy, and the executive committee was disbanded. One of Mackworth-Young's most important talents was the ability to hold together a rapidly growing, disparate organization. He was concerned about the rivalry between banking and investment on the one hand and corporate finance on the other, and accordingly he positioned himself in a very small room at the end of a corridor, putting himself geographically midway between the two. His was not an innovative mind, but he was a reconciler and a catalyst.

When he first joined his reaction had been that Morgans had too many committees and not enough individual decision-making, but by the end of the 1970s he had apparently come to agree with the others that this collegiate and consensual approach was one of Morgans' strengths. His tenure saw the introduction of a management committee in January 1978, a decision-taking body which would meet weekly and whose brief would be management matters rather than day-to-day business. The Holdings Board remained as a supervisory body, and this was underlined with another reorganization in November 1979: members of the management committee would no longer be members of the Holdings Board, although the group chief executive normally attended meetings of the latter. The daily management of the bank would be the responsibility of the chief executive along with the board of the bank, made up of all the bank's directors; the board would meet monthly. The management responsibility for the group as a whole would remain with the management committee, made up of the heads of the various business activities plus the finance director and secretary; the committee would meet weekly. Finally, the supervision of the group as a whole would be the responsibility of the Holdings Board, which would meet quarterly. Catto now became non-executive chairman of the Holdings Board, Mackworth-Young became chairman of Morgan Grenfell & Co. (the bank), and Reeves became group chief executive, all from 1 January 1980.[27]

Further Expansion Overseas

Major reasons for the management changes were the growth in the number and range of Morgans' activities and the rapidity with which Stevens's international plans were being made manifest. Bendall took over Stevens's role as the godfather of the Indo-Suez relationship, and in August 1974 a protocol was signed which established an operating relationship between Morgans and Suez. The two organizations wanted to give a 'certain immediate reality' to the relationship, and Morgans fell in with Suez's suggestion that they look at joint ventures in the Far East. Compagnie Financière de Suez was structured like an investment trust, and they had, through the branches of Banque Indochine (a commercial bank), a presence throughout South-East Asia. The theory was that there were merchant banking and financing opportunities in Hong Kong, Singapore, Kuala Lumpur, and elsewhere: Indo-Suez would provide the clients and Morgans would provide the know-how.[28]

In Singapore, Indo-Suez and Morgan Grenfell (Singapore) Limited was duly established in August 1975, owned 40% each by Indo-Suez and Morgans and 20% by the Development Bank of Singapore; the relationship with the Development Bank gave status to the organization in Singapore and helped facilitate the acquisition of the necessary licences. (In due course Morgans and Indo-Suez bought them out.) A good staff was recruited, and it is clear that most of Morgans' efforts in the Far East went into Singapore. This meant that the parallel joint venture in Hong Kong developed very slowly and not nearly as effectively: with the expansion going on in London, and the consequent lack of people available to go out to the Far East, it was very difficult to give it the necessary support.

By 1976 it was clear that the Morgan–Suez relationship was not working, primarily because there was a conflict of national interest. The idea had been that project finance would be developed and served from, for example, Singapore, but it became increasingly obvious that an Anglo-French bank would suffer because French and British contractors were frequently in competition for contracts. In 1976 Rawlinson went out to decide what to do about the situation, with the result that in June 1976 there was an amicable parting in the Far East, with Morgans buying Indo-Suez out of Singapore and Indo-Suez buying Morgans out of Hong Kong.

In Singapore Morgans inherited a very good staff and a going concern, which they renamed Morgan Grenfell (Asia). One reason for its success was that unlike many other such overseas organizations, Morgans limited the number of London-based staff sent out to run it—there were never more than three—and consciously tried to bring on able and hard-working local staff. They also had the inestimable advantage of coinciding with the bull market of the late 1970s. This enabled Morgan Grenfell (Asia) to become firmly enough established to ride out the downturn between 1983 and 1985.[29] But equally important was the high management quality and entrepreneurial skills of the Singaporean directors and staff. Indeed, profitability continued to grow, and by the end of 1988 MG (Asia) had a big role in Morgans' future strategy for the Asian-Pacific region.[30]

For some years after 1976 Morgans ceased to have any representation in Hong Kong, but the possibilities held out to Western business by the opening up of the People's Republic of China led Morgans to look at it again. In January 1984 the management committee decided in favour of returning to Hong Kong, and in March the Holdings Board approved the proposal to purchase Euromanagement Limited, a tax advisory and trust business, in order to use it as the basis for a new subsidiary, Morgan Grenfell (Hong Kong).[31]

The Far East was only one area of expansion, and it was poignant that within a year of Stevens's death so much of what he had planned came to fruition, with new offices set up on three continents. Europe had been a priority, and in January 1974 a representative office was set up in Rome. Bendall had decided to use the only real contact Morgans had in Italy, a former legal counsel to the British embassy, Guy Hannaford. After the

Second World War Hannaford had served for some years on a commission sorting out desequestrations, a position which ensured that he
met nearly every major Italian industrialist, and he introduced Morgans
to some of his friends, who were captains of industry. Georgio Cefis, the
son of the president of Montedison, was recruited from Mediobanca, and
on Hannaford's death in 1975 Cefis set up an office in Milan (the Rome
office was closed). By the later 1970s Morgans had an assured place in
Italy. A major reason for this was that Morgans exported the idea of
buyer credits, and indeed helped the Italian government to set up a
system modelled on that of the ECGD; appropriately, a significant part
of Morgans' work in Italy was project finance. Because of this, Morgans
in 1982 upgraded the representative office to a subsidiary, Morgan
Grenfell Italia SpA, which enabled Italian clients to pay in lira rather than
pounds.[32]

Morgans also decided to open an office in Switzerland, although less
for the business it would generate than for the services offered by the
banking system. In 1974 Morgan Grenfell Finance was established in
Geneva, in order to increase the bank's ability to manage private portfolios for non-UK residents (there was a gentlemen's agreement that they
would not take as clients any UK residents until UK exchange controls
were lifted). As a finance company Morgans' Swiss operation was not
allowed to engage in any real banking—i.e. it could not take deposits
outside the group or lend money, although it could manage it. Two years
later the operation was upgraded to what was called a finance company
with banking character: this was the origin of Morgan Grenfell (Switzerland) SA., which could now book loans and borrow to a limited extent,
and by the mid-1980s had an established position in the secondary Swiss
franc capital market.

In October 1979 the question of whether to upgrade Morgan Grenfell
(Switzerland) to full banking status was discussed. It was decided that on
balance it would not then be an advantage, but that the question should
be considered again in a year's time. When it was discussed again the
conclusion was different, and in 1980 Morgans applied for full banking
status. In the end Morgan Grenfell (Switzerland) remained a finance
company with banking character able to underwrite and trade, and a new
organization, Banque Morgan Grenfell en Suisse SA. was established. Its
principal business was the management of the portfolios of private clients
of significant means. The advantage of full banking status, with its more
onerous capital and reporting requirements, lay primarily in the higher
profile given to an asset management business: investment clients often

showed strong preference for placing their affairs in the hands of a bank rather than those of a finance company.[33]

Another area in which Stevens had taken a particular interest was the Middle East. He had been, in his personal capacity, adviser to the Central Bank of Iran, and others in the bank, such as Douglas-Home and McAfee, had contacts in, for example, the Gulf and Oman. Once the oil boom began the business possibilities increased considerably, and Morgans soon felt they should have a base out there. One possibility was Beirut as a financial and communications centre, but there were two arguments against it: it appeared to some in the bank to be inherently unstable, and Morgans had for a while an important joint venture with the Arab Bank, which was quite strong there. Eventually Morgans set up an office in Cairo: the Egyptian balance of payments was improving and a number of big projects were being discussed, while communications with the rest of the Middle East were good. But relations between Egypt and the Gulf States were sometimes difficult, and the Egyptian economy remained one of the weakest in the region. In the end these problems, combined with those of finding staff prepared to go there, made it impossible to justify the high cost of maintaining an office in Cairo, and in 1986 it was closed.[34]

There were also problems in Iran. Stevens's connections in the country had facilitated Morgans' doing business there, and in February 1972, for example, they arranged the finance (US$21 million) for the Ahwaz–Rey second oil pipeline. Because of the oil boom and the Shah's development plans, a study team visited Iran in 1973; it was decided to open up a representative office in Tehran, and in September 1974 Desmond Harney, a member of the Diplomatic Service who was already working in the Embassy, became Morgans' representative. By late 1978, however, it was problematical whether or not there was any future for the office. Harney had returned to London for discussions in the autumn, and it was decided that he should return to Tehran for a few weeks, both to assess the situation and to demonstrate to Iranian clients that Morgans had no intention of leaving unless the situation became too dangerous. However, the return of Ayatollah Khomeini in February 1979 led to the formal overthrow of the old regime within two weeks and the answer was clear; the office was finally closed at the end of the year.[35]

Morgans had many fewer contacts in South America than in the Middle East. Representative offices, manned as a rule by locals, were set up there both to generate business in what was then a fruitful territory for export and project finance, and to support Morgans' contractor-clients in what was a highly competitive field. The office in Venezuela was the only one to be staffed from the UK, and it was authorized in February 1976 largely because of a pending major project. By August the same year Morgans had agreed a proposal, in conjunction with two Venezuelan private banks and the Kuwait International Investment Company, to organize international finance for capital projects in Venezuela. Offices elsewhere, in Chile and Colombia, for example, were opened in due course.[36]

One redeeming virtue of representative offices in South America was that they were not too costly: it was the horrific prospective cost of opening an office in Tokyo—estimated in 1978 to be £250,000 a year —which helped keep Morgans out of Japan for years. It was again Stevens who was responsible for Morgans' first tentative venture into Japan: he argued that everyone was forming a link with a Japanese partner, and accordingly Reeves and Adrian Hohler were sent off to Japan to identify a suitable partner. The Mitsubishi Bank was a favoured possibility, but it was found to be impossible to come to an agreement. Morgans then decided upon a trilateral rather than a bilateral arrangement: discussions with Tokai Bank, whose strength lay in the Japanese provinces, went well, and Tokai brought in Kyowa Bank. Thus in August 1974 Tokai Kyowa Morgan Grenfell Limited was set up. The arrangement was a useful one for all three partners: Morgan Grenfell 'saw it as a means of cementing our relationship with the banks. They saw it as a means of building up a merchant/investment banking expertise in London.'[37]

The question of whether the bank ought to be more active in Japan was debated in August 1978 by the management committee: if Morgans were to present themselves as having full international coverage, it would be difficult to explain why they were not represented in one of the richest industrialized countries in the world. Indeed, Japanese advice was always that Morgans should set up in Japan if they were serious about attracting Japanese clients. But the cost of doing so would be horrendous, and the prospects of recouping the cost within less than four years not very good. A decision was put off, as it was again in December 1980. But the bank was aware that Japanese companies were increasingly looking overseas for capital investment opportunities. Morgans would not be successful if they tried advising Japanese companies from London: Japanese corporations would not take them seriously unless they had a presence in Tokyo, since the Japanese themselves believed that local representation was necessary in any market in which it was hoped to transact business effectively. But if the bank were to decide to set up an office in Tokyo, each division would have to be prepared both to bear a proportion of the costs and to justify the cost in terms of potential fee income. By mid-January 1981 internal soundings had been completed, and the management committee decided on 14 January that it was worth while opening a representative office for a three-year trial period. Raymond Highman then went out as Morgans' first representative in Tokyo.[38]

Finally, there was the question of representation in the US, a question complicated not only by the Morgan family relationship, but even more by the fact that Morgan Guaranty were, with their one-third holding in Morgan Grenfell, the largest single shareholder. Again, Stevens was very keen on the US—he tended to seek relaxation by going off on his own to explore provincial banks in Wisconsin—but it was the failure of Triangle which triggered Morgan Grenfell's decision to open a representative office in New York. Yet this decision must be seen in the context of the changing nature of the relationship between the London and New York houses.

Divorce in the Family

The merger in 1959 between J. P. Morgan & Co. and the Guaranty Trust Company opened the final act in the relationship. The Guaranty Trust had had an office in London since the early years of the century, and this office became Morgan Guaranty Trust's London branch. At first it was thought that the two London offices would be complementary, and a merger of Morgan Grenfell and Morgan Guaranty's London offices was opposed by Harcourt in 1963 on these grounds, as well as on those of the loss of British business which would result. But gradually over the 1960s relations became more difficult: in an argument over the Ford UK Pension Fund, for example, for whom Morgan Grenfell had acted as adviser since 1953, Morgan Guaranty accused Morgan Grenfell of trying to poach a client (they both advised their respective national Ford companies) and apparently tried to persuade Morgan Grenfell not to set up a trust department in competition with their own in London. There was usually good will at the top on both sides, but the imperatives of business seemed more and more to hold sway.[39]

Over the century Morgan Grenfell had benefited from falling heir to the London business of Morgan Guaranty's American clients, but this became increasingly less likely now that the New York bank continued to develop its London branch. This meant that if Morgan Grenfell wished to retain or increase the numbers of their American clients, they had to go out and find them. Unfortunately,

. . . recent experience has shown that a new relationship with a U.S. Corporation most often starts with some banking business, usually in the U.K., or with preliminary work in the acquisition field; it is very hard to obtain investment or other corporate finance business without a less significant relationship having first been achieved. M.G.T. unavoidably gets the pick of any banking business (other than leasing) in most cases. . . .

We are at a disadvantage compared with many of our competitors in not having our own operation in New York and M.G.T.'s domestic banking officers, who are of course M.G.T.'s main contact with their U.S. corporate clients, and potentially a network of salesmen for us second to none, are at present really in no way selling our services. . . .[40]

By the time the Triangle negotiations were in train, the old order of things, by which the two cousins did not trespass on each other's preserve, had gone.

Morgan Grenfell had never had any representation of their own in the US. Partly this was because of the family relationship, and the fact that before 1959 'each was content to transact the major part of its business, both nationally- and internationally-sourced in its own country'.[41] But sentimental notions had not prevented Morgan Guaranty from expanding its services in London, and it is probable that American legal restrictions were a more important reason for keeping Morgan Grenfell out of the US. One restriction was the Banking Act of 1933, by which Morgan Grenfell was prevented from operating in the US as an investment bank because of Morgan Guaranty's one-third shareholding. The other restriction was the Interest Equalization Tax of 1963, which imposed a tax on American investment in foreign securities in an attempt to stem capital outflows; so long as it was in force, there was little point in Morgan Grenfell's setting up as a distributor of securities in the US. Therefore, when in February 1973 the announcement was made that the tax would be phased out by the end of 1974, the reaction within the bank was immediate, with Chappell and Reeves telexing to Hardman and Stevens in New York that

events of this week and probable . . . changes enormously strengthen argument that our means of representation in US market must be reinforced. Our overnight thoughts are purely on basis that if family links cannot be cemented through present exercise (which still remains our first preference) then we must repeat must find technique of opening business-doing office as compared with mere representation in US, with all that this means for existing shareholders.[42]

Mere representation, however, would be the first step.

But before this step was taken, Morgan Grenfell received the first of what would be two invitations from Morgan Guaranty during the 1970s to take part in a London-based joint venture. Morgan Guaranty wanted to establish an international investment advisory company in Europe, and they thought that it made sense to combine their Paris and Geneva investment businesses with Morgan Grenfell's in London; indeed, a desire to rationalize their investment advisory business had apparently been their primary motive in arguing for a Morgan International. Once that proposal had been torpedoed at the Bermuda meetings in June 1973, the possibility remained that Morgan Grenfell might agree to a limited combined venture. But the London bank did not: they insisted that their funds managed for UK clients must be in a wholly owned operation; besides, a joint venture with an American bank would probably lead to the loss of prestigious Post Office and other government-related funds. Morgan Grenfell accepted with equanimity that the two would now be in competition, deciding in the first instance that they had better actively cultivate those funds originally brought to them by Morgan Guaranty. Morgan Guaranty then went ahead with their own arrangements.[43]

Meanwhile, plans were developed for a Morgan Grenfell representative to go out to New York, and in September 1973 the subject was broached to Morgan Guaranty. They 'responded enthusiastically to this idea', and agreed to Morgan Grenfell's suggestion that he have an office in one of their buildings, although in fact that suggestion was never acted upon. By October, it had been decided that Christopher Whittington would be the manager, and that he would take up residence on 1 April 1974. Morgan Guaranty was co-operative, and from the beginning Whittington was invited to attend the weekly meeting of its international banking division.[44] Largely because of American regulatory obstacles, Morgan Grenfell 'drifted along with a representative office' until 1980, when the question would arise as to whether it should be upgraded.[45]

But before that decision was taken, Morgan Guaranty made a second suggestion to Morgan Grenfell to join in a London-based venture, this time to participate in the secondary Eurobond business. Morgan Grenfell had been involved in primary issuing since the mid-1960s; in 1968, for example, the bank were joint managers for three Eurodollar issues and one Euro-Deutschmark issue, and helped to underwrite seventy-four issues.[46] But this business grew naturally out of their work in issuing fixed-interest stocks in sterling, and those involved reported to a corporate finance director. In 1972 through January 1973 Morgan Grenfell had a booming new issue business; then the bottom fell out of the Eurobond market, and there were virtually no more issues for the rest of 1973. The bank cut back on their Eurobond department. Then in 1974 the market came back to life, but in a different form. Previously it had been predominantly an international market for American corporations selling to Swiss-based investors, while it was now predominantly a government-centred market. Morgan Grenfell decided in 1974 to intensify efforts to establish themselves in all aspects of the Eurobond market, and the capability was built up. However, to some extent they still approached it as a corporate market, rather than recognizing that the market and the market-place had changed.

In February 1976 Chappell mooted the possibility that Morgan Grenfell and Morgan Guaranty might co-operate more closely in the Eurobond market: Morgan Guaranty had now withdrawn from MECI, which then became Morgan Stanley International, and they would presumably have to build up a capability of their own. However, at the summit meeting held at Morgan Grenfell in May 1976, Morgan Guaranty said that they 'were not ready to expand into the underwriting business [of Eurobonds] at the present time'.[47]

In the same month, however, Morgan Stanley decided to build up a fully-fledged trading capability in the secondary Eurobond market, and to site it in London. The following year they sounded out Morgan Grenfell on the possibility of the two firms' co-operating in the UK market, although Mackworth-Young later wrote that Reeves and he

were not quite sure whether we were being wooed or raped, but it felt very like the former. . . . They said that they would particularly like to be involved in Eurobond issues for UK companies now that these were again happening. . . . They denied hotly any suggestion that they didn't like two Morgan houses being in the same management group. They clearly want us to introduce them into management positions for UK companies.

The bargain offered was that if Morgan Grenfell introduced them into Eurobond issues for UK companies, they in return would refer American companies to Morgan Grenfell when the Americans wished to acquire UK companies.[48]

In June 1977 Reeves, Mackworth-Young, and Whittington met with Morgan Guaranty for the summit, and

it was felt by MGT that there should be some way in which all three of the houses should be able to cooperate in the area of Eurobonds and floating rate issues. We [Morgan Grenfell] pointed out that . . . there could well be some point in MGT and MG jointly making bids for certain pieces of business. . . . Regarding the future of longterm cooperation one should be able to utilise MGT's branch network to build up placing power as they come in contact with many more potential purchasers of bonds than MG could hope to meet. It was agreed that we should continue the dialogue on this subject, with a view eventually to working jointly on an issue.[49]

This discussion clearly stimulated the same thoughts in both banks: if the two were to co-operate in the primary market, why not the secondary? H. C. Tilley, a Morgan Grenfell director, wrote that

perhaps we should actively consider the establishment jointly with MGT of a Eurobond secondary market trading operation since in my view one can never really achieve long term credibility as an issuing house without being prepared to operate in the secondary market. . . . We have always shrunk from this due to the amount of capital required but if MGT were to be our partners then all this would change.[50]

By January 1978 Morgan Guaranty was 'making noises which indicate that it is thinking of entering the area of international issues'. W. J. Hopper, the head of the Eurobonds department in Morgan Grenfell, assessed the options open to Morgan Guaranty, one of which was to participate in a jointly owned investment bank. For this purpose, Morgan Grenfell might be seen as its partly owned investment bank:

it is difficult to assemble a fully trained eurobond team and MG has one. Furthermore, in 1978 MG may branch out modestly from primary market activities into secondary market activities and placing. . . . [On the other hand,] MGT has a natural fear, by no means unjustified, that if it introduces issue business to MG, it is difficult to prevent MG doing banking business with the same company—possibly at the wish of that company rather than MG. . . . From MG's point of view it would be highly beneficial to have MGT stand behind its international issuing activities . . . [I]f the market thought that MG's issuing activities were backed by MGT's financial muscle, we would be in the same league as the Deutsche Bank![51]

By October 1978 Morgan Guaranty had decided to enter the secondary market in London, and they proposed that they should do it jointly with Morgan Grenfell. During a long meeting on 2 November 1978, the management committee, with Hopper and Whittington in attendance, debated the question at length. On the one hand, the proposal would have definite advantages: business in Eurobonds was going increasingly to the bigger banks, and their combined size and skills would have a far greater effect than the individual effort of either; and further, Morgan

Grenfell would get access to Morgan Guaranty's client list and marketing effort in what could be a very profitable area. Yet the disadvantages appeared commanding: 'it was difficult to envisage how, if the venture were carried out through a joint company, MG could in the long term retain either control or an equal share in the management of the operation. It was felt that MG should not go down a route which would result in its losing control over the team which it had built up'; and besides this, 'MG's history of joint ventures had not been good. Such ventures had either had to be wound up or we have eventually been bought out.'

In conclusion it was agreed:

that GWM-Y should show a positive interest in carrying the proposal further but only on the basis that we were not prepared to exchange a good, viable, profitable Eurobond capability and team for a dividend. We would only be prepared to go ahead if we could ensure at the outset that what was ours would remain so.[52]

The discussions with Morgan Guaranty were ended soon thereafter, much to the disappointment of Catto and Collins, and the American bank set up Morgan Guaranty Limited in London.[53]

If Morgan Grenfell were going to go it alone, they would have to strengthen their Eurobond capability. In June 1979 it was decided to take Eurobonds out of Corporate Finance and set up a new Eurobond Division; by this time the option of co-operation with Morgan Guaranty no longer existed, although they did not object to the London bank's plans (nor to Morgan Grenfell's asking Morgan Stanley for advice). By March 1981 the basic sales team and half the trading team necessary for a secondary capacity were in place.[54]

Morgan Guaranty were now almost fully competitive with Morgan Grenfell on the latter's home ground, with only merger and acquisition activities still out of their reach. Increasingly, the argument for upgrading representation in the US, which had been decided against in 1977, strengthened. The probability that this path, if taken, would soon lead to a break between the two banks was accepted and indeed, in some quarters, welcomed: the time was fast approaching when the restrictions implied by the Morgan Guaranty shareholding would be perceived as outweighing the advantages. This was especially true in the US.[55]

In March 1979 the New York representative office came up for review in the management committee. The work being done was changing, with personnel spending greater amounts of time on specific business; this meant that there was less time to develop new business, and new staff were needed, which was very expensive under the present structure.

At the same time our credibility in the U.S.A. is adversely affected by our inability to do business there. There was further a danger that because we could not assist our clients in U.S. acquisitions and had to introduce them to U.S. investment banks, our role in this area would cease. . . . As a result . . . . it was recommended and agreed that we should again review the methods by which we could do business in the U.S.A. and be prepared to speak frankly to MGT on the subject. Such a review . . . would include all possibilities. . . .[56]

In July 1979 the management committee considered the report on US prospects produced at their request by Whittington and Jonathan Perry. First of all, Morgan Grenfell's scope for business consisted primarily in advising British clients on US acquisitions, possibly in advising small and medium-sized US businesses on US mergers and acquisitions, in private placings and general financial advice, and in portfolio management for US domestic pension funds. Unfortunately, not all of these activities could be carried out whilst Morgan Guaranty was a shareholder. For example, mergers and acquisitions would be restricted to agreed cash offers since only registered broker dealers, and not commercial banks, were allowed to solicit shareholders and to arrange share-for-share exchanges. However, as long as the borrower was a foreign entity, private placements would not fall foul of US law. The report recommended that Morgan Grenfell should talk to the Federal Reserve Board to see if they could register as a broker dealer in order to carry on those merger and acquisition and private placement activities which would be incidental to foreign or international business; they would have to agree not to engage in domestic underwriting. It also recommended that Morgan Guaranty be told exactly what they proposed to discuss with the Federal Reserve Board. If the discussions with the Board were successful, the recommendation was that Morgans should establish Morgan Grenfell Incorporated in New York and register it as a broker dealer. After some discussion, the management committee decided to proceed exactly as suggested, and in March 1980 the principle of incorporation was approved.[57]

Morgan Guaranty were told of the decision, and over the next few months negotiations were carried out with the Federal Reserve Board. The object was to ensure that Morgan Grenfell Inc. would be able to engage in a far wider spectrum of business than could the representative office, while not disturbing Morgan Guaranty's shareholding. In the end this was done, and permission was received for the proposed New York subsidiary to register as a broker dealer. An American, John B. Fraser of the First Boston Corporation, became the first president, and by April 1981 the new subsidiary was in operation.[58]

The refusal of Morgan Grenfell to agree on a joint venture in Eurobonds, and the decision to incorporate in New York, appear finally to have decided Morgan Guaranty to sell its one-third shareholding. The possibility that this might one day happen had been part of Morgan Grenfell's calculations since at least 1973, when in the aftermath of the Triangle negotiations the London Bank proposed that the shareholding be reduced to 15%. In February 1977 a memorandum circulating within Morgan Grenfell recommended that Morgan Guaranty be replaced as a shareholder by one or two British institutions, primarily on the grounds that increasing expansion on both sides would lead to their bumping into each other more and more often. But all these discussions were theoretical; when, however, Morgan Guaranty notified Morgan Grenfell of their decision, the need to consider the practical alternatives became urgent. There seemed to be two: merger with a friendly insurance broker, or the placing of Morgan Guaranty's shares with a number of institutions.

From 1934 until the capitalization issue in January 1961, Morgan Guaranty was the only institutional shareholder, the remainder of the shares being held by directors past and present and their families; there were then 1 million ordinary shares and 249, 997 6% preference shares. With the 1961 issue, a further 250, 000 6% preference shares were created, and these were placed with four new institutional shareholders: the Legal and General Assurance Society (50, 000 shares), the Prudential Assurance Company (50,000 shares), Prudential Nominees Limited (50, 000 shares), and the Sun Life Assurance Company (100, 000 shares). In 1967 Morgan Grenfell and Willis, Faber & Dumas, the Lloyd's insurance broker, exchanged shareholdings, with Willis Faber taking a 10% stake in Morgans; this was increased to 22% in 1974. With the various exercises in capitalization and authorization of new share capital over the two decades, the number of institutional shareholders increased and the proportion of the shares held by the families substantially decreased: by May 1980 the ratio was nearly 86 : 14.[59]

With contacts and even friendship at the highest level, Morgan Grenfell and Willis Faber had had a close relationship for years, in 1968 jointly setting up two unit trusts for the benefit of Lloyd's insurers. Thus when the bank had to decide what to do, the favoured option at first was a merger with Willis Faber, to result in a financial conglomerate which would allow Morgan Grenfell operational independence. However, the drawback was that Willis Faber, which has become a public limited company in 1976, might be taken over and Morgans would in that way be swallowed up by a predator. If the idea was proposed to Willis Faber, it was not taken up; at any rate the fall-back option, which was a placing of the shares with friendly institutions, was soon decided upon.

Morgan Guaranty wanted a premium for their shares, and this could have proved dangerous, since the best way to secure a premium would have been to sell the shareholding as a single block. But the overriding priority for Morgan Grenfell was to retain their independence, and the purchase of 33% of their shares would, because of the Takeover Code, have necessarily triggered off a full bid for Morgans. For this reason, and the danger that the world would interpret Morgan Guaranty's sale of 100% of their shareholding as a failure of confidence in Morgan Grenfell, they were prevailed upon to sell only 29.02% in the first instance. But they still wanted the premium, and Morgan Grenfell came up with the ingenious idea of converting a proportion of Morgan Guaranty's ordinary shares into $11\frac{1}{4}$% cumulative preference shares and placing those with the institutions. In the end Morgan Guaranty received 255p per share for their holding, compared with a price of 175p at which ordinary shares had changed hands in November 1980.

Therefore, in May 1981 a three-part transaction was announced: the placing of part of Morgan Guaranty's ordinary shareholding with existing institutional shareholders; the placing with institutional investors of £12 million of new $11\frac{1}{4}$% cumulative preference shares; and a rights issue of new ordinary shares, to be subscribed at 200p per share, which would raise approximately £12.5 million. The result was that Morgan Guaranty retained 3.98% of the enlarged share capital, Willis Faber now had 24%, and the Prudential Assurance Company now nearly $9\frac{1}{2}$% (up from 3.35%). Nine insurance companies, including the Prudential, owned 29.11%; six investment trusts owned 12.69%; and three pension funds owned 8.81%. There were four new institutional investors, the London and Manchester Assurance Company, the Industrial and General Investment Trust, the Church Commissioners, and the Merchant Navy Officers' Pension Fund. There was very little adverse press comment, with the perception dominating that the withdrawal made good business sense, since the two Morgan banks were competing all over the world. In May 1982 Morgan Guaranty's remaining shares were quietly placed with friendly institutions.[60]

And so the wheel came full circle. From the original American-owned but London-based merchant bank had grown three organizations: Morgan Grenfell, the direct heir of the legacy of George Peabody and J. S. Morgan, and J. P. Morgan & Co., the American-based branch set up by J. S. Morgan and his son Pierpont, which shared the same roots as the London bank, and which itself had spawned Morgan Stanley. For over a century Morgan Grenfell and J. P. Morgan & Co., had been bound by ties of interest and even of affection unusual in the world of banking. Each had strong claims to be dominant in its own sphere, J. P. Morgan & Co. as a commercial bank, Morgan Grenfell as a merchant bank, and each held sway in the respective home markets. But these markets changed, and business drew both banks overseas, and with these developments the gradual disengagement began. Yet, even during the period of growing competition, the two co-operated in many ways, in jointly arranging projects all over the world, referring business to each other, and generally facilitating each other's interests. But banks are businesses, not social networks, and when the conflict, or anticipation of future conflict, outweighed the benefits of the link, it was time to part. The fact that the parting was arranged amicably and with due consideration on both sides was a tribute to the century of shared history.

EPILOGUE
1981–1988

IN the 1980s, Morgan Grenfell took off: from net profits of £4.4 million in 1979 and £7.2 million in 1980, the figures leapt to £17 million in 1982 to £24 million in 1984 to almost £55 million in 1986. Banking, asset management, and corporate finance all contributed to profits, but it was the extraordinarily powerful and successful Corporate Finance Division which helped to make Morgan Grenfell almost a household name. By mid-decade Morgan Grenfell were regularly referred to in the press as the leading merchant bank in London.

During this period phenomenal changes were taking place in the financial services sector, as the Office of Fair Trading forced the Stock Exchange to eliminate its restrictive practices and allow banks as well as brokers to deal in equities and government securities. The conventional wisdom then insisted that merchant banks had two choices: they could develop such a capacity in order to play a role in the new world of continuous, global trading in securities, deemed vital to any merchant bank which wished to play in the first division, or they could retreat to being a niche player, profitable, but of a different status entirely. Those in the middle, it was feared, would be squeezed out. After much thought and discussion, Morgan Grenfell opted for the first choice, and this would require them to develop or acquire the capacity to trade and distribute securities.

The 1980s then saw major developments in the organization of Morgan Grenfell. The separation in May 1981 from Morgan Guaranty eliminated legal constraints on their development in the US, and over this period there was a progressive building-up of the organization in New York; this culminated in the purchase in December 1986 of Cyrus J. Lawrence Incorporated, a broker well known for the high quality of its research. The same period also saw a change in the presence in Tokyo, from representative office to branch; in 1986 Morgan Grenfell received the coveted securities licence from the Japanese government, and in 1987 a discretionary fund management licence. Both of these organizations were developed as profit centres in their own right, but they had another equally important function: situated in the two other major financial centres, they were intended to support a move into the international securities business.

The risks involved in trading in securities, whether equities or government stocks, meant that a much larger capital base was required. The decisions made in 1984, which included the purchase of a jobber, Pinchin, Denny & Co., and a gilt-edged broker, Pember & Boyle, and the consequent establishment of Morgan Grenfell Securities and Morgan Grenfell Government Securities, had as one consequence the need for more capital. This was met temporarily by a rights issue and the introduction of a new shareholder, the Deutsche Bank, in 1984. One way of acquiring capital is by selling equity to the public and becoming a listed company, and this had been repeatedly discussed over the years. After a diversion provided by abortive merger discussions with Exco International in January and February 1986, Morgan Grenfell Holdings in June 1986 took the momentous step of becoming a listed company.

But then, with the group at the height of its reputation for corporate finance prowess, a Department of Trade and Industry investigation began into the takeover of the Distillers Co. Ltd. by Guinness plc, for whom Morgans had acted as advisers. The chief executive and others resigned, and for a period the Group was run by an executive committee, rather as had been the case upon the death of Stevens. But within four months a new chief executive, John Craven, had joined the Group, and within a year of becoming listed it was clear that the wounds inflicted upon the bank's business had been very far from terminal. Indeed, the recovery demonstrated the depth of quality in Morgans, with neither business nor profits depending upon a few.

Craven had inherited the Group objective that they develop into an integrated, international investment house, alongside a separate but related investment management organization. For some months Morgan Grenfell Securities and Morgan Grenfell Government Securities, aided by the last leg of the bull market, traded reasonably successfully. But expansion of the market came to an abrupt halt with the stock-market crash on 19 October 1987. For some time after the crash their market share grew satisfactorily, but the decision of several of the bigger securities houses to trim margins to the bone meant that the business they had was increasingly unprofitable. By the late autumn of 1988, the decision was taken: in order to safeguard the profitability of the rest of the Group, Morgans had to withdraw from securities, both equities and gilts, except in New York and Singapore.

By the end of 1988, then, Morgan Grenfell had decided to concentrate on developing its traditional areas of quality and strength: banking, asset management, and corporate finance. What was required—and indeed had always been required throughout the Group's history—was high morale and continuing responsiveness to a changing environment. An organization dependent on the external political and economic climate, the changing needs of its clients, and the quality of its staff must necessarily have peaks and troughs, and for that reason many of the London merchant banks have gone through difficult times. Morgan Grenfell over the years had been no exception to this. But they had recovered and thrived, and as the Group began the second half of their second century, there was every indication that they would continue to do so.

Appendices

COMPILED BY JUDY SLINN

Appendix 1. George Peabody, George Peabody & Co. 1838–1864

Year	Capital	Gross earnings	Commission[1]	P/L stocks	Interest	Net profit[2]	Reserve[3]	Partners[4]		
								George Peabody	C. P. Gooch	J. S. Morgan
1845		12,656	1,430		358	11,486				
1846		29,592	2,562		1,053	22,821				
1851	250,000									
1852		41,681	30,170			37,625		34,615	3,010	
1853		29,527[5]			6,259	40,533		37,290	3,243	
1855	450,000		30,612	20,475	(2,021)[6]	42,515				
1856			47,881	41,927	1,385	87,469				
1857	637,823		55,805	22,618	10,747	50,000	33,268	32,500	3,500	14,000
1858	710,999		29,959	37,388	19,789	43,043	40,000	27,979	3,013	12,052
1859	862,008		30,661	39,096	3,104	60,000	9,006	39,000	4,200	16,800
1860	981,706		37,452	36,493	7,204	76,437		49,685	5,350	21,403
1861	964,322		42,360	(13,911)	4,748		26,084		No distribution made	
1862 old[7]	823,567		47,531	(2,730)	4,535		15,209			
1862 new			8,484	3,041	2,267		12,589			
1863 old	206,792	104,826	4,378	3,126	23	10,004	22,597	6,503	700	2,801
1863 new			31,049	61,217	9,679	75,000	894	22,500	10,500	42,000
1864 old	206,195		952	562					No distribution made	
1864 new			39,176	26,319	20,679		81,156			

[1] The main sources of income were commission (including acceptance commission), interest, and P/L stocks.

[2] Net profit = gross earnings less counting house expenses and losses and bad debts.

[3] From 1857 the amounts were put aside in a suspense account.

[4] Partners were paid a sum consisting partly of interest on their capital and partly the share of the profit.

[5] 1854 = 9 months to September 1854 (the end of the financial year was changed from December to September).

[6] ( ) indicates loss.

[7] From 1862 to 1864 the partnership accounts were kept separately as old and new.

NOTES TO APPENDIX I

Until 1851 George Peabody was the sole proprietor of the business. In the ledgers and papers which survive there are complete profit and loss accounts only for 1845 and 1846 and then from 1852 onwards. It is unclear whether this is because the accounts were not formalized, or because they have not survived. Although there are a considerable number of George Peabody's ledgers and papers at the Essex Institute, Salem, Mass., the series is incomplete, and it is therefore impossible to provide a complete run of figures to compare with the later ones (see Appendices II and III).

Nor is it clear what Peabody counted as his capital in these years. In January 1845 he opened in his books a new Capital account, which was credited with £20,000, to bear interest at 6% and to be made up every 6 months. The interest was to be paid into his No. 1 account, opened at the same time and credited with £23,000 at opening, to bear interest at 5%.

TABLE A. *Acceptances 1845–1851 (£)*

Year	Total amount	Amount outstanding at end of year
1845	193,557	65,187
1846	613,714	119,411
1847	708,005	187,237
1848	273,265	16,287
1849	552,176	
1850	953,334	
1851	1,901,854	614,374

It is abundantly clear, however, that he made most of his money out of dealing in stocks and bonds. His acceptance business also grew, as Table A indicates.

From 1851, when he formed George Peabody & Co. and took his clerk C. P. Gooch as a partner, and in particular from 1854, when J. S. Morgan joined him, the figures become more substantial.

Capital. From late in 1854 when J. S. Morgan became a partner, the capital was nominally £450,000; but from 1857 onwards it has been calculated as the total sum in the partners' accounts at the end of the year. It dropped sharply in 1863 when Peabody's £400,000 was withdrawn to a separate account. It was repaid to him in seven quarterly instalments between April 1864 and October 1865, with interest—a total sum of £446,512. He was also paid his share of the lease of 22 Old Broad Street, valued at £19,500, and paid in five annual instalments of £3,900. From 1862 to 1864 the partnership accounts were kept separately as old and new and because of payments owing it was not until July 1877 that the accounts of G. Peabody & Co. in liquidation were finally closed.

Sources. MS 181, various volumes, George Peabody Papers, Essex Institute, Salem, Mass. MSS 21761 and 21768, Morgan Grenfell Papers, Guildhall Library. Private ledgers, Morgan Grenfell Papers, MGC.

APPENDIX II. J. S. Morgan & Co. 1865–1909

Year	Capital	Gross earnings	Commission	P/L stocks	Interest	Other	Net profit	J. S. Morgan	C. P. Gooch	J. E. Peabody	J. C. Rogers	Reserve
1865		50,794	17,775	26,057	5,747	8,564 Erie loan	49,949	37,462	12,487			
1866		93,561	62,003	(18,278)[1]	12,283		27,457	20,593	6,864			40,000
1867		121,114	71,274	7,226	17,364	19,541 Chilean loan	100,000	75,000	25,000			12,249
1868	471,284	116,065	48,330	20,770	16,604	16,985 Dabney Morgan / 8,095 Gold profit	70,000	52,500	17,500			36,351
1869	529,686	97,238	62,011	(6,681)	12,778		40,000	30,000	10,000			36,823
1870	655,468	136,513	73,490	5,784	20,797	8,841 Chilean loan / 19,033 Illinois & St Louis	115,000	86,250	28,750			7,813
1871	1,057,200	374,363	159,527	122,669	41,881	14,130 French loan / 14,071 French 6%	352,274	264,206	88,069	8,000		1,000
1872	1,376,428	231,703	104,476	43,933	26,638		200,000	130,000	35,000	35,000		15,738
1873	1,560,805	175,165	88,215	(12,751)	22,306		100,000	65,000	17,500	17,500		44,172
1874	1,416,892	252,074	125,043	55,668	22,515	12,673 Dabney Morgan / 17,260 Allegheny Bonds	180,000	121,500		31,500	27,000	56,015
1875	1,460,853	164,277	84,231	(49,453)	21,885	10,228 New Jersey Bonds	75,184	50,749		13,157	11,278	15,000
1876	1,486,243	176,842	86,107	(21,106)	19,696	33,618 US 3%	120,822	81,555		21,144	18,123	
1877	1,670,415	202,477	90,333	1,024	18,115		168,000	113,400		29,400	25,200	
1878	1,762,416	137,014	47,906	41,794	13,721[2]	17,012 US 4% Syndicates	99,992	99,992	*W. H. Burns*			
1879	1,905,482	181,863	44,237	71,497	9,015		130,784	98,088	32,696			30,000
1880	2,330,887	279,566	59,332	79,482	16,909	94,807 V. & C. Rail Stocks	180,863	135,661	45,202			70,000
1881	2,726,719	334,330	109,205	160,670	24,547	10,469 Dabney Morgan	185,533	139,150	46,383			100,000
1882	2,913,995	159,064	64,817	23,449	28,421		127,771	95,828	31,943			
1883	3,126,450	175,782	59,020	61,437	8,876	11,600 Dabney Morgan	120,975	90,731	30,244			
1884	2,735,952	115,914	65,585	(41,078)	(166)			(4,178)	(2,089)			25,000 (Spec. Res.)

[1] ( ) indicates loss.

[2] In 1878 the interest account also shows a payment of £78,181 direct to J. S. Morgan.

APPENDIX II. *(cont.)*

Year	Capital	Gross earnings	Commission	P/L stocks	Interest	Other	Net Profit	J. S. Morgan / J. P. Morgan	W. H. Burns / W. S. M. Burns	Robert Gordon / C. E. Dawkins	F. W. Lawrence / E. C. Grenfell	J. P. Morgan, Jr.
1885	2,903,013	143,420	38,280	91,364	(10,979)[1]		112,670	65,512	31,804	15,354		
1886	2,923,986	194,361	52,272	123,943	(3,482)		162,034	92,359	46,990	22,685		
1887	2,698,426	204,834	86,564	47,704	17,326	18,249 Argentine 5%	159,724	91,100	46,349	22,375		
1888	2,382,026	161,950	36,222	104,426	5,771		132,716	75,648	38,488	18,580		
1889	2,386,468	173,974	39,160	107,803	10,339		146,413	83,455	42,460	20,498		
1890	1,772,889	43,641	26,842	(5,559)	6,724		32,384	4,813[2] / 8,141 J.P.M.	8,141	4,070		
								J. P. Morgan				
1891	1,809,555	125,268	52,262	22,580	10,275		97,045	38,818	38,818	19,409		
1892	1,920,955	211,047	67,712	99,102	8,316		180,720	72,288	72,288	36,144		
1893	1,866,613	97,763	57,607	(57,444)	4,927			(10,945)	(10,945)	(5,472)		
1894	1,897,944	108,264	42,441	39,194	8,854		76,075	30,430	30,430	15,215		
1895	2,188,187	363,683	90,081	220,766	15,969	16,263 Erie Reorganization	323,485	129,394	129,394	66,697		
1896	2,249,531	264,762	78,758	146,239	19,997		137,365	54,946	54,946	27,473	*F. W. Lawrence*	
1897	2,124,849	362,581	96,754	225,913	17,656		312,308	124,923	124,923	62,462		
1898	2,043,317	261,216	60,699	170,723	13,790		230,476	163,638	*W. S. M. Burns*[3]	66,838	13,828	
1899	2,212,106	243,336	87,729	115,785	21,003		209,839	148,986		60,853		
1900	2,260,735	208,745	48,606	130,021	11,570		185,657	92,829	23,207	46,414	12,590	23,207
1901	2,489,090	488,831	135,902	307,737	33,794		449,270	224,635	56,159	112,317		56,159
1902	2,330,810	388,849	54,996	275,253	43,670		343,446	171,723	42,931	85,861		42,931
1903	1,910,651		70,419	(240,779)	23,147	50,000 United Collieries Special Reserve		(80,879)	(20,220)	(40,439)	*E. C. Grenfell*	(20,220)
1904	1,914,811	203,839	51,320	119,977	22,104	50,000 United Collieries	122,708	61,354	15,338	30,677	5,113	15,338
1905	1,721,563	143,107	56,594	(220,859)	30,923		147,483	(53,387)	(13,347)	(26,694)	(4,449)	(13,347)
1906	1,554,019	481,651	97,407	40,349	30,174			70,792	17,698		5,899	17,698
1907	1,129,313	119,242	66,303	(413,421)	14,574	34,694 Reserve Kessler & Co.		(260,283)	(43,380)		(14,460)	(43,380)
1908	1,258,219	139,166	92,438	(26,334)	26,498		32,921	32,921	8,230		2,743	8,230
1909	1,382,082		64,279	147,226	41,066		283,779	32,921	Balance carried forward, no distribution			

[1] ( ) indicates loss. [2] In 1890 J. S. Morgan died; profits were low in that year of the Baring crisis, and only a proportion of the year's share was paid to J. S. Morgan's estate, the rest going to J. P. Morgan. [3] In 1898 W. H. Burns died.

NOTES TO APPENDIX II

Capital. This is calculated on the amount in partners' capital accounts at the end of each financial year. Most of J. S. Morgan's capital was transferred to his son, J. P. Morgan, so that the capital of the bank dropped by £613,579 between 1889 and 1890; not until 1900/1 did it again reach the level of 1889. The deaths of Robert Gordon and W. H. Burns made no appreciable difference.

Income, profit, and appropriation. The major contributors to gross earnings were the commission, stocks, and interest accounts, and they are therefore set out in this appendix in detail. Of these, the stocks account was the most variable, making in some years large losses—for example 1875, 1884, and 1893, and then most conspicuously in 1903, 1905, and 1907. In all those years except 1875, other income was insufficient to make up the loss and the partners had to pay in. E. C. Grenfell was particularly unfortunate in his first six years as a partner. His share of the profits in three paying years totalled £13,755, but in 1905 his account was debited with £14,449 towards the losses and again in 1907 with £14,460, and then there was no distribution in 1909; over the six years his share of the profits was negative: −£5,154.

Additionally, P/L stocks were written down by £89,885 in 1884 and by £40,746 in 1889. As well as the three major earning accounts, there were other sources of income which varied from year to year for particular issues etc.; large earnings are in the 'other' column; but there were other smaller amounts too, not detailed here.

Profit was calculated after the deduction of counting-house expenses (in the 1860s about £7,000, rising to £12,000–£13,000 in the 1870s, to £15,000 in the 1880s, £17,000–£18,000 in the 1890s, £20,000 in 1900, £30,000 in 1908, and £36,000 in 1909) and bad debts and losses. In this appendix, net profit appears as the amount divided between the partners, but sums (detailed in the appendix) were also put to reserve between 1866 and 1883. After that there seems to have been no general reserve fund, only specific reserve sums (detailed in the 'other' column) in 1904, 1905, and 1907. Additionally, J. P. Morgan had a special account; in 1906 £35,396 was paid into it and in 1909 £16,461.

Partners were paid a sum consisting of interest on their capital and their share of the rest of the profits, according to agreed ratios.

Sources. MS 21768, vols. 1–13, plus other ledgers, Morgan Grenfell Papers, Guildhall Library. Annual balance sheets, and chief accountant's files, Treasury Safe Surround Boxes, MGP, MGC.

APPENDIX III. Morgan Grenfell & Co. 1910–1945

Year	Capital	Gross earnings	Commission	P/L stocks	Interest	Dividends	Issues	Exchange	Other
1910	1,020,264		58,077	(15,769)[1]	27,769				
1911	1,097,576	199,322	37,865	48,467	25,229				23,604 Kentucky & Indiana issu 28,097 Mogyana R
1912	1,127,414	120,864	41,515	28,046	19,933				
1913	1,053,201		43,091	(194,954)	23,749				
1914	924,490		56,348	(302,723)	30,446				
1915	1,127,367	643,875	547,222	(80,685)	36,114				19,556 Chile loan 33,419 Argentine issue
1916	1,185,942	361,989	307,921	(43,242)	28,457				20,000 Chilean Go loan
1917	1,413,702	252,966	195,792	84,491	27,449				
1918	1,454,205	230,241	40,908	80,183	82,884				23,538 EPD Refun
1919	1,538,374		116,823	(17,494)	104,279				21,750 EPD Refun
1920	1,480,933	257,605	116,902	(117,080)	119,316				
1921	1,472,141	387,259	46,358	110,462	110,334			10,202	86,868 EPD Refun
1922	1,513,841	394,572	28,307	127,802	137,723		78,020	4,790	
1923	1,509,532	294,459	31,293	63,028	110,257		53,810	2,941	23,388 Bad debts written bac
1924	1,559,045	431,107	47,506	162,135	107,504	99,074	107,507	6,455	
1925	1,841,063	332,364	47,043	54,848	12,264	95,878	70,451	9,924	21,860 Diamond S
1926	1,873,555	370,116	45,018	71,099	132,045	95,878			34,333 Diamond S
1927	1,957,983	610,777	112,682	266,238	68,020	80,695	72,003	8,545	
1928	2,443,574	540,107	80,402	209,659	169,597		12,837		40,943 Diamond S
1929	2,582,958	670,039	87,743	68,806	228,147		30,328		2,361 Diamond S
1930	2,381,903	327,695	94,175	(101,733)	169,350		41,449		
1931	1,959,462		72,463	(209,780)	136,370		19,971		
1932	2,025,096	229,001	52,894	49,017	103,337				
1933	2,118,044	275,831	54,976	88,958	101,447				13,000 Income tax refund
1934	1,700,000	463,744	74,332	137,235	108,655		117,163		
1935	1,700,000	293,752	75,316	(23,528)	141,929		68,381		
1936	2,500,000	782,522	71,399	12,914	226,398		157,878		
1937	2,500,000	480,485	77,974	(223,972)	248,806		40,030		
1938	2,500,000	303,666	60,072	(112,626)	200,744		20,886		
1939	2,500,000	173,734	56,690	57,511	15,051		21,845		
				(1)[3]		Income (2)[3]			
1940	2,000,000	207,797	56,115	(32,428)	18,403	87,015		3,615	
1941	2,000,000	167,229	32,915	3,457	15,150	98,687			
1942	2,000,000	298,473	36,772	121,701	16,263	82,421	26,542		
1943	1,500,000	817,876	30,747	23,835	22,978	731,095	17,054		
1944	1,500,000	282,567	31,169	26,900	17,371	167,756	21,564		
1945	1,500,000	460,612	39,073	124,557	(2,514)	187,172	68,650		

[1] ( ) indicates loss.
[2] 1932, 1933, and 1940 sundry profit included issues.
[3] From 1940 separated as (1) = net profits on sales of investments less net depreciation on valuation, and (2) = income from inve ments.

ᴘᴇɴᴅɪx III. (*cont.*)

ry s	Net profit	J. P. M. & Drexel	E. C. Grenfell	V. H. Smith	C. F. Whigham	M. Herbert	T. Catto	R. V. Smith
		27,514	16,508	11,005				
	169,424	84,712	50,827	33,885				
	89,392	44,696	26,818	17,878				
		(54,459)	(29,952)	(24,506)				
		(114,871)	(63,179)	(51,692)				
	438,782	219,391	120,665	98,726				
	185,942	6,095	98,916	80,931				
	177,508	56,236	68,868	52,404				
	191,748	93,124	49,975	36,637	12,012			
	195,561	46,574	70,665	52,178	26,144			
	96,469	13,949	40,048	26,267	16,205			
	231,633	75,221	80,453	58,606	17,353			
73	308,185	149,671	71,735	52,705	34,074			
94	240,257	118,491	55,162	39,161	27,442			
	353,791	173,098	78,715	59,595	39,665			
08	277,293	121,507	48,272	48,415	41,419	17,680		
	312,499	141,934	51,324	51,695	46,157	21,389		
95	519,775	252,100	68,509	78,634	68,491	24,974		
68	469,653	150,589	69,906	89,827	86,109	41,975	31,247	
59	533,370	170,834	77,640	97,145	99,497	50,970	37,284	
20	54,492	12,003	18,638	196	3,855	10,041	5,061	4,699
89		(106,181)	(26,931)	(71,676)	(68,912)	(20,254)	(20,719)	(907)
53²	36,640		18,172			6,649 (died)	3,622	4,888
46²	173,341	62,897	40,643	21,422	26,624		13,965	7,791
50	346,381				See Notes			
	126,335							
	542,192							
	109,776							
	43,580							
	29,233							
09²	32,176							
	23,884							
	142,994							
	528,511							
	146,606							
	276,088							

NOTES TO APPENDIX III

Capital. From 1910 J. P. Morgan, Drexel & Co., had £1 million capital in the bank, the surplus over that being the amount in the London partners' capital accounts at the end of each year. Total capital fell in 1913 and 1914 because the London partners had debit balances reflecting the amounts they had to bear of their shares of the losses of those years.

In 1934 the capital was reorganized and separated into ordinary shares and management shares divided among the partners. Thereafter they received salaries (which they had been receiving since before the war), listed as managing directors' remuneration in the profit and loss account, and dividends on their shares. The old-style appropriation accounts, from which the details on these tables have been drawn, no longer appear.

Profits. The profit and loss accounts became more detailed in this period, other contributors to gross earnings, dividends, exchange, issues, etc. being listed in some years. The remittance for London partners is listed in three years: 1921 (£22,591); 1922 (£12,657); 1923 (£6,347). Commission includes commission on acceptances, itemized separately in Appendix V. Net profit continued to be, for most of this period, gross earnings less counting-house expenses (by the 1930s approaching £100,000), provision for bad debts, donations, and, in some years after 1929, income tax (in 1929 it was £20,557).

Sources. The sources for Appendix III are varied. Some figures come from the private ledgers, some from the annual (unpublished, as Morgan Grenfell & Co. was a private company) accounts drawn up by Spicer & Pegler, some from the Chairman's Report, and some from the miscellaneous papers, accounts, and statements to be found in the Accountants' Boxes in the Treasury Surround at the bank. The accounts for the years 1914–18 were particularly confused because they were reworked several times for Excess Profits Duty(EPD).

APPENDIX IV. Morgan Grenfell 1946–1980

Year	Paid-up capital	Published reserves	Inner reserves	Total capital reserves	Gross earnings	Sources of income		
						Interest	Income from investments	Commi
1946	1,500,000	556,157	n.a.	n.a.	672,399	25,926	275,773	78,724
1947	1,500,000	560,006	n.a.	n.a.	771,907	11,464	237,063	102,651
1948	1,500,000	567,452	n.a.	n.a.	505,774	2,099	218,322	109,487
1949	1,500,000	572,672	n.a.	n.a.	597,504	(4,068)[1]	243,840	98,440
1950	1,500,000	576,123	400,000	2,476,123	820,721	1,088	194,092	100,889
1951	1,500,000	582,068	450,000	2,532,068	731,677	13,834	192,654	129,355
1952	1,500,000	589,536	460,000	2,549,536	554,023	14,000	178,082	135,690
1953	1,500,000	843,890	260,000	2,603,890	660,339	8,349	190,455	135,069
1954	1,500,000	845,524	420,000	2,765,524	910,855	7,693	265,386	140,611
1955	1,500,000	848,506	430,000	2,778,506	811,688	19,912	214,306	145,409
1956	1,500,000	852,556	585,000	2,937,556	953,468	76,403	156,805	153,537
1957	1,500,000	1,104,177	510,000	3,114,177	1,023,936	79,982	152,864	202,088
1958	1,750,000	856,214	615,000	3,221,214	1,013,575	116,652	154,475	170,498
1959	1,750,000	857,180	785,000	3,392,180	1,024,732	136,928	186,248	173,382
1960	2,000,000	1,110,843	465,000	3,575,843	1,080,809	173,065	206,736	174,000
1961	2,000,000	1,112,672	680,000	3,792,672	1,408,318	124,402	235,579	234,286
1962	2,250,000	1,114,230	870,000	4,234,230	1,383,918	57,571	428,393	247,113
1963	2,250,000	1,117,979	890,000	4,257,979	1,276,137	241,000	193,273	269,364
1964	2,250,000	1,371,735	670,000	4,291,735	1,148,665	341,237	159,657	280,815
1965	2,250,000	1,376,760	935,000	4,561,760	1,473,326	239,345	154,628	331,383
1966	2,250,000	1,387,331	1,235,000	4,872,331	1,674,704	365,137	133,012	371,124

[1] ( ) indicates loss.

APPENDIX IV. *(cont.)*

Year	Paid-up capital	Published reserves	Inner reserves	Loan capital	Total capital resources (£000)	Sources of Income		
							Interest & discounts	Divid
1967	3,475,000	2,569,768	885,000		6,930			
1968	3,475,000	2,971,009	1,135,000		7,581			
1969	4,000,000	2,698,429	1,370,000		8,068		876,389	220,72
1970	4,105,000	2,831,000	737,000		7,673		1,178,045	242,42
1971	4,105,000	5,187,000	2,663,000	3,000,000	14,955		2,782,335	195,0
1972	4,157,500	5,536,000	5,584,000	6,961,704	22,239		2,308,111	84,9
1973	7,315,000	5,334,000	5,584,000	9,579,129	27,812		4,297,191	228,1
1974	10,472,500	5,426,000	7,112,000	10,617,195	33,628		5,201,028	317,7
						Investment commission	Interest	Divid
1975	10,520,000	6,525,000	10,487,000	14,305,031	41,837	1,169,033	3,364,718	376,4
1976	10,520,000	8,596,000	12,363,000	17,292,400	48,777	1,487,061	4,148,078	203,2
1977	12,900,000	12,504,000	17,103,000	14,304,715	56,812	1,919,487	8,179,472	269,4
1978	15,875,000	13,806,000	22,286,000	14,136,573	66,104	2,107,131	3,471,884	524,2
1979	15,876,250	15,604,000	28,381,000	19,251,498	79,113	3,313,251	7,197,258	716,7
1980	30,811,000	25,624,000	29,267,000	21,187,410	106,889	4,545,675	9,914,896	897,5

[1] ( ) indicates loss.

PENDIX IV. *(cont.)*

s	Underwriting	Realization of investments	Gross profit	Gross profit (% return on capital)	Transfer to contingency	Net profit	Net profit (% return on capital)
453	51,786	166,070	406,314		130,000	46,089	n.a.
069	19,229	147,194	464,708		140,000	45,099	n.a.
503	34,478	197,862	310,793		80,000	48,696	n.a.
254	12,929	(262,027)	104,634		5,000	46,470	n.a.
056	35,866	282,807	483,519	19.5	160,000	52,951	2
428	23,471	150,776	307,208	12	50,000	53,195	2
295	28,333	39,532	237,976	9	10,000	56,218	2
297	11,536	167,050	337,413	13	50,000	53,854	2
912	36,068	102,912	580,091	21	160,000	61,259	2
063	20,195	80,712	215,914	8	10,000	63,357	2
939	19,165	150,195	532,942	18	155,000	64,425	2
486	31,828	44,937	644,996	21	175,000	61,996	2
795	23,018	161,553	559,537	17	105,000	80,537	2.5
723	26,697	130,724	589,590	17	165,000	80,590	2.5
191	30,389	122,622	646,735	18	180,000	83,288	2.5
217	33,223	168,935	884,789	23	185,000	90,642	2.5
617	29,963	219,046	870,524	21	190,000	120,996	3
368	36,728	(179,017)	906,013	21	270,000	146,150	3.5
695	29,134	(156,736)	380,275	9	30,000	143,042	3.5
960	33,120	46,637	818,398	18	265,000	224,431	5
500	25,175	103,818	954,925	20	300,000	274,321	5.5

PENDIX IV. *(cont.)*

nmission	Financial adv. fees / Corporate fin.	Underwriting / Currency	Dealing in securities / Profit (loss) realization	Gross earnings	Gross profit	Net profit	Gross profit (% return on capital)	Net profit (% return on capital)
				2,332,433	1,455,187	369,187	21	5.5
				3,119,509	2,059,516	415,516	27	5.5
2,716	801,062	(100,195)[1]	256,290	3,272,563	1,839,420	407,420	23	5
1,463	899,599	41,163	346,981	3,670,279	(1,154,050)	403,286		n.a.
1,252	784,874	42,151	491,374	5,606,156	(1,519,649)	420,017		n.a.
4,479	913,863	29,055	441,835	5,734,304	3,262,350	1,001,864	15	4.5
8,345	1,595,257	36,597	(448,132)	8,427,805	4,744,021	1,375,214	17	5
5,850	1,807,747	(18,362)	(1,266,807)	8,984,401	3,373,156	1,133,009	10	3.5
6,830	1,895,976	4,278,277	457,976	14,280,070	6,196,014	1,983,594	15	5
3,065	3,224,197	2,975,417	(526,828)	15,549,024	6,502,820	2,496,093	13.5	5
7,804	3,867,774	4,913,137	410,852	25,645,706	12,912,979	5,452,187	23	9.5
1,316	3,201,002	3,886,901	436,886	18,229,904	6,877,630	3,691,704	10.5	5.5
1,839	4,237,013	2,703,226	493,100	22,987,892	7,967,769	4,405,524	10	5.5
05,137	5,076,580	4,135,890	1,415,997	33,580,253	13,173,997	7,211,738	12.5	6.5

NOTES TO APPENDIX IV

Paid-up capital. Figures given for issued and fully paid-up capital from the published balance sheets. From 1971 the figures are for the Morgan Grenfell Group.

Reserves. In 1946, £500,000 was transferred from the contingency reserve account to establish the general reserve, which appeared on the balance sheet for the first time in that year. The published reserves thereafter consist of the general reserve, plus share premium in some years and the balance unappropriated in the profit and loss account.

Inner reserves (1950–70) consist of the contingency reserve (the amounts credited to that account are shown each year from 1946 to 1966) and the investment reserve (£100,000) as shown in the Chairman's Report each year.

From 1971 to 1980 the inner reserves also included the amount calculated to be the difference between net book value and market value of investments. The figures are taken from the annual statements made by the group to the Bank of England (chief accountant's files). There was no loan capital until 1971.

Income. Gross earnings are shown and then major contributions to earnings. (Smaller amounts have been left out from 1946 to 1966.) The figures come from the files of the chief accountant and the schedules sent to New York and are, as far as can be seen, consistent.

For 1967 and 1968 no full set has been found. The total figures are in the schedule. Major contributors as given in the Annual Review can be seen in Table B.

TABLE B. *Major contributors 1967–1968*

	1967	1968
Income on investments	421,833	437,038
Interest (gross)	5,863,168	7,893,403
Interest on investments	569,992	847,789
Commission	377,197	443,315
Issues	552,620	738,839
Underwriting	24,035	56,593

The nomenclature and the way in which the figures were shown changed from time to time. Those for 1969–74 inclusive come from the detailed profit and loss accounts (chief accountant's file), while those for 1975–80 inclusive come from Private Ledger No. 12. Currency, separated out, was formerly included in interest. Some contributors became significant only in the last few years—for example, oil fees and energy services.

Because of the different sources and because of restatements, comparison of year on year would not always be valid.

Gross profit. Gross profit is income after the deduction of expenses, managing directors' payments, and provision for bad or doubtful debts. In 1970 bad debt provision was particularly high at £2,966,649. Net profit is the amount available for appropriation after taxation.

Return on capital employed. This has been calculated using total capital resources, for both gross profit and net profit. In 1970 and 1971 there was a deficit, and a net profit figure was produced by transferring from reserves. Accordingly, no percentage has been calculated.

Sources. Published Annual Reports and Accounts; chief accountant's files; detailed (unpublished) annual accounts; private ledgers.

APPENDIX v(1). Morgan Grenfell Group plc 1981–1986 (£000)

Year	Issued share capital	Reserves	Loan capital	Capital resources	Profit before tax	Profit after tax	Profit attributable to ordinary shareholders	Retained profit
1981	44,427	43,387	35,253	123,067	20,241	12,144	11,200	9,440
1982	44,554	58,540	35,388	138,482	26,586	17,340	15,959	13,750
1983	55,317	65,581	35,834	156,732	33,792	20,172	19,672	16,878
1984	65,164	116,010	70,107	251,281	46,395	24,372	10,870	6,875
1985	70,560	158,008	57,392	286,332	68,821	41,401	39,925	33,039
1986[1]	171,251	199,748	69,082	576,448	82,185	54,932	52,805	36,938

[1] In 1986 the consolidated accounts were restated for the offer to the public of ordinary shares. The figures shown are on the same basis for the six years.

Sources: Prospectus 1986, Annual Report and Accounts 1986.

APPENDIX V(II). Morgan Grenfell Group revenue: Contribution by major activity (%)

	1981	1982	1983	1984	1985
Banking	69	68	56	52	44
Corporate finance	14	15	20	24	32
Investment management	16	16	21	21	21
Other	1	1	3	3	3

Source: Prospectus 1986, p. 23.

APPENDIX VI. Acceptances

Year	Total annual acceptances divided by 4	Acceptances outstanding[1]	Commission
1892	4,175,000		
1893	4,200,000		
1894	3,250,000		
1895	5,800,000		
1896	3,175,000		
1897	2,575,000		
1898	2,575,000		
1899	3,275,000		
1900	4,150,000		
1901	5,300,000		
1910		3,021,978	n.a.
1911		2,312,320	
1912		2,652,819	
1913		2,815,416	
1914		2,086,271	
1915		1,426,901	
1916		654,326	
1917		548,867	
1918		217,839	
1919		434,026	
1920		1,643,226	
1921		795,666	
1922		486,818	
1923		546,796	
1924		1,366,052	
1925		1,564,661	
1926		1,592,474	
1927		1,758,496	
1928		2,691,098	40,687
1929		3,492,328	45,261
1930		3,892,761	59,862
1931		2,880,113	46,515
1932		1,283,782	30,000
1933		1,443,895	25,000
1934		1,327,710	30,800
1935		2,223,409	21,788
1936		3,040,903	26,801
1937		2,595,586	34,153
1938		2,346,724	30,509
1939		1,964,081	28,987

APPENDIX VI. *(cont.)*

Year	Total annual acceptances divided by 4	Acceptances outstanding	Commission
1940		1,278,906	27,310
1941		1,241,779	17,948
1942		1,026,511	16,271
1943		668,379	12,958
1944		411,344	10,033
1945		738,151	10,512
1946		3,905,205	36,487
1947		5,321,485	56,680
1948		6,329,674	80,667
1949		5,833,431	70,001
1950		6,002,442	73,044
1951		8,594,930	94,091
1952		5,819,193	104,543
1953		6,302,833	94,330
1954		7,081,696	89,379
1955		5,336,727	79,095
1956		7,449,428	102,160
1957		9,674,047	128,858
1958		9,465,173	110,672
1959		6,261,749	100,296
1960		6,787,473	90,224
1961		12,247,354	138,298
1962		12,541,925	162,470
1963		10,868,947	146,853
1964		13,917,918	135,144
1965		16,608,906	188,018
1966		16,584,914	198,126
1967		14,471,423	180,082
1968		15,944,859	155,077
1969		15,417,138	152,332
1970		20,526,932	n.a.
1971		19,870,414	
1972		30,502,703	
1973		71,292,996	
1974		97,499,919	
1975		92,387,329	1,206,366
1976		73,772,703	1,015,255
1977		110,370,296	1,257,485
1978		136,900,119	1,111,265
1979		184,227,160	1,441,408
1980		241,126,326	1,486,672

APPENDIX VI. *(cont.)*

Year	Total annual acceptances divided by 4	Acceptances outstanding	Commission
1981		364,049,000	1,425,366
1982		416,405,000	1,422,721
1983		424,745,000	1,248,345
1984		460,509,000	1,149,900
1985		413,883,000	1,248,843
1986		513,551,000	

[1] Amount outstanding at the end of the year
Source: Guildhall Lib. MS 21799, fo. 197 (see Ch. 3 n. 22), Annual Reports and Accounts, balance sheets, Chairman's Speeches, private ledgers.

APPENDIX VII. Balance sheet totals 1900–1986

Balance sheet totals give a crude picture of the growth (and the set-backs) of the Morgan Group.

Year	Total	Year	Total
1900	6,272,500	1938	13,703,524
1901	6,487,248	1939	8,418,294
1902	6,696,172	1940	7,169,517
1903	4,282,168	1941	7,050,922
1904	4,639,266	1942	6,828,735
1905	10,193,288[1]	1943	9,670,848
1906	4,970,983	1944	10,008,427
1907	4,610,455	1945	10,459,531
1908	5,798,973	1946	15,382,709
1909	8,212,214	1947	17,881,293
1910	6,834,119	1948	19,891,440
1911	5,185,230	1949	19,192,457
1912	6,189,868	1950	19,425,642
1913	6,300,293	1951	20,139,355
1914	5,409,641	1952	18,018,725
1915	6,834,119	1953	21,805,279
1916	5,638,070	1954	26,288,881
1917	4,186,972	1955	22,866,833
1918	3,661,748	1956	20,008,808
1919	3,909,201	1957	25,385,597
1920	5,613,712	1958	26,013,921
1921	4,826,667	1959	24,003,734
1922	4,131,711	1960	25,159,430
1923	3,965,356	1961	34,074,809
1924	5,524,057	1962	52,128,814
1925	7,909,098	1963	86,100,494
1926	7,302,124	1964	108,277,155
1927	10,870,590	1965	96,747,921
1928	14,573,236	1966	111,870,202
1929	11,604,581	1967	139,498,836
1930	12,618,900	1968	155,148,642
1931	12,917,338	1969	176,582,612
1932	9,200,185	1970	204,158,306
1933	13,121,616	1971	214,738,218[2]
1934	14,091,100	1972	278,420,000
1935	14,857,376	1973	352,754,071
1936	20,025,986	1974	447,195,629
1937	16,676,939	1975	536,344,485

APPENDIX VII. *(cont.)*

Year	Total	Year	Total
1976	698,751,384	1982	2,598,813,000
1977	862,886,584	1983	3,160,790,000
1978	1,047,900,189	1984	3,941,198,000
1979	1,264,873,200	1985	4,027,271,000
1980	1,818,837,186	1986	6,034,906,000
1981	2,129,923,718		

[1] The unusually high total in 1905 (not achieved again until 1927) was attributable to £5 million on the Argentine 6% Redemption Account.
[2] From 1971 totals from the consolidated group balance sheet.

Sources: Balance sheets, private ledgers, annual accounts.

APPENDIX VIII. Number of people employed.

For the years 1873 through 1927, the figures are based on information from an incomplete salary and bonuses ledger. From 1968 the bank gave the number in the Annual Report.

Year	Average number employed (UK)	Year	Average number employed (UK)
1873	21	1922	47 + 13
1874	22	1923	52 + 15
1875	22	1924	50 + 11
1876	24	1925	48 + 16
1877	25	1926	48 + 14
1878	24	1927	55 + 26[3]
1879	24	1939	132
1880	25	1950	105
1881	29	1968	243
1882	26	1969	317
1883	28	1970	378
1884	28	1971	400
1885	25	1972	419
1893	33	1973	456
1894	33	1974	528
1895	33	1975	558
1896	33	1976	554
1910	41	1977	564
1911	40	1978	597
1912	40	1979	639
1913	42	1980	713
1914	47	1981	787
1915	49 + 21[1]	1982	816
1916	49 + 25	1983	881
1917	48 − 20	1984	968
1918	47 + 20	1985	1,144
1919	47 + 13	1986	1,802
1920	46 + 3[2]	1987	2,057
1921	47	1988	1,658

[1] In this and other entries the figure after the plus sign indicates the number of temporary staff.
[2] Temporary staff who then joined permanent staff.
[3] Large increase in numbers of messengers plus the innovation of three watchmen.

Notes

Chapter 1

1. Franklin Parker, *George Peabody: A Biography* (Nashville: Vanderbilt University Press, 1971), 7. Muriel Emmie Hidy, *George Peabody Merchant and Financier 1829–1854* (New York: Arno Press, 1978), 6.
2. Hidy, *Peabody*, pp. 15–16.
3. Hidy, *Peabody*, p. 70. For the capital of some other Anglo-American houses in 1836 see Stanley Chapman, *The Rise of Merchant Banking* (London: George Allen & Unwin, 1984), table on p. 41. Baring Bros. had capital of £0.78m. and Brown, Shipley & Co. had capital of £1.35m., for example.
4. Thomas C. Cochran and William Miller, *The Age of Enterprise: A Social History of Industrial America* (New York: Harper & Row, 1961), 43–7.
5. R. C. O. Matthews, *A Study in Trade Cycle History 1833–42* (Cambridge: Cambridge University Press, 1954), 199.
6. Hidy, *Peabody*, pp. 74–6. Sir John Clapham, *The Bank of England: A History 1694–1914*, 2 vols. (Cambridge: Cambridge University Press, 1970), ii. 154–5.
7. Hidy, *Peabody*, pp. 70–90. W. Marston Acres, *The Bank of England from Within 1694–1900*, 2 vols. (London: Oxford University Press for the Bank of England, 1931), ii. 463–4
8. Hidy, *Peabody*, p. 90.
9. List of Guarantors of Loan by Bank of England to W. & J. Brown & Co. Liverpool, HC 1.1, Morgan Grenfell Papers, Guildhall Library, London (hereafter MGP, GhL). Hidy, *Peabody*, pp. 84–6. Peabody's ledger for 1837–9 shows considerable dealings in 1837–8 with James Brown & Co., Liverpool. Vol. 43, MS 181, George Peabody Papers, Essex Institute Library, Salem, Mass.
10. G. Peabody to S. Riggs, 27 May 1837, Business Correspondence, Peabody Papers.
11. Hidy, *Peabody*, pp. 92–4.
12. Hidy, *Peabody*, p. 96.
13. Petty Cash Books, 1838–1846, Account Books, Peabody Papers.
14. Thanks to Dr Stefanie Diaper for emphasizing this point to me.
15. Cochran and Miller, *Age of Enterprise*, p. 46.
16. R. G. McGrane, *Foreign Bondholders and American State Debts* (London: Macmillan, 1935), 59.
17. Leland H. Jenks, *The Migration of British Capital, to 1875* (New York: Alfred Knopf, 1927), 106.
18. Ralph W. Hidy, *The House of Baring in American Trade and Finance: English Merchant Bankers at Work 1763–1861* (New York: Russell & Russell, 1970), 309. M. Hidy, *Peabody*, p. 301 for Reform Club.
19. Hidy, *Peabody*, pp. 111–16, 175–82, 135–8, 122.
20. G. Peabody to W. Bend, 3 Mar. 1847, Business Correspondence, Peabody Papers.
21. Information from Dr Stefanie Diaper. Sir John Mallabar has pointed out that as late as 1918 Morgan Grenfell, as well as other leading houses, still referred to themselves as 'merchants', not as merchant bankers. Interview with Sir John Mallabar, 24 July 1986.
22. On 28 Nov. 1838 he purchased bill stamps for £1. 10s., while in Jan. 1839 the

TABLE I. *Acceptances (bills payable) (£)*

Date	Amount of 6 mths. cumulative	Outstanding
June 1845	193,557	65,187
June 1846	613,714	119,411
June 1847	708,005	187,237
June 1848	400,000	n.a.
June 1849	522,175	n.a.

cost for bill stamps was £3. 16s. Petty Cash Books, 1838–1846, Account Books, Peabody Papers. By 1840 the level of acceptances had risen considerably: 10 acceptances dated June 1840 and due in Sept. totalled just over £10,000, while 13 dated in July/Aug. and due in Nov. 1840 totalled some £20,000. Bills Payable, 1840, Peabody Papers. By 1845, acceptances formed a very significant element of the business, as can be seen from Table 1 (Ledger Bills Payable, 1845, 1846, 1847, 1848, 1849, Peabody Papers).

23. Hidy, *Peabody*, pp. 139–45.
24. W. P. Ledward, 'Monetary Policy 1833–9: With Special Reference to the Anglo-American Crisis of 1839', D.Phil. thesis (Oxford, 1983), 894–91. Ledward notes (pp. 109–10) that with regard to the bill of lading, the theory was that these would be sent to the accepting house in London, who would then send them on to their agent in the US; the latter would hand the documents over to the American importing house only when given sufficient funds to pay off the value of the acceptance. The bill of lading gave the accepting house absolute control over the destiny of the goods. However, what was happening in the late 1830s was that bills of lading were going straight to the importer rather than to the American agent, and the accepting house no longer possessed any 'real' collateral (the 'open credit system').
25. Hidy, *Peabody*, pp. 194, 190.
26. Quoted in Hidy, *Peabody*, p. 261.
27. G. Peabody to Wetmore & Cryder, 15 July 1845, Business Correspondence, Peabody Papers. Also quoted in Hidy, *Peabody*, p. 225. The letter is very difficult to read, and I am taking Hidy's word for the exact quotation.
28. Hidy, *Peabody*, pp. 216–51.
29. Hidy, *Peabody*, pp. 257–9.
30. Hidy, *Peabody*, p. 261.
31. G. Peabody to Miss Clagett, 27 Apr. 1849, Business Correspondence, Peabody Papers, Hidy, *Peabody*, pp. 259–62, 305.
32. Chapman, *Rise of Merchant Banking*, p. 92.
33. Quoted in Hidy, *Peabody*, p. 269.
34. I owe this point to Mr. Jeremy Wormell.
35. Hidy, *Peabody*, p. 269.
36. Hidy, *Peabody*, pp. 285–6.

37. G. Peabody to W. W. Corcoran, 6 Oct. 1848, Business Correspondence, Peabody Papers.
38. Hidy, *Peabody*, pp. 292–3.
40. David Landes, *Bankers and Padshas: International Finance and Economic Imperialism in Egypt* (Cambridge: Harvard University Press, 1979), 15.
41. Quoted in Hidy, *Peabody*, p. 312.
42. G. Peabody to G. B. Blake, 6 Apr. 1852, Business Correspondence, Peabody Papers.
43. Hidy, *Peabody*, pp. 327–43. Between Dec. 1849 and Feb. 1850, Peabody completed several iron rail contracts totalling $467,785; 19 different ships carried the rails from Britain to the US. For one contract alone, with the Nashville and Chatanooga Railroad, Peabody received to June 1851 £100,000 plus 5% interest. Folder 5, Box 178, Peabody Papers.
44. G. Peabody to W. Moore, 24 Apr. 1851, Business Correspondence, Peabody Papers. Hidy, *Peabody*, p. 306.
45. Hidy, *Peabody*, pp. 327–43.
46. Articles of Partnership, printed as Appendix H in Hidy, *Peabody*, pp. 383–4.
47. Co-Partnership Agreement, 8 Feb. 1836, HC 1.2, MGP, GhL.
48. Vincent P. Carosso, *The Morgans: Private International Bankers 1854–1913* (Cambridge: Harvard University Press, 1987), 15–27; quotation on pp. 26–7. I am very grateful to Professor Carosso for letting me read the work in manuscript.
49. Carosso, *Morgans*, p. 27.
50.
51. Carosso, *Morgans*, pp. 29–30. Copy of Co-Partnership Agreement, 29 Apr. 1851, HC 1.2, MPG, GhL.
52. Carosso, *Morgans*, p. 34.
53. Parker, *Peabody*, pp. 65–7.
54. For the negotiations see HC 1.3, MGP, GhL.
55. Parker, *Peabody*, pp. 67–8; Carosso, *Morgans*, p. 35.
56. A. M. Chadboone to J. S. Morgan, 28 Apr. 1854, HC 1.2.4, MGP, GhL.
57. Baring Brothers & Co. MSS, Public Archives, Ottawa, quoted in Carosso, *Morgans*, p. 36.
58. Both quotations from Parker, *Peabody*, p. 66.
59. G. Peabody to the Revd Binney, 28 July 1855, Business Correspondence, Peabody Papers.
60. Hidy, *Peabody*, pp. 356–7.
61. Carosso, *Morgans*, pp. 44–5. Co-Partnership Agreement, 30 Sept. 1854, HC 1.3.23, MGP, GhL.

TABLE 2. *Acceptances (bills payable)*

Date	Amount 6 mths. cumulative (£)
30 June 1850	953,334
30 June 1851	1,901,854
31 Dec. 1851	2,461,921
Apr. 1853–30 June 1854	6,049,021 (15 mths.)

62. Carosso, *Morgans*, p. 48.

63. Edwin J. Perkins, *Financing Anglo-American Trade: The House of Brown, 1800–1880* (Cambridge: Harvard University Press, 1975), 14. The value of acceptances can be seen from Table 2 (Overseas Vol. A, 1849–51, Vol. 51, 1851, and Overs. Vol. c, 1854, all Peabody Papers).

64. G. Peabody to J. S. Morgan, 23 June 1854, MGP, GhL. Carosso, *Morgans*, pp. 38–9.

65. Perkins, *House of Brown*, pp. 121–2.

66. R. Hidy, *House of Baring*, pp. 439–40.

67. Clapham, *Bank of England*, ii. 226–7.

68. Carosso, *Morgans*, p. 63.

69. Parker, *Peabody*, pp. 93–4; Carosso, *Morgans*, p. 63, Clapham, *Bank of England*, ii. 226–7.

70. Clapham, *Bank of England*, ii. 227–32.

71. Diary of Bonomy Dobree, 17 Nov. 1857, Bank of England Archives, London.

72. Carosso, *Morgans*, p. 65. Perkins, *House of Brown*, pp. 257–8.

73. G. Peabody to the *New York Times*, 9 Feb. 1858; Parker, *Peabody*, p. 96; Carosso, *Morgans*, p. 66.

74. The loan's guarantors, with the amounts pledged, were as follows: the London Joint Stock Bank (£300,000); the Union Bank of London (£150,000); the Oriental Bank Corporation (£100,000); the Bank of Manchester (£50,000); the Bank of Liverpool (£15,000); Overend, Gurney & Co. (£50,000); Cunliffe & Co. (£25,000); Brown, Shipley & Co. (£20,000); Phipps & Co. (£5,000); Curtis M. Lampson (£24,000); E. Moon of Liverpool (£50,000); and two other friends of the firm who pledged £5,000 each. 'Agreement . . . Between . . . G. Peabody . . . William Butler Duncan . . . The Governor and Company of the Bank of England', 25 Nov. 1857, MGP, GhL, printed in Carosso, *Morgans*, p. 667. Dobree's Diary, 17, 18, 19, 20, 23 Nov. 1857, and Court Minutes, G4/80, 1158/1, both Bank of England. According to Carosso (p. 667), citing a letter from Brown, Shipley to its New York house, Peabody refused to have any help from Barings, requesting the withdrawal of their name, presumably because of their pressure to pay them when he was in difficulties. He also refused help from Huth & Co.

75. Parker, *Peabody*, p. 95. Lewis Corey, *The House of Morgan: A Social History of the Masters of Money* (New York: AMS Press, 1969), claims that it was the Bank of England who made this offer; the only possible source for this story which I can find—and it is far-fetched—stems from a meeting at the Bank of England on Monday, 23 Nov. 1857. Dobree wrote in his Diary that at a meeting with Mr Morgan, Mr Clarke, and J. W. Freshfield, the Governor 'explained to Mr Morgan that the Bank consented to the advance of £250,000 on the understanding that Messrs G. Peabody & Co. only to use it for the purpose of liquidating existing engagements and not as capital to enable them to enter upon new business'.

76. Quoted in Carosso, *Morgans*, p. 667.

77. G. Peabody to the *New York Times*, 9 February 1858; George Peabody & Co., 'Sketch of Out-turn of Business . . . Between 30 September 1854 & 30 September 1864', AC 1, MGP, GhL.

78. J. P. Morgan, Jr., 'Reminiscences', Mar. 1938, Morgan Grenfell Papers, Morgan Grenfell & Co. Ltd. (hereafter MGP, MGC).

79. Carosso, *Morgans*, pp. 69–70, 73–4.

80. Carosso, *Morgans*, pp. 70–1.
81. Morgan, 'Reminiscences', Mar. 1938, MGP, MGC.
82. Parker, *Peabody*, pp. 105–7, 120–8. Intentions and results do not, unfortunately, always go together. Professor L. S. Pressnell has pointed out that 'Without in any way questioning Peabody's good intentions and the undoubted benefit he brought to poorly housed Londoners, they (Peabody Buildings) became horrors to many people. In matters of housing, working class fears of having to live in "the buildings" were rivalled (in the inter-war years) only by fears of having to go to live in the bleak wilderness of a London County Council estate in a place such as Dagenham.' Letter to the author, 4 Sept. 1986.
83. Parker, *Peabody*, pp. 128, 170, 201. Although the first American to receive the honour, he was the second to have been offered it (Andrew Stevenson, American Minister in London in 1838, had turned it down).
84. Carosso, *Morgans*, pp. 76–80.
85. Carosso, *Morgans*, pp. 81–3. In 1907 J. S. Morgan & Co. and Barings co-managed an American Telephone & Telegraph Co. issue of 4% convertible gold bonds of $1,000 each.
86. Carosso, *Morgans*, pp. 95–7.
87. Carosso, *Morgans*, pp. 97–9.
88. Carosso, *Morgans*, pp. 99–100.
89. Parker, *Peabody*, pp. 144–5; Carosso, *Morgans*, pp. 103–4.
90. Note on partnership arrangements on 1 Oct. 1864, HC 1.4.1, MGP, GhL.
91. Hidy, *Peabody*, pp. 348–50.
92. Parker, *Peabody*, pp. 181–7.

Chapter 2

1. Landes, *Bankers and Pashas*, p. 33.
2. John Moody, *The Long Road Home* (New York: Macmillan, 1946), 136.
3. Moody, *Long Road*, p. 61.
4. Notes by Sir John Mallabar, 24 July 1986.
5. Landes, *Bankers and Pashas*, p. 3.
6. Landes, *Bankers and Pashas*, p. 34.
7. Landes, *Bankers and Pashas*, p. 33.
8. Landes, *Bankers and Pashas*, p. 40.
9. Carosso, *Morgans*, p. 105. Chapman, *Rise of Merchant Banking*, p. 40, table 3.1. The concept of partnerships having a fixed amount of capital is one which must be taken with a certain amount of salt. As Jeremy Wormell has noted, 'A capital must be fixed, and this determines each partner's share of profits. But this can be, and usually is, purely nominal. The bulk of the working capital is provided by balances kept by the partners in the firm. These go up and down according to whether they have recently bought West Yorkshire. In any case the credit of the bank rests on the entire worth of the partners—money, securities, land, pictures. The idea that the full capital of Barings was £2.1m is absurd.' Dr John Orbell states that Barings' partnership capital was as follows: Dec. 1870—£2.099m.; Dec. 1875 —£1.629m.; Dec. 1879—£1.940m. He also points out that at Barings the partners did not always keep balances in the firm: rather, they merely accepted liability to meet a share of any losses.
10. Carosso, *Morgans*, p. 106.

11. Carosso, *Morgans*, p. 107.

12. J. S. Morgan & Co. to Dabney, Morgan & Co., 10 July 1869 for the first two quotes and ibid., 11 June 1868, for the third quote, both letters in MGP, GhL, quoted in Carosso, *Morgans*, p. 112.

13. Carosso, *Morgans*, pp. 112–19.

14. Carosso, *Morgans*, p. 115. Dr J. Orbell's impression is that Barings' dealings in commodities fell off dramatically in the 1870s.

15. My thanks to Dr John Orbell for emphasizing this point.

16. Jenks, *British Capital*, p. 264, J. S. Morgan & Co. lost £260,000 on their first European loan, the Spanish Government 3% Loan 1869. See typescript entitled 'Loans Issued by J. S. Morgan & Co. 1865/1885 and approximate result' in 'Loans and Options', MS 21,793, no. 1, MGP, GhL.

17. See HC 4.3.1 and HC 4.3.2, MGP, GhL for the contracts, prospectuses, etc. for these two loans. For the profits made see the typescript list in MS 21,793, no. 1, MGP, GhL. Dr J. Orbell comments that these were 'exceptionally large profits even by Barings' standards!' Note to author, 11 Feb. 1987.

18. Carosso, *Morgans*, p. 126. See MS 21,760, HC 4.3.4, MGP, GhL for the details of the 1870 loan. On this they earned a profit of £131,650. See typescript in MS 21,793, no. 1, MGP, GhL. Chapman, *Rise of Merchant Banking*, pp. 87, 89. In 1909 Morgans and Rothschilds co-managed the £3m. Chilean 5% Government Loan.

19. In short, they mispriced it. See MS 21,760, HC 4.10.1 for papers on the loan, and typescript in MS 21,793, no. 1 for the loss sustained by J. S. Morgan & Co., both MGP, GhL. Carosso, *Morgans*, pp. 129–30.

20. J. P. T. Bury, *Napolean III and the Second Empire* (London: The English Universities Press Ltd., 1964), 181–5. Carosso, *Morgans*, p. 131.

21. France, Assemblée Nationale, *Rapport fait au nom de la Commission d'enquête sur les actes du gouvernement de la défense nationale . . . emprunt Morgan* (Versailles, 1873), 11–14, 83, 131,, quoted in Carosso, *Morgans*, p. 131.

22. See MS 21,760, HC 9.1(2) and (3), MGP, GhL for the disposition of the funds and the payment of contracts for supplies for France from Britain and the US.

23. George W. Smalley, *Anglo-American Memoirs, Second Series* (London: Duckworth & Co., 1912), 216–17.

24. The papers covering the negotiations of the £10m. French Government 6% Loan 1870 can be found in MS 21,760, HC 9.1(1), MGP, GhL. *George Peabody & Co., J. S. Morgan & Co., Morgan Grenfell & Co., Morgan Grenfell & Co. Ltd., 1838–1958* (Oxford: Oxford University Press, 1958, for private circulation), 9. Carosso, *Morgans*, p. 132.

25. Carosso, *Morgans*, p. 132. For Morgans' net profit see typescript in 'Loans and Options', MS 21,793, no. 1, MGP, GhL.

26. George Peabody & Co., and then J. S. Morgan & Co., had been Drexel & Co.'s London correspondent since 1854, when Barings turned them down. Carosso, *Morgans*, p. 133.

27. A. J. Drexel to J. S. Morgan, 27 Jan. 1871, MS 21, 760, HC 1.9(a), MGP, GhL.

28. Quoted in J. P. Morgan, Jr., 'Reminiscences', May 1938, MGP, MGC.

29. J. P. Morgan, Jr., 'Reminiscences'; A. J. Drexel to J. S. Morgan, 27 Jan. 1871, MS 21,760, HC 1.9(a), MGP, GhL. Carosso, *Morgans*, pp. 135–7.

30. Carosso, *Morgans*, pp. 148, 155–8.

31. Carosso, *Morgans*, pp. 159–62.
32. Carosso, *Morgans*, pp. 162–74. Carosso has noted elsewhere that 'The extended business family was the private bankers' chief source of talent.' *Investment Banking in America* (Cambridge: Harvard University Press, 1970), 16.
33. J. P. Morgan to J. S. Morgan, 19 Oct. 1875, Morgan Family Papers, Pierpont Morgan Library, New York City, printed in Carosso, *Morgans*, p. 163.
34. J. S. Morgan to S. Endicott Peabody, 16 July 1870, for the quotation, quoted in Carosso, *Morgans*, p. 163. Peabody's share of the profits totalled £147,000 (see Appendix II). For the letters from Melton to Peabody and the other partners see MS 21,760, HC 1.10.2, MGP, GhL.
35. During his last nine years his share of the profits totalled £240,969 (see Appendix II).
36. Carosso, *Morgans*, p. 164, quotes the assessment of R. G. Dun & Co. from their credit ledgers in the Baker Library, Harvard Business School, Boston, Mass. It is not clear whether this was the income or capital value of the firm.
37. J. P. Morgan, Jr., 'Reminiscences'; Carosso, *Morgans*, pp. 163–4. The correspondence over this episode contains a hint that what Pierpont Morgan thought of as constituting the real partnership was the London and New York firms. As he wrote to J. S. Morgan on 28 Mar. 1873, his preference was for the London and New York firms to establish themselves in Boston 'with our own name and credit'. His idea 'was to have an organization there, working within but quite as independent as Paris and Phila. are now'. Quoted in Carosso, *Morgans*, p. 164.
38. Jacob C. Rogers to J. S. Morgan, 30 Sept. 1878, MS 21,760, HC 1.6.7, MGP, GhL.
39. Carosso, *Morgans*, pp. 164–5.
40. Carosso, *Morgans*, p. 165. J. P. Morgan, Jr., 'Reminiscences', MGP, MGC.
41. Carosso, *Morgans*, pp. 165–6, 400. Chief accountant's private (coded) notebook, Treasury Surround Box J.M., MGP, MGC.
42. Carosso, *Morgans*, p. 166.
43. Carosso, *Morgans*, pp. 169–71.
44. Chapman, *Rise of Merchant Banking*, p. 82.
45. 'In connection with the payment of the War indemnity to Germany, for which the proceeds of this Loan as well as those of the 1872 Loan, were applied, N. M. Rothschild & Sons, at the head of a group of bankers and financiers, guaranteed to maintain the stability of the foreign exchanges and thus greatly facilitated the payment of the indemnity. The transmission of the funds to Germany, which was effected chiefly by remittances in bills of exchange, was carried out in conjunction with Baron Alphonse de Rothschild, of Paris, and this immense operation called into play all the resources and energies of the Rothschild family and its allies. The work and anxiety involved in this vast undertaking would have prostrated any man of inferior calibre.' Jules Ayer, *A Century of Finance 1804–1904: The London House of Rothschild* (London: William Neely, 1905, privately printed), 55.
46. Carosso, *Morgans*, pp. 202–4.
47. Carosso, *Morgans*, pp. 175–90 for details. The papers concerning these issues can be found in MS 21,760, HC 3.1.1(1), MGP, GhL.
48. Carosso, *Morgans*, pp. 184–99.
49. Carosso, *Morgans*, p. 204.
50. Everard Hambro was also a close friend of Hugh Colin Smith, head of Hay's

Wharf and sometime Governor of the Bank of England, whose son Vivian would become a partner in J. S. Morgan & Co. in 1905. Bo Bramsen and Kathleen Wain, *The Hambros 1779–1979* (London: Michael Joseph, 1979), 300–1. Carosso, *Morgans*, p. 205. For a list of those Hambros' syndicated loans in which J. S. Morgan & Co. participated (May 1876–Aug. 1899) see MS 21,760, HC 2.39, MGP, GhL. With regard to the Italian loan, the 1881 tranche in fact went well, but the 1882 tranche got into severe difficulties. Information from Dr J. Orbell.

51. Carosso, *Morgans*, pp. 209–11. For the 1870 Chilean loan see HC 4.3.4, MGP, GhL.

52. Hidy, *House of Baring*, p. 326.

53. H. S. Ferns, *Britain and Argentina in the Nineteenth Century* (Oxford: Clarendon Press, 1960), 397–400. Michael G. Mulhall, *The English in South America* (Buenos Aires: 'Standard', 1875), 534 for quotation. This may well have been a bit of special pleading—or memories were short—since Argentina was in default c. 1828–57. Information from Dr J. Orbell. Net imigration into Argentina 1881–90 totalled 680,000, compared with 85,000 the previous decade. Bill Albert, *South America and the World Economy from Independence to 1930* (London: Macmillan, 1983), table xv (p. 66).

54. Carosso, *Morgans*, p. 212.

55. Typescript list of loans, MS 21,793, no. 1, MGP, GhL.

56. Ferns, *Britain and Argentina*, pp. 401–4. See MS 21,760, HC 4.1.5, MGP, GhL for papers on various Argentine government loans. Carosso, *Morgans*, pp. 214–15. Moreover, as loans became larger, the resources needed to launch them exceeded the amount which could be invested by just one house. And governments always preferred two friendly banks to just one.

57. Chapman, *Rise of Merchant Banking*, p. 88.

58. Typescript in 'Loans and Options', MS 21,793, no. 1, MGP, GhL.

59. Chapman, *Rise of Merchant Banking*, pp. 95 and 96. Table 6.2 (p. 97) shows that for US and Canadian railroad stocks issued through the London merchant banks 1865–90, Baring Bros. had issued 28.7% for a value of £34.68m., while J. S. Morgan & Co. had issued 21.6% for a value of £26.09m.

60. Carosso, *Morgans*, p. 246. See also D. A. Adler, *British Investment in American Railways 1834–1898* (Charlottesville: University Press of Virginia, 1970) and Dolores Greenberg, *Financiers and Railroads 1869–1889: A Study of Morton, Bliss & Co.* (Newark: University of Delaware Press, 1981).

61 Letter in Morgan Family Papers, Morgan Library, New York City, quoted in Carosso, *Morgans*, p. 250. One reason for ascribing the occasional timidity of J. S. Morgan & Co. to the elder Morgan is that things do appear to have changed after his death. It is noticeable, for example, that although most of the Morgan firms' non-railway business of the 1890s was for established corporations in heavy, capital-intensive industry, all the houses, and in particular London and New York, also started financing some smaller, potentially promising companies. In one area of considerable future importance, that of the motor car, London was far ahead of New York: it was only after considerable effort that J. S. Morgan & Co. managed to persuade Pierpont Morgan in July 1896 to take at par $2m. of the Studebaker Brothers Manufacturing Company's first mortgage bonds. The company, the world's largest wagon and carriage makers, had begun experiment-

ing with horseless vehicles and had relied for the previous three years on J. S. Morgan & Co. for its credit requirements. Each firm took £1m. of the bonds. Pierpont probably felt justified in his reluctance, since the business proved to be unprofitable and each house posted a net loss of £7,800. See the exchange of cables between the two houses between 25 June and 3 July 1896, MS 21,802/8. MGP, GhL. Carosso, *Morgans*, p. 395.

62. Carosso, *Morgans*, p. 241.

63. Drexel, Morgan & Co. to J. S. Morgan & Co., 10 Dec. 1880, MS 21,802/5, MGP, GhL. Carosso, *Morgans*, pp. 249–51.

64. Chapman, *Rise of Merchant Banking*, p. 101. Carosso, *Morgans*, pp. 267–8, for the quotation.

65. Carosso, *Morgans*, pp. 270–2.

66. Gordon letter in Morgan Family Papers, Morgan Library, New York, quoted in Carosso, *Morgans*, p. 278.

67. Capital at the end of Dec. 1889 can be found in Private Ledger L-834, MGP, MGC. Carosso, *Morgans*, p. 276. At the time the partnership was renewed in Oct. 1889, it was agreed that after the elder Morgan retired or died at least £1.5m. of his capital would stay in the firm if his son decided to carry on the business.

68. Carosso, *Morgans*, table 5 (p. 303).

69. Clapham, *Bank of England*, ii. 326.

70. Clapham, *Bank of England*, ii. 326–7.

71. Clapham, *Bank of England*, ii. 327–38. Other houses contributing to the guarantee included the Bank of England itself (£1m.), Rothschilds (£500,000), Glyn, Mills, Currie (£500,000), Raphael and Sons (£250,000), Antony Gibbs and Sons (£200,000), Brown, Shipley (£200,000), Smith, Payne and Smith (£100,000), Barclays (£100,000), Robarts (£100,000), and Hambros (£100,000). Clapham, *Bank of England*, ii. 333.

72. *Bankers' Magazine*, 65 (1891), 811, printed in Carosso, *Morgans*, p. 300.

73. In fairness to Barings it should be remembered that Morgans were not as threatened by the consequences of Barings' position in 1890 as Barings probably felt they were by Peabody's in 1857. It is also impossible to know if the Bank of England had had to pressure Morgans to join the lifeboat.

74. J. S. Morgan & Co. to J. P. Morgan, 27 Oct. 1899, MS 21,802/8, MGP, GhL.

75. Carosso, *Morgans*, pp. 405–11. There were of course good business reasons for the two firms to work together, as a cable from J. S. Morgan & Co. to J. P. Morgan dated 13 July 1900 makes clear: 'Baring's called, anxious get our views on proposed Argentine business. After long and most friendly talk we have arrived at nothing definite except necessity our pulling together avoid continental interference and make business success.' MS 21,802/8, MGP, GhL.

76. J. P. Morgan, Jr., to Curzonfel, 5 Mar. 1907, MS 21,802/11, MGP, GhL.

77. E. C. Grenfell and V. H. Smith to J. P. Morgan, Jr., 12 Dec. 1908, MS 21,802/12, MGP, GhL.

78. J. P. Morgan, Jr., to E. C. Grenfell, 9 Jan. 1909, MS 21,802/12, MGP, GhL.

79. Quoted in John Douglas Forbes, *J. P. Morgan Jr. 1867–1943* (Charlottesville: University Press of Virginia, 1981), 64.

80. Grenfell to Jack Morgan, 15 Jan. 1909, MS 21,802/12, MGP, GhL. Carosso, *Morgans*, pp. 578–81. Barings tried in various ways to get one up on J. S. Morgan

& Co.: in Mar. 1910, for example, Barings arranged a dinner for the Argentine ambassador, and Grenfell was quite cross because the Morgan partners were not asked to help plan the dinner and in fact received only a very off-hand invitation. During the years before 1914 Grenfell made special efforts to ensure that in matters great and small, Barings accorded Morgans the consideration and recognition warranted by its newly established position. Grenfell to Jack Morgan, 26 Mar. 1910, Box Hist. 10, Book 1, MGP, MGC. Carosso, *Morgans*, p. 844.

81. C. E. Dawkins to Sir A. Milner, 21 Dec. 1900, Box 213, fo. 163, Milner Papers, Bodleian Library, Oxford (hereafter Bod. Lib.).

82. This was clearly a widespread problem, as Mark W. Collett of Brown, Shipley wrote to John Crosby Brown, his New York partner, on 25 July 1899: 'If Mr Morgan with the exceptional position he holds & with the advantage of having Mr Hambro (himself an able man who knows the London *business* community more intimately than most) to enquire, look out & suggest without in any way committing himself, has failed to find a man of Mercantile & Banking training, and has had to be content to fall back upon a capable Treasury official, who has his work to learn, is it surprising that we have not been more successful?' Brown Brothers Harriman Historical File, New York Historical Society, New York. Professor Vincent Carosso kindly provided him with a transcript of this eight-page letter, on which this paragraph is based.

83. Dawkins to Milner, 8 Feb. 1901, Box 214, fo. 42, Milner Papers.

84. Dawkins to Curzon, 5 Oct. 1900, vol. 181, fo. 174, Curzon Papers, India Office Library, London. G. R. Searle, *The Quest for National Efficiency: A Study in British Politics and British Political Thought 1899–1914* (Berkeley: University of California Press, 1971), 161.

85. Andrew Boyle, *Montagu Norman: A Biography* (London: Cassell, 1967), 30.

86. See the entry on Grenfell by the author in the *Dictionary of Business Biography* (hereafter *DBB*), 5 vols. (London: Butterworths, 1984), ii. 655–6. For further details of Grenfell's background, both familial and social, see Youssef Cassis, 'Bankers in English Society in the Late Nineteenth Century', *Economic History Review*, 2nd ser., 38/2 (1985), 210–29. Grenfell's aunt, Constance Hugh Smith, attributed to the friendship between Junius Morgan and her husband Hugh Colin Smith, 'which has descended to the IIId generation, . . . the taking of Edward Grenfell into the Morgan House, and so making his fortune, and later the entrance of Vivian into the Firm'. V. H. Smith was her son. Constance Hugh Smith, MS 'Autobiography', vol. 3, fo. 168, in the possession of Mrs Fortune Stanley.

87. Farrer to Revelstoke, 6 Apr. 1904, Lord Revelstoke's Private Letters 1904, file COF/05/1/12, Baring Brothers & Co. Limited Archives, London.

88. On 8 Feb. 1901 Dawkins had written to Milner that 'Revelstoke—this is exceedingly confidential—wants to amalgamate with us in some ways. I don't think it is very likely to happen.' Box 214, fo. 42, Milner Papers. It is unlikely that Dawkins knew about the 1904–5 discussions.

89. John Orbell, *Baring Brothers & Co., Limited: A History to 1939* (London: Baring Bros. & Co. Ltd., 1985), 72.

90. Revelstoke to Farrer, 16 Apr. 1904, file COF/05/1/12, Baring Archives.

91. Telegram from Winsor in London to George Perkins of J. P. Morgan & Co. in New York, 28 Apr. 1904, file COF/05/1/12, Baring Archives.

92. Carosso, *Morgans*, p. 447, refers to the letter of 18 Oct., which is not in the Baring Archives. Revelstoke to Winsor, 17 Mar. 1905, file COF/05/1/12, Baring Archives, for the quotation.

93. Farrer to Hugo Baring, 29 July 1905, file COF/05/1/12, Baring Archives.

94. Revelstoke to Hugo Baring, 8 Aug. 1905, file COF/05/1/12, Baring Archives.

95. Farrer to Hugo Baring, 4 Aug. 1905, file COF/05/2/2, Baring Archives.

96. Winsor to Revelstoke, 4 Apr. 1905, file COF/05/1/12, Baring Archives. Searle, *National Efficiency*, p. 161. Farrer to Hugo Baring, 2 Aug. 1905, file COF/05/1/12, Baring Archives.

97. Lancelot Hugh Smith wrote in pencil opposite fo. 27, vol. 5, of his mother's MS 'Autobiography' that 'I went to America with Walter Burns in the spring 1897. . . . It was then I made friends with Jack Morgan, a friendship which has had such an effect on the career of the family . . . . When Walter Burns (father) died Jack came over for several years, which resulted in Vivian ultimately joining the firm of Morgans . . . .' In the same hand but in a darker pencil is added 'It is curious now to realise that possibly he would have been a richer man had he stayed at Hays Wharf.' Hays Wharf was the family firm. Vivian Hugh Smith was the eldest of six brothers, all of whom were a credit to their mother: two were the managing directors of Morgan, Grenfell, and Hambros, one became a senior partner of a leading Stock Exchange firm, and one head of Hays Wharf; the other two became admirals in the Royal Navy. See J. A. S. L. Leighton-Boyce, *Smiths the Bankers 1658–1958* (London: National Provincial Bank Ltd., 1958), 309–10.

98. Carosso, *Morgans*, pp. 449–50. Appendix I.

Chapter 3

1. Grenfell to Jack Morgan, 6 Feb. 1923, fos. 441–2, E.C.G.'s Letter Book 1897–1930, MGP, MGC.

2. Whigham began in May 1908 with a salary of £3,000 per year, with rises of £250 on 1 Jan. 1910 and 1 Jan. 1911. Whigham to Grenfell, 13 Jan. 1908, fos. 65–7, C.F.W.'s Letters Book (unnumbered, largely pre-MGC), MGP, MGC.

3. Grenfell to H. H. Harjes, 13 Dec. 1910, fo. 434, Private Letters Book 3, Box Hist. 10, MGP, MGC.

4. Carosso, *Morgans*, pp. 550–64.

5. Smith to Jack Morgan, 26 July 1911, fos. 1–3, Private Letters Book 6, Box Hist. 10, MGP, MGC.

6. Carosso, *Morgans*, pp. 573–5. See also E. W. Edwards, *British Diplomacy and Finance in China, 1895–1914* (Oxford: Clarendon Press, 1987), 174, and Roberta Allbert Dayer, *Bankers and Diplomats in China 1917–1925: The Anglo-American Relationship* (London: Frank Cass, 1981), ch. 1.

7. Grenfell to Harjes, 26 Mar. 1913, Private Tels/China Book, MGP, MGC, quoted in Carosso, *Morgans*, pp. 576–7.

8. Grenfell to Perkins, 22 June 1910, fo. 247, and Morgan Grenfell & Co. to J. P. Morgan & Co., Private, 22 June 1910, fos. 243–5, both Private Letters Book 2, Box Hist. 10, MGP, MGC.

9. With regard to an issue of Illinois Steel Co. 4.5% Debenture Bonds, Vivian Smith wrote to Thomas Lamont on 20 July 1911 that 'It is a subject of comment that Higginson & Co. are able to distribute a printed prospectus with J.P.M. & Co.

as first of the issuing Banks whilst we not only do not appear thereon but actually know nothing of the matter except what is contained in two lines of the newspaper. Higginson & Co here are a small newly-established house of no importance except as being correspondents of Lee, Higginson & Co., and yet have known about this deal for some days before we see it in the press, and now come in to offer us a complimentary participation in the business out of their share.' Private Letters Book 5, fo. 485, Box Hist. 10, MGP, MGC.

10. 21 June 1910, fos. 232–3, Private Letters Book 2, Box Hist. 10, MGP, MGC.
11. Dawkins to Milner, 8 Feb. 1901, Box 214, fo. 42, Milner Papers. It is only fair to add, as Dr J. Orbell has pointed out, that Dawkins and Revelstoke did not get on.
12. The Diary of Sir Edward Hamilton, Permanent Secretary to the Treasury, reveals that the Rothschilds were consulted by the Treasury on 4 Feb., 6 Feb., 27 Feb., 7 Mar., and 24 July 1900, Add. MS 48676; 18 Apr. 1901, Add. MS 48678; and 14 Apr. and 15 Apr. 1902, Add. MS 48679, all British Library, London (hereafter BL). There were doubtless other occasions.
13. Hamilton Diary, 14 Apr. 1903, Add. MS 48680, BL.
14. Grenfell to Porter, 18 Oct. 1913, fo. 358, Private Letters Book 10, Box Hist. 10, and Grenfell to Porter, 16 Mar. 1914, fo. 289, Private Letters Book 11, Box Hist. 11, both MGP, MGC.
15. Grenfell Correspondence 1900–36, fo. 79, MS 21,799, MGP, GhL.
16. See the cable from J. S. Morgan & Co. to J. P. Morgan dated 13 July 1900, which refers to the necessity of Barings and J. S. Morgan & Co. 'pulling together [to] avoid Continental interference . . . .', MS 21,802/8, MGP, GhL.
17. Dawkins to Milner, 8 Feb. 1901. Box 214, fo. 42, Milner Papers.
18. Grenfell wrote to Harjes on 26 July 1910 that '. . . since 1909 we, on behalf of J.P.M. & Co. and ourselves, agreed not to take Provincial or Government loans in Argentina except with Barings here, who are allied with the 4 French Banks for Argentine business'. Private Letters Book 2, fo. 406, Box Hist. 10, MGP, MGC. Barings and Morgan Grenfell co-managed issues for Argentina in 1909, 1910, 1915, 1923, 1934, 1935, 1936, and 1937.
19. This was the Caucasus Coffee Company, set up in August 1901 to develop mining properties in the Morgoul Valley. It was distinctly unprofitable, even before it was severely damaged during the First World War. Carosso, *Morgans*, p. 462; letters in MS 21,802/11, MGP, GhL; and letters in Private Letters Books, Box Hist. 10–12, MGP, MGC. As Grenfell wrote in Jan. 1916, 'This mine has had even more than the ordinary vicissitudes, and we all wish we had never heard of it.' Grenfell to Porter, 7 Jan. 1916, File Closing Entries, Treasury Surround Boxes, Box J.M., MGP, MGC.
20. Chapman, *Rise of Merchant Banking*, table 7.2 (p. 121) for the figures for Schröders, Brown, Shipley, and Rothschilds. For the figures for Kleinworts, Barings, and Hambros see Stefanie Diaper, 'The History of Kleinwort, Sons & Co. in Merchant Banking, 1855–1961' Ph.D. thesis (University of Nottingham, 1983), table 4.1 (pp. 144–6).
21. For the amount of Morgan Grenfell acceptances at 1 Aug. 1914 see E. C. Grenfell Correspondence 1900–36, fo. 78, MS 21,799, MGP, GhL. For City reaction to Kleinwort acceptances see Stefanie Diaper, 'Merchant Banking Growth in the

TABLE 3. *Ratio of acceptances to capital*

	Capital (£)	Total acceptances divided by 4	Ratio of acceptances to capital	
			Morgan Grenfell	Kleinwort
1892	1,920,955	4,175,000	2.2 : 1	5.9 : 1
1893	1,867,239	4,200,000	2.25 : 1	5.5 : 1
1894	1,897,944	3,250,000	1.7 : 1	5.0 : 1
1895	2,188,187	5,800,000	2.65 : 1	5.6 : 1
1896	2,249,531	3,175,000	1.49 : 1	5.0 : 1
1897	2,124,849	2,575,000	1.21 : 1	4.7 : 1
1898	2,043,317	2,575,000	1.26 : 1	5.1 : 1
1899	2,252,106	3,275,000	1.45 : 1	4.8 : 1
1900	2,260,735	4,150,000	1.84 : 1	4.7 : 1
1901	2,489,097	5,300,000	2.13 : 1	5.0 : 1

Second Half of the Nineteenth Century: The Case of Kleinwort, Sons & Co.', unpublished paper (1985), 20–5. Kleinworts had £14.8m, of acceptances running at the end of July 1914. Information from Dr S. Diaper.

22. The *locus classicus* for the ratio of acceptances to capital is Sir Robert Kindersley's evidence to the Macmillan Committee in 1931, when he explained that it was conventional wisdom amongst the merchant banks that a firm's acceptances should not exceed three or four times its capital. *Committee on Finance and Industry* (PP 9131, Cmd. 3897), 73. The only run of numbers for acceptances 1864–1910 extant for Morgan Grenfell covers the period 1892 through 1901, and they are cumulative annual totals. But if, on very rough and ready calculations, the totals are divided by 4 to give the amount of 3-month bills outstanding, and then compared with the amount of partners' capital on 31 Dec., it is possible to get some rough idea of the ratio of capital to acceptances, as can be seen from Table 3. (Morgan Grenfell numbers from MS 21,799, fo. 197, MGP, GhL; I am indebted to Rob Turrell for bringing them to my attention. Kleinwort numbers from Diaper, 'History of Kleinwort', table 2.3 (pp. 78–9). Grenfell noted that in June 1901 JSMC acceptances amounted to 6 millions, 'being more than double the normal amount'. MS 21,799, fo. 78, MGP, GhL.)

23. In 1905 MGC were apparently charging $\frac{7}{8}$% on 4-month drafts; in May 1913 they proposed opening a credit for an American firm for $\frac{1}{2}$% plus stamp and other expenses for 3-month drafts. Smith to Porter, 8 May 1913, fos. 367–71, and 6 May 1913, fos. 351–2, both Private Letters Book 9, Box Hist. 10, MGP, MGC. Grenfell wrote to Porter on 7 Jan. 1916 with regard to acceptances that 'The rates have been so reduced in the last twenty years that we have largely retired from the business . . .'. File Closing Entries, Box J.M., Treasury Surround Boxes, MGP, MGC.

24. Grenfell to Willard Straight, 1 Jan. 1914, fos. 806–7, Private Letters Book 10, Box Hist. 10, MGP, MGC.

25. Barings and Morgans had worked together for decades, in the US (when Morgans was still George Peabody & Co.) as well as in Argentina. For example, in 1907 the two houses had co-managed the London end of a $40m. American Telephone

& Telegraph issue of 4% convertible gold bonds. Morgan Grenfell took great care not to conflict with Barings in areas which Morgans considered belonged to them, such as Russia. See Smith to James Wishaw in St Petersburg, 31 Jan. 1912: 'I think this might be arranged without in any way conflicting with Messrs Baring's interests; we are just as anxious as you are yourself to avoid that in every way possible.' Private Letters Book 7, fo. 36, Box Hist. 10, MGP, MGC. For Schröders see Morgan Grenfell & Co. to Morgan Harjes et Cie, 11 Oct. 1913, fo. 319, Private Letters Book 10, Box Hist. 10, MGP, MGC, and Notes by Sir John Mallabar, 24 July 1986 (in the possession of the author). For Panmure Gordon, Robert Fleming, Huth, and Wagg see J. R. Carter to H. Harjes, 7 Mar. 1914, fo. 213, Private Letters Book 11, Box Hist. 11, MGP, MGC. For the Lazards quotation see Smith to Davison, 3 Sept. 1912, fo. 303, Private Letters Book 8, Box Hist. 10; for the Canadian syndicate see Grenfell to Harjes, 12 Jan. 1911, fos. 80–1, Private Letters Book 4, Box Hist. 10, both MGP, MGC.

26. Youssef Cassis, 'Bankers in English Society in the Late Nineteenth Century', *Economic History Review*, 2nd ser., 38/2 (1985), 210–29.

27. Notes by Mallabar, 24 July 1986. It is worth noting that virtually all the letters in the Private Letters Books from 1910 on are typed, the majority of the exceptions being letters from one of the London partners to their senior, Pierpont Morgan. All the letters are certainly on copybook paper, which resembles strong tissue paper. One of the managers at Rothschilds wrote a memoir which gave a similar sort of picture with regards to physical surrounds. He emphasizes the autocratic nature of relations between partners and staff. Ronald Palin, *Rothschild Relish* (London: Cassell, 1970).

28. Mallabar, Notes, 24 July 1986.

29. Diary of Edward Holden, 18 Apr. 1912, Midland Bank Archives, Midland Bank Ltd., London. (The London Joint Stock Bank amalgamated with the London Joint City and Midland Bank in 1918; it was renamed Midland Bank Ltd. in 1923.)

30. Mallabar, Notes, 24 July 1986. John Izard recalls that when he joined the bank in 1926 as a junior staff member he was paid £100 p.a. Letter from John Izard to the author, 12 May 1987.

31. R. G. Smith to S. T. J. Warren, 13 Nov. 1912, fo. 622, Private Letters Book 8, Box Hist. 10, MGP, MGC.

32. Grenfell to Mrs William Miller, 29 Aug. 1912, fo. 284, Private Letters Book 8, Box Hist. 10, MGP, MGC. Dr S. Diaper notes that Kleinworts, Anthony Gibbs, and Barings (and perhaps others as well) paid pensions to retiring staff, and to their widows, even before formal schemes became common this century.

33. Morgan Grenfell & Co. to Mrs William Miller, 9 Sept. 1912, fo. 338; R. G. Smith to Mrs William Miller, 7 Oct. 1912, fo. 445; and Morgan Grenfell & Co. to H. G. Brown of Messrs Linklater & Co., 28 Nov. 1912, fo. 698, all Private Letters Book 8, Box Hist. 10, MGP, MGC.

34. Grenfell to Mr West, 6 Feb. 1917, fos. 334–6. E.C.G.'s Letter Book 1897–1930, MGP, MGC, for quotation. Chairman's Speech for 1937, given 12 July 1938, held in the Secretariat, MGC. Kleinworts also set up a formal pension fund in 1927. Information from Dr S. Diaper.

35. Small Leather Book, Box J.M., Treasury Surround, MGP, MGC.

36. Grenfell to Morgan, 19 Nov. 1917, E.C.G.'s Letter Book 1897–1930, MGP, MGC.

37. Material on 1923–6 from ledgers in Treasury Surround Boxes. For 1928–30 see E. C. Grenfell Correspondence 1900–36, fo. 137, MS 21,799, MGP, GhL.

38. For 1910 the partners made losses on Southern Railway Development Bonds and on American stocks. See Grenfell to Davison, 2 Jan. 1911, fo. 42, Private Letters Book 4, Box Hist. 10. Again, there was what Grenfell called a 'depressing finish' to 1912 because of the losses on American stocks. Grenfell to Carter, 2 Jan. 1913, fo. 807–8, Private Letters Book 8, Box Hist. 10. For 1913 the London partners suffered a loss on the P/L stocks account of £194,854 (see Appendix III), and Grenfell wrote to Porter in New York in some detail about it. The total cost of stocks and bonds invested in by the London partnership was £2,130,926, and of this total more than half was invested in US stocks and bonds. With regard to the debit side, 'the total is accounted for largely by the shrinkage in all securities. The principal balances in the shrinkage occur in what we may call Second Class American Bonds, such as Southern Pacific Convertibles, Southern Railway Developments and Atchison Convertibles, with A. T. & T. 4.5% Convertibles. There is of course a further considerable loss in U.S. Stocks, principally U.S. Steel and Ore Lands.' The firm also had £156,000 in Mexican Government 6% 10-Year Bonds, which had been written down to 86, as well as several other substantial investments in Mexican transport utilities. They had considerable holdings in Canada, where there had been 'great depression and a fall in value', as well as strikes in Canadian Collieries. They had also made an advance of $350,000 to the Cuban North Coast Railway, but they were hopeful of its eventual profitability. Grenfell to Porter, 7 Jan. 1914, File Closing Entries, Box J.M., Treasury Surround, all MGP, MGC.

39. E. V. Morgan, *Studies in British Financial Policy, 1914–25* (London: Macmillan, 1952), 7–8.

40. David French, *British Economic and Strategic Planning 1905–1915* (London: George Allen & Unwin, 1982), 90–1.

41. Whigham to Porter, 7 Oct. 1914, fo. 372, Private Letters Book 12, Box Hist. 11, MGP, MGC. The two versions, 'Acceptance' and 'Accepting', are in the original letter.

42. Morgan Grenfell & Co. to Frederick Huth Jackson, 4 Aug. 1914, fo. 58a, Private Letters Book 12, Box Hist. 11, MGP, MGC. After a burst of activity the committee continued for some years on an informal basis, being run in the early 1930s from the office of F. Huth and Co., whose senior partner (L. Huth Walters) was its chairman. In 1936 the firm disappeared, and the committee was rearranged, establishing an office of its own with a permanent secretary. R. S. Sayers, *The Bank of England 1891–1944* (Cambridge: Cambridge University Press, 1986, first published 1976), 534.

43. Grenfell to Davison, 20 Aug. 1914, fo. 145, Private Letters Book 12, Box Hist. 11, MGP, MGC.

44. Grenfell to Porter, 7 Jan. 1916, File Closing Entries, Box J.M., Treasury Surround Boxes, MGP, MGC. For Barings' safety see Orbell, *Baring Brothers*, p. 76. E. C. Grenfell Correspondence 1900–36, fo. 120, MS 21,799, MGP, MGC.

45. Kathleen Burk, 'The Treasury: From Impotence to Power', in Kathleen Burk (ed.), *War and the State: The Transformation of British Government 1914–1919* (London: George Allen & Unwin, 1982), 87.

46. Dr Orbell has pointed out that this was a refunding operation, undertaken in London and New York, which resulted in an inflow of funds into the UK.

47. Carosso, *Morgans*, p. 461.

48. Smith to Morgan, 3 July 1916, File 1, Bundle 120, Box P.930, MGP, MGC.

49. Smith to Davison, 4 Nov. 1916, File 1, Bundle 120, Box P.930, MGP, MGC.

50. Grenfell to Smith, 20 Aug. 1917, File 1, Bundle 120, Box P.930, MGP, MGC.

51. Details of Catto's career taken from his memoir, *Thomas Sivewright Catto 1879–1959* (privately printed, 1962), *passim*. R. Davenport-Hines has extracted most of the best stories from this for his article on Catto in *DBB*, vol. i. Quotation from Catto, *Catto*, p. 63.

52. Catto to Smith, 13 May 1919, File 1, Bundle 120, Box P.930, MGP, MGC.

53. Letter of 26 May 1919 [? to ?], File 1, and 'Shares in Andrew Yule & Co. Ltd', 19 Sept. 1922, File 2, Bundle 120, Box P.930, MGP, MGC.

54. Grenfell to Jack Morgan, 2 Jan. 1929, fos. 466–7, E.C.G.'s Letter Book 1897–1930, MGP, MGC, for quotation. Catto, *Catto*, p. 85. Grenfell to Morgan, 4 Jan. 1927, fo. 461, E.C.G.'s Letter Book 1897–1930.

55. Chairman's Speeches at AGM, 25 May 1935 (covering 1934) and 17 June 1959 (covering 1958), the Secretariat, MGC.

56. Grenfell to Morgan, 23 Aug. 1917, fo. 385, and Grenfell to Jack Morgan, 8 Nov. 1911, fos. 391–95, E.C.G.'s Letter Book 1897–1930; Morgan Grenfell & Co. Minute Book 1918–34, Treasury Surround Boxes, MGP, MGC. Allocation of 1,000 shares: J. P. Morgan 160 (159 transferred to J. P. Morgan & Co. 17 Dec. 1919); E. C. Grenfell 270; V. H. Smith 180; C. F. Whigham 50; J. P. Morgan & Co. 279; Drexel & Co. 50; individual American partners 11. From entry for 17 July 1918, Minute Book 1918–34, ibid.

57. J. P. Morgan & Co. to Morgan Grenfell & Co., 12 Oct. 1918, File 1, Bundle 120, Box P.930, MGP, MGC.

58. Information to the author.

59. E. C. Grenfell Correspondence 1900–36, fo. 76, MS 21,799, MGP, GhL. Grenfell to Morgan, 4 Jan. 1927, fo. 459–60, E.C.G.'s Letter Book 1897–1930, MGP, MGC for the quotation.

60. But Grenfell might well have been depressed to learn that Barings' credit commissions were £100,472 in 1924 and £151,164 in 1925. Information from Dr J. Orbell.

61. 'Report of Visit of G.W., N.D.J. and M.H. to Brussels in Friday, 3 Dec. 1926', p. 3, File Commercial Credits, 1 (1912–32), Box P.546, MGP, MGC.

62. Michael Herbert to George Whitney, 19 Mar. 1926, and memo by Herbert, 'European Business', 27 Mar. 1929, both File Commercial Credits, 1, Box P.546, MGP, MGC.

63. Smith to Grenfell, 27 May 1926, no. 26/4729, File Commercial Credits, 1, Box P.546, MGP, MGC.

64. Grenfell to Smith, 28 May 1926, no. 26/2218, and memo by R.H.V.S. and J.B. on visits to Amsterdam, dated 10 June 1926, both File Commercial Credits, 1, Box P.546, MGP, MGC.

65. Whigham to Morgan, 5 Jan. 1926, fos. 455–8; Grenfell to Morgan, 4 Jan. 1927, fos. 458–61, for the quotation, both E.C.G.'s Letter Book 1897–1930, MGP, MGC. Dr S. Diaper notes that 1926 saw a drop in the acceptance business of several accepting houses.

66. Grenfell to Morgan, 2 Jan. 1928, fos. 462–5, E.C.G.'s Letter Book 1897–1930, MGP, MGC.

67. They emphasized in Oct. 1930 that Morgan Grenfell would accept no agency or shipping bills. E. C. Grenfell Correspondence 1900–36, fo. 23, MS 21,799, MGP, GhL. Numbers for acceptance commissions from Chairman's Speeches for appropriate years, the Secretariat, MGC. Barings' credit commissions were £114,889 for 1928, £101,912 for 1929, and £81,605 for 1930. Information from Dr J. Orbell.

68. Harold van B. Cleveland and Thomas F. Huertas, *Citibank 1812–1970* (Cambridge: Harvard University Press, 1985), 146.

69. Derek Aldcroft, *From Versailles to Wall Street 1919–1929* (London: Allen Lane, 1977), 240–2.

70. Lamont to J.P.M. & Co., 11 Aug. 1924, no. 4943, file 32, Box Hist. 6 (Private Telegrams), MGP, MGC.

71. Stephen A. Schuker, *The End of French Predominance in Europe: The Financial Crisis of 1924 and the Adoption of the Dawes Plan* (Chapel Hill: University of North Carolina Press, 1976), 349.

72. Sir Henry Clay, *Lord Norman* (London: Macmillan, 1957), 144.

73. D. E. Moggridge, *British Monetary Policy 1924–1931: The Norman Conquest of $4.86* (Cambridge: Cambridge University Press, 1972), ch. 9.

74. Quoted in the memorandum by Sir Henry Clay, 'Embargo on Foreign Capital Issues' 15 June 1930, Box 34, Clay Papers, Nuffield College, Oxford. This paragraph is largely based on this memorandum, and I am indebted to Philip Williamson for bringing it to my notice.

75. Clay, *Norman*, pp. 239, 368, 416–17.

76. M.N.'s Commentary, 2 Feb. 1925, Series 172, file 1500A, fo. 51, Treasury Papers, Public Record Office, London (hereafter PRO).

77. Moggridge, *British Monetary Policy*, pp. 213–14.

78. Aldcroft, *Versailles to Wall Street*, p. 242, and Cleveland and Huertas, *Citibank*, p. 385, argue that it was cheaper to borrow in New York than in London; Moggridge, *British Monetary Policy*, p. 200, states the opposite.

79. Sir Otto Niemeyer of the Treasury certainly believed that long-term loans would always be cheaper in London because of 'our greater skill in the foreign loan business'. Commentary by O.E.N. on the Chancellor's Exercise, Feb. 1925, fo. 45, T.172/1500A.

80. Paul Einzig, *The Fight for Financial Supremacy* (London: Macmillan, 1931), 52. If one substitutes 'Japanese' for 'American' in this quotation, it has a very contemporary ring.

81. Stephen V. O. Clarke, *Central Bank Cooperation 1924–31* (New York: Federal Reserve Bank of New York, 1967), 77.

82. Einzig, *Financial Supremacy*, pp. 73–5.

83. With regard to the credit to be extended to the British government in aid of the return to gold, Grenfell wrote to Morgan that 'It would be essential that your participants be confined to the U.S.A. without direct or indirect passing on.' 21 Mar. 1925, no. 4585, File British Government Gold Standard Credit 1925, MGP, MGC. With regard to the Dawes loan, it was 'to be understood as an absolute condition by all underwriters that no participation be passed on to anyone in

another country in which an issue of the German loan is also to be made'. Morgan Grenfell & Co. to J. P. Morgan & Co., 8 Oct. 1924, no. 24/5090, file 4, Bundle 54 (German Government Loan in USA 1924), MGP, MGC.

84. Clay, *Norman*, 144.
85. See cables on New South Wales loan, file 39, and cables on Australia, file 40, both Box Hist. 7 (Private Telegrams), MGP, MGC. London continued to be a much more important capital market for Australia than New York; during Mar. 1927–Mar. 1928 Australia borrowed £35m. in London and approximately £8m. in New York. T.W.L. to J. P. Morgan & Co., 27 Mar. 1928, no. 4624, file 42, Box Hist. 8, MGP, MGC. It is also interesting to note that the negotiations for the Commonwealth of Australia 4.5% External G. Loan 1956, issued in New York by J. P. Morgan & Co. in June 1928, were, at the request of the Australian representatives, carried out entirely in London by Morgan Grenfell & Co. via cables to J. P. Morgan & Co., files 42–3, Box Hist. 8, MGP, MGC.
86. J. P. Morgan & Co. to Morgan Grenfell & Co., 21 Dec. 1927, no. 2527, file 41, Box Hist. 7, MGP, MGC. 'Our experience . . . showed that evidence of cooperation with Great Britain particularly was of great influence with the investors throughout this Country . . .'. J. P. Morgan & Co. to Morgan Grenfell & Co., 23 Jan. 1924, no. 2050, file 31, Box Hist. 5, MGP, MGC.
87. Einzig, *Financial Supremacy*, p. 47. Dr S. Diaper points out that domestic issues increased very markedly in London between 1922 and 1929.
88. Midi Railway Co. offer of £3m. 6% sterling bonds of the Compagnie des Chemins de fer du Midi and Orleans Railway Co. offer of £2m. 6% sterling bonds. The three firms issued loans for the two railway companies again in 1935.
89. Government of Argentina Issue of £2m. 5% bonds.
90. Orbell, *Baring Brothers*, pp. 80–1. For the 1924 and 1930 Japanese loans the syndicate also included the Hong Kong and Shanghai Bank; the Yokohama Specie Bank Ltd. joined for the 1924 loan. Grenfell to Morgan, 1 Jan. 1925, fos. 453–4, E.G.C.'s Letter Book 1897–1930, MGP, MGC.
91. Morgan Grenfell & Co. to General Motors Acceptance Corp., 2 July 1925, fo. 502, Private Letters Book 32, Box Hist. 13, MGP, MGC. M. Miller and R. A. Church, 'Motor Manufacturing', in Neil K. Buxton and Derek H. Aldcroft (eds.), *British Industry Between the Wars* (London: Scolar Press, 1982), 179–215, 193.
92. Roy Church and Michael Miller, 'The British Motor Industry, 1922–1939', in Barry Supple (ed.), *Essays in British Business History* (Oxford: Clarendon Press, 1977), 166. Morgan Grenfell Minute Book 1918–34, entry for 2 Sept. 1925, Treasury Surround Boxes, MGP, MGC.
93. Whigham to Grenfell, 7 Sept. 1925, fos. 799–800, Private Letters Book 32, Box Hist. 13, MGP, MGC.
94. *The Times*, 19 Sept. 1925.
95. The Secretary, Vauxhall Motors Ltd., to Shareholders, 19 Oct. 1925, File Vauxhall Motors Ltd., MGP, MGC. The shares rose from 4s. to 7s. during the negotiations.
96. Agreement, dated 20 Oct. 1925; report of the shareholders' meeting, reprinted from *The Times* of 31 Oct. 1925; the *Telegraph*, 31 Oct. 1925; all in File Vauxhall Motors Ltd., MGP, MGC.
97. The payment was for advice given during the negotiations, for being a party to the agreement as trustees, and for carrying through the details of the cash

payments and exchange of shares. Morgan Grenfell & Co. to J. D. Mooney, 21 Oct. 1925, File Vauxhall Motors Ltd., MGP, MGC.

98. File General Motors Corp. 1929, Box 87, and File Vauxhall Motors Ltd. 1934/37, Box 236, both MGP, MGC. The profits made on the placings came to £7,395 in 1949, £27,631 in 1954, £28,313.15 in 1955, and £17,857.10 in 1957, a total of £81,197.10. Chairman's Speeches for relevant years, the Secretariat, MG.

99. John Campbell, *Lloyd George: The Goat in the Wilderness 1922–1931* (London: Jonathan Cape, 1977), 36, 90, 157. Denis Judd, *Lord Reading* (London: Weidenfeld and Nicolson, 1982), 234. Philip Williamson to the author, Sept. 1987. Daily Chronicle Investment Corporation Limited, Prospectus for 800,000 7% first cumulative preference shares of £1 each; Memoranda by C.F.W., 25 Mar. 1927 and 4 June 1927, all File Daily Chronicle Investment Corporation Ltd., Box 137, MGP, MGC.

100. Catto, *Catto*, p. 91. File Daily Chronicle Investment Corporation Ltd., Box 137, MGP, MGC. On the role of the City MP see Philip Williamson, 'Financiers, the Gold Standard and British Politics, 1925–1931', in John Turner (ed.), *Businessmen and Politics: Studies of Business Activity in British Politics, 1900–1945* (London: Heinemann, 1984), 105–29.

101. Sayers, *Bank of England*, 320–4.

102. Chairman's Speech at the AGM, 14 June 1929 (for 1928), held in the Secretariat, MGC. Grenfell to Morgan, 2 Jan. 1929, fos. 466–7, E.C.G.'s Letter Book 1897–1930, MGP, MGC for quotation.

103. Sayers, *Bank of England*, 330. *The Times*, 11 Jan. 1930, for the quotation.

104. Thomas to Grenfell, 22 Jan. 1930; Memorandum by Grenfell dated 30 Jan. of meeting held 29 Jan. 1930 in Thomas's office, both File Bankers' Industrial Development Company Limited [BID Co.], Box 497, MGP, MGC. The others who attended were Lord Bearstead of Marcus Samuel & Co., Baron d'Erlanger of Erlanger & Co., Baron Schröder of J.H. Schröder & Co., and Alfred Wagg of Helbert, Wagg & Co.

105. Grenfell to T. Newhall of Drexel & Co., 7 Dec. 1932, File BID Co., Box 497, MGP, MGC.

106. File BID Co., Box 497, MGP, MGC. Richard Kellett, *The Merchant Banking Arena with Case Studies* (London: Macmillan, 1967), 43.

107. Grenfell to Morgan, 7 Jan. 1931, E.G.C.'s Letter Book 1897–1930, MGP, MGC.

108. Whigham to Morrow, 13 Aug. 1925, fo. 677, Private Letters Book 32, Box Hist. 13. MGP, MGC.

109. Chapman, *Rise of Merchant Banking*, p. 101.

TABLE 4. *Shares and salaries*

	Shares (%)		Salaries (£)	
	Present	Future	Present	Future
E.C.G.	22	12	10,800	5,000
V.H.S.	18	18	8,600	8,000
C.F.W.	10	15	6,600	8,000
J.P.M. & Co./D. & Co.	50	50		
M.H.	—	5	—	5,000

TABLE 5. *Redivision of London profits*

	Shares (%)	
	Present	Future
E.C.G.	12	12
V.H.S.	18	20
C.F.W.	15	20
M.H.	5	8
T.C.	—	7
TOTAL	50	67

110. Herbert's joining the firm necessitated a redivision of the profits and a change in salaries. In the end Whigham got an increase, and this, plus Herbert's share, came out of Grenfell's share, as can be seen from Table 4. Grenfell to Morgan, 6 June 1924, fos. 451–2, E.C.G.'s Letter Book 1897–1930, MGP; MGC; Chairman's Speech, 12 Oct. 1933 (for 1932), the Secretariat, MGC.

111. Catto, *Catto*, p. 85.

112. This can be seen from Table 5. Grenfell to Morgan, 2 Jan. 1928, fos. 462–3, E.C.G.'s Letter Book 1897–1930, MGP, MGC.

113. Grenfell to Morgan, 6 Feb. 1923, fos. 441–3, E.C.G.'s Letter Book 1897–1930, MGP, MGC. Information on Smith (and Rodd) from A. E. Weighill.

114. Selina Hastings, *Nancy Mitford* (London: Hamish Hamilton, 1985), 82–91, p. 81 for the quotation.

115. Grenfell to Morgan, 23 Mar. 1923, fo. 445, E.C.G.'s Letter Book 1897–1930, MGP, MGC. This is a useful reminder that profitable property speculation is a relatively recent phenomenon; in the earlier part of the century people often preferred not to tie up their money in property because there were more profitable ways to utilize it.

116. Morgan Grenfell & Co. to the controller, London Telephone Service, 28 Aug. 1925, fo. 753, Private Letters Book 32, Box Hist. 13, MGP, MGC.

117. It might also imply that like other houses at the time Morgans were getting into currency and stock arbitrage, which demanded swift communications to make consistent profits. Thanks to Dr S. Diaper for making this point.

118. Grenfell to Morgan, 4 Jan. 1927, fo. 459, E.C.G.'s Letter Book 1897–1930, MGP, MGC.

119. Federal Reserve Committee on Branch, Group and Chain Banking, *225 Bank Suspensions: Case Histories from Examiners' Reports* (Washington, DC: US Government Printing Office, 1932). Cleveland and Huertas in *Citibank*, p. 401, argue that the Federal Reserve Study was incorrect in its conclusion and that the Depression, not banks' investments in bonds, caused the failures: 'The depression reduced the value of both loans and investments, reducing banks' net worth. It was merely easier to measure the depreciation in banks' bond accounts than in their loans, since bonds generally traded on a secondary market and could therefore be readily priced.'

120. Chairman's Speech for 1934, given 24 May 1935, the Secretariat, MGC. Morgan Grenfell & Co. Minute Book 1918–34, entry for 12 June 1934, Treasury Surround Boxes, MGP, MGC.

121. Barings reconstituted themselves a limited company after their crash, but Dr J. Orbell states that this was not for fear of unlimited liability but because it was the only way to raise capital to continue the business. See Orbell, *Baring Brothers*, p. 60.

Chapter 4

1. Frederick Lewis Allen, *The Great Pierpont Morgan* (New York: Bantam Books Inc., 1956 (1st pub. 1949), 82. New York partner Robert Bacon was one example.

2. See Carosso, *Morgans*, pp. 466–74.

3. Thomas R. Navin and Marion V. Sears, 'A Study in Merger: Formation of the International Mercantile Marine Company', *Business History Review*, 28 (1954), 291–302.

4. J. P. Morgan to J. S. Morgan & Co., 18 July 1900, MS 21,802/8, MGP, GhL.

5. Carosso, *Morgans*, p. 482.

6. Navin and Sears, 'A Study in Merger', pp. 303–11.

7. J. P. Morgan to C. Steele and G. W. Perkins, 10 Apr. 1902, and J. P. Morgan to C. Steele, 11 Apr. 1902, both MS 21,802/9, MGP, GhL.

8. Inverclyde passed the information, which he had just learnt from Cunard's agent in New York, on to Lord Selborne, the First Lord of the Admiralty, on 8 Mar. 1902. Vivian Vale, *The American Peril: Challenge to Britain on the North Atlantic 1901–04* (Manchester: Manchester University Press, 1984), 123. For Cunard's manoeuvres, see Vale, ch. 5.

9. Dawkins to Jack Morgan, 9 July 1901; Jack Morgan to Dawkins, 19 Nov. 1901; J. P. Morgan to Perkins, 17 Apr. 1902; Dawkins to Perkins, 18 Apr. 1902; Perkins to Jack Morgan, 21 Apr. 1902; J. P. Morgan & Co. to J. S. Morgan & Co., 22 Apr. 1902; and J. S. Morgan & Co. to J. P. Morgan & Co., 22 Apr. 1902, all MS 21,802/9, MGP, GhL. Many of the London bonds went to Dutch investors. Navin and Sears, 'A Study in Merger', p. 316.

10. Navin and Sears, 'A Study in Merger', pp. 312–3.

11. 'So far as contemporary opinion was concerned, it was the naval question above everything else which exacerbated Anglo-German relations. The history of British policy towards maritime affairs over the previous three centuries revealed how much the preservation of naval supremacy had been ingrained into the national consciousness.' Paul Kennedy, *The Rise of the Anglo-German Antagonism 1860–1914* (London: George Allen & Unwin, 1980), 416. Dawkins to Milner, 23 May 1902, Box 215, fo. 50, Milner Papers, Bod. Lib.

12. Ismay had passed the 4 Feb. agreement to Selborne on 26 Mar., and the Cabinet had the text before them for their discussion on 7 Apr. The decision then was that although the White Star Line had broken an agreement with the Admiralty by agreeing to sell their ships, there was nothing the government could do until the shipping trust was called into existence. Vale, *American Peril*, p. 123. Dawkins to J. P. Morgan, 6 May 1902, MS 21,802/9, MGP, GhL.

13. Dawkins to Milner, 9 May 1902, Box 215, fos. 44–5, Milner Papers.

14. Debates were held on 16, 18, and 29 May 1902. Dawkins to Milner, 23 May 1902, Box 215, fos. 51–3, Milner Papers.

15. Hamilton Diary, 2 June 1902, Add. MS 48676, BL.

16. Dawkins to Steele, 18 June 1902, MS 21,800/1, MGP, GhL.

17. Steele and Perkins to J. S. Morgan & Co., 21 May 1902, MS 21,802/9, MGP, GhL.

18. Dawkins and Jack Morgan to Steele, 23 May 1902, MS 21,802/9, MGP, GhL.

19. J. S. Morgan & Co. to Steele, 11 June 1902, MS 21,802/10, MGP, GhL.

20. Dawkins, 'Memorandum', 11 June 1902, MS 21,800/1, MGP, GhL. Dawkins to Milner, 13 June 1902, Box 215, fos. 54–5, Milner Papers.

21. Dawkins to Milner, 13 June 1902, Box 215, fo. 54, Milner Papers.

22. Hamilton Diary, 12 June 1902, Add. MS 48679, BL.

23. Quoted in Vale, *American Peril*, p. 134.

24. Vale, *American Peril*, pp. 135–6. Dawkins to J. P. Morgan, 1 Sept. 1902 and 9 Sept. 1902; J. S. Morgan & Co. to Dawkins (NY), 23 Sept. 1902; Dawkins and Jack Morgan for Gerald Balfour, 27 Sept. 1902; Dawkins to J. P. Morgan, 3 Oct. 1902, all MS 21,802/10, MGP, GhL. Dawkins to Milner, 9 Oct. 1902, Box 215, fo. 57, Milner Papers. Parliamentary Papers, Cd. 1704 (1903).

25. Dawkins to Milner, 6 Oct. 1902, Box 215, fo. 58, Milner Papers. Navin and Sears, 'A Study in Merger', pp. 320–4. Carosso, *Morgans*, p. 486.

26. Sayers, *Bank of England*, p. 15. Sayers adds in n. 2 that 'Banks (both London and country) could always borrow on Consols for very short terms—even overnight —and therefore regarded them as the first reinforcement for their cash reserves. This continued until 1914.' J. Wormell has noted that 'The Bank of England would always believe in issuing the longest dated piece of paper possible. It is the way of central bankers.'

27. Hamilton Diary, 4 Feb. 1900, Add. MS 48676, BL.

28. E. Hamilton, 'Taxation *versus* Loans', 20 Feb. 1900, T.170/31/141343.

29. For an outline of the Boer War from the standpoint of economics and imperialism see D. K. Fieldhouse, *Economics and Empire 1830–1914* (London: Weidenfeld and Nicolson, 1976), 354–62. Hamilton Diary, 31 July 1900, Add. MS 48676, BL.

30. J. S. Morgan & Co. to J. P. Morgan, 30 Jan. and 31 Jan. 1900, J. P. Morgan, Jr., to J. P. Morgan, 16 Feb. 1900 (2 cables), and J. S. Morgan & Co. to J. P. Morgan, 17 Feb. 1900, all MS 21,802/8, MGP, GhL.

31. Hamilton Diary, 9 Dec. 1903, Add. MS 48681, BL. For information on Cassel see the entry by Pat Thane in *DBB* i. 604–14.

32. Sayers, *Bank of England*, p. 16.

33. Hamilton Diary, 4 Feb., 12 Feb., 27 Feb., and 4 Mar. 1900, Add. MS 48676, BL.

34. J. P. Morgan to Jack Morgan, 19 Feb. 1900, Jack Morgan to J. P. Morgan, 16 Feb. 1900 (second cable) and 8 Mar. 1900, MS 21,802/8, MGP, GhL.

35. Hamilton Diary, 6 Feb., 12 Feb., 26 Feb., 4 Mar. 1900, Add. MS 48676, BL.

36. R. Bacon to Jack Morgan, 9 Mar. 1900, 12 Mar. 1900, and 13 Mar. 1900; J. S. Morgan & Co. to J. P. Morgan, 19 Mar. 1900; J. P. Morgan & Co. to J. S. Morgan & Co., 20 Mar. 1900 (2 cables); J. S. Morgan & Co. to J. P. Morgan & Co., 21 Mar. 1900, all MS 21,802/8, MGP, GhL. Carosso, *Morgans*, pp. 510–11.

37. Sayers, *Bank of England*, p. 14. Hamilton Diary, 16 Mar. 1900, Add. MS 48676, BL.

38. Hamilton Diary, 21 Mar. 1900, Add. MS 48676, BL.

39. Hamilton Diary, 24 July 1900, Add. MS 48676, BL. Sayers, *Bank of England*, p. 16.
40. Dawkins to Milner, 26 July 1900, Box 213, fo. 158, Milner Papers. Dawkins would later write to Milner that 'the gold we are bringing over will arrest what would have been a 7 p.c. Bank rate and considerable trouble'. 16 Aug. 1900, Box 177, fo. 155, Milner Papers.
41. J. S. Morgan & Co. to J. P. Morgan, 26 July 1900, MS 21,802/8, MGP, GhL.
42. J. P. Morgan to Dawkins, 27 July 1900, MS 21,802/8, MGP, GhL.
43. J. S. Morgan & Co. to J. P. Morgan, 27 July 1900, and J. S. Morgan & Co. to J. P. Morgan, 28 July 1900, both MS 21,802/8, MGP, GhL.
44. J. P. Morgan to Dawkins, 30 July 1900, MS 21/802/8, MGP, GhL.
45. J. S. Morgan & Co. to J. P. Morgan, 30 July 1900, MS 21,802/8, MGP, GhL.
46. J. P. Morgan to Dawkins, 31 July 1900, MS 21,802/8, MGP, GhL.
47. J. S. Morgan & Co. to J. P. Morgan, 28 July 1900, MS 21,802/8, MGP, GhL. Hamilton Diary, 31 July 1900, Add. MS 48676, BL.
48. Hamilton Diary, 31 July 1900, Add. MS 48676, BL.
49. Hamilton Diary, 2 Aug. 1900, Add. MS 48676, BL.
50. J. P. Morgan to Dawkins, 31 July 1900 and 3 Aug. 1900, MS 21,802/8, MGP, GhL. Hamilton Diary, 2 Aug. 1900, Add. MS 48676, BL. J. S. Morgan & Co. to J. P. Morgan, 3 Aug. 1900, MS 21,802/9, MGP, GhL.
51. Hamilton Diary, 2 Aug. 1900, Add. MS 48676, BL. Dawkins to Milner, 16 Aug. 1900, Box 177, fo. 155, Milner Papers. J. P. Morgan & Co. to J. S. Morgan & Co., 9 Aug. and 8 Aug. 1900 (second letter), MS 21,802/9, MGP, GhL.
52. Quoted in Chapman, *Rise of Merchant Banking*, p. 160.
53. Hamilton Diary, 11 Jan. 1901, Add. MS 48677, BL.
54. Dawkins to Milner, 25 Jan. 1901, Box 214, fo. 40, Milner Papers.
55. Hamilton Diary, 14 Apr. 1901, Add. MS 48678, BL.
56. Hamilton Diary, 11 Feb. 1901, Add. MS 48677, BL. Dawkins to J. P. Morgan, 19 Jan. 1901; J. P. Morgan & Co. and Baring Magoun & Co. to Dawkins, 21 Jan. 1901; and J. S. Morgan & Co. to J. P. Morgan, 21 Jan. 1901, all MS 21,802/9, MGP, GhL.
57. Dawkins to Milner, 25 Jan. 1901, Box 214, fo. 40, Milner Papers.
58. J. S. Morgan to J. P. Morgan, 5 Feb. 1901, MS 21,802/9, MGP, GhL.
59. Hamilton Diary, 6 Feb. 1901, Add. MS 48677, BL.
60. Hamilton Diary, 8 Feb. and 11 Feb. 1901, Add. MS 48677, BL.
61. Hamilton Diary, 25 Mar. 1901, Add. MS 48678, BL.
62. Hamilton Diary, 2 Apr. 1901, Add. MS 48678, BL.
63. Hamilton Diary, 17 Apr. 1901, Add. MS 48678, BL.
64. Hamilton Diary, 18 Apr. 1901, Add. MS 48678, BL.
65. J. P. Morgan to C. Steele, 19 Apr. 1901, MS 21,802/9, MGP, GhL.
66. Carosso, *Morgans*, p. 513.
67. Hamilton Diary, 19 Apr. 1901, Add. MS 48678, BL.
68. Dawkins to Jack Morgan, 6 Dec. 1901, fo. 89, and Dawkins to Perkins, 3 Jan. 1902, fos. 118–20, both MS 21,800/1; J. S. Morgan & Co. to J. P. Morgan & Co., 13 Jan. 1902 and 16 Jan. 1902, both MS 21,802/9, all MGP, GhL.
69. Dawkins to Milner, 21 Mar. 1902, Box 215, fo. 40, Milner Papers.
70. Hamilton Diary, 20 Mar. and 24 Mar. 1902, Add. MS 48679, BL. Dawkins to Perkins, 10 Apr. 1902, MS 21,802/9, MGP, GhL. Hamilton Diary, 11 Apr. and

14 Apr. 1902, Add. MS 48679, BL. Perkins to Dawkins, 11 Apr. and 12 Apr. 1902, MS 21,802/9, MGP, GhL.

71. Hamilton Diary, 11 Apr. 1902, Add. MS 48679, BL.

72. Hamilton Diary, 14 Apr. 1902, Add. MS 48679, BL.

73. Hamilton Diary, 14 Apr. 1902, Add. MS 48679, BL.

74. J. S. Morgan & Co. to J. P. Morgan & Co., 15 Apr. 1902, MS 21,802/9, MGP, GhL.

75. Dawkins to Hamilton, 15 Apr. 1902, Private, MS 21,800/1, MGP, GhL. J.P.M. kept $600,000 of the Consols for his own house, and these were subsequently sold on joint account with J. S. Morgan & Co. and C. J. Hambro & Son. J. P. Morgan & Co. to J. P. Morgan (in Paris), 24 Apr. 1902, MS 21,802/9, MGP, GhL.

76. Hamilton Diary, 15 Apr. 1902, Add. MS 48679, BL.

77. Hamilton Diary, 15 Apr. and 17 Apr. 1902, Add. MS 48679, BL. Dawkins to Hamilton, 16 Apr. 1902, Private, MS 21,800/1, MGP, GhL.

78. Dawkins to Milner, 25 Apr. 1902, Box 215, fo. 41, Milner Papers. J.P.M. had clearly engaged in a bit of bluff in offering to take as many Consols as the Chancellor wanted, since his New York partners had cabled they could handle only £5m.'s worth, and at $92\frac{1}{2}$ at that.

79. Carosso, *Morgans*, p. 513.

80. David McLean, 'Finance and "Informal Empire" before the First World War', *Economic History Review*, 2nd ser., 29/2 1976), 291–305, 292–3. For Morgan's very frustrating Chinese experience see Carosso, *Morgans*, pp. 50–78.

81. Karl Erich Born, *International Banking in the 19th and 20th Centuries* (Leamington Spa: Berg Publishers Limited, 1983), 142–3. E.C.G. Correspondence 1900–36, p. 25, MS 21,799; and Dawkins to H. Babington Smith, 26 Mar. 1902, MS 21,800/1, both MGP, GhL.

82. Dawkins to Lansdowne, 12 Sept. 1902, MS 21,800/2, MGP, GhL. The secretary was the Marquess of Lansdowne.

83. Dawkins to Gewinner (Deutsche Bank), 23 Apr. 1903, and Dawkins to Babington Smith, 27 Apr. 1903, both MS 21,800/2, MGP, GhL.

84. Hamilton Diary, 21 Apr. 1903, Add. MS 48680, BL.

85. McLean, 'Finance and "Informal Empire"', pp. 284–6. Minute by Hardinge, 20 Nov. 1908, Series 371, vol. 549, file 45717, Foreign Office Papers, PRO. This was awkward for Morgans because J. P. Morgan & Co. had special arrangements with the Dresdner Bank to expand the market for each other's securities. Carosso, *Morgans*, p. 516.

86. Carosso, *Morgans*, p. 594.

87. Carosso, *Morgans*, pp. 513–15.

88. Kathleen Burk, *Britain, America and the Sinews of War 1914–1918* (London: George Allen & Unwin, 1985), 13–14.

89. Sir Cecil Spring Rice to Sir Edward Grey, 21 Oct. 1914, and Spring Rice to Grey, 27 Oct. 1914, both FO 371/2224. Jack Morgan to Grenfell, 2 Nov. 1914, Box Hist. I, file 5, MGP, MGC; Basil Blackett, 'Purchase of War Supplies in the United States', 27 Nov. 1914, Series II, vol. 26, fos. 166–74, H. H. Asquith Papers, Bod. Lib. Burk, *Sinews of War*, pp. 14–18.

90. War Office to Foreign Office, 3 Nov. 1914 and Admiralty to Foreign Office, 30

Oct. 1914, both FO 371/2224. H. P. Davison to J. P. Morgan & Co., 16 Dec. 1914, Folder J. P. Morgan & Co.—Cables 1914–1919, Dwight Morrow Papers, Amherst College, Connecticut. Davison to J. P. Morgan & Co., 19 Dec. 1914, United States Senate, *Munitions Industry: Supplemental Report . . . of the Special Committee on Investigation of the Munitions Industry* (74th Congress, 2nd Session, Senate Report 944, 1936), exhibit no. 2166, xxvi. 7800. 'Commercial Agreement', 15 Jan. 1915, Series D, vol. 12, file 2, no. 1, David Lloyd George Papers, House of Lords Record Office, London.

91. Thomas Lamont, 'Historical Memorandum', 12 Sept. 1939, Series II, file 84-19, Thomas Lamont Papers, Harvard Business School, Boston. Sayers, *Bank of England*, p. 87. US Senate, *Munitions Industry*, v. 71.

92. John Douglas Forbes, *Stettinius, Sn.: Portrait of a Morgan Partner* (Charlottesville: University Press of Virginia, 1974), 47–52. Davison to Grenfell, 27 Feb. 1915, no. 1323, and Davison to Morgan Grenfell & Co., 1 Mar. 1915, no. 1332, Box Hist. 1, file 5, MGP, MGC.

93. Notes by Sir John Mallabar, 24 July 1986.

94. Grenfell to Morgan, 18 Mar. 1918, Box Hist. 3, file 17, no. 52388, and Grenfell to Lamont, 14 Oct. 1915, Box Hist. 11—Letters, file 12, both MGP, MGC. George Booth called it an amazing code. Duncan Crow, *A Man of Push and Go: The Life of George Macaulay Booth* (London: Rupert Hart-Davis, 1965), 123.

95. Memorandum by Grenfell, 20 July 1915, T.170/62; and Board of Trade, 'A Brief Note on the Dependence of the United Kingdom on United States Supplies', 6 Nov. 1916, Series 42, vol. 23, no. 7, Cabinet Papers, PRO. Burk, *Sinews of War*, pp. 61–2, 80–1.

96. Burk, 'The Treasury', in Burk (ed.), *War and the State*, pp. 90–2.

97. Grenfell to Davison, 5 Aug. 1915, Box Hist. 11—Letters, file 13, fo. 736, MGP, MGC. A few weeks later he was driven to write that 'As regards Finance, undoubtedly McKenna is a very ignorant man . . . [who is] inclined to try to appear wise.' Grenfell to Morgan, 24 Aug. 1915, Box Hist. 11—Letters, file 13, fo. 277, MGP, MGC.

98. Burk, *Sinews of War*, pp. 65–75. For the amount of securities sold to mid-July 1917 and a list of collateral loans see Kathleen Burk, 'J. M. Keynes and the Exchange Rate Crisis of July 1917', *Economic History Review*, 2nd ser, 32/3 (1979), 405–16, 407.

99. J. P. Morgan & Co. to Northcliffe, 19 July 1917, Box 84, folder Northcliffe, Stettinius Papers, University of Virginia, Charlottesville, Va. For a list of outstanding amounts of the demand loan on selected dates, see T. Chadwick, 'British Government Transactions in America', File JMP Misc. 18E/1, MGP, MGC, partially printed in Kathleen Burk, 'The Mobilization of Anglo-American Finance During World War I', in N. F. Dreisziger (ed.), *Mobilization for Total War* (Waterloo: Wilfrid Laurier University Press, 1981), 23–42, 39.

100. Davison and Lamont to Morgan, 22 Nov. 1916, Box British Govt. Loan 3, file Nov.–Dec. 1916, no. 31458, and Morgan to J. P. Morgan & Co., 30 Oct. 1916, Box Hist. 2, F.12, no 24877, both MGP, MGC. Charles Hamlin Diary, vol. 4: entries for 19 Nov., 24 Nov., 25 Nov., and 27 Nov. 1916, Hamlin Papers, Library of Congress, Washington (hereafter Lib. of Cong.). *New York Times*, 28 Nov. 1916. Burk, *Sinews of War*, pp. 82–5.

101. Spring Rice to Grey, 5 Dec. 1916, FO Minutes dated 20 Dec. 1916, FO 371/2800.
102. Bradbury to Balfour, 13 Jan. 1917, FO 371/3070.
103. Department of the Treasury, *Annual Report of the Secretary of the Treasury on the State of the Finances for the Fiscal Year ended June 30, 1919* (Washington: Government Printing Office, 1920).
104. Lamont to Morgan, 18 Dec. 1917, Box Hist. 3, F.17, no. 46687, and Cravath to Lamont, 22 May 1918, Box Hist. 3, F.18, no. 56556, both MGP, MGC. Forbes, *Stettinius*, pp. 71–3. For an example of McAdoo's suspicions of Morgans see the handwritten letter from McAdoo to the president, 27 Jan. 1918, as quoted in Forbes, *Stettinius*, pp. 71–2.
105. Crawford to FO, 4 July 1917, FO 371/3115. Department of State, *Papers Relating to the Foreign Relations of the United States, 1917*, Suppl. 2, *The World War* (Washington: Government Printing Office, 1932), 539–43. Grenfell to J. P. Morgan & Co., 4 July 1917, Box Hist. 2, F.16, no. 38709, MGP, MGC.
106. Crosby to Lansing, 28 June 1917, Box 119, GB 132/17-3, US Treasury Papers, National Archives, Washington. Diary of Hardman Lever, 28 June 1917, T.172/429, fos. 151–2.
107. Lord Northcliffe to the Chancellor, 5 July 1917, Drawer 91, file 91, William Wisemen Papers, Yale University Library, New Haven, Conn.
108. J. P. Morgan & Co. to Grenfell, 3 Aug. 1917, Box Hist. 2, F.16, no. 49272, MGP, MGC. Lever to the Chancellor, 1 Aug. 1917, FO 371/3116, PRO. Diary of Basil Blackett, 31 July 1917, fo. 23; Lever's Diary, 1 Aug. 1917, fo. 23; Blackett's Diary, 10 Aug. 1917, fo. 26; and Blackett's Diary, 22 Aug. 1917, fo. 30, all T.172/430. Lever to Chancellor, 15 Aug. 1917, FO 371/3116, PRO. Morgan to McAdoo, 16 Aug. 1917, and McAdoo to Morgan, 20 Aug. 1917, both Box 185, William Gibbs McAdoo Papers, Lib. of Cong. Morgan to Grenfell, 17 Aug. 1917, Box Hist. 2, F16, no. 49662, MGP, MGC.
109. Reading to Churchill, 27 May 1918, FO 800/223.
110. Grenfell to Morgan, 24 Aug. 1915, Box Hist. 11—Letters, F.13, fo. 277, and Grenfell to Morgan, 14 Jan. 1916, E.C.G.'s Letter Book, 1897–1930, both MGP, MGC.

Chapter 5

1. Clarke, *Central Bank Cooperation*, pp. 79–80. For the whole question of Britain's return to gold see Moggridge, *British Monetary Policy, passim*.
2. B. Strong to M. Norman, 9 July 1924, printed in Clarke, *Central Bank Cooperation*, p. 77. Frederick Leith-Ross of the Treasury wrote to a member of the Japanese Financial Mission on 29 May 1929 that '. . . as to the credit opened in 1925, I find that, as I thought, the credits were raised partly with the Federal Reserve Bank of New York and partly with Messrs J. P. Morgan to meet the wishes of the Federal Reserve Bank.' T.172/1500A, fo. 186.
3. M. Norman to Morgan, 30 Apr. 1925, and Morgan to Grenfell, 6 Jan. 1925, both File Brit. Govt. Gold Standard Credit 1925, MGP, MGC.
4. T.W.L., 'Aide-Memoire', May 1925; E.C.G. Minute, 8 May 1925, both File Brit. Govt. Gold Standard Credit 1925, MGP, MGC. F. Leith-Ross in 1929 confirmed that Morgans and their syndicate cost the British government £500,000 'in

commission'. F. Leith-Ross to Mr Tsushima, 22 May 1929, T.172/1500A, fos. 184–5.

5. N. D. Jay to George Whitney, 5 Oct. 1925, no. 2431; Morgan and George Whitney to J. P. Morgan & Co., 6 Oct. 1925, no. 4806; Belgian plan is in Morgan Grenfell & Co. to J. P. Morgan & Co., 6 Oct. 1925, no. 4807, all in Box Hist. 6, file 36, MGP, MGC.

6. J. P. Morgan & Co. to Morgan and Whitney, 9 Oct. 1925, no. 2328; J. P. Morgan & Co. to Morgan, Whitney, and F. D. Bartow, 14 Oct. 1925, no. 2335; Morgan and Whitney to J. P. Morgan & Co., 14 Oct. 1925, no. 4824; Morgan and Whitney to J. P. Morgan & Co., 16 Oct. 1925, no. 4826; J. P. Morgan & Co. to Morgan, 5 Nov. 1925, no. 2366; J. P. Morgan & Co. to Morgan, 20 Nov. 1925, no. 2389; Morgan Grenfell & Co. to J. P. Morgan & Co., 21 Nov. 1925, no. 4876; J. P. Morgan & Co. and Guaranty Trust Co. to Whigham, 24 Nov. 1925, no. 2399, all Box Hist. 6, file 36, MGP, MGC. Bartow was a partner in the New York firm.

7. Clay, *Norman*, p. 256. Leffingwell was subsequently proved correct.

8. Whigham to J. P. Morgan & Co., 27 Nov. 1925, nos. 4887 and 4888; J. P. Morgan & Co. and Guaranty Trust Co. to Whigham, 28 Nov. 1925, no. 2416; J. P. Morgan & Co. to Whigham, 3 Dec. 1925, no. 2429, all Box Hist. 6, file 36, MGP, MGC.

9. For details on the 1926 Kingdom of Belgium Stabilization Loan 7% Sterling Bonds, see Box Hist. 7, files 38–9, MGP, MGC.

10. Clarke, *Central Bank Cooperation*, p. 33, and Clay, *Norman*, pp. 284–6, for example.

11. J. P. Morgan & Co. to Whitney, 23 Oct. 1926, no. 2441; J. P. Morgan & Co. to Morgan, 4 Nov. 1926, no. 2483; Morgan to J. P. Morgan & Co., 4 Nov. 1926, no. 5015, all Box Hist. 7, file 39, MGP, MGC.

12. J. P. Morgan & Co. to Morgan, 6 Nov. 1926, no. 2484, Box Hist. 7, file 39, MGP, MGC.

13. Clay, *Norman*, p. 257.

14. Clay, *Norman*, p. 258.

15. The other partner was George Whitney. Morgan Grenfell & Co. to J. P. Morgan & Co., 6 Oct. 1925, no. 4806, Box Hist. 6, file 36, MGP, MGC.

16. 17 July 1924, no. 2431, Box Hist. 6, file 32, MGP, MGC.

17. J. P. Morgan & Co. and Guaranty Trust Co. to C. F. Whigham, 24 Nov. 1925, no. 2399, Box Hist. 6, file 36, MGP, MGC.

18. Michael J. Hogan, *Informal Entente: The Private Structure of Cooperation in Anglo-American Economic Diplomacy, 1918–1928* (Columbia: University of Missouri Press, 1977), 60–2; Eduard März, *Austrian Banking & Financial Policy: Creditanstalt at a Turning Point, 1913–1923*, trans. Charles Kessler (London: Weidenfeld & Nicolson, 1984), part 5, ch. 2. Lamont in Paris to D. W. Morrow in New York, 15 May 1921, file 1, Bundle 156 (Austria. Reconstruction. 1923/24 Loan), MGP, MGC.

19. J. P. Morgan & Co. to Grenfell, 3 Dec. 1921, no. 2255, file 1, Bundle 156, MGP, MGC.

20. Lamont to J. P. Morgan & Co., 12 May 1922, no. 4715, file 1; Morgan Grenfell & Co. to Baron Franckenstein, the Austrian Minister of Finance, 22 May 1922, file 1; and G. M. Young to Whigham, 23 June 1922, file 1, all Bundle 156, MGP,

MGC. März, *Austrian Banking & Financial Policy*, pp. 480–1. The Lamont cable of 12 May can also be found in 2/82-17, Austria, Lamont Papers.

21. Morgan Grenfell & Co. to J. P. Morgan & Co., 16 Jan. 1923, no. 4511, file 2, Bundle 156, MGP, MGC. Hogan, *Informal Entente*, p. 165. Smith and Whigham to Morgan, 16 Jan. 1923, no. 4512, and Morgan to Morgan Grenfell & Co., 18 Jan. 1923, no. 2013, both file 2, Bundle 156, MGP, MGC.

22. Lamont to Grenfell, 10 Mar. 1923, file 2; Morgan Grenfell & Co. to J. P. Morgan & Co., 21 Apr. 1923, no. 4585, file 2; J. P. Morgan & Co. to Austrian Loan Commission, enclosed in Lamont to J. P. Morgan & Co., 10 May 1923, no. 82307, file 2; Morgan Grenfell & Co. to J. P. Morgan & Co., 11 June 1923, no. 4700, file 3; and J. P. Morgan & Co. to Morgan Grenfell & Co., 11 June 1923, no. 2200, file 3, all Bundle 156, MGP, MGC. Hogan, *Informal Entente*, pp. 65–6.

23. Schuker, *End of French Predominance, passim.*

24. 'As regards public offering of German Loan in U.S.A. it is essential that principal European Powers should be bound by Protocol to refrain from any interference with Germany which would impair the security or the service of the loan.' J. P. Morgan & Co. to Morgan Grenfell & Co., 10 July 1924, no. 24/2406; Lamont cabled J. P. Morgan & Co. on 15 July 1924 that there would be no possibility of such a protocol. No. 24/4874. Grenfell and Lamont to J. P. Morgan & Co., 22 July 1924, no. 24/4896, reported that the British contended that the situation would be impossible for the investor should any Allied Power have authority to enforce isolated sanctions. All from file 2, Bundle 54 (German Government Loan in USA, 1924), MGP, MGC.

25. Grenfell and Lamont to J. P. Morgan & Co., 23 July 1924, no. 24/4899, and Lamont to J. P. Morgan & Co., 20 July 1924, no. 24/4892, for shaky British and French governments, both file 2, Bundle 54, MGP, MGC.

26. D. W. Morrow, T. Cochran and R. C. Leffingwell to Lamont, 24 July 1924, no. 24/2459, and ?T. W. Lamont to J. P. Morgan & Co., 20 July 1924, no. 24/4892 for M. Norman's stiffness, both file 2, Bundle 54, MGP, MGC. Cochran was a New York partner. Schuker, *End of French Predominance*, ch. 8.

27. Oct. 1924, no. 24/5097, file 4, Bundle 54, MGP, MGC.

28. Clarke, *Central Bank Cooperation*, p. 68.

29. 8 Oct. 1924, no. 24/5097, file 4, Bundle 54, MGP, MGC.

30. Clarke, *Central Bank Cooperation*, p. 68.

31. Morgan Grenfell & Co. to J. P. Morgan & Co., 22 Oct. 1924, no. 24/2707, and Harjes to Morgan, 13 Oct. 1924, no. 24/2009, both file 5, Bundle 54, MGP, MGC.

32. J. P. Morgan & Co. to Morgan, 14 Oct. 1924, no. 24/2667, and A. M. Anderson to Lamont, 16 Oct. 1924, no. 24/5172, both file 5, Bundle 54, MGP, MGC. Anderson was a New York partner. Clarke, *Central Bank Cooperation*, p. 69.

33. Schuker notes that Grenfell wrote to Lamont that he could not take an active part in negotiations for fear of political attacks on Morgans if things went badly; however, this did not prevent Grenfell from keeping his ear to the ground, and he helped Lamont draft many of the cables. *End of French Predominance*, p. 291.

34. Clay, *Norman*, pp. 266–7. Stephen A. Schuker 'American Foreign Policy and the Young Plan', in Gustav Schmidt (ed.), *Konstellationen internationaler Politik: Politische und wirtschaftliche Faktoren in den Beziehungen zwischen Westeuropa und den USA, 1924–1932* (Bochum: Studienverlag Dr N. Brockmeyer, 1983), 122.

35. Clay, *Norman*, pp. 267–8. Sally Marks, *The Illusion of Peace: International Relations in Europe 1918–1933* (London: Macmillan, 1976), 102.

36. Lamont wrote to Owen D. Young (via J. P. Morgan & Co) on 31 July 1929 that 'I find very strong criticism here of the plan in so far as it affects British interests and very strong opposition both in political and financial circles . . . . I had over an hour with the Chancellor and . . . he says he is determined to improve Britain's percentage and may not hesitate to break the conference on this issue.' No. 29/4893; Morgan wrote to Young on 9 Aug. that '. . . [Philip] Snowden's extraordinary methods of negotiation have thrown the whole thing into such confusion that no one can see his way anywhere and the whole thing is clouded by the fear of the complete rupture of the Conference before it has fairly begun.' No. 29/4925, both File International Bank (BIS), Bundle 213, MGP, MGC. Marks, *Illusion of Peace*, p. 104. David Carleton, *MacDonald versus Henderson: The Foreign Policy of the Second Labour Government* (London: Macmillan, 1970), 40–9. Sir Frederick Leith-Ross, *Money Talks: Fifty Years of International Finance* (London: Hutchinson & Co. Ltd., 1968), 110–23.

37. Marks, *Illusion of Peace*, pp. 102–6.

38. Lamont to P. Quesnay, Personal, 14 Aug. and 19 Aug. 1929, both File International Bank (BIS), Bundle 213, MGP, MGC.

39. Clay, *Norman*, pp. 364–7. In his evidence to the Macmillan Committee on 26 Mar. 1930, Norman emphasized how useful the BIS had been in 'taking Reparations from the political arena and putting them into a back room in the BIS' (p. 243), and in particular how useful the BIS was proving to be as a routine and therefore nearly unpublicized meeting-place for central bankers. His evidence is printed as an appendix in Paul Einzig, *Montagu Norman: A Study in Financial Statesmanship* (London: Kegan Paul, Trench, Trubner & Co., Ltd., 1932), esp. pp. 241–7. Frank C. Costigliola, 'The Other Side of Isolation: The Establishment of the First World Bank, 1929–1930', *Journal of American History*, 59/3 (1972), 602–20, emphasizes Norman's disillusionment.

40. Lamont to the Chancellor of the Exchequer, Personal, 20 Aug. 1929, and Morgan to J. P. Morgan & Co., 31 Oct. 1929, no. 29/5071, both File International Bank (BIS), Bundle 213, MGP, MGC.

41. Lamont to P. Quesnay, Personal, 14 Aug. 1929, and Lamont to the Chancellor of the Exchequer, Personal, 20 Aug. 1929, both File International Bank (BIS), Bundle 213, MGP, MGC.

42. Morgan to Young, 9 Aug. 1929, no. 29/4925, for the quotation, and Morgan to J. P. Morgan & Co., 31 Oct. 1929, no. 29/5071, both File International Bank (BIS), Bundle 213, MGP, MGC.

43. Costigliola, 'Other Side of Isolationism', p. 620.

44. Morgan to J. P. Morgan & Co., 2 Sept. 1929, File German Railway Financing, MGP, MGC.

45. J. P. Morgan & Co. to Morgan Grenfell & Co., 10 July 1931, no. 2312, File German Crisis 1931, MGP, MGC.

46. Memorandum by R. H. Brand, 1931, File Acceptance Houses Committee, 1A, Documents and Memoranda, MGP, MGC.

47. Memorandum by Michael Herbert, File Acceptance Houses Committee, German Indebtedness, MGP, MGC. This section is based on Kathleen Burk, 'Supplemen-

tary Remarks to Gerd Hardach, "The 1931 German Banking Crisis"', unpublished paper, 1981.

48. Phillip Williamson, 'A "Bankers' Ramp"? Financiers and the British Political Crisis of August 1931', *English Historical Review*, 99/343 (1984), 770–806, 777.

49. Morgan to J. P. Morgan & Co., 29 July 1931, no. 31/4894, File German Crisis 1931, MGP, MGC. Williamson, 'A "Bankers' Ramp"?', pp. 778–81.

50. Williamson, 'A "Bankers' Ramp"?', pp. 782–4.

51. Comment by Harry A. Siepmann, head of the central banking section, Bank of England, as reported in a memorandum by George L. Harrison, Governor of the Federal Reserve Bank of New York, quoted in Williamson, 'A "Bankers' Ramp"?', pp. 786, 795.

52. Quoted in Williamson, 'A "Bankers' Ramp"?', pp. 786–7.

53. Williamson, 'A "Bankers' Ramp"?', p. 790. J. P. Morgan & Co. to Morgan in England, 8 Aug. 1931, no. 2371, File Brit. Govt. Credit 1931, No. 1, MGP, MGC.

54. Grenfell to Morgan, 19 Aug. 1931, File Brit. Govt. Credit 1931, No. 1, MGP, MGC.

55. Grenfell to J. P. Morgan & Co., 20 Aug. 1931, 5.20 p.m., no. 4922, File Brit. Govt. Credit 1931, No. 1, MGP, MGC.

56. B. R. Mitchell, *British Historical Statistics* (Cambridge: Cambridge University Press, 1988), 645.

57. Williamson, 'A "Bankers' Ramp"?', pp. 796–7. Quote on p. 797.

58. J. P. Morgan & Co. to Grenfell, 21 Aug. 1931, 10 a.m., no. 2380, File Brit. Govt. Credit 1931, No. 1, MGP, MGC. Williamson, 'A "Bankers' Ramp"?', p. 798.

59. Williamson, 'A "Bankers' Ramp"?', pp. 799–800.

60. J. P. Morgan & Co. to Morgan Grenfell & Co., rec. 7.50 a.m., 22 Aug. 1931, no. 2382, File Brit. Govt. Credit 1931, No. 1, MGP, MGC.

61. Grenfell to J. P. Morgan & Co., 22 Aug. 1931, sent 9.30 p.m., no. 4926, File Brit. Govt. Credit 1931, No. 1, MGP, MGC.

62. Sir E. M. Harvey, Deputy Governor, to Morgan Grenfell & Co. to J. P. Morgan & Co., 23 Aug. 1931, no. 4930, and Grenfell to J. P. Morgan & Co., 23 Aug. 1931, 2.40 p.m., no. 4929 for the quote, both File Brit. Govt. Credit 1931, No. 1, MGP, MGC.

63. Memorandum (covering events 22 Aug–18 Sept. 1931), no date, no name, but probably by Grenfell, File Brit. Govt. Credit 1931, Documents and Memoranda, MGP, MGC.

64. Harrison, telephone conversation with Norman, 23 Aug. 1931, quoted in Williamson, 'A "Bankers' Ramp"?', p. 801.

65. J. P. Morgan & Co. to Grenfell, 23 Aug. 1931, rec. 10 p.m., no. 2383, File Brit. Govt. Credit 1931, No. 1, MGP, MGC. Cable confirmation of telephone message Whitney to Grenfell.

66. Williamson, 'A "Bankers' Ramp"?', pp. 802–3. Quote from Memorandum, no name, no date, File Brit. Govt. Credit 1931, Documents and Memoranda, MGP, MGC.

67. Williamson, 'A "Bankers' Ramp"?', pp. 770–1. Grenfell to Lamont, Private, 27 Aug. 1931, File Brit. Govt. Credit 1931, No. 1, MGP, MGC.

68. Grenfell to Lamont, 25 Jan. 1932, File Brit. Govt. Credit 1931, No. 2, MGP, MGC.

69. Grenfell to J. P. Morgan & Co., 24 Aug. 1931, 8 p.m., no. 4934, File Brit. Govt. Credit 1931, No. 1, MGP, MGC. Sayers, *Bank of England*, p. 399.

70. J. P. Morgan & Co. to Grenfell, 25 Aug. 1931, no. 2386 (confirming telephone conversation), File Brit. Govt. Credit 1931, No. 1, MGP, MGC.

71. Memorandum, no name, no date, File Brit. Govt. Credit 1931, Documents and Memoranda, and J. P. Morgan & Co. to Morgan (in London), 27 Aug. 1931, rec. 7.40 p.m., no. 2401 for quote, File Brit. Govt. Credit 1931, No. 1, both MGP, MGC.

72. Morgan Grenfell & Co. to J. P. Morgan & Co., 28 Aug. 1931, 11.20 p.m., no. 4954, MGP, MGC.

73. Sayers, *Bank of England*, pp. 400–1.

74. Sayers, *Bank of England*, pp. 402–4.

Chapter 6

1. Held in the Secretariat, MGC.

2. Interview with John Izard, 10 Apr. 1986.

3. Kellett, *Merchant Banking Arena*, p. 60.

4. A general awareness in industry of the need for rationalization meant that mergers of this sort were then rather fashionable.

5. P. W. S. Andrews and Elizabeth Brunner, *Capital Development in Steel: A Study of The United Steel Companies, Ltd.* (Oxford: Basil Blackwell, 1951), 102–18.

6. Jonathan S. Boswell, 'Sir Walter Benton Jones', *DBB* iii. 539.

7. Memorandum by E.C.G., 5 June 1929, and Memorandum by C.F.W., 6 June 1929, both File Steel Industry—GB-Reorganisation, Bundle 274, MGP, MGC.

8. David Fanning, 'Clarence Charles Hatry', *DBB* iii. 111–13.

9. Boswell, 'Jones', *DBB* iii. 540. Chris Beauman has pointed out that United Steel was the outstanding leader amongst the steel companies in the quality of its management and 'post-nationalisation its managers colonised most of the industry . . .'. C. B. B. Beauman to the author, 24 Nov. 1987.

10. Memorandum by C.F.W., 1 Nov. 1933, File United Steel Companies (hereafter USC) Issue of 4% Debenture Stock, Box 8, MGP, MGC.

11. Memorandum by C.F.W., n.d., covering 2 and 3 Nov. 1933, and Memorandum by E.C.G., 8 Nov. 1933, both File USC Oct. 1934 Issue of 4% Debenture Stock, Memoranda, Box 8, MGP, MGC.

12. Memorandum by C.F.W., 9 Nov. 1933, File USC Oct. 1934 Issue of 4% Debenture Stock, Memoranda, Box 8, MGP, MGC.

13. Memorandum by E.C.G., 4 May 1934. The nine syndicate members were Morgan Grenfell; Barings; Hambros; Rothschilds; M. Samuel; Helbert, Wagg; Robert Fleming; Prudential Assurance Company; and Tobacco Securities Trust Company. Minutes of meeting, 7 May 1934, both File USC May 1934 Purchase and Resale of 4.5m. Shares, Memoranda, Bundle 6, MGP, MGC.

14. Memorandum for meeting of syndicate members on 27 Sept. 1934 and Summary of Operation, File USC Option to Purchase 2,077,223 Shares, Box 8, MGP, MGC. *The Times*, 10 Oct. 1934. *Financial Times*, 10 Oct. 1934 and 29 Nov. 1934. Morgan Grenfell derived £65,200 from the two operations. Chairman's Speech for 1934, the Secretariat, MGC.

15. File USC Oct. 1934 Issue of 4% Debenture Stock, Box 7, MGP, MGC. *Financial Times*, 8 Oct. 1934. The two principal subsidiaries were Appleby-Frodingham Steel Co. and Samuel Fry and Co. The proceeds of the issue were to be used (1) to repay the existing £1.3m. of 6% debentures and (2) to redeem a temporary bank loan of £977,169. *Investors Chronicle*, 13 Oct. 1934. Morgan Grenfell's profit was £28,840. Chairman's Speech for 1934, the Secretariat, MGC.

16. Memorandum by T.S.C. of discussions with Spens and Benton Jones on 3 Apr. 1935, dated 5 Apr. 1935, File USC Oct. 1934 Issue of 4% Debenture Stock, Memoranda; and Memoranda by C.F.W. of meeting between Benton Jones, Spens, Catto, and Whigham on 1 Aug. 1935, same date, File USC 1935 Proposed Purchase of Lancashire Steel Corp., both Box 8, MGP, MGC.

17. Memorandum by Whigham of meeting on 28 Apr. 1934 with the Governor, 28 Apr. 1934, and Summary, both File USC 1936 Increase of Capital, Box 8, MGP, MGC. *Financial Times,* 12 May and 23 May 1936.

18. Sayers, *Bank of England*, pp. 549–50. Andrews and Brunner, *Capital Development in Steel*, p. 206, made the judgement. File John Summers & Sons Ltd. Issue of £2,000,000 4½% First Mortgage Debenture Stock 1939, MGP, MGC. Morgans made a profit on the Summers issue of £11,211; they also received a fee of £5,250 from United Steel. Chairman's Speech for 1939, the Secretariat, MGC.

19. The notes were placed by Rowe & Pitman, Cazenove Akroyds & Greenwood & Co., Robert Fleming & Co., Royal Exchange Assurance, and Barings, with Morgans retaining £175,000 for themselves and their clients. Morgan Grenfell's profit on the notes was £16,100. Chairman's Speech for 1938, the Secretariat, MGC.

20. Morgans made a profit of £82,353 on the Colvilles issue. Chairman's Speech for 1936, the Secretariat, MGC.

21. *George Peabody & Co., J. S. Morgan & Co., Morgan Grenfell & Co., Morgan Grenfell & Co. Ltd. 1838–1958* (Oxford: Oxford University Press, 1958, for private circulation), 20.

22. Interview with John Izard, 10 Apr. 1986. It is rather surprising that Morgans left things that late, as many City firms, according to Dr S. Diaper, had started making plans much earlier in the year. As she notes, 'All those partners' country houses came in jolly useful!' Note to the author, 3 July 1987.

23. Chairman's Speech for 1945, the Secretariat, MGC.

24. Interview with J. E. H. Collins, 10 June 1987.

25. Chairman's Speech for 1945, the Seretariat, MGC.

26. *Financial Times*, 12 July 1943, and *Financial News*, 9 July 1943.

27. Palin, *Rothschild Relish*, pp. 163–4.

28. *Daily Telegraph*, 2 July 1940.

29. *The Times*, 8 May 1939. Memorandum on Morgan Grenfell's assets as of 25 Mar. 1939; Secret Memorandum by the Discount Office, Bank of England, 28 Nov. 1942; letter from Lord Bicester to the Bank of England, 24 Dec. 1942, all File C48/41, Morgan Grenfell 1934–62, Bank of England Archives.

30. Memorandum given to Lord Bicester, 19 Nov. 1942; for lists of capital and reserves as of Nov. 1942 (before Morgans' reduction), showing that Morgans' was 35% of Barings' and 62% of Kleinworts; see Secret Memorandum by the Discount Office, 28 Nov. 1942, both File C48/41, Bank of England.

31. Chairman's Speeches for 1940, 1941, 1942, the Secretariat, MGC.
32. Chairman's Speech for 1942, the Secretariat, MGC. *Star*, 10 May 1944.
33. R. Smith to M. Pesson-Didion, 10 Oct. 1944, File Change of Firm 7, Bundle 154, MGP, MGC.
34. Chairman's Speech for 1943, the Secretariat, MGC.
35. Interview with J. E. H. Collins, 10 June 1987.
36. Interviews with Lord Catto, 27 May and 4 June 1967. Thanks to J. Wormell for useful comments on floating charge loans.
37. The profit on the 1945 issue was £14,909. Chairman's Speech for 1945, the Secretariat, MGC.
38. Summary, File USC 1938 Issue of 4½% 10-Year Notes 1948, Box 9; Memorandum of meetings on 30 Oct. and 31 Oct. 1944, Memorandum on United Steel's wishes and requirements, 26 Oct. 1944, and Summary, all File USC Issue of 1,500,000 4½% Cumulative Preference Shares, Box 8, both MGP, MGC. Sayers, *Bank of England*, p. 550.
39. *Daily Telegraph*, 17 May 1946. File USC 1946 Issue to Debenture Stockholders, Box 9, MGP, and Chairman's Speech for 1946, the Secretariat, both MGC.
40. *Stock Exchange Gazette*, 11 Jan. 1947. Memorandum by R.G.E., 26 Nov. 1946, and Summary, both File USC Issue of 1,713,546 4½% Cumulative Preference Shares, Box 9, MGP, and Chairman's Speech for 1947, the Secretariat, MGC.
41. Memorandum by R.H.V.S., 12 June 1950, and Memorandum by R.G.E., 13 Oct. 1950, both File USC 1950 Proposed Issue, Box 9, MGP, MGC.
42. Harold S. Kent, *In on the Act: Memoirs of a Lawmaker* (London: Macmillan, 1979), 202. Kent had helped to draft both the 1949 and the 1953 Acts.
43. Notes of a meeting held in the Ministry of Supply, 18 July 1950, Box 011612, File July–Dec. 1950, and BISF Council Minutes, 7 Nov. 1950, Box 01546, both British Iron and Steel Federation Papers, British Steel Corporation Record Centre, Irthlingborough. For further information on the whole steel denationalization episode 1950–69, see Kathleen Burk, *The First Privatisation: The Politicians, the City and the Denationalisation of Steel* (London: The Historians' Press, 1988).
44. Notes of meeting, 27 Oct. 1950, fos. 1–3, and Memorandum of meeting, 5 Dec. 1950, fos. 8–11, both Partner's File 65A—Steel Industry, Barings Archives. The relevant file in the Conservative Research Department Papers is silent on the subject of working parties on steel denationalization, whether their own or the City's. File CRD 2/3:1, Conservative Party Archives, Bod. Lib. Forbes had also been Chairman of the Labour government's Iron and Steel Board 1946–9 and would be Chairman of the second Iron and Steel Board 1953–9.
45. Minutes of Working Committee, 19 Dec. 1950, fo. 13; 8 Mar. 1951; and 19 Mar. 1951, all Partner's File 65A, Barings Archives.
46. File G1/125, Bank of England.
47. File G1/125, Bank of England.
48. Memorandum by A. Bull on 'Unscrambling of Steel', for Sir K. Peppiatt and Lord Cobbold, 28 Sept. 1951; seen and agreed to by a number of high Bank officials. File G1/125, Bank of England.
49. Cobbold to Bridges, 29 Oct. 1951, File G1/125, Bank of England.
50. Note by the Governor, 9 Nov. 1951, File G1/125, Bank of England.
51. Hansard, *Parliamentary Debates*, 5th ser., vol. 493 (1951–2), cols. 52, 663–4.

52. Note by the Governor, 19 Nov. 1951, and Cobbold to Butler, 19 or 20 Nov. 1951, both File G1/125, Bank of England.
53. Note by the Governor, 23 Nov. 1951, and top secret memorandum by H. C. B. M[ynors] on steel, 23 Nov. 1951, both File G1/125, Bank of England.
54. Anthony Seldon, *Churchill's Indian Summer: The Conservative Government, 1951–55* (London: Hodder and Stoughton, 1981), 189–191. Sandys was Churchill's son-in-law.
55. Sandys to Cobbold, Personal, 14 Aug. 1952, with Cobbold's minutes on it, File G1/125, Bank of England.
56. Memorandum by Cobbold of meeting on 16 Sept. with the Chancellor and the Minister of Supply, 18 Sept. 1952, and memorandum by Cobbold of meeting with Sir John Morison, 18 Sept. 1952, both File G1/125, Bank of England.
57. Seldon, *Churchill's Indian Summer*, pp. 190–1.
58. Kent, *In on the Act*, p. 236.
59. Mynors's momorandum to the Governor, 'Steel Working Party', 25 Nov. 1952, and Mynors's memorandum for the Governor of his talk with Morison, 25 Feb. 1953, and Cobbold's scribbled note—'. . . this is very tricky', 27 Feb. 1953, all File G1/125, Bank of England.
60. R. Peddie of United Steel to Erskine, 27 Feb. 1953; Erskine to Peddie, 2 Mar. 1953; and Erskine to Peddie plus memorandum, 2 Apr. 1953, all File USC 1953 Offer for Sale of £14m. Ordinary Shares, General File, Box 377, MGP, MGC.
61. H.C.B.M., 'Steel. Note of a conversation with Sir John Morison', 6 Mar. 1953, seen by the Governor and the Deputy Governor, File G1/125, Bank of England. Erskine reported on 27 Aug. 1953 that Pearl Assurance planned to take $2\frac{1}{2}\%$ of each issue, one-quarter of the amount the Prudential was prepared to take. Memorandum on Steel by R.G.E., 27 Aug. 1953, File Steel Industry 1953 *et seq.* Denationalisation. General. Documents and Memoranda, Box 369, MGP, MGC.
62. Secret memorandum by H. C. B. Mynors, 17 Mar. 1953, File G1/125, Bank of England.
63. Draft memorandum by H.C.B.M., 20 Mar. 1953, File G1/125, Bank of England.
64. Cobbold to Butler, Secret, 25 Mar. 1953, File G1/125, Bank of England.
65. Governor's Note, 27 Mar. 1953, File G1/125, Bank of England.
66. File G1/125, Bank of England.
67. Confidential Memorandum on the meeting of 9 Apr. 1953, received from the Bank 13 Apr. 1953, File Steel Industry 1953 *et seq.* Denationalisation. General. Documents and Memoranda, Box 369, MGP, MGC.
68. David Colville, Private and Confidential Memorandum on Steel, 14 Apr. 1953, File Steel Industry Denationalisation. General. Documents and Memoranda, Box 369, MGP, MGC.
69. Confidential memorandum on meeting of 9 Apr. 1953, and Cobbold to Butler, 14 Apr. 1953 (for quotation), both File G1/125, Bank of England.
70. Interview with J. E. H. Collins, 10 June 1987.
71. Governor's Note, 1 May 1953, File G1/125, Bank of England.
72. Note by Mynors for the Governor of a conversation with Sir John Morison, 22 Apr. 1953, File G1/125, Bank of England. The members of the Sub-Committee on Steel were Erskine (Chairman), J. Backhouse of Schröders, J. H. Hambro, P. Horsfall of Lazards, and A. Russell of Helbert, Wagg. Minutes of the Meeting on

13 Apr. 1953 of the Issuing Houses Steel Committee, the Hon. R. H. V. Smith of Morgan Grenfell in the Chair.

73. Sandys to Forbes, 7 Dec. 1953, BT 255/123, file E69, Board of Trade Papers, PRO. Most of the relevant Treasury files appear not to have survived.

74. The Report of the Sub-Committee on Steel of the Issuing Houses had insisted that 'The Consortium of Issuing Houses should not be asked to enter into a commitment in respect of the first public Offer for Sale until it is known that the reacquisition of the major privately owned companies is in an advanced stage of negotiation and that the negotiations relating to some at least will have been completed and publicly known to have been completed when the first public Offer is made . . . . We accept the fact that insistence upon this point may delay the date of the first public Offer.' 13 May 1953, File Steel Industry 1953 *et seq.* Denationalisation. General. Documents and Memoranda, Box 369, MGP, MGC. The first public offer, which it had been hoped would take place at the end of July, in fact took place on 23 Oct. 1953.

75. United Steel, 'Memorandum for Reorganised Capital Structure and Sale of the Company's Securities . . .', received with letter from Peddie to Erskine, 1 May 1953, both File USC 1953 Offer for Sale. Documents and Memoranda; Memo by K. Barrington of telephone call from Peddie, 14 May 1953, and Peddie to Erskine, 11 July 1953, for quotation, both File USC 1953 Offer for Sale; Benton Jones to Erskine, 16 Sept. 1953, File USC 1953 Offer for Sale, General, all Box 377. MGP, MGC. The Sub-Committee on Steel of the Issuing Houses had pointed out that Stewarts & Lloyds 'has probably the greatest investment appeal and, notwithstanding the size, we favour it as the subject of the first Offer for Sale'. Report of the Sub-Committee on Steel, 13 May 1953, File Steel Industry 1953 *et seq.* Denationalisation. General. Documents and Memoranda, Box 369, MGP, MGC. It is unclear why United Steel was selected in its place; in any case Morgan Grenfell would still have led the Consortium, and did so when Stewarts & Lloyds was denationalized in June 1954. The Sub-Committee's Report had also 'noted that the Agency will expect a loading over the take-over price to take into account some part of the profits retained during the period of State ownership'.

76. File USC 1953 Offer for Sale, Box 377, MGP, MGC.

77. H.C.B.M.'s Secret Memorandum on talks with Randal [Rufus] Smith and George Erskine, 16 July 1953, File G1/125, Bank of England. Sun Insurance Office to Morgan Grenfell, 13 Oct. 1953, File USC 1953 Offer for Sale, Box 377, MGP, MGC.

78. Managing Director of Brown Knight and Truscott Ltd. to the Editor, *Daily Mail*, 26 Oct. 1953, with a copy to Morgan Grenfell. File USC 1953 Offer for Sale, Box 377, MGP, MGC.

79. File USC 1953 Offer for Sale, Box 377, MGP, MGC.

80. The prospectus noted that loans of £7,030,000 were obtained from the Iron and Steel Corporation. These loans had been reduced by the acquisition by the Corporation of USC's holdings of £2,805,822 ordinary shares in John Summers & Sons Ltd. at a price of 34s., yielding approximately £4,770,000. To repay the balance of £2,260,000 and to provide for future capital expenditure and working capital, the directors of USC issued to the Agency for cash 1.5 million $5\frac{3}{4}$% £1 preference shares at par and £10m. $4\frac{3}{4}$% debenture stock 1968/78 at 98. The

debenture stock had been prepaid to the extent of 23 and the balance would be paid by the Agency by 30 Apr. 1955.

81. Chairman's Speech for 1953, the Secretariat, MGC.

82. 'We wholly concur with the Governor's request that care should be taken to avoid any accusation that "the City" is making undue profit and we are of the opinion that the percentage spread chargeable to the Agency should be kept as low as possible . . .'. Report by the Sub-Committee on Steel appointed by the eight issuing houses, 13 May 1953, File Steel Industry 1953. Denationalisation. General. Documents and Memoranda, Box 369, MGP, MGC.

83. Chairman's Speech for 1953, the Secretariat, MGC.

84. Chairman's Speech for 1954, the Secretariat, MGC.

85. Chairman's Speech for 1955, the Secretariat, MGC. Morgans' profits on the English Steel operation was £40,321·17.3.

86. File Steel Company of Wales 1957 40 million £1 shares at par, Box 368, MGP, MGC. File USC 1957 Issue of 6 million ordinary shares, Box 367, MGP, MGC; Morgan Grenfell's profit was £48,950. Chairman's Speech for 1957. The profit on the issue of debenture stocks for Colvilles was £42,937·10.0 and for South Durham £58,312·10.0. Chairman's Speech for 1958, both in the Secretariat, MGC. File USC 1961 Rights issue and File USC 1963 Acquisition by Strapping Associates, both Box 376, MGP, MGC. *The Times*, 8 Mar. 1963.

87. Kent, *In on the Act*, pp. 245–6.

88. T. C. Barker and C. I. Savage, *An Economic History of Transport in Britain* (London: Hutchinson University Library 1959; 3rd rev. edn., 1974), 228–30.

89. Interview with Lord Catto, 27 May 1987.

90. Kellett, *Merchant Banking Arena*, pp. 94–5.

91. Kellett, *Merchant Banking Arena*, p. 161.

92. Interview with Lord Catto, 27 May 1987.

93. Interview with J. E. H. Collins, 10 June 1987.

94. Interview with Lord Catto, 27 May 1987. Clay, *Norman*, p. 16, for the quotation.

95. Interview with Lord Catto, 27 May 1987.

96. David Robinson, 'The Strategy, Structure and Financial Performance of Some Major Merchant Banking Groups, 1958 to 1974', M.B.Sc. thesis (Manchester Business School, 1976), 11.

97. Kellett, *Merchant Banking Arena*, p. 67. Chairman's Speeches for 1957, 1961, and 1962, the Secretariat, MGC.

98. And, of course, G. P. Gooch and F. W. Lawrence had done so the previous century in J. S. Morgan & Co.

99. Interview with Donald Wells, 22 May 1987.

100. Minutes of the meeting of the Sub-Committee on Steel, 13 Apr. 1953 *et seq.* Denationalisation, Box 369, MGP, MGC.

101. Interview with Donald Wells, 22 May 1987.

102. Interview with Sir John Sparrow, 5 June 1987.

Chapter 7

1. Interview with Blaise Hardman, 10 June 1987.

2. Interviews with Dorothy Beech and Eileen Izard, both 28 July 1987.

3. Chairman's Speech for 1961, given 26 June 1962, the Secretariat, MGC. Interview with Charles Rawlinson, 16 July 1987.
4. D. Robinson, 'The Strategy, Structure and Financial Performance of Some Major Merchant Banking Groups, 1958 to 1974', p. 162.
5. Annual Reviews (formerly Chairman's Speech) for 1965 and 1966, the Secretariat, MGC.
6. Interview with Charles Rawlinson 16 July 1987. Annual Review for 1967 and Minutes of Board Meeting, 22 Sept. 1964, Morgan Grenfell & Co. Minute Book 1959–1969, both the Secretariat, MGC.
7. Letter from Lady Stevens to the author, 6 Sept. 1987. Interviews with Lord O'Brien, Governor of the Bank 1966–73, 17 June 1987, and with Sir George Blunden, Deputy Governor of the Bank from 1986, 6 July 1987.
8. Chairman's Speech for 1962, given 27 June 1963, and Annual Review for 1963, both the Secretariat, MGC. Interviews with Donald Wells, 22 May 1987, and Blaise Hardman, 10 June 1987.
9. The numbers are all based on MG balance sheets and private ledgers (for inner reserves). Table 6 gives the Morgan Grenfell ratios for 1965 and 1966.
10. Interview with Sir George Blunden, 6 July 1987.
11. Board Meeting, 28 Mar. 1967, MG Minute Book 1959–1969, the Secretariat, MGC. Interview with Christopher Reeves, 8 July 1987.
12. Robinson, 'Strategy, Structure and Financial Performance', table 3.7 (p. 51).
13. Board meeting, 22 Sept. 1964, MG Minute Book 1959–1969, the Secretariat, MGC. Interview with Donald Wells, 22 May 1987.
14. *Financial Times*, 17 July 1968. C. M. J. Whittington, 'Morgan Grenfell's Involvement in Film Finance' [memorandum for Slaughter and May], 26 May 1971, File De Grunwald Productions Ltd., No. 4, Memos, Box 512, MGP, MGC. Interview with Christopher Whittington, 8 June 1987.
15. Interviews with Christopher Whittington, 8 June 1987, and Lord Catto, 4 June

TABLE 6. *Morgan Grenfell gearing ratios: calculations for two particularly high years*

	1965	1966
Deposits etc.	76,356,005	91,594,547
less reserves	2,046,760	2,502,009
	74,309,245 (1)	89,092,538 (1)
Share capital	2,250,000	2,250,000
plus reserves	2,046,760	2,502,009
	4,296,760	4,752,009
less fixed assets	3,348,473	3,557,200
	948,287 (2)	1,194,809 (2)
(1) divided by (2)	78.36	74.56

Note: 'Reserves' = general, contingency, and investment reserves plus unappropriated profit.

1987. Whittington, 'Morgan Grenfell's Involvement in Film Finance', 26 May 1971, and Syndicate to Morgan Grenfell, 'Film International Limited', 12 Mar. 1971. The ten films financed by Morgan Grenfell were *Shalako, The Girl Who Couldn't Say No, Connecting Rooms, The McMasters, The Last Grenade, The Virgin and the Gypsy, Perfect Friday, Cactus in the Snow, Murphy's War,* and *A Room in Paris.* Whittington, 'Morgan Grenfell's Involvement in Film Finance', Appendix A, 26 May 1971, all File De Grunwald, No. 4, Box 512, MGP, MGC.

16. Whittington, 'Morgan Grenfell's Involvement in Film Finance', 26 May 1971, File De Grunwald, No. 4, Box 512, MGP, MGC. Interview with Lord Catto, 4 June 1987.

17. Letter from J. C. Smith to the author, 19 Oct. 1987. Interviews with Christopher Whittington, 8 June 1987, and Lord Catto, 4 June 1987.

18. Whittington, 'Morgan Grenfell's Involvement in Film Finance', 26 May 1971, File De Grunwald, No. 4, Box 512, MGP, MGC. Interview with Christopher Whittingon, 8 June 1987.

19. C. Whittington to C. R. Reeves, 'Note on the Bank of England position re Films International', 24 May 1971, File De Grunwald, No. 4, Box 512, MGP.

20. Morgan Grenfell & Co. Ltd. to the Syndicate, 'Memorandum. Films Syndicate', 12 Feb. 1971; Morgan Grenfell & Co. Ltd. to the Film Syndicate, 1 Mar. 1971; Syndicate to Morgan Grenfell & Co. Ltd., 'Films International Limited', 12 Mar. 1971 (for the quotation); interview with Christopher Whittington, 8 June 1987; and Whittington, 'Morgan Grenfell's Involvement in Film Finance', 26 May 1971, all (except interview) File De Grunwald, No. 4, Box 512, MGP, MGC.

21. Interviews with Lord Catto, 4 June 1987; Christopher Whittington, 8 June 1987; John Smith, 8 June 1987; E. A. Bradman, 23 July 1987; and Blaise Hardman, 10 June 1987. Bradman, Hardman, and Smith all agree that the eventual loss was £6m.

22. A. R. Holmes and Edwin Green, *Midland: 150 Years of Banking Business* (London: B. T. Batsford Ltd., 1986), 274–5. Lazards had extended a credit of £2.75m.; Hill Samuel and Warburgs each £2m.; Barings, Kleinworts, Samuel Montagu, Rothschild, and Schröder each £1.75m.; Morgan Grenfell £1.5m.; Guinness Mahon £1m.; Bank of London and South America and the Canadian Imperial Bank of Commerce each £0.75m.; and the Toronto Dominion Bank £0.5m. J. G. Stanford, 'Rolls-Royce Limited. Revolving Syndicate Acceptance Credit for £20,000,000', 14 Oct. 1970; Memorandum by Reeves for Harcourt, 14 Oct. 1970; and A.N.G., Report of a meeting on 12 Oct. 1970 in the Bank of England to discuss Rolls-Royce's financial problems, 12 Oct. 1970, all File Rolls-Royce Limited 1970 Negotiations, Box P.793, MGP, MGC.

23. Memorandum by Kearns to Harcourt, 14 Oct. 1970, File Rolls-Royce Limited, Box P. 793, MGP, MGC.

24. Memorandum by Reeves of 'Meetings at Lazards on 9 November 1970 and at the Bank of England on 10 November 1970, 12 November 1970, File Rolls-Royce Limited, Box P.793, MGP, MGC.

25. Memorandum by Reeves on the meeting at Lazards, 3 Feb. 1971, and memorandum by Collins on the meeting at the Bank of England, 3 Feb. 1971, both File Rolls-Royce Limited, Box P.793, MGP, MGC.

26. J.G.S[tanford], Memorandum of meeting at Hill Samuel Ltd. of Representatives

of the Acceptance Credit Syndicate, 25 June 1973, File Rolls-Royce Limited, Box P.793, MGP, MGC. 'Notes on Capital and Reserves of 31st December 1971', File Annual Banking Returns, Chief Accountant's Office, MGC.

27. Minutes of Board meetings, 19 Apr. 1971 and 25 Apr. 1972, MG Minute Book 1970–1976, the Secretariat, and File Annual Banking Returns 1966–1986, Chief Accountant's Office, both MGC. Interview with E. A. Bradman, 10 Aug. 1987.

28. Minutes of Board meeting, 1 Dec. 1971, Minute Book 1971–1980, Morgan Grenfell Holdings Limited, and Informal Minutes of Board meeting, 13 Oct. 1976, MG Holdings, the Secretariat, MGC.

29. Interviews with David Bendall, 4 June 1987, and Christopher Reeves, 14 July 1987. The quotation is from Bendall.

30. Interview with Christopher Whittington, 8 June 1987. Fox-Pitt, Kelton Inc., 'Morgan Grenfell Holdings', Oct. 1977, File Relations with MGT after July 1973, Part 2, Christopher Reeves Papers (private possession).

31. Interviews with Christopher Reeves, 14 July 1987, and Donald Wells, 2 June 1987. Board Meetings, 29 Nov. 1971, Minute Book 1971–1980, MG Holdings; Minutes of Board meetings, 6 Dec. 1971, 31 Dec. 1971, and 28 June 1971, MG Minute Book 1970–1976; and Minutes of Board meeting, 19 Dec. 1969, MG Minute Book 1959–1969, all the Secretariat, MGC.

32. Interview with Lord O'Brien, 17 June 1987.

33. Interview with Sir George Blunden, 6 July 1967.

34. Interview with J. E. H. Collins, 10 June 1987. For information on mergers see John Grady and Martin Weale, *British Banking, 1960–85* (London: Macmillan, 1986), 99–101.

35. Interview with Sir George Blunden, 6 July 1987.

36. Interview with J. E. H. Collins, 10 June 1987.

37. Interviews with Lord Catto, 27 May 1987; David Bendall, 2 June and 4 June 1987; and J. E. H. Collins, 10 June 1987. 'Report of a meeting held on Thursday, 18th October, 1973 at 9:45 a.m.', File Relations with M.G. After July 1973, Part I, Reeves Papers.

38. Interviews with Sir John Sparrow, 5 June 1987, Blaise Hardman, 10 June 1987, David Bendall, 4 June 1987, and Michael Hildesley, 30 Aug. 1987. Note from Sir John Sparrow to the author, 8 Sept. 1987. Minutes of Board meeting, 28 May 1975, MG Minute Book 1970–1976, the Secretariat, MGC. Quotation from interview with Christopher Reeves, 8 July 1987. In 1970 MG's basic fee for fund management services started at $2\frac{1}{2}$ per mille. E.R.K., 'Report of a meeting at 23 Great Winchester Street on 27 Nov. 1970' [between MG and MGT Investment people], File Morgan Houses' relations, Box P.680, MGP, MGC. Interview with James Norton, 10 Nov. 1987.

39. Interview with M. Bullock, 30 Jan. 1989.

40. Grady and Weale, *British Banking, 1960–85*, table 5.2 (p. 102).

41. Interviews with M. Bullock, 30 Jan. 1989, and James Norton, 10 Nov. 1987.

42. Interviews with David Bendall, 2 June 1987, and Sir George Blunden, 6 July 1987.

43. Grady and Weale, *British Banking, 1960–85*, p. 108.

44. Interviews with David Bendall, 2 June 1987, and E. A. Bradman, 23 July 1987. Annual Reviews for 1967, 1968, and 1969, the Secretariat, MGC.

45. Interview with Christopher Whittington, 8 June 1987.

46. Preston to Stevens, Personal and Confidential, 18 Dec. 1972, File Office Business, 40, Box P.597, MGP, MGC.

47. Stevens to Preston, Personal and Confidential, 2 Jan. 1973, and Reeves to Stevens, 28 Dec. 1972, both File Office Business, 40, Box P.597, MGP, MGC.

48. Munn to Stevens, 4 Jan. 1973, and Stevens to Munn, 9 Jan. 1973 (for quote), both File Office Business, 40, Box P.597, MGP, MGC.

49. Private Ledger 12, Accounts Dept., MGC.

50. Chairman's Speech for 1958, given 17 June 1959, and Annual Reports for 1968 and 1969, the Secretariat, MGC. C. J. J. Clay and B. S. Wheble, *Modern Merchant Banking* (Cambridge: Woodhead-Faulkner, 2nd edn., 1983), 51, 45–6. Interviews with Christopher Whittington, 8 June 1987, Christopher Reeves, 8 July 1987, and Michael Hildesley, 30 Aug. 1987. Angus Dunn and Martin Knight, *Export Finance* (London: Euromoney Publications Limited, 1982).

51. Interviews with Christopher Reeves, 8 July 1987, Lord O'Brien, 17 June 1987, and Michael Hildesley, 30 Aug. 1987. Board meeting, 12 Nov. 1975, MG Holdings Minute Book 1971–1980; committee meeting, 24 May 1978, Management Committee Minutes 1978; and Board meeting, 27 Sept. 1972, MG Minute Book 1970–1976, all the Secretariat, MGC.

52. Interview with David Douglas-Home, 11 Nov. 1987.

53. *Financial Times*, 13 Oct. 1987. Grenfell to Morgan, 4 Mar. 1929, Harcourt to Lamont, 9 July 1957, and C. Means to Harcourt, 25 Nov. 1957, all File Channel Tunnel Project 1, Box P.461, MGP, MGC. Barbara Castle, *The Castle Diaries 1974–76* (London: Weidenfeld & Nicolson, 1980), 281. S. W. Fogarty (D.o.E.) to Lord Harcourt, 4 Mar. 1975, File Channel Tunnel Project: Minutes of Directors' Meetings 3, Box P.457, MGP, MGC.

54. Castle, *Diaries 1974–76*, p. 281. Interview with Angus Dunn, 11 Nov. 1987. Nicholas Henderson, *Channels and Tunnels* (London: Weidenfeld & Nicolson, 1987), 7–8. Note by Rory Macnamara, *c.* 21 Dec. 1987.

55. Interviews with John Franklin, 7 Dec. 1987, and Sir George Blunden, 6 July 1987. Henderson, *Channels and Tunnels*, p. 63. Note by Rory Macnamara, *c.* 21 Dec. 1987.

56. A loan of US$21,413,935 for the imperial government of Iran in connection with the Ahwaz–Rey second crude oil pipeline, Feb. 1972; two agreements to place at disposal of Emirate of Abu Dhabi facilities of US$140m. and US$40m., Nov. 1973; a loan of $5m. for the Bulgarian Bank for Foreign Trade, Jan. 1974; financial agreements between the Moscow Narodny Bank Limited (the bank for foreign trade of the USSR) and Morgan Grenfell to make sums available to assist financing of two contracts for Soviet purchases of UK machinery, July 1975; agreement between Morgan Grenfell and National Westminster Bank on one part and the Rumanian Bank for Foreign Trade to finance a contract between Elliott Turbomachinery Limited of London and ICE Romchim of Bucharest, Mar. 1976; and financial agreement between Morgan Grenfell and Bank Handlowy w Warszawie for £11,906,619·10 *re* a contract between GKN Contractors Limited and p.p. Metalexport, Sept. 1976. MG Minute Book 1970–1976, the Secretariat, MGC. Project finance did not always depend on government guarantees. One example was Woodside Petroleum Ltd., the project to tap offshore gas on Australia's north-west shelf. Morgans in 1981 organized a US$1.4 billion credit syndicate

with the banks accepting the completion risk—the biggest non-recourse (i.e. without government guarantees) project finance ever done.

57. Interviews with David Bendall, 4 June 1987, J. E. H. Collins, 10 June 1987, Christopher Whittington, 8 June 1987, Blaise Hardman, 10 June 1987, and Donald Wells, 2 June 1987.

58. 'Strengths and Weaknesses of M.G. & Co.', *c.* 1972, File Triangle, Reeves Papers for the quotation. Interview with Donald Wells, 22 May 1987.

59. Interviews with Donald Wells, 22 May 1987, Charles Rawlinson, 16 July 1987 and J. E. H. Collins, 10 June 1987.

60. Interview with George Law, 15 July 1987. Annual Reviews for 1967 and 1968, the Secretariat, MGC.

61. *The Economist*, 18 May, 29 June, and 20 July 1968. Interview with J. E. H. Collins, 15 July 1987. Note from George Law to the author, 22 Sept. 1987.

62. David Kynaston, 'A City at War with Itself', *Financial Times*, 7/8 Jan. 1989. Interview with Lord O'Brien, 17 June 1987. *The Economist*, 2 Nov. 1968.

63. *The Economist*, 20 July, 27 July, 17 Aug. 1968, and 25 Jan. 1969.

64. *The Economist*, 26 Apr. 1969.

65. Interview with George Law, 15 July 1987. Annual Review for 1969, the Secretariat, MGC.

66. Interview with George Law, 15 July 1987.

67. Douglas Moffitt, 'The Hundred Incredible Days', pt. 2, *Investors Review*, 22 Mar.–4 Apr. 1974, pp. 29–36, 34.

68. David Howarth and Stephen Howarth, *The Story of P & O* (London: Weidenfeld & Nicolson, 1986), 185–6.

69. Howarth and Howarth, *P & O*, p. 186, Moffitt, 'The Hundred Incredible Days', pt. 2, pp. 30, 29 for the quotation.

70. Morgan Grenfell & Co. Limited, 'The Peninsular and Oriental Steam Navigation Company and Bovis Limited', 1 Oct. 1972, and D.A.P., 'P & O', 14 Nov. 1972, both File Peninsular and Oriental Steam Navigation Company, Memoranda, Box P.771, MGP, MGC. Moffitt, 'The Hundred Incredible Days', pt. 2, p. 34. Interview with Lord Catto, 4 June 1987, for the quotation. Williams and Glyn also advised P & O, while, once the bid was announced, Warburgs were appointed advisers to Bovis.

71. Moffitt, 'The Hundred Incredible Days', pt. 2, pp. 35–6. Morgan Grenfell & Co., 'The P & O and Bovis', 1 Oct. 1972, File P & O, Memoranda, Box P.771, MGP, MGC.

72. Morgan Grenfell & Co., 'The P & O and Bovis', 1 Oct. 1972, and 'Resolutions of those attending a meeting of P & O Institutional Stockholders, Thursday, 28th September, 1972 at 3.00 p.m.', both File P & O, Memoranda, Box P.771, MGP, MGC. Moffitt, 'The Hundred Incredible Days', pt. 2, p. 36.

73. Howarth and Howarth, P & O, pp. 187–8. Interview with George Law reported in *The Times*, 25 Oct. 1972. *Daily Telegraph*, 14 Oct. 1972.

74. R.A.C., 'Timetable', 8 Nov. 1972, File P & O, Memoranda, Box P.771, MGP, MGC. Moffitt, 'The Hundred Incredible Days', pt. 3, *Investors Review*, 5–18 Apr. 1974, pp. 23–30, 24.

75. *The Times*, 14 Nov. 1972. Moffitt, 'The Hundred Incredible Days', pt. 3, p. 27.

76. Moffitt, 'The Hundred Incredible Days', pt. 3, p. 27.

77. Moffitt, 'The Hundred Incredible Days', pt 3, p. 27. Howarth and Howarth, *P & O*, pp. 189–90.
78. Moffitt, 'The Hundred Incredible Days', pt. 3, p. 26.
79. *Evening Standard*, 20 Nov. 1972; *Daily Telegraph*, 1 Dec. 1972; Moffitt, 'The Hundred Incredible Days', pt. 3, p. 28. Interview with George Law, 15 July 1987.
80. Moffitt, 'The Hundred Incredible Days', pt. 2, p. 35, and pt. 3, p. 28. Interview with George Law, 15 July 1987.
81. 20 Nov. 1972.
82. Hamish McRae and Frances Cairncross, *Capital City: London as a Financial Centre* (London: Metheun London Ltd., 2nd rev. edn. 1985), p. 153. Interview with Hamish McRae, 9 June 1987. In 1969 there was a merger negotiated between Robert Maxwell's Pergamon and Saul Steinberg's Leasco; the details were arranged 'by the principals meeting face to face in a hotel lobby without the presence of advisers . . . . When exposed to professional scrutiny the proposed deal quickly fell apart at the seams. Robert Fleming & Co., who had been advising Pergamon, resigned.' Frank Welsh, *Uneasy City: An Insider's View of the City of London* (London: Weidenfeld & Nicolson, 1986), 26.
83. See Margaret Reid, *The Secondary Banking Crisis, 1973–75* (London: Macmillan, 1982), 123. Interview with George Law, 15 July 1987. The *FT* 30 Share Index reached a record 543.6 on 19 May 1972. Reid, *Secondary Banking Crisis*, p. 61.
84. Note from George Law to the author, 22 Sept. 1987.
85. 'Strengths and Weaknesses of M.G. & Co.', *c*.1972, File Triangle, Reeves Papers.

Chapter 8

1. Chairman's Speech for 1949, given 29 June 1950, and for 1962, given 27 June 1963; board meeting, 21 Sept. 1977, MG Holdings Minute Book 1971–1980, all the Secretariat, MGC. *The Economist*, 23 Feb. 1963. Interview with Lord Catto, 27 May 1987.
2. Board meeting, 21 Sept. 1977, Minute Book 1971–1980, MG Holdings, the Secretariat, MGC. Interview with Julien Prevett, 10 Aug. 1987.
3. Committee meeting 18 May 1988, File Jan.–May 1988, committee meetings 15 June, 22 June, 24 Aug. 1988, File May–Oct. 1988, and committee meetings 2 Nov. and 30 Nov. 1988, File Oct. 1988– , all Group Management Committee Meetings; Group Directors' meeting, 5 Oct. 1988, File Informal Minutes Jan. 1988– ; and Michael Dobson, Group Board Paper 2/05.10.88, on Australia, 27 Sept. 1988, File Agendas and Papers, No. 13, Group Board, all the Secretariat, MGC. *The Times*, 1 Dec. 1988. Note from Nicholas Bull, 6 Feb. 1989.
4. Chairman's Speeches for 1952, 1953, 1955, 1956, 1959, 1960, and 1961, and Annual Review for 1967, all the Secretariat, MGC. Interview with Lord Catto, 27 May 1987.
5. Chairman's Speeches for 1957, 1958, 1960, and 1961, and the Annual Review for 1965, the Secretariat, MGC. Interview with Lord Catto, 27 May 1987.
6. Lord Catto for MGC to P. R. Legh, Bank of England, 30 Jan. 1962, File Morgan & Cie S.A., 1961 Formation and Subsequent Developments, Box. P.667, MGP, MGC.
7. Allen to Collins, 7 Dec. 1960; Catto to G. F. Verbeck, 30 Oct. 1961; Catto to

P. R. Legh, Bank of England, 30 Jan. 1962; Bank of England to MGC, 14 Feb. 1962; and Verbeck to Harcourt, 23 Feb. 1962, all File Morgan & Cie S.A., 1961 Formation etc., Box P.667, MGP, MGC. Annual Review for 1966, the Secretariat, MGC.

8. A. M. Vagliano, 'Memorandum', Strictly Confidential, 30 Nov. 1961, File Morgan & Cie S.A., 1961 Formation etc., Memos, Box P.667, MGP, MGC.

9. 'Morgan-Dämmerung', *Capital*, Sept. 1965, translation under title 'Breakthrough for Morgan', File Morgan & Cie S.A., Memos, Box P.667, MGP, MGC.

10. Harcourt, 'Memorandum: Morgan et Cie', 18 Sept. 1963, File Morgan & Cie S.A., Memos, Box P.667, MGP, MGC.

11. *New York Times*, 16 Aug. 1966. Interviews with Blaise Hardman, 10 June 1987, and Donald Wells, 2 June 1987.

12. *New York Times*, 16 and 17 Aug. 1966. Interview with J. E. H. Collins, 15 July 1987. File Schwab 1965 London Group Pool, Box P.482, MGP, MGC.

13. 'Morgan et Cie: Proposed Participation of Morgan Stanley & Co.', 18 Sept. 1963; 'Morgan & Cie: Comments and questions on the numbered paragraphs of Morgan Stanley & Co. Memorandum of March 15, 1966', circulated in MGC 27 Apr. 1966; 'Re: Morgan & Cie', 1 Nov. 1966, all File Morgan & Cie S.A., Memos, Box P.667, MGP, MGC. *New York Times*, 16 and 17 Aug. 1966. Annual Review for 1966, board meeting, 29 Nov. 1974, MG Minute Book 1970–1976, and board meeting, 7 Feb. 1980, MG Holdings Minute Book 1971–1980, all the Secretariat, MGC.

14. Annual Reports for 1965 and 1966, and board meeting, 8 Mar. 1978, MG Holding Minute Book 1971–1980, both the Secretariat, MGC. Interview with Charles Rawlinson, 16 July 1987. The profit was £3m., a useful and timely addition to capital. Summit meeting, 20 June 1977, File Relations with MGT after July 1973, Part 2, Reeves Papers.

15. Interview with David Bendall, 2 June 1987. Committee meeting, 24 May 1978, Management Committee Minutes 1978, the Secretariat, MGC.

16. Board meeting, 26 July 1972, MG Holdings Minute Book 1971–1980, the Secretariat, MGC.

17. 'Record of a meeting on 16/17 Jan. 1972'; K. C. Barrington, 'Private and Confidential memorandum to Holding Company Directors', 21 Jan. 1972; and 'Secret Memorandum from JMS on his visit to Morgan Stanley in New York, 10/11 Feb. 1972', all File Triangle, Reeves Papers.

18. 'JMS Secret Memorandum', 2 Mar. 1972, File Triangle, Reeves Papers.

19. 'Visit of JMS and EPC to New York, 10 August 1972', Strictly Confidential, to all Holdings and Bank Board Directors, 16 Aug. 1972, File Triangle, Reeves Papers.

20. 'Triangle Meeting at Morgan Guaranty, New York, Friday, 10th November 1972'; Bank of England, 'Banking Mergers and Participation', Nov. 1972; J.M.S., E.P.C., C.R.R., 'Triangle', 8 Mar. 1973; J. Stevens, 'Note of conversation with the Governor of the Bank of England—7th May 1973', 8 May 1973, all File Triangle, Reeves Papers. Interview with Sir George Blunden, 6 July 1987.

21. J.M.S., 'Memorandum to members of the Holdings Board', 16 Mar. 1973, File Triangle, Reeves Papers.

22. File Triangle, Reeves Papers.

23. Bendall to Reeves, copies to J.M.S., P.F. [P.F.P.], E.P.C., 4 May 1973. Peter

Phillips pointed out that under the plan effective control of Morgan Grenfell would pass to the two American firms, which the Bank of England had already made clear would not be allowed, and therefore, 'an overall Triangle operation' was necessarily put 'into abeyance for the time being'. P.F.P., 'Triangle: An Appraisal', 20 May 1973, both File Triangle, Reeves Papers.

24. Note from George Law to the author, 22 Sept. 1987. C.R.R., 'Record of a meeting on 6th May with Walter Page [of MGT]', attended by Harcourt, Stevens, Chappell, and Reeves, File Triangle, Reeves Papers. Interviews with Michael Hildesley, 11 June 1987, and David Bendall, 2 June 1987.

25. 'Triangle Talks in Bermuda on 20–22nd June with MGT and MI', 25 June 1973 (for the quotation), and C.R.R. and E.P.C., 'Triangle', 31 July 1973, both File Relations with MGT after July 1973, Part 1, Reeves Papers. Interview with David Bendall, 2 June 1987, and Christopher Reeves, 8 July 1987.

26. P.F.P., 'Triangle 2', 10 Apr. 1973, File Triangle, Reeves Papers. Board meeting 19 Dec. 1969, MG Minute Book 1959–1969, the Secretariat, MGC. Interview with David Bendall, 10 June 1987. The capitalization of Suez was nearly 35 times that of Morgan Grenfell.

27. Interviews with David Bendall, 4 June 1987, George Law, 15 July 1987, and Charles Rawlinson, 16 July 1987. Note from Sir John Sparrow to the author, 8 Sept. 1987, and note from George Law to the author, 22 Sept. 1987. Board meetings 25 Oct. 1973, 30 Oct. 1973, and 19 Dec. 1974, MG Minute Book 1970–1976; board meetings 30 Oct. 1973, 11 Dec. 1974, and 14 Nov. 1979, MG Holdings Minute Book 1971–1980; and committee meeting, 4 Jan. 1978, Management Committee Minutes 1978, all the Secretariat, MGC. Summit meeting, 13 Jan. 1978, File Relations with MGT after July 1973, Part 2, Reeves Papers.

28. Interview with David Bendall, 10 June 1987. Board meeting, 14 Aug. 1974, MG Holdings Minutes Book 1971–1980, the Secretariat, MGC.

29. Interviews with David Bendall, 10 June 1987, Michael Hildesley, 11 June 1987, and Hsieh Fu Hua, 21 June 1986. Board meetings 20 May and 9 June 1976, MG Holdings Minute Book 1971–1980, the Secretariat, MGC.

30. Committee meeting, 11 May 1988, File Jan.–May 1988, and committee meeting, 9 Nov. 1988, File Oct. 1988– , both Group Management Committee Minutes 1988, the Secretariat, MGC.

31. Committee meeting, 11 Jun. 1984, Management Committee Minutes 1984, and board meeting, 28 Mar. 1984, MG Holdings Minutes Book Sept. 1984–June 1986, both the Secretariat, MGC.

32. Interview with David Bendall, 2 June 1987. Board meeting, 24 Jan. 1974, MG Minute Book 1970–1976, the Secretariat, MGC.

33. Interview with David Bendall, 19 Aug. 1987. Committee meeting, 17 Oct. 1979, Management Committee Minutes 1979, the Secretariat, MGC.

34. Interview with David Bendall, 10 June 1987.

35. Board meetings 3 Feb. 1972 and 2 Sept. 1974, MG Minute Book 1970–1976; D. Douglas-Home, 'Teheran', 6 Feb. 1979, Management Committee Agendas and Papers 1979; and committee meetings 7 Feb. and 20 June 1979, Management Committee Minutes 1979, all the Secretariat, MGC. 'First Monthly Meeting Between MG and MGT', 24 Oct. 1973, File Relations with MGT after July 1973, Part 1, Reeves Papers.

36. Interview with David Bendall, 10 June 1987. Board meetings 11 Feb. and 11 Aug. 1976 and 27 Aug. 1980, MG Holdings Minute Book 1971–1980, the Secretariat, MGC. 'Venezuela–Middle East Joint Venture', File Relations with MGT after July 1973, Part 1, Reeves Papers.

37 Interviews with Christopher Reeves, 14 July 1987, and Christopher Whittington, 8 June 1987. Board meeting, 13 Aug. 1974, MG Minute Book 1970–1976, and committee meeting, 4 Apr. 1979, Management Committee Minutes 1979 (for quotation), both the Secretariat, MGC.

38. Committee meeting 30 Aug. 1978, Management Committee Minutes 1978; board meeting, 27 Aug. 1980, MG Holdings Informal Minutes 1975–1986; committee meeting, 3 Dec. 1980, Management Committee Minutes 1980; and committee meeting, 14 Jan. 1981, Management Committee Minutes 1981, all the Secretariat, MGC.

39. J.D.D.B., 'Memorandum' [of meeting on 9 Oct. 1959 in New York between MGT and MG people], 15 Oct. 1959; Harcourt, 'Thoughts on a possible merger between M.G. & Co. and the London office of M.G.T. Co. of New York', 20 Sept. 1963; Harcourt to John Meyer, 10 May 1963; Meyer to Harcourt, 7 June 1963; and Harcourt to Meyer, 10 June 1963, all File Morgan Houses Relations, Box P.680, MGP, MGC.

40. Barry McFadzean, 31 July 1970, File Morgan Houses Relations, Box P.680, MGP, MGC.

41. G.W.M.-Y. [G. W. Mackworth-Young], 'Morgan Grenfell/Morgan Guaranty Relationship', 14 Feb. 1977, File Relations with MGT after July 1973, Part 2, Reeves Papers.

42. Chappell and Reeves, telex to Hardman, 14 Feb. 1973, File Triangle, Reeves Papers.

43. Patterson to Harcourt and Stevens, 13 Aug. 1973; 'Note of Morgan Grenfell/MGT meeting on Thursday, 6 Dec. 1973', and 'Routine meeting with MGT', all File Relations with MGT after July 1973, Part 1, Reeves Papers.

44. 'Triangle. Record of a Meeting in New York on 11th September 1973', for quotation; 'First Monthly Meeting between MG and MGT', 24 Oct. 1973; and 'Record of Meeting at MGT. New York, Thursday, 14 March 1974', all File Relations with MGT after July 1973, Part 1, Reeves Papers.

45. Interview with Christopher Whittington, 8 June 1987 (for quotation), and board meeting, 27 Aug. 1980, MG Holdings Informal Minutes 1975–1986, the Secretariat, MGC.

46. Annual Reports for 1968 and 1969, the Secretariat, MGC. The profit made on Eurobonds that year was £182,451, an increase of 75% over 1967. In 1969 the profit was £354,001, an increase of 94%.

47. W. J. Hopper, 'Eurobonds—Review of Activities', 24 Oct. 1977, File Relations with MGT after July 1973, Part 2; E.P.C., 'Aide Memoire: MGT/MG Co-operation in the Eurobond Market', 2 Feb. 1976; and summit meeting, 27 May 1976 (for quotation), both File Relations with MGT after July 1973, Part 1, all Reeves Papers. Interview with Michael Hildesley, 30 Aug. 1987.

48. G.W.M.-Y., Memorandum on meeting with Morgan Stanley International, 26 May 1976, File Relations with MGT after July 1973, Part 1; and G.W.M.-Y. to Directors, 'Morgan Stanley', 23 May 1977 (for the quotation), File Relations with

MGT after July 1973, Part 2, both Reeves Papers. 'Timeo Danaos et dona ferentis' was scribbled on the bottom of the 1977 memorandum.

49. C.M.J.W., 'Meeting . . . on June 20, 1977', 22 June 1977, File Relations with MGT after July 1973, Part 2, Reeves Papers.

50. H. C. Tilley, 'Possibility of joint marketing of Eurobonds with MGT & MS', 17 June 1977, File Relations with MGT after July 1973, Part 2, Reeves Papers.

51. W.J.H., 'Relations Between MG and MGT with Regard to International Issues', 6 Jan. 1978, File Relations with MGT after July 1973, Part 2, Reeves Papers.

52. Management Committee Minutes 1978, the Secretariat, MGC.

53. Interviews with Lord Catto, 4 June 1987, and J. E. H. Collins, 10 June 1987.

54. Committee meetings 9 May, 16 May, 23 May, and 27 June 1979, Management Committee Minutes 1979; and committee meeting, 18 March 1981, Management Committee Minutes 1981, both the Secretariat, MGC.

55. Committee meeting, 3 May 1978, Management Committee Minutes 1978, the Secretariat, MGC.

56. Committee meeting, 28 Mar. 1979, Management Committee Minutes 1979, the Secretariat, MGC.

57. Committee meeting 25 July 1979, Management Committee Minutes 1979; committee meeting 26 Mar. 1980, Management Committee Minutes 1980; and board meeting, 26 Mar. 1980, MG Holdings Minute Book, 1971–1980, all the Secretariat, MGC.

58. John Franklin to Reeves, 15 May 1980; 'Minutes of Morgan Grenfell/Morgan Guaranty Meeting', 20 May 1980; Catto to A. Vagliano, 18 July 1980, all File Relations with MGT after July 1973, Part 3, Reeves Papers. Board meeting, 27 Aug. 1980, MG Holdings Minute Book 1971–1980, and committee meeting, 15 Apr. 1981, Management Committee Minutes 1981, both the Secretariat, MGC.

59. Reeves to all Holdings Directors, 16 July 1973, File Relations with MGT after July 1973, Part 1; C.M.J.W., Memorandum, 16 Feb. 1977, File Relations with MGT after July 1973, Part 2; 'Draft', 20 Feb. 1981; 'Some thoughts for ART [of Willis Faber]'; and R. M. J. Taylor to Reeves, lists of Holdings' shareholders in May 1980, 16 May 1980, all File Relations with MGT after July 1973, Part 4, all Reeves Papers. Board meetings 9 Dec. 1960 and 31 Jan. 1961, MG Minute Book 1959–1969, and Annual Review for 1967, both the Secretariat, MGC.

60. Annual Review for 1968, the Secretariat, MGC. 'Draft', 20 Feb. 1981; 'Merger Example'; 'Proposed Scheme—1st May, 1981'; 'List of Shareholders before Scheme'; and 'Shareholders in MG following Scheme', all File Relations with MGT after July 1973, Part 4, Reeves Papers. 'Corporate Finance Master Shareholding List', May 1981, the Secretariat, MGC. Interviews with Charles Rawlinson, 16 July 1987, and Donald Wells, 2 June 1987. Committee meeting, 26 May 1982, Management Committee Minutes 1982, the Secretariat, MGC.

Select Bibliography and Sources

MANUSCRIPT SOURCES

H. H. Asquith Papers (Bodleian Library, Oxford).

Bank of England Archives (Bank of England, London).

Baring Brothers Papers (Baring Brothers & Co., London).

British Iron and Steel Federation Papers, (British Steel Corporation Record Centre, Irthlingborough).

Brown Brothers Harriman Papers (New York Historical Society, New York).

Cabinet Papers (Public Record Office, London).

Sir Henry Clay Papers (Nuffield College, Oxford).

Foreign Office Papers (Public Record Office, London).

David Lloyd George Papers (House of Lords Record Office, London).

Edward Hamilton Papers (British Library, London).

Charles Hamlin Papers (Library of Congress, Washington, DC).

Thomas Lamont Papers (Harvard Business School, Boston).

William Gibbs McAdoo Papers (Library of Congress, Washington, DC).

Midland Bank Archives (Midland Bank Ltd., London).

Milner Papers (Bodleian Library, Oxford).

Morgan Grenfell Papers 1838–1909 (Guildhall Library, London).

Morgan Grenfell Papers 1910 and on (Morgan Grenfell Group, London).

Dwight Morrow Papers (Amherst College, Amherst, Mass.).

George Peabody Papers (Essex Institute Library, Salem, Mass.).

Christopher Reeves Papers (private possession).

Constance Hugh Smith Papers (Mrs Fortune Stanley, London).

Edward Stettinius Papers (University of Virginia, Charlotsville, Va.).

Treasury Papers (Public Record Office, London).

US Treasury Papers (National Archives, Washington, DC).

William Wiseman Papers (Yale University, New Haven, Conn.).

PRINTED SOURCES

Department of State, *Papers Relating to the Foreign Relations of the United States, 1917*, Supplement 2. *The World War* (Washington, DC: United States Government Printing Office, 1932.

Department of the Treasury, *Annual Report of the Secretary of the Treasury on the State of the Finances for the Fiscal Year Ended June 30, 1919* (Washington, DC: United States Government Printing Office, 1920.

Hansard, *Parliamentary Debates*, 5th series.

United States Senate, 74th Congress, 2nd Session, Special Committee on Investigation of the Munitions Industry, *Munitions Industry*, Report no. 944, 7 vols. (Washington, DC: United States Government Printing Office, 1936.

BOOKS

ACRES, D. W. MARSTON, *The Bank of England from within 1694–1900* 2 vols. (London: Oxford University Press for the Bank of England, 1931).

ADLER, D. A., *British Investment in American Railways 1834–1898* (Charlottesville: University Press of Virginia, 1970).

ALBERT, BILL, *South America and the World Economy from Independence to 1930* (London: Macmillan, 1983).

ALDCROFT, DEREK, *From Versailles to Wall Street 1919–1929* (London: Allen Lane, 1977).

ATTALI, JACQUES, *A Man of Importance: Sir Siegmund Warburg 1902–82* (London: Weidenfeld & Nicolson, 1986).

AYER, JULES, *A Century of Finance 1804–1904: The London House of Rothschild* (London: William Neely, 1905, privately printed).

BOLTON, SIR GEORGE, *A Bankers World*, ed. R. Fry (London: Hutchinson, 1970).

BORN, KARL ERICH, *International Banking in the 19th and 20th Centuries* (Leamington Spa: Berg Publishers Limited, 1983).

BOYLE, ANDREW, *Montagu Norman: A Biography* (London: Cassell, 1967).

BRAMSEN, BO, and WAIN, KATHLEEN, *The Hambros 1779–1979* (London: Michael Joseph, 1979).

BURK, KATHLEEN, *Britain, America and the Sinews of War 1914–1918* (London: George Allen & Unwin, 1985).

—— *The First Privatisation: The Politicians, the City and the Denationalisation of Steel* (London: The Historians' Press, 1988).

—— (ed.), *War and the State: The Transformation of British Government, 1914–1919* (London: George Allen & Unwin, 1982).

BUXTON, NEIL, and ALDCROFT, DEREK H. (eds.), *British Industry Between the Wars* (London: Scholar Press, 1982).

CAMPBELL, JOHN, *Lloyd George: The Goat in the Wilderness 1922–1931* (London: Jonathan Cape, 1977.

CARLETON, DAVID, *MacDonald versus Henderson: The Foreign Policy of the Second Labour Government* (London: Macmillan, 1970).

CAROSSO, VINCENT P., *Investment Banking in America* (Cambridge: Harvard University Press, 1970).

—— *The Morgans: Private International Bankers* 1854–1913 (Cambridge: Harvard University Press, 1987).

CASSIS, YOUSSEF, *Les Banquiers de la City à l'époque edouardienne* (Geneva: Librairie Droz SA, 1984).

—— *La City de Londres 1870–1914* (Aleçon: Librairie Belin, 1987).

CASTLE, BARBARA, *The Castle Diaries 1974–76* (London: Weidenfeld & Nicolson, 1980).

CHAPMAN, STANLEY, *The Rise of Merchant Banking* (London: George Allen & Unwin, 1984).

CLAPHAM, SIR JOHN, *The Bank of England: A History 1694–1914*, 2 vols. (Cambridge: Cambridge University Press, 1970).

CLARKE, STEPHEN V. O., *Central Bank Cooperation 1924–31* (New York: Federal Reserve Bank of New York, 1967).

CLAY, SIR HENRY, *Lord Norman* (London: Macmillan, 1957).

COCHRAN, THOMAS C., and MILLER, WILLIAM, *The Age of Enterprise: A Social History of Industrial America* (New York: Harper & Row, 1961 rev. edn.).

COREY, LEWIS, *The House of Morgan: A Social History of the Masters of Money* (New York: AMS Press, 1969 (reprint of 1930 edn.)).

CROW, DUNCAN, *A Man of Push and Go: The Life of George Macaulay Booth* (London: Rupert Hart-Davis, 1965).

DAVIS, RICHARD, *The English Rothschilds* (London: Collins, 1983).

DAYER, ROBERTA ALBERTA, *Bankers and Diplomats in China 1917–1925: The Anglo-American Relationship* (London: Frank Cass, 1981).

DREISZIGER, N. F. (ed.). *Mobilization for Total War* (Waterloo: Wilfrid Laurier University Press, 1981).

DUNN, ANGUS, and KNIGHT, MARTIN, *Export Finance* (London: Euromoney Publications Limited, 1982).

EDWARDS, E. W., *British Diplomacy and Finance in China 1895–1914* (Oxford: Clarendon Press, 1987).

ELLINGER, BERNARD, *The City: The London Financial Markets* (London: P. S. King & Son, Ltd., 1940).

ELLIS, AYTOUN, *Heir of Adventure: The Story of Brown, Shipley & Co. Merchant Bankers 1810–1960* (privately printed, 1960).

FALLON, IVAN, and SRODES, JAMES S., *Takeovers* (London: Hamish Hamilton, 1987).

FAY, STEPHEN, *Portrait of an Old Lady: Turmoil at the Bank of England* (Harmondsworth: Viking, 1987).

FERNS, H. S. *Britain and Argentina in the Nineteenth Century* (Oxford: Clarendon Press, 1960).

FORBES, JOHN DOUGLAS, *Stettinius, Sr.: Portrait of a Morgan Partner* (Charlottesville: University Press of Virginia, 1974).

——*J. P. Morgan, Jr. 1867–1943* (Charlottesville: University Press of Virginia, 1981).

FRENCH, DAVID, *British Economic and Strategic Planning 1905–1915* (London: George Allen & Unwin, 1982).

FULFORD. ROGER, *Glyn's 1753–1953: Six Generations in Lombard Street* (Macmillan, 1953).

George Peabody & Co., J. S. Morgan & Co., Morgan Grenfell & Co., Morgan Grenfell & Co. Ltd., 1835–1958 (Oxford: Oxford University Press, 1958, for private circulation).

GRADY, JOHN and WEALE, MARTIN, *British Banking, 1960–85* (London: Macmillan, 1986).

GREEN, EDWIN, and MOSS, MICHAEL, *A Business of National Importance: The Royal Mail Shipping Group, 1902–1937* (London: Methuen, 1982).

GREENBURG, DOLORES, *Financiers and Railroads 1869–1889: A Study of Morton, Bliss & Company* (Newark: University of Delaware Press, 1981).

HAMILTON, ADRIAN, *The Financial Revolution: The Big Bang Worldwide* (New York: Viking, 1986).

HENDERSON, NICHOLAS, *Channels and Tunnels* (Weidenfeld & Nicolson, 1986).

HIDY, MURIEL EMMIE, *George Peabody Merchant and Financier 1829–1854* (New York: Arno Press, 1978).

HIDY, RALPH W., *The House of Baring in American Trade and Finance: English Merchant Bankers at Work 1763–1861* (New York: Russell & Russel, 1970 (1st edn. 1949)).

HOGAN, MICHAEL J., *Informal Entente: The Private Structure of Cooperation in Anglo-American Economic Diplomacy, 1918–1928* (Columbia: University of Missouri Press, 1977).

HOLMES, A. R., and GREEN, EDWIN, *Midland: 150 Years of Banking Business* (London: B. T. Batsford Ltd., 1986).

HOWARTH, DAVID and HOWARTH, STEPHEN, *The Story of P & O* (London: Weidenfeld & Nicholson, 1986).

JENKS, LELAND H., *The Migration of British Capital, to 1875* (New York: Alfred Knopf, 1927).

KAY, WILLIAM, *The Big Bang* (London: Weidenfeld & Nicolson, 1986).

KELLETT, RICHARD, *The Merchant Banking Arena with Case Studies* (London: Macmillan, 1967).

KENNEDY, PAUL, *The Rise of the Anglo-German Antagonism 1860–1914* (London: George Allen & Unwin, *1980*).

KENT, SIR HAROLD S., *In on the Act: Memoirs of a Lawmaker* (London: Macmillan, 1979).

KINROSS, JOHN, *Fifty Years in the City: Financing Small Business* (London: John Murray, 1982).

LANDES, DAVID S., *Bankers and Pashas: International Finance and Economic Imperialism in Egypt* (Cambridge: Harvard University Press, 1979).

LEIGHTON-BOYCE, J. A. S. L., *Smiths the Bankers 1658–1958* (London: National Provincial Bank Ltd., 1958).

LEITH-ROSS, SIR FREDERICK., *Money Talks: Fifty Years of International Finance* (London: Hutchinson & Co. Ltd., 1968).

MCGRANE, R.G., *Foreign Bondholders and American State Debts* (London: Macmillan, 1935).

MARKS, SALLY, *The Illusion of Peace: International Relations in Europe 1918–1933* (London: Macmillan, 1976).

MÄRZ, EDUARD, *Austrian Banking & Financial Policy: Creditanstalt at a Turning Point, 1913–1923*, trans. Charles Kessler (London: Weidenfeld & Nicolson, 1984).

MATTHEWS, R. C. O., *A Study in Trade Cycle History: Economic Fluctuations in Great Britain, 1833–1842* (Cambridge: Cambridge University Press, 1954).

MEYER, RICHARD HEMMING, *Bankers' Diplomacy: Monetary Stabilization in the Twenties* (New York: Columbia University Press, 1970).

MICHIE, R. C., *The London and New York Stock Exchanges 1850–1914* (London: George Allen & Unwin, 1987).

MITCHELL, B. R., *British Historical Statistics* (Cambridge: Cambridge University Press, 1988).

MOGGRIDGE, D. E., *British Monetary Policy 1924–1931: The Norman Conquest of $4.86* (Cambridge: Cambridge University Press, 1972).

MOODY, JOHN, *The Long Road Home* (New York: Macmillan, 1946).

MORGAN, E. V., *Studies in British Financial Policy, 1914–25* (London: Macmillan, 1952).

MOTTRAM, R. H., *A Last Glance at the old Country Banking* (London: Hutchinson & Co. Ltd., 1940).

MULHALL, MICHAEL G., *The English in South America* (Buenos Aires: 'Standard', 1875).

O'HAGAN, H. OSBORNE, *Leaves from my Life*, 2 vols. (London: John Lane at the Bodley Head Limited, 1929).

OLDHAM, WILTON J., *The Ismay Line: The White Star Line and the Ismay Family Story* (Liverpool: The Journal of Commerce, 1961).

ORBELL, JOHN, *Baring Brothers & Co., Limited: A History to 1939* (London: Baring Brothers & Co. Ltd., 1985).

PAKENHAM, THOMAS, *The Boer War* (London: Weidenfeld and Nicolson, 1979).

PALIN, RONALD, *Rothschild Relish* (London: Cassell, 1970).

PARKER, FRANKLIN, *George Peabody: A Biography* (Nashville: Vanderbilt University Press, 1971).

PERKINS, EDWIN J., *Financing Anglo-American Trade: The House of Brown, 1800–1880* (Cambridge: Harvard University Press, 1975).

PLENDER, JOHN, and WALLACE, PAUL, *The Square Mile: A Guide to the New City of London* (London: Century Publishing, 1985).

PUGH, PETER, *Is Guinness Good for You?* (London: Financial Training Publications Limited, 1987).

REID, MARGARET, *The Secondary Banking Crisis, 1973–75* (London: Macmillan, 1982).

RUBENSTEIN, W. D., *Men of Property* (London: Croom Helm, 1981).

SATTERLEE, HERBERT L., *J. Pierpont Morgan: An Intimate Portrait* (New York: Macmillan, 1939).

SAYERS, R. S., *The Bank of England 1891–1944* 3 vols. (Cambridge: Cambridge University Press, 1976).

SCHMIDT, GUSTAV (ed.), *Konstellationen internationaler Politik: Politische und Wirtschaftliche Faktoren in den Beziehungen zwischen Westeuropa und den USA, 1924–1932* (Bochum: Studienverlag Dr N. Brockmeyer, 1983).

SCHUKER, STEPHEN A., *The End of French Predominance in Europe: The Financial Crisis of 1924 and the Adoption of the Dawes Plan* (Chapel Hill: University of North Carolina Press, 1976).

SEARLE, G. R., *The Quest for National Efficiency: A Study in British Politics and British Political Thought 1899–1914* (Berkeley: University of California Press, 1971).

SELDON, ANTHONY, *Churchill's Indian Summer: The Conservative Government, 1951–55* (London: Hodder & Stoughton, 1981).

SILVERMAN, DAN P., *Reconstructing Europe After the Great War* (Cambridge: Harvard University Press, 1982).

SKINNER, THOMAS, *The London Banks and Kindred Companies and Firms* (London: The Bullionist, November 1881).

SMALLEY, GEORGE W., *Anglo-American Memoirs, Second Series* (London: Duckworth & Co., 1912).

SUPPLE, BARRY (ed.), *Essays in British Business History* (Oxford: Clarendon Press, 1977).

TRUPTIL, R. J., *British Banks and the London Money Market* (London: Jonathan Cape, 1936).

WELSH, FRANK, *Uneasy City: An Insiders View of the City of London* (London: Weidenfeld & Nicolson, 1986).

ZIEGLER, PHILIP, *The Sixth Great Power of Europe: Barings 1763–1929* (London: Collins, 1988).

ARTICLES

ABRAHAMS, PAUL, 'American Bankers and the Economic Tactics of Peace: 1919', *Journal of American History*, 56 (1969), 572–83.

BURKE, KATHLEEN, 'J. M. Keynes and the Exchange Rate Crisis of July 1917', *Economic History Review*, 2nd ser., 32/3 (1979), 405–16.

—— 'The Mobilization of Anglo-American Finance During World War I', in N. F. Dreisziger (ed.), *Mobilization for Total War* (Waterloo: Wilfred Laurier University

Press, 1981), 25–42.

—— 'The Treasury: From Impotence to Power', in ead. (ed.), *War and the State: The transformation of British Government, 1914–1919* (London: George Allen & Unwin, 1982), 84–107.

CARROLL, JOHN M., 'The Paris Bankers' Conference of 1992 and America's Design for a Peaceful Europe', *International Review of History and Political Science*, 10 (1973), 39–47.

CASSIS, YOUSSEF, 'Bankers in English Society in the Late Nineteenth Century', *Economic History Review*, 2nd ser., 38/42 (1985), 210–29.

COSTIGLIOLA, FRANK C., 'The Other Side of Isolation: The Establishment of the First World Bank, 1929–1930', *Journal of American History*, 59/3 (1972), 602–20..

—— 'Anglo-American Financial Rivalry in the 1920s', *Journal of Economic History*, 37 (1977), 911–34.

DIAPER, STEFANIE, 'Merchant Banking Growth in the Second Half of the Nineteenth Century: The Case of Kleinwort, Sons & Co.', unpublished paper, 1985.

—— 'Merchant Banking in the Inter-War Period: The Case of Kleinwort, Sons & Co.', *Business History*, 28/1 (1986), 55–76.

HARRIS, JOSÉ and THANE, PAT, 'British and European Bankers, 1880–1914: An "aristocratic bourgeoisie"?', in Pat Thane, G. J. Crossic, and Roderick Floud (eds.), *The Power of the Past: Essays for Eric Hobsbawm* (Cambridge: Cambridge University Press, 1984), 215–34.

JONES, GEOFFREY, 'Lombard Street on the Riviera: The British Clearing Banks and Europe 1900–1960', *Business History*, 24/2 (1982), 186–210.

KYNASTON, DAVID, 'A City at War with Itself', *Financial Times*, 7/8 Jan. 1989.

McLEAN, DAVID, 'Finance and "Informal Empire" before the First World War', *Economic History Review*, 2nd ser., 29/2, (1976), 291–305.

OFFER, AVNER, 'Empire and Social Reform: British Overseas Investment and Domestic Politics, 1908–1914', *The Historical Journal*, 26/1 (1983), 119–38.

SCHUKER, S. A., 'American Foreign Policy and the Young Plan' in Gustav Schmidt (ed.), *Konstellationen internationaler Politik: 1924–1932* (Bochum: Studienverlag Dr N. Brockmeyer, 1983), 122–30.

SKIDELSKY, ROBERT, 'Retreat from Leadership: The Evolution of British Economic Foreign Policy, 1870–1939', in Benjamin M. Rowland (ed.), *Balance of Power or Hegemony: The Interwar Monetary System* (New York: University Press, 1976), 147–92.

THANE, PAT, 'Financiers and the British State: The Case of Sir Ernest Cassel', *Business History*, 28/1 (1986), 80–99.

TURRELL, ROB, with VAN HELTEN, JEAN-JACQUES, 'The Rothschilds, the Exploration Company and Mining Finance', *Business History*, 28/2 (1986), 181–205.

WILLIAMSON, PHILIP, 'A "Bankers Ramp"? Financiers and the British Political Crisis of August 1931', *English Historical Review*, 99/343 (1984), 770–806.

—— 'Financiers, the Gold Standard and British Politics, 1925–1931', in John Turner (ed.), *Businessmen and Politics: Studies of Business Activity in British Politics, 1900–1945* (London: Heinemann, 1984), 105–29.

THESES

DIAPER, STEFANIE, 'The History of Kleinwort, Sons & Co. in Merchant Banking, 1855–1961', Ph.D. thesis (University of Nottingham, 1983).

LEDWARD, W. P., 'Monetary Policy 1833–9: With Special Reference to the Anglo-American Crisis of 1839', D. Phil Thesis (Oxford, 1983).

ROBINSON, DAVID, 'The Strategy, Structure and Financial Performance of Some Major Merchant Banking Groups, 1958–1974', M. B.Sc. thesis (Manchester Business School, 1976).

PERODICALS

Acquisition Monthly
Banker
Bankers' Magazine
Daily Telegraph
The Economist
Financial News
Financial Times
Investors Chronicle
Investors Review
Observer
Stock Exchange Gazette
The Times
Wall Street Journal

INTERVIEWS

John Baylis
C.B.B. Beauman
Dorothy Beech
David Bendall
Robert Binyon
Sir George Blunden
E. A. Bradman
M. Bullock
Sir Peter Carey
Lord Catto
J. E. H. Collins

John Craven
Lord Donoughue
David Douglas-Home
Angus Dunn
John Forsyth
John Franklin
Desmond Harney
M. E. Hildesley
Hsieh Fu Hua
Eileen Izard
John Izard
George Law
Hamish McRae
P. J. McAfee
Janet McCurrie
Sir John Mallabar
James Norton
Lord O'Brien
Bryan Pennington
Julien Previtt
Charles Rawlinson
Christopher Reeves
Anthony Richmond-Watson
John Smith
Sir John Sparrow
Richard Webb
Donald Wells
Christopher Whittington
Jeremy Wormell

Index